# Banking on Data

**International Banking and Finance Law Series**

VOLUME 37

*Series Editors*

Professor Joseph Norton, Professor Ross Buckley and Professor Douglas Arner.

*Subjects*

Topical issues in international banking and financial services law, such as regulatory responses to the global financial crisis or regulation of alternative investment funds.

*Objective & Readership*

To provide authoritative analysis of trends and complex subjects for academics, regulators and practitioners involved in international banking and financial services law.

*The titles published in this series are listed at the end of this volume.*

# Banking on Data

## Evaluating Open Banking and Data Rights in Banking Law

Scott Farrell

Wolters Kluwer

*Published by:*
Kluwer Law International B.V.
PO Box 316
2400 AH Alphen aan den Rijn
The Netherlands
E-mail: lrs-sales@wolterskluwer.com
Website: www.wolterskluwer.com/en/solutions/kluwerlawinternational

*Sold and distributed by:*
Wolters Kluwer Legal & Regulatory U.S.
920 Links Avenue
Landisville, PA 17538
United States of America
E-mail: customer.service@wolterskluwer.com

ISBN 978-94-035-3116-8

e-Book: ISBN 978-94-035-3186-1
web-PDF: ISBN 978-94-035-3196-0

*This book is dedicated to the memory of my mother and my father, the latter of whom passed away between this book's completion and publication. I am forever thankful for their resolve that their children would have the education to which they were not granted the opportunity.*

# Table of Contents

# List of Figures

# List of Tables

# Preface

Anyone with a recent history in retail banking, fintech or financial information technology should have heard the phrase 'open banking'. It has grown from its birth in the European Union and the United Kingdom to develop across many places with diverse legal and banking systems, from Australia, Brazil, Canada, China, Hong Kong, India, Israel and Japan, to Malaysia, Mexico, New Zealand, Nigeria, Russia, Singapore, South Korea, and the United States of America, to name just a few.

Although established in different jurisdictions at different times in different ways, open banking has a common purpose – to enable bank customers to benefit from safely sharing their banking data with others they choose. This simple concept is anticipated to have an extensive impact. Even long-established global banking institutions such as the Bank for International Settlements (BIS) believe that open banking will change the traditional business model of banking, change the relationship between bank and customer and revolutionise how customers manage their finances. Other predictions are more ebullient, forecasting that it will create a new paradigm and a new ecosystem for financial services through a wave of digital transformation. Although the ultimate impact of open banking is unknown, it is clear that open banking will change banking significantly for banks, for their customers, and for those who work with them.

This book explains open banking and analyses its legal foundations. It takes a perspective aligned with the functions which open banking performs with respect to customer data as valuable information, evaluating its foundations by reference to banking law, rather than privacy or competition laws. In doing so, it aims to provide a unique and detailed legal analysis of the open banking systems of the leading common law jurisdictions, Australia and the United Kingdom, and a framework which can be used to evaluate, and design, open banking in other jurisdictions too. By enabling banking law to serve as a benchmark for the legal foundations of open banking, the lessons learned over centuries in banking and payments can be incorporated into the design of emerging open banking systems, so that 'banking on data' can be as safe and effective as banking with money.

*Scott Farrell*

# Acknowledgements

I would like thank Professor Ross Buckley, Professor Douglas Arner, and Dr Anton Didenko for their ideas and guidance. I would also like to thank King & Wood Mallesons, the University of New South Wales, the Australian Research Council Laureate Fellowship for their support of the research which led to this book, Dr Jenny Jarret for her invaluable assistance with that work, and Max Allan for his counsel and consideration.

The views expressed in this book are mine, and not necessarily those of any person, agency, or entity with whom I have worked in connection with the subject matter.

I would also like to express my heartfelt thanks for the tremendous patience and support of my wife, Delia, without whom I could never have started or completed this book, the research on which it is based, or any of my work in open banking and consumer data rights.

CHAPTER 1

# Introducing Open Banking

This chapter introduces open banking by explaining its meaning, objectives, and functions. It also introduces open banking systems and their foundations, the connection between open banking systems and banking payment systems and the benefits of analysing the legal foundations of open banking systems from a banking law perspective. It further introduces the importance of trust in the context of open banking. This chapter finishes by introducing the coverage of the following chapters of this book.

## 1.1 WHAT IS OPEN BANKING?

### 1.1.1 Meaning of Open Banking

Open banking has no accepted legal definition. It is not, for example, defined in the laws which establish and govern open banking in the two open banking jurisdictions which are the focus of the analysis in this book, Australia and the UK.[1] Nor is it defined in the laws of open banking's foundation in the EU (known as *PSD2*),[2] the legislative basis of its proposed implementation in the US,[3] or the semi-regulatory documents on which it is based in Hong Kong,[4] or Singapore.[5]

1. For Australia, *see Competition and Consumer Act 2010* (Cth) ('*CCA*'); *Competition and Consumer (Consumer Data Right) Rules 2020* ('*CDR Rules*'). For the UK, *see Retail Banking Market Investigation Order 2017* (UK) ('*CMA Order*'); *Payment Services Regulation 2017* (UK) ('*PSR*'). These are explained further in Chapter 2.
2. *Directive 2015/2366/EU of the European Parliament and of the Council of 25 November 2015 on Payment Services in the Internal Market, amending Directives 2002/65/EC, 2009/110/EC, and 2013/36/EU and Regulation (EU) No 1093/2010 and repealing Directive 2007/64/EC* OJ L 337/35 ('*PSD2*').
3. *Dodd-Frank Wall Street Reform and Consumer Protection Act*, Pub L No. 111-203, 124 Stat. 1376, s. 1033 (2010) ('*Dodd-Frank Act*').
4. Hong Kong Monetary Authority, 'Open API Framework for the Hong Kong Banking Sector', 18 July 2018) https://www.hkma.gov.hk/media/eng/doc/key-information/press-release/2018/20180718e5a2.pdf.

Instead, it is more common for open banking to be described than defined. Some descriptions are highly technical and technological, focussing on the use of Application Programming Interfaces (APIs) to enable access to customer data.[6] Fortunately, for those not familiar with software engineering and data science, most descriptions are functional and purposive, focussing on the outcomes to be achieved and the methods used to do so. These descriptions can be found in reports prepared for governments or other bodies implementing open banking. For example, a report in the UK described open banking as having the purpose to:

> allow bank customers to securely share their data with third parties so a broad range of businesses can compete to provide bank customers with better financial services, more choice and lower prices.[7]

With the intention, according to an Australian government report:

> to give customers more *control* over their information, leading to more *choice* in their banking and more *convenience* in managing their money, and resulting in more *confidence* in the use and value of an asset mostly undiscovered by customers – their data'.[8]

A similar, purposive, approach has been taken in Canada where an official report into open banking described it as:

> a system that allows consumers to securely and efficiently transfer their financial data between financial institutions and accredited third party service providers in order to access services that can help them improve their financial outcomes.[9]

A functional description of open banking is also used by the BIS:

> [T]he sharing and leveraging of customer-permissioned data by banks with third party developers and firms to build applications and services, such as those that provide real-time payments, greater financial transparency options for account holders, and marketing and cross-selling opportunities.[10]

Other descriptions developed by scholars take a similar approach.[11] Although these descriptions explain what open banking *does* more than defining what it *is,* they reveal both the subject and object of open banking – bank customers and their banking data, respectively. They also describe important functions of open banking, namely the

5. Association of Banking in Singapore and Monetary Authority of Singapore, 'ABS-MAS Financial World: Finance-as-a-Service API Playbook', November 2016) https://abs.org.sg/docs/library/abs-api-playbook.pdf.
6. *See* section 1.2.2 below.
7. Open Data Institute and Fingleton, 'Open Banking, Preparing for Lift Off' (Report, 2019) 4.
8. Australian Treasury, 'Review into Open Banking: Giving Customers Choice, Convenience and Confidence' (Report, December 2017) v (emphasis in original). The review was led by the author and this quote is from the author's foreword.
9. Advisory Committee on Open Banking, 'Final Report of Advisory Committee on Open Banking' (Report, April 2021) 29 https://www.canada.ca/content/dam/fin/consultations/2021/acob-ccsbo-eng.pdf.
10. Bank for International Settlements, 'Report on Open Banking and Application Programming Interfaces' (Report, November 2019) 4.
11. *See*, for example, Linda Jeng (ed.), *Open Banking* (Oxford University Press, 2022).

sharing of that data, the use of the data shared, and the customer's control over both. With these descriptions in mind, this book defines open banking as:

> sharing customer banking data as the customer directs, for use as the customer desires.

This definition is chosen because it is simple, places the customer and their data at the centre and relies on neither open banking's purpose nor the technology used. It is also easily adapted to other customer data to be shared, beyond open banking. Although this definition does not rely on open banking's purpose or how that purpose is achieved, each of these is important in understanding open banking. The next sections show this by explaining the objectives of open banking and the functions which enable those objectives to be achieved.

### 1.1.2 Objectives of Open Banking

Despite the differences in the way that open banking is implemented in different places, four purposes are commonly asserted: to improve competition, to encourage innovation, to foster inclusion and to enhance consumer protection. These are not mutually exclusive, and many jurisdictions share some, if not all, of them. They are each explained in turn.

#### *(a) Improving Competition*

In many jurisdictions a primary objective of open banking is to improve competition in banking services. This includes the UK, where it was designed to increase the rivalry between banks and remedy the problem that larger, incumbent banks do not need to compete whilst smaller, newer banks find it difficult to establish themselves.[12] Similar goals of encouraging competition were also fundamental for developing open banking in Australia.[13]

This objective of open banking arises from the competition problems which have emerged in banking and the failure of more customary competition regulation to fully address the competitive advantages of controlling banking data. Customer account information has a central role in banking. Banks rely on the use and reuse of this information to assess, manage and price credit risk and the processing of data is at the core of banking business. Because of its importance, banks control access to customer account information and, in doing so, perform a 'gatekeeper role' with respect to it. This represents a substantial advantage to banks in providing financial services, and a barrier to entry to other competitors, including emerging financial technology firms ('fintechs'), seeking to offer competing financial services to banks' customers. This is

12. *See* Competition and Markets Authority, 'Retail Banking Market Investigation' (Final Report, 9 August 2016). *See also* Financial Conduct Authority, 'Open Finance' (Feedback Statement No. FS21/7, March 2021) [1.4].
13. *See* Australian Treasury (n. 8).

known as the 'data bottleneck' problem, and it leads to market failures in banking competition such as information asymmetry and high search and switch costs.

The sharing of banking data enabled by open banking is intended to mitigate this problem by reducing barriers to entry and expansion. Enabling customers to share their account data with alternative providers can reduce the associated switching costs and the 'lock-in' to current service providers. Providing customers with easy access to their banking data enables them to choose alternative providers and overcomes the reluctance which customers have in changing their provider of retail banking services. By mitigating the information asymmetry problems which have traditionally impacted banking, open banking seeks to increase competition on the 'merits' in banking, particularly because banking is increasingly 'powered' by data and the technologies which analyse them.

### *(b) Encouraging Innovation*

Encouraging innovation is fundamental to the benefits of the new, competitive financial services which are expected to grow from open banking. This has been an important purpose of open banking in the EU, where it is intended to develop user-friendly, accessible and innovative payment methods,[14] and in Australia, where it is to establish a framework for the growth of new ideas and business.[15] This objective of open banking distinguishes it from other legal and regulatory interventions because it is designed to facilitate innovation, rather than to respond to it.

Open banking is intended to enable fintechs to develop new intermediary businesses using the increased accessibility of customer account data. These data are a valuable resource for the provision of new products and services to customers because they allow banking services to be 'unbundled' so that customers can, for example, separate the making of deposits and the organisation of payments. This permits customers to make different choices for each unbundled element, facilitates greater efficiency, and enables the creation of new banking business models.

The unbundling of banking services assisted by open banking also presents strategic challenges for banks. Banks could lose the direct interface with their customers if open banking enables a 'platform business model' to be established in banking, which separates the manufacture and distribution of the bank's financial products and services. This changed relationship between banks and their customers could be intermediated by technology-enabled competitors, such as fintechs and large technology companies (or 'bigtechs'). The result could be that banks are relegated to subordinate functions of holding deposits and operating underlying infrastructure (like utilities or the 'pipes') without any interaction with the customer. On the other hand, open banking also offers opportunities for banks to innovate, to change their product and service offering to customers, and to grow their business and market share.

14. *PSD2* (n. 2) Art. 98(2)(e).
15. Australian Treasury, 'Consumer Data Right Overview' (Explanatory Guide, 9 May 2018) 5.

### (c) *Fostering Inclusion*

Jurisdictions such as Mexico, Brazil and India have undertaken open banking for the express purpose of improving financial inclusion.[16] The increased competition and innovation from enabling access to customer data is intended to empower new entrants in the market to create new products and services which are adapted to the needs of those who are unserved or underserved by existing providers. Open banking's potential for servicing those customers increases if customer data beyond banking, such as utility and telecommunications data, are included within its scope to complement the insufficiently reliable traditional assessments of creditworthiness. In this way, open banking is intended to foster credit inclusion and to lower financial inequalities.

Open banking is hoped also to foster financial inclusion by enabling improvement in financial management, particularly through sharing data with trusted intermediaries. In the UK, open banking has led to services that can identify upcoming bills and allocate funding from inexpensive sources rather than overdrafts, and services that can alert friends and family to help a consumer in financial difficulties. Financial inclusion has also been an important consideration in the design of open banking in Canada,[17] and developments to enable further inclusion have been recommended in Australia.[18]

### (d) *Enhancing Consumer Protection*

Open banking achieves its primary consumer protection objective by providing a safer, more reliable alternative to other ways of sharing customer banking data. Before open banking, customers had to provide their online banking login credentials to those with whom they wanted to share their banking information. This process is commonly known as 'screen scraping' and it is a controversial method of accessing customer account data, although it remains used in many jurisdictions, including the United States and Canada.[19] Screen scraping is argued to be a slow and unstable technology with potential inaccuracies in the data collected (due to the lack of standardisation in the bank interfaces being 'scraped'), which exposes customers to increased cybersecurity risk, and increases the opportunity to take advantage of vulnerable customers and cause financial hardship. Open banking avoids these risks as customer credentials are only shared with their bank and, for this reason, banks and many fintechs prefer the

16. *See, e.g.*, Yan Carriere-Swallow, Vikram Haksar and Manasa Patnam, 'India's Approach to Open Banking: Some Implications for Financial Inclusion', *Open Banking* (Oxford University Press, 2022).
17. Advisory Committee on Open Banking (n. 9).
18. *See* Australian Treasury, 'Inquiry into Future Directions for the Consumer Data Right: Giving Consumers Choice, Convenience and Confidence' (Report, October 2020) 171. The author led this inquiry. *See also* Australian Treasury, 'Statutory Review of the Consumer Data Right' (Report, 2022).
19. *See* Advisory Committee on Open Banking (n. 9), Congressional Research Service, 'Open Banking, Data Sharing, and the CFPB's 1033 Rulemaking' (Insight, CRS Report, 9 September 2021) https://crsreports.congress.gov/product/pdf/IN/IN11745.

use of open banking to screen scraping. This has been expressed to be a key factor in its adoption in Canada, India, the UK and the EU. Open banking systems also have other consumer protection objectives such as improving consumers' comprehension of the risks and benefits in sharing their data. This aspect of consumer protection is a key objective in Australia.

### *(e) Relationship Between Objectives*

These objectives of open banking are not independent of each other. They are related and can be paired and categorised from different perspectives. For example:

- *Impact*: The competition and innovation objectives can be seen as being focussed on the *supply* of goods and services by businesses to customers, whilst the inclusion and consumer protection objectives can be seen as being focussed on the *demand* for goods and services by customers from those businesses.
- *Purpose*: The competition and consumer protection objectives can be seen as *improving* sub-optimal use of data either by banks acting as gateways, or bad actors seeking to take advantage of customers' data, whilst the innovation and inclusion objectives can be seen as *developing* new uses of data to achieve a better outcome.

These perspectives of impact and purpose are illustrated in the diagram at Figure 1.1. This representation of the objectives of open banking is used to compare the purposes of Australian and UK open banking in Chapter 2.

*Figure 1.1 Impact and Purpose of Objectives of Open Banking*

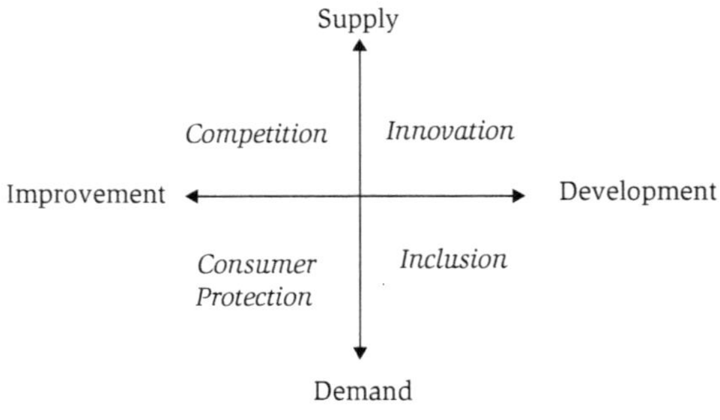


This understanding of the objectives of open banking is important because it enables an examination of the functions required to be performed by open banking to be *effective* in achieving them.

### 1.1.3 Functions Performed by Open Banking

The objectives of open banking described above are achieved by the performance of three functions:

- granting customers *autonomy* so that they may require their banks to share their data with recipients chosen by customers;
- enabling *portability* of those data so that they can be safely shared by those banks with those recipients; and
- ensuring the *accountability* of those recipients to the customers for the custody and use of the shared data.

These are explained in turn below. The development of portability into a fourth function of providing connectivity between participants is explained in the context of open banking systems in section 1.2.2.

#### *(a) Customer Autonomy: The Choice to Share Data*

For open banking to achieve its objectives, customers must be able to *choose* to share their banking data with recipients. In this way, open banking provides customers with control over their data, which is a form of data autonomy.[20]

This autonomy provided by open banking can be likened to concepts of data ownership, data sovereignty or informational self-determination.[21] However, the customer autonomy granted by open banking does not seek to reach as far. It includes the choice to share customer data for selected uses, but it does not control or exclude use by others who have received the data through some other means. Also, instead of being supported by fundamental individual rights, customer autonomy in open banking is supported by a combination of the customer's legal rights to share their data and the technological arrangements (such as customer experience standards) which enable them to do so.

A further important distinction to make is between the customer autonomy provided by open banking and that provided by commercial data sharing arrangements that customers might otherwise choose to enter into with service providers. Whilst these arrangements appear to (and sometimes can) provide customers with choices to share their data, they do not offer the customer the accountability provided by an open banking system.

20. *See* Cesare Fracassi and William J Magnuson, 'Data Autonomy' (2021) 74(2) *Vanderbilt Law Review* 327.
21. *See, e.g.*, Nadezhda Purtova, 'Default Entitlements in Personal Data in the Proposed Regulation: Informational Self-Determination Off the Table ... And Back on Again?' (2014) 30(1) *Computer Law & Security Review* 6-24.

### (b) Data Portability: The Means of Sharing Data

In addition to providing customers with the choice to share their data, open banking provides the *means* by which those customer data can be shared by the bank with the recipient chosen by the customer. This can be characterised as a form of data portability.[22]

Data portability is not a new concept and legal support for a different form of data portability can be found in the right to transmit data under privacy laws such as the EU's *General Data Protection Regulation* (*GDPR*).[23] However, the data portability provided by open banking is more extensive than a consumer's rights to transmit their personal data found in privacy laws. This is because open banking requires that data be shared in a standardised form which is interoperable between technology systems (referred to as syntactic portability) and meaningful to the recipient (referred to as semantic interoperability). These requirements are fundamental in meeting the objectives of open banking, as the customer data must be readily receivable, comprehensible and usable by the recipient with whom the customer has chosen to share their data. This standardised data portability of open banking is supported by a combination of the technological arrangements between banks and data recipients (including the APIs described in the next part of this chapter) and the legal relationships which support them.

It is important to distinguish the data portability of open banking from the broader concept of 'open data', which permits data to be accessible to anyone for their own use for any purpose, and from transfers of customer data made between entities for regulated purposes, such as those made to guard against the prevention of fraud. This is because the data portability of open banking remains subject to the customer's control, through the customer autonomy explained above.

### (c) Recipient Accountability: The Safekeeping and Use of Shared Data

Achievement of the objectives of open banking requires not only that customers can share their data with whom they choose and a means by which those data can be shared, it also requires that the shared data be *kept safely and used* by the chosen recipient only as the customer desires. In other words, there needs to be accountability to the customer for their data which has been shared.

---

22. It might also be described as a form of data access, but the distinction is not relevant here, *see* See Inge Graef, Martin Husovec and Jasper van den Boom, 'Spill-Overs in Data Governance: The Relationship Between the GDPR's Right to Data Portability and EU Sector-Specific Data Access Regimes' (TILEC Discussion Paper No DP 2019-005, Tilburg University, April 2019). *See also* Paul De Hert et al., 'The Right to Data Portability in the GDPR: Towards User-Centric Interoperability of Digital Services' (2018) 34(2) *Computer Law & Security Review* 193-203.
23. *Regulation (EU) 2016/679 of the European Parliament and of the Council of 27 April 2016 on the Protection Of Natural Persons with regard to the Processing Of Personal Data and on the Free Movement of such Data, and repealing Directive 95/46/EC (General Data Protection Regulation)* OJ L119/1 ('*GDPR*'). Article 20 of *GDPR* includes a general right for the individual to require the transfer of their personal information in a 'structured, commonly used and machine-readable format'.

Accountability for data is at the foundation of privacy laws, like the *GDPR*. However, the accountability in open banking is not the same as the concept of data protection on which those laws are customarily based. This is because the focus of recipient accountability in open banking is to enable the provision of a particular good or service requested by the customer, rather than the protection of fundamental rights of privacy, or general rights of control. Open banking also differs from the right of access to data contained in privacy laws such as Australia's *Privacy Act 1998* (Cth) ('*Privacy Act*'),[24] as it provides customers with data portability in enabling them to share their data with others, rather than obtaining access to it themselves.

Recipient accountability is supported by data recipients' legal responsibilities to customers for shared data, the authorisation requirements to be a recipient of customer data under open banking and the technological arrangements (such as cyber-security requirements) which ensures that they are met.

Figure 1.2 illustrates how these three functions combine to produce open banking, and the distinction with other data-related relationships and frameworks described in this section.

*Figure 1.2 Functions of Open Banking*

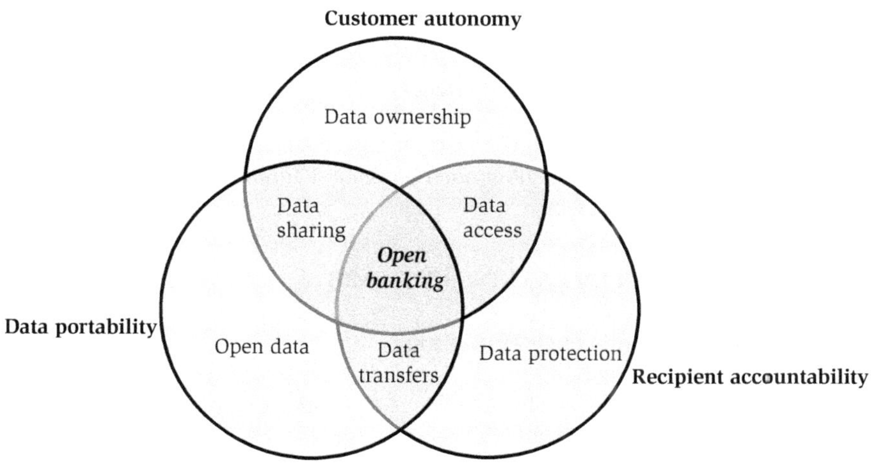


### 1.1.4 Summary

This part of the chapter has explained the meaning, objectives and functions of open banking systems. The objectives, and the functions which need to be performed to achieve them are illustrated in Figure 1.3.

24. *Privacy Act 1998* (Cth) ('*Privacy Act*'). Australian Privacy Principle 12 ('APP12') created under the *Privacy Act* provides a framework for individuals to get access to their personal information.

*Figure 1.3 Objectives and Functions of Open Banking*

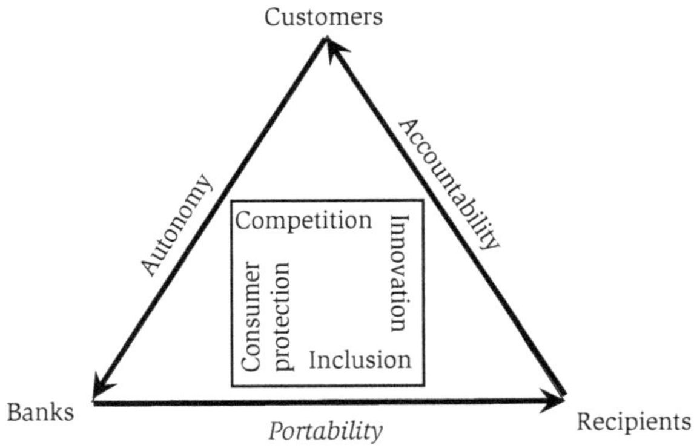


It can now be seen how the functions required to be performed in order for open banking to be effective in achieving its objectives are encapsulated in the definition of open banking provided at the beginning of this chapter:

*sharing customer banking data* (Portability) *as the customer directs,* (Autonomy) *for use as the customer desires.* (Accountability)

Based on this understanding of the meaning, objectives and functions of open banking, the next part introduces how open banking is implemented in a jurisdiction through its open banking system.

## 1.2 WHAT ARE OPEN BANKING SYSTEMS?

### 1.2.1 Implementations of Open Banking

The meaning of open banking established above does not explain how open banking is implemented in the jurisdictions which seek to achieve its objectives. This is done by establishing an open banking system, which can be defined as:

> the system of rules and technology used by participants for open banking.

This definition comprises the three foundations of open banking systems: technology, rules and participation, explained in the next section. This definition can be combined with the definition of open banking established in the previous part of this chapter, to provide the following more comprehensive definition of an open banking system:

> the system of rules and technology used by participants for sharing customer banking data as the customer directs, for use as the customer desires.

This definition of an open banking system is explained further below by reference to the foundations of open banking systems which enable the performance of their functions and some of the features which distinguish different open banking systems.

### 1.2.2 Foundations of Open Banking Systems

Open banking systems implement open banking through a combination of technology, rules and participation. These form three foundations of open banking systems and are supported by standards, enforceability and regulation, respectively.

#### *(a) Technology and Standards*

Open banking is often considered to be first and foremost a technology innovation. This is because the portability, autonomy and accountability functions of open banking are operationally performed through the use of interoperable data technology, primarily APIs. APIs are a set of protocols which enable communication between computer applications, by setting out data available for retrieval and how it can be retrieved. Although APIs are not new, they are considered to be the most reliable technological foundation for open banking and are fundamental to the interoperability required for open banking to be effective. In fact, APIs are so commonly used that open banking systems are, in some jurisdictions such as Singapore and Hong Kong, referred to as 'open API' systems.

The use of APIs ensures that open banking is not confined to the use of any particular technology platform. Indeed, there is no 'operator' of an open banking system that is responsible for the operation of such a platform. Instead, different participants operate their own technology with the help of other entities as needed. The technical coordination required for these different technological frameworks to interact effectively is conducted through *standards*. These standards ensure that the autonomy, portability and accountability functions can be operationally performed. As explained earlier in this chapter, customer autonomy is supported by the customer experience standards which enables customers to control the sharing of their data, data portability is supported by the standards applicable to the APIs which enables recipients to obtain access to customer data, and recipient accountability is supported by the standards which protect the shared data from misuse, such as cyber-security controls. Accordingly, the extent of standardisation achieved in an open banking system directly affects its efficacy in achieving its objectives. The role of standards in open banking systems is analysed in Chapter 6.

#### *(b) Rules and Enforceability*

Whilst the technology of open banking systems govern their operational performance, it does not govern other matters, such as what data should be sharable by customers, who must share those data, what rights and obligations are associated with sharing data and who is responsible if something goes wrong. These matters are determined by the rules of an open banking system. From an engineering perspective, these are 'non-functional requirements' because they are not expressed as the relationship between observable inputs and outputs. Nevertheless, they are fundamental to the performance of the functions of open banking, and they are fundamental in establishing the trust needed for customers and others to participate in open banking.

Whilst rules enable the performance of the functions of open banking, they cannot ensure the performance of these functions on their own. In order to make the rules effective they need to be legally *enforceable*. The laws which ensure the enforceability of the rules of an open banking system act in the same way that standards do for the technology of an open banking system, by facilitating the coordination of participants. Customer autonomy is supported by the *legal rights* which customers have to share data, data portability is supported by the *legal relationships* between banks and data recipients, and recipient accountability is supported by the *legal responsibilities* of recipients for the safekeeping and use of shared customer data. Accordingly, the extent of enforceability of these legal rights, responsibilities and relationships directly affects the system's efficacy in achieving its objectives. The legal rights, responsibilities and relationships which underpin open banking are analysed in Chapters 5 to 11.

### *(c) Participation and Regulation*

A further foundation of open banking systems is participation. Without participation by banks and recipients, open banking systems cannot perform their functions or achieve their objectives. In order to be effective, an open banking system must have many customers using it to require many banks to share data with many recipients. The more banks which participate, the more sources of data available for customers to share. The more recipients which participate, the more goods and services offered to customers by recipients using the shared customer data. To enable this participation, banks and recipients may need to use third parties and some participants may need to work with banks and recipients. The scale of participation directly affects the data portability in an open banking system and, as explained in Chapter 3, is fundamental to establish the connections needed for an open banking system to develop into the ecosystem required for it to achieve its objectives. For this reason, this book treats the *participant connectivity* it provides as an additional, related function of open banking. This is illustrated in Figure 1.4.

*Figure 1.4 Relationship Between Participant Connectivity and Other Functions*

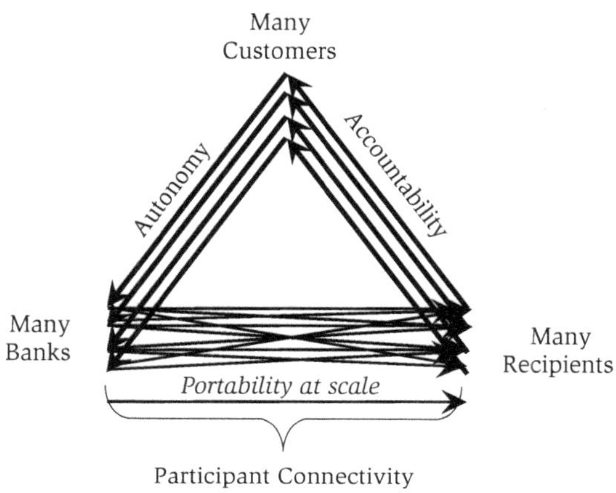


In order to be effective, participation in open banking must follow the standards and the rules. In fact, the standards and rules at the foundation of open banking systems are themselves supported by the extent of regulatory involvement and oversight with respect to participation in the system. Whilst regulatory oversight of participation might not be necessary if participants comply themselves, self-interest can mitigate against voluntary compliance. Also, regulatory supervision can encourage participants to coordinate and progress the development of open banking, as well as establish trust in participants that the system will be fairly governed beyond influence from participants. Accordingly *regulation of participation* in the admission of participants to the open banking system, or in monitoring compliance of participants with the standards and rules, or in taking action against participants when there is non-compliance, is important in ensuring the efficacy of an open banking system. Participation is analysed further in Chapters 9 to 11.

In summary, the three foundations of open banking systems, technology, rules and participation, are supported by three frameworks, standardisation, enforceability and regulation. These are illustrated in Figure 1.5.

*Figure 1.5 Foundations of an Open Banking System*

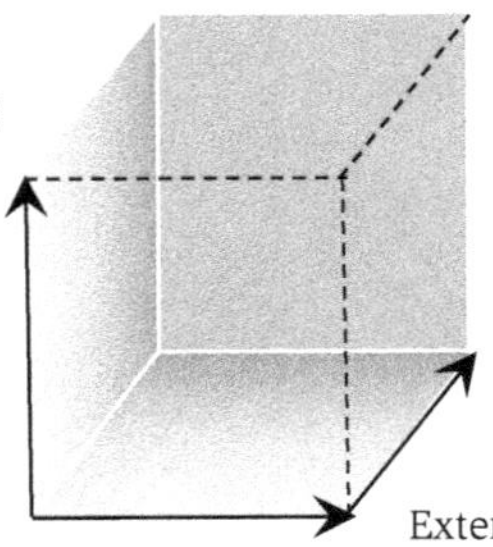


This representation of the foundations of open banking systems can also serve as a basis for comparing different open banking systems. An example is set out in the next chapter.

### 1.2.3 Features of Different Open Banking Systems

As noted earlier, open banking is implemented differently in different jurisdictions and, as a result, open banking systems differ across the world. There are many ways to distinguish them from each other, including the differing objectives sought to be achieved, the difference in outcomes already achieved and the state of progress in their development. Another is to compare that extent of their technology, rule and participation foundations described above. A further basis is to distinguish them by reference to the features which arise from those foundations. Three often used are the scope of the data which can be shared, the depth of functionality available with that data, and the scale of participation.

#### *(a) Scope of Data Able to Be Shared*

The scope of the data able to be shared through an open banking system is a critical feature arising from its design. The more sources of data available to be shared under an open banking system then the greater the potential choices which the customers could make and the greater the potential benefits which they could be offered through increased innovation and inclusion. The scope differs in different jurisdictions. As explained in Chapter 5, the data able to be shared under UK open banking is limited to payment accounts (as it is in the EU) whilst data from a broad range of bank accounts is able to be shared under Australian open banking.

#### *(b) Depth of Functionality Enabled with Shared Data*

The depth of functionality provided by an open banking system is also a critical feature arising from its design. The primary distinction is whether only what is known as 'read access' is provided meaning that data can be shared, but it cannot be acted upon within the system. The alternative is what is known as 'read and write access' meaning that actions can also be initiated through the system, such as the initiation of payments. The greater the depth of functionality offered; the more convenience open banking can provide customers because the consequences of choices can be acted upon within the same system. This depth of functionality also differs between jurisdictions. For example, also as explained in Chapter 5, under Australian open banking this is currently limited to data sharing whereas payments can also be initiated in the UK and the EU systems.

### *(c) Scale of Participation Accessible in Data Sharing*

A further critical design feature of an open banking system is the scale of participation at which it can be implemented. As explained above, participation is essential for open banking's efficacy. Different open banking systems enable different participation based on who is required to share customer data and who is able to receive customer data under the system. For example, in Chapter 5 it is explained that the Australian system requires all banks to share customer data, as well as some recipients (through reciprocity), whereas the EU system is limited to the providers of payment accounts, to which the UK adds nine specified banks.

These three features are illustrated as different dimensions in Figure 1.6. In the next chapter, they are used to illustrate the differences in the scope, scale and depth of the open banking systems of Australia and the UK.

*Figure 1.6 Features of Scope, Scale and Depth of an Open Banking System*

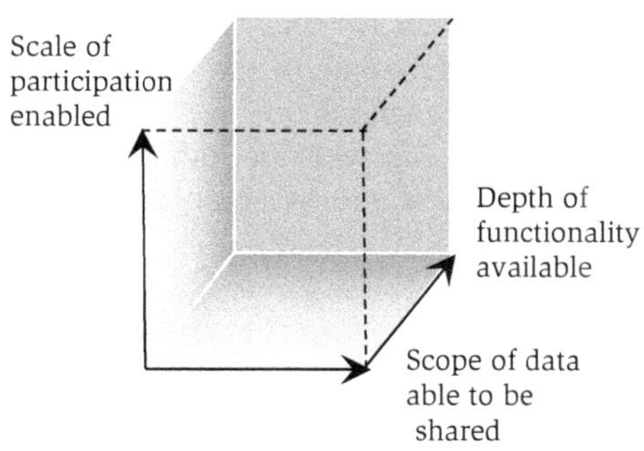


## 1.2.4 Summary

This part of this chapter has explained the meaning of open banking and the functions, foundations and features of open banking systems. These can be described as the *Why, How, What* and *Where* of open banking systems, as illustrated in Figure 1.7.

*Figure 1.7 Relationship Between Objectives, Functions, Foundations and Features*

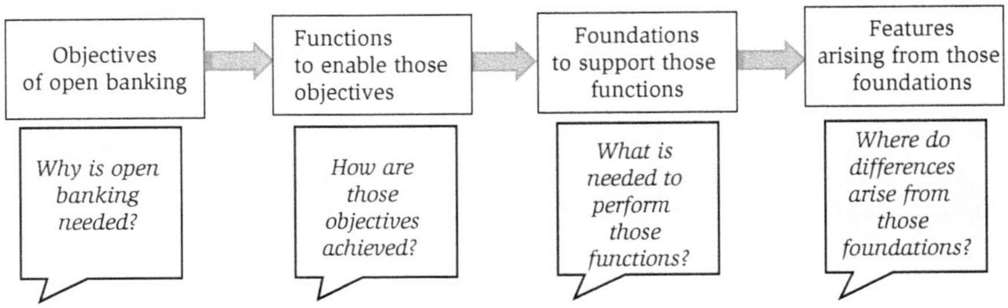


This analysis is fundamental in the evaluation of open banking from a banking law context conducted in this book. Before explaining this, it is necessary to introduce the role of trust in open banking.

## 1.3 WHAT IS THE ROLE OF TRUST IN OPEN BANKING?

### 1.3.1 Importance of Trust in Open Banking

Although customers are likely to share data about themselves often in their digital lives, and consent to sharing their data regularly when online, open banking provides transparency on the choice to share data and its consequences. The analysis in this book shows different sources of uncertainty in open banking including the use of new technology, the complexity of understanding data and information, and the need to rely on others when their performance cannot be easily verified. Open banking depends on customers choosing to share their data despite this uncertainty and, as a result, trust is critical to the efficacy of open banking systems.[25]

Trust has many definitions but some of the most relevant to its role in open banking are that trust 'gives people confidence to place their faith in strangers and systems',[26] 'is a confident relationship with the unknown',[27] and is 'a judgment of confident reliance on another person, group, organization or system when there is

25. *See, e.g.*, Daniel Gozman, Jonas Hedman and Kasper Sylvest Olsen, 'Open Banking: Emergent Roles, Risks & Opportunities' (2018) (183) *Research Papers;* Ine van Zeeland and Jo Pierson, 'In Banks We Trust: Banks as Custodians of Personal Data in Open Banking Ecosystems', SSRN (Research Paper, 30 July 2021) https://papers.ssrn.com/sol3/papers.cfm?abstract_id=3896405; Faith Reynolds et al., 'Consumer Priorities for Open Banking' (Research Report, June 2019) https://www.openbanking.org.uk/wp-content/uploads/Consumer-Priorities-for-Open-Banking-report-June-2019.pdf; Data Standards Body and Consumer Policy Research Centre, 'Stepping Towards Trust' (Research Report, August 2020) https://consumerdatastandards.gov.au/wp-content/uploads/2020/09/20200902_CPRC-Report-1_Publication.pdf.
26. Philippa Ryan, *Trust and Distrust in Digital Economies* (Routledge, 2019) 13.
27. Rachel Botsman, *Who Can You Trust?: How Technology Brought Us Together – And Why It Could Drive Us Apart* (Penguin UK, 2017) 18.

uncertainty and risk'.[28] Importantly, each of these refers to the related concept of confidence. This book refers to different levels of confidence in referring to the aspects of trust required for open banking to be effective, as explained in the next section.

### 1.3.2 Difference Levels of Confidence in Open Banking

From the customer's perspective, the different aspects of trust related to open banking considered in this book can be characterised as confidence at different levels (adapted from the 'trust stack' developed by Botsman):[29]

- Customers need to have confidence in open banking itself, so that they are prepared to engage with it and share their banking data with others they choose. The focus of this trust is the *concept* of open banking, and it is based on the awareness and acceptance of open banking as holding potential benefits through enhanced choice and convenience. It is supported by the legal rights of customers to share their data, disclosure of the consequences of doing so, and education as to the objectives of open banking which seek to ensure that there is *transparency*.
- Customers need to have confidence in those with whom they have chosen to share their data, so that they do share their data with them. The focus of this trust is the *recipient* who receives shared customer data, and it is based on their competence and reliability in performing their obligations to the customer under open banking. It is supported by the legal responsibilities of recipients to customers, the accreditation requirements for recipients and the customer compensation arrangements, which seek to ensure that recipients are *trustworthy*.
- Customers need to have confidence in the arrangements between participants which facilitate and govern the sharing of their data and in which their banks and recipients participate. The focus of this trust is the open banking *system* as a whole, including its participants and regulators. It is based on the integrity and dependability of that system. It is supported by the legal relationships between participants and regulators, the allocation of liability between participants, and framework for managing defaults in open banking systems, which seek to ensure the system's *credibility*.

These confidence levels are dependent on each other. For example, without confidence in the concept of open banking, there would be no willingness to share data and, as a result no need for confidence in the recipients who receive the shared data. Also, without confidence in recipients there would be no sharing of data and, as a result, no need for confidence in the open banking system. Further, as explained in later chapters, if a participant fails to perform its obligations, then confidence in the

28. Nicole Gillespie and Robert Hurley, 'Trust and the Global Financial Crisis', *Handbook of Advances in Trust Research* (Edward Elgar Publishing, 2013), 178.
29. Botsman (n. 27) 60.

system can be impaired, which then causes a loss in confidence in other participants, and potentially the concept of open banking itself. Each of the levels of confidence can reinforce the other levels or undermine them. This relationship is illustrated in Figure 1.8.

*Figure 1.8 Interrelationship of Confidence Levels in Open Banking*

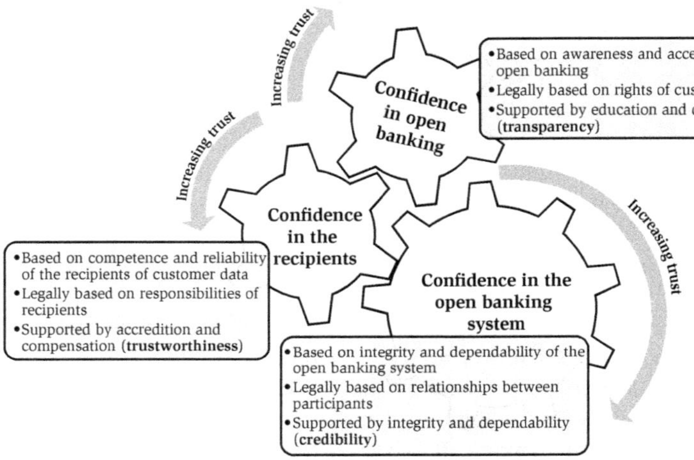


Increasing confidence in each of open banking, recipients and the open banking system increases trust and confidence in each other. However, this also works in reverse as decreasing confidence in any of them also decreases trust and confidence in the others.

## 1.4 WHAT IS A BANKING LAW PERSPECTIVE ON OPEN BANKING?

### 1.4.1 Need for a Different Perspective on Open Banking

Despite open banking's broad emergence in different jurisdictions and the ambition evident from its objectives, in-depth analysis of the legal structure of open banking systems has been limited. Instead, analysis commonly focuses on the outcomes desired from open banking's implementation or technological aspects. Although these perspectives are important, this chapter has shown that they relate only to objectives without consideration of the functions required to be performed to achieve them, or to only one of the foundations which support the performance of those functions.

The limited amount of legal analysis of open banking which has been conducted is also incomplete in its coverage. There is a rich body of academic thinking in privacy law, particularly with respect to the *GDPR,* some of which addresses the data portability rights contained in those laws. However, this has not developed into comprehensive legal analysis of open banking. Most of the published legal research into open banking has been conducted on the EU's *PSD2,* but this is often confined to its comparison with data portability under *GDPR*, or how it seeks to achieve its competition goals. Legal analysis of UK open banking or Australia's Consumer Data Right (CDR), of which Australian open banking forms part, is also primarily devoted to comparisons with *GDPR* and other privacy laws. Other legal analysis of open banking systems focuses on its use to remedy competition issues in contrast to more traditional competition regulatory tools. In the context of the different components of open banking introduced in this chapter, the analysis of the legal foundations of open banking systems is limited to privacy aspects of the accountability function, associated aspects of its consumer protection objective, or its use to achieve its competition objective in contrast to other competition law tools. This is illustrated in Figure 1.9.

*Figure 1.9 Focus of Current Legal Analysis of Open Banking*

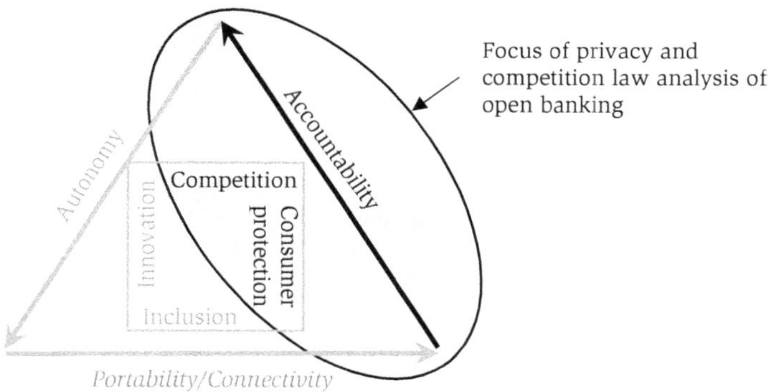


This book argues that a different perspective needs to be taken in analysing open banking, one which more comprehensively considers the legal foundations required for it to perform the functions needed to be effective in achieving its objectives. This perspective arises from some simple, but related questions:

- If data are valuable, shouldn't open banking be designed as banking systems for data, rather than merely technological frameworks for sharing data on banking?
- Shouldn't open banking's support for this value be assessed separately from the protection of the content from which this value is derived?
- If customers are 'banking on data', shouldn't open banking laws be evaluated in a banking law context?

Answers to these questions can be derived from the considerable amount of legal analysis which already underpins banking payment systems. For this to happen, the relationship between open banking systems and banking payment systems needs further explanation.

### 1.4.2 Relationships Between Open Banking Systems and Banking Payment Systems

The relationship between the open banking systems which enable the sharing and custody of customer data, and the banking payment systems which enable the banking and payment of customer funds, arises on two different conceptual levels, transactional connection and functional equivalence.

#### *(a) Transactional Connection*

There is a clear transactional connection between open banking systems and banking payment systems. The customer account data which are shared through open banking systems are generated from transactions in banking payment systems. As explained in the earlier part of this chapter, this can be described as 'read access' as it enables data to be read by those with whom it is shared. As explained in Chapter 5, it can also be described as factual information as it discloses information about things which have happened. In addition, open banking systems can also be used to initiate transactions in banking payment systems such as payments where that functionality is provided. This can be described as 'write access' as it enables the account information to be changed. Also as explained in Chapter 3, it can also be described as the sharing of instructional information which enables things to happen. In this way, the sharing of data generated in either an open banking system or a banking payment system can enable transactions in the other. This is illustrated in Figure 1.10.

*Figure 1.10 Transactional Connection Between Open Banking and Banking Payment Systems*

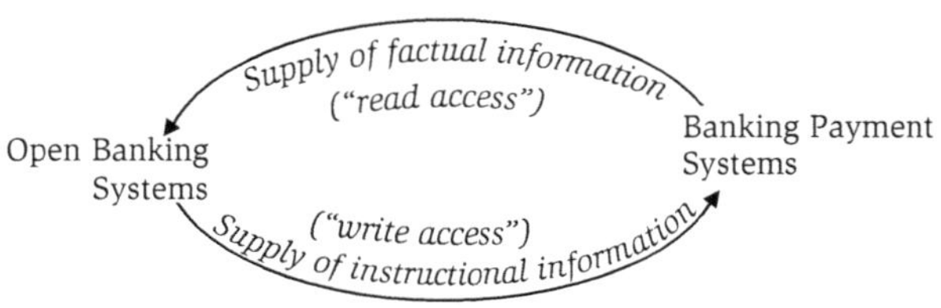


However, this transactional connection is not a sufficient basis to evaluate open banking from a banking law perspective. Instead, functional equivalence is needed.

#### *(b) Functional Equivalence*

As the previous parts of this chapter have shown, open banking systems enable customers to require their banks to share their data with recipients the customers choose, who then are accountable to the customer for the use of the data shared. Banking payment systems perform equivalent functions, enabling customers to require their banks to transfer funds which have been received on their behalf. This functional equivalence between open banking systems and banking payment systems is explained in Chapters 3 and 4. It is based on three premises. The first is that the customer data which are shared under open banking are valuable. The second is that customer funds in modern banking payment systems are comprised of bank accounts, which are also data. The third is that because payments of customer funds are conducted as funds transfers, which are made by communication of messages, both banking payment systems and open banking systems are networks for the communication of valuable information, customer data in the case of open banking systems and customer funds in the case of banking payment systems. The relationship of functional equivalence which results from this is illustrated in Figure 1.11.

*Figure 1.11 Functional Equivalence Between Systems*

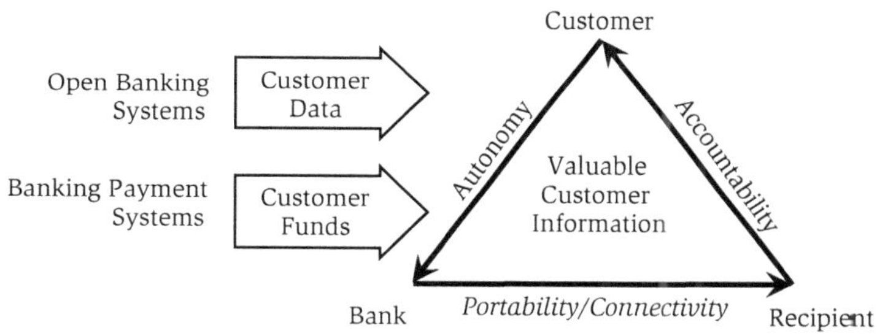


This relationship enables the perspective of banking payment systems to be taken to the legal analysis of open banking systems. The legal features which support autonomy, portability, connectivity and accountability in banking payment systems are well developed. Over the centuries of their evolution, an understanding of the risks in banking payment systems has also developed, together with the role that legal rights, responsibilities and relationships perform in their management and in designing them for resilience. The lessons learned from the experiences of crises and failures have been incorporated into the legal design of these systems, in order to mitigate the impact of crises and failures in the future. Consequently, the principles of legal design needed for the efficiency and safety of banking payment systems can be used as a benchmark against which open banking system can be assessed.

### 1.4.3 Value of a Banking Perspective on Open Banking

This book demonstrates how the legal principles which underpin the transfer and use of money under banking payment systems can be used to assess the legal foundation of open banking systems. Based on the functional equivalence of open banking systems and banking payment systems, the legal features of banking payment systems are used to serve as a benchmark, against which the legal features of the open banking systems can be evaluated. This book takes this approach to compare the legal foundations of the two leading common-law open banking systems with each other, then evaluating those of banking payment systems.

In doing so, it shows how important legal features from banking payment systems can be included in open banking systems. Treating open banking as a banking system *for* data (instead of merely providing data *on* banking) should allow new open banking systems to benefit from lessons learned in protecting and promoting banking of customer funds. This should allow these open banking systems not only to 'work as well as the systems we have for money',[30] but to be as effective and as safe as them too.

## 1.5 HOW TO NAVIGATE THIS BOOK

### 1.5.1 Chapter Summary

The eleven other chapters in this book are briefly summarised below.

- Chapter 2, *Australian and UK Open Banking*, introduces open banking in Australia and the UK and explains why they have been selected for analysis by reference to similarities in their objectives, functions, and extensiveness of their foundations, differences in the structure and substance of their legal foundations, and commonality in their banking laws.
- Chapter 3, *Data, Money and Networks,* develops the equivalence of the functions performed by open banking for customer data and those performed in banking payment systems for customer funds. It explains the nature of customer banking data as valuable information and how customer funds also constitute valuable information. It also explains the communication of information under both open banking and banking payment systems. It concludes by showing how both open banking systems and banking payment systems are networks for the communication of valuable information.
- Chapter 4, *Functions, Foundations and Risks,* completes the development of the functional equivalence between open banking systems and banking payment systems. Using the foundation of both open banking systems and banking payment systems comprising networks for the communication of valuable information developed in the previous chapter, it identifies the comparable functions performed by each and the legal foundations which support that performance. It concludes by developing a framework to categorise the risks which arise in open banking systems.
- Chapter 5, *Supplying Customer Data for Sharing,* commences the analysis of the legal foundations of open banking systems by comparing the legal rights which support making data available for customers to share under the open banking systems and evaluating them against equivalent rights in banking payment systems. It analyses what data customers should have the right to share and who should be required to share customer data, and includes

30. Department of Finance Canada, 'Consumer-Directed Finance: The Future of Financial Services' (Report, February 2020) 20.

consideration of the scope, scale and functionality of open banking systems and the concept of reciprocity.

- Chapter 6, *Sharing Customer Data,* examines the legal foundations of open banking systems for sharing customer data by comparing the legal rights which support the sharing of customer data under the open banking systems and evaluating them against equivalent rights of banking payment systems. It analyses how customer data should be shared and how the rights to share data should be established and includes consideration of screen scraping and the role of standards.
- Chapter 7, *Utilising Shared Customer Data,* examines the legal foundations for governance of the use of shared customer data by comparing the legal responsibilities supporting use of customer data under Australian and UK open banking and evaluating them against the equivalent legal responsibilities under banking payment systems. It analyses limits on the data requested for sharing and how shared customer data should be used and includes consideration of data minimisation and the role of consent.
- Chapter 8, *Preserving Value of Shared Data,* examines the legal foundations for preservation of value of shared customer data by comparing the legal responsibilities supporting the value of customer data under Australian and UK open banking and evaluating them against the equivalent legal responsibilities under banking payment systems. It analyses the legal foundations for the maintenance of the quality, and the management of security, of shared data, and includes consideration of deletion and de-identification of shared data.
- Chapter 9, *Facilitating Participation in Open Banking,* examines the legal foundations for facilitating participation in open banking by comparing the legal relationships which support participation under Australian and UK open banking and evaluating them against the equivalent legal relationships under banking payment systems. It analyses the legal foundations for direct and indirect participation, and outsourcing arrangements, and includes consideration of the disclosure of customer data beyond open banking's regulatory perimeter.
- Chapter 10, *Allocating Liability in Open Banking,* examines the legal foundations for allocating liability in open banking by comparing the legal relationships which establish liability under Australian and UK open banking and evaluating them against the equivalent legal relationships under banking payment systems. It analyses the legal relationships and the allocation of liability between participants, and the compensation arrangements for their customers, and includes consideration of multilateral contracts and depositor protection.
- Chapter 11, *Ensuring Credibility in Open Banking,* examines the legal foundations for ensuring the credibility in open banking by comparing the legal relationships which support stability under Australian and UK open banking and evaluating them against the equivalent legal relationships under banking payment systems. It analyses when participants should be removed from open

banking and the management of participant default and includes consideration of the status of data-related obligations in insolvency.
- Chapter 12, *Open Banking and Banking Laws*, summarises the analysis of the previous chapters in an assessment of the legal foundations of the Australian and UK open banking systems and extracts themes for designing open banking systems. It draws conclusions on the need for a banking law foundation for open banking laws and finishes by identifying opportunities for further research.

The Bibliography after Chapter 12 includes further resources beyond those specifically referenced in footnotes, particularly in relation to the historical illustrations of risks banking and payment systems.

### 1.5.2 Interpretation

In this thesis, unless a contrary intention appears:

- **ACCC** means the Australian Competition and Consumer Commission.
- **API** or **Application Programming Interface** means a set of technological protocols which enable software applications to communicate with each other and to exchange data.
- **Australian system** means the open banking system implemented in Australia.
- **Australian Standards** means the data standards applicable to the Australian system.
- **ADI** or **Authorised Deposit-taking Institution** means an entity which is authorised to carry on banking business under the *Banking Act 1959* (Cth).
- **bank** means the bank that holds the account data of the customer. Under the Australian system, the relevant legislative term is **data holder** and under the UK system it is **Account Servicing Payment Service Provider**.
- **banking payment system** means a legislative, regulatory, contractual, participation and technological arrangements which facilitate the storage and liquidity of customer bank funds.
- ***CCA*** means the *Competition and Consumer Act 2010* (Cth), Part IVD of which establishes and governs the Australian system.
- **CDR** means the Australian Consumer Data Right, of which the Australian system forms the first component.
- **customer** means the customer of the bank who wants to share their account data with a data recipient. Under the Australian system, the relevant legislative term is **CDR consumer** and under the UK system it is **Payment Service User**.
- **DSB** means the Data Standards Body responsible for the creation of the Australian Standards.
- ***GDPR*** means the *General Data Protection Regulation*,[31] as incorporated into UK law.

31. *GDPR* (n. 23).

- **OBIE** means the Open Banking Implementation Entity, which was responsible for implementing the UK open banking system.
- **open banking** means the sharing of customer banking data through standardised technology at the customer's request for use only as the customer directs.
- **open banking system** or **system** means the legislative, regulatory, participation and standardisation arrangements which implement open banking in a jurisdiction.
- ***PSD2*** means the revised *Payment Services Directive* of the European Union.[32]
- ***PSR*** means the *Payment Services Regulation 2017* (UK).
- **recipient** means the person with whom the customer wants to share their account data. Under the Australian system, the relevant legislative term is **data recipient** and under the UK system it is **Account Information Service Provider** or **AISP**.
- **screen scraping** means a process to enable a customer to share bank account data where the customer provides its bank login credentials to the data recipient.
- **UK** means the United Kingdom.
- **UK system** means the open banking system implemented in the United Kingdom.
- **UK Standards** means the data standards applicable to the UK system.

In this book, the first of the three numbers in a section reference is the chapter in which the section is found, the second is the relevant part of that chapter.

32. *PSD2* (n. 2).

CHAPTER 2

# Australian and UK Open Banking

The later chapters of this book compare the legal foundations of the Australian and UK open banking systems and evaluate them against the equivalent legal foundations of banking payment systems. This chapter introduces open banking in Australia and the UK and explains why they have been selected for this comparison and evaluation by reference to:

- similarities in their *objectives* and *functions*;
- similarities in the *extensiveness* of their foundations; and
- differences in the *structure and substance* of their legal foundations.

This chapter concludes by explaining the commonality in the banking laws of Australia and the UK and their relevance to the analysis conducted in this book.

## 2.1 HOW DEVELOPED IS OPEN BANKING IN AUSTRALIA AND THE UK?

Open banking is a relatively recent development in Australia and the UK, as it is elsewhere. It was established in the UK in 2017 although some requirements did not come fully into force until September 2019. Open banking was established in Australia in 2019, although the sharing of customer transaction data did not commence until July 2020, and it was progressively applied to more banks and more banking products until July 2022.

Although the open banking systems in both jurisdictions are barely established when compared to their banking payment systems, they are two of the most developed open banking systems globally. This is due to the strong development of open banking in both jurisdictions. As of March 2022, the participation in open banking in the UK included more than 90 payment account service providers (banks) representing more than 95% of current accounts in the UK. There were more than 230 regulated recipients of customer data and more than 5 million users of open banking services.[1] Payments have been a significant driver of the growth in the use of open banking in the UK, including its use to pay taxes. In Australia, by July 2022, open banking applied to 76 different Australian banks and 114 different banking brands, representing more than 99% of Australian household deposits. At this time, there were 32 recipients of data accredited under the Australian system, of which three acted as principals for a further 31 representatives.[2] In addition to the wide range of bank accounts (including mortgage and savings accounts), data sharing on energy accounts commenced in November 2022.

There is a continuing commitment to the further development of open banking in both jurisdictions. In the UK, work is underway to expand open banking into open finance, by including bank accounts currently excluded from its operation, such as mortgage and savings accounts.[3] In addition, through the 'smart data' initiative the UK government is intending to expand data sharing to other services, such as utilities.[4] Australia's CDR already covers other banking accounts and energy accounts, and it is to be extended to telecommunications accounts and then to non-bank lending, general insurance and superannuation accounts too.[5] Draft legislation has also been released in Australia to enable 'action initiation' so that the CDR can be used by customers to authorise others to take actions on their behalf, such as changing accounts and making payments.[6] In both Australia and the UK, government agencies and regulators see clear benefits of open banking for customers and wider potential benefits for the economy. These are seen in the similarities in their objectives, as explained next.

## 2.2 HOW SIMILAR ARE THEIR OBJECTIVES AND FUNCTIONS?

Australian and UK open banking were established in order to achieve similar objectives, primarily to improve competition and to encourage innovation, although other objectives have developed in importance after the systems were established. The two systems also emphasise similar functions to be performed to achieve those objectives.

### 2.2.1 Australian CDR

Open banking in Australia is the first stage of the CDR. This is an economy-wide right, proposed by the Australian Productivity Commission in 2017 to be 'an avenue to

1. Competition and Markets Authority, 'The Future Oversight of the CMA's Open Banking Remedies' (Reponse to Consultation, 21 March 2022).
2. Australian Treasury, 'Statutory Review of the Consumer Data Right' (Report, 2022).
3. *See* Financial Conduct Authority, 'Open Finance' (Feedback Statement No. FS21/7, March 2021) [3.65], [3.72].
4. *See* Department for Business Energy & Industrial Strategy, 'Next Steps for Smart Data' (Report, September 2020) https://assets.publishing.service.gov.uk/government/uploads/system/uploads/attachment_data/file/915973/smart-data-consultation-response.pdf.
5. Australian Treasury, 'Strategic Assessment: Outcomes' (Report, January 2022).
6. 'Consumer Data Right – Exposure Draft Legislation to Enable Action Initiation', *Australian Government, The Treasury* (Exposure Draft Legislation, 26 September 2022) https://treasury.gov.au/consultation/c2022-317468.

improve market competitiveness and innovation' and 'take Australia beyond the stage of viewing data availability solely through a privacy lens'.[7] Establishing open banking in Australia through the implementation of the CDR was recommended by the review into open banking conducted by the Australian Treasury in 2017.[8] The explanatory material which accompanied the legislation which enacted its legal foundation summarises the purpose of the CDR as follows:

> The primary aim of the CDR is to give consumers the ability to access and use more information about themselves, and about their use of goods and services in a manner that allows them to make more informed decisions about both themselves and the goods and services they use. By doing so, the CDR aims to increase competition, enable consumers to fairly harvest the value of their data, and enhance consumer welfare.
>
> The CDR places the value of consumer data in the hands of the consumer and will enable a range of business opportunities to emerge as new ways of using the data are created. Consumers will be the decision makers in the CDR system and will be able to direct where their data goes in order to obtain the most value from it.[9]

Although competition and innovation objectives were key drivers of open banking in Australia, there was also a strong focus on customer autonomy being foundational to these objectives, which not only related to choice and convenience, but also safety and the need for privacy safeguards. Accordingly, there was a consumer protection objective present too. This has been reinforced since the commencement of open banking, and also lent itself to the development of inclusion as an objective, with recent reviews recommending both the banning of screen scraping and the development of use cases that drive social benefit.[10]

### 2.2.2 UK Open Banking

Open banking in the UK is the outcome of two different processes. The first was the investigation into retail banking conducted by the UK Competition and Markets Authority (CMA). This found that there to be competition problems in retail banking in the UK and that part of the solution was an open API standard for UK banking:

> The aim is to increase consumer engagement by making it easier for customers to see where they could get a better deal. It also aims to increase competitive intensity by supporting the growth of technology that can be adopted by banks and non-bank providers to compete to offer new products.[11]

---

7. Productivity Commission, *Data Availability and Use* (Report No. 82, 2017) 14, 15
8. Australian Treasury, 'Review into Open Banking: Giving Customers Choice, Convenience and Confidence' (Report, December 2017).
9. Explanatory Memorandum, Treasury Laws Amendment (Consumer Data Right) Bill 2018 (Cth) 5 ('CDR Bill EM').
10. *See* Australian Treasury, 'Statutory Review of the Consumer Data Right' (n 2). *See also* Australian Treasury, 'Inquiry into Future Directions for the Consumer Data Right: Giving Consumers Choice, Convenience and Confidence' (Report, October 2020).
11. Competition and Markets Authority (n. 1) 55.

The order issued by the CMA following its report, known as the *CMA Order*,[12] imposed obligations on the nine largest banks in Great Britain and Northern Ireland at the time (known as the 'CMA9') to remedy the competition problems, including by requiring those banks:

> [T]o create and pay for an Open Banking Implementation Entity (OBIE) to agree, consult upon, implement, maintain and make widely available, with charge, open and common banking standards.[13]

The second process that led to open banking was the need to implement the EU's *PSD2* which was intended to continue the development of an integrated internal market for safe electronic payments, in part to ensure 'that consumers, merchants and companies enjoy choice and transparency of payment services'.[14] *PSD2* extends beyond payment services to cover services which were 'complementary' to them including sharing account information. This extended coverage was 'to provide consumers with adequate protection for their payment and account data as well as legal certainty about the status of account information service providers'.[15]

The two processes were not independent of each other. In making its findings, the CMA was conscious of *PSD2* and envisaged that compliance with its requirements would also allow compliance with PSD2. It also saw PSD2 as a means to 'address the risk that consumer confidence in services using API technology will be undermined'.[16] Accordingly, the *CMA Order* had a primary focus on competition and innovation as its objectives, whilst *PSD2* complemented this with an additional focus on consumer protection. Both have a distinct emphasis on achieving these objectives through encouraging and enhancing the effectiveness of customer choice. This has been reinforced by reports of UK regulators which have emphasised that UK open banking 'should continue to support innovation and greater competition for consumers and businesses'.[17] Since its operation, a financial inclusion purpose has emerged in UK open banking, particularly as a result of the supervisory role undertaken by the Financial Conduct Authority (FCA).

### 2.2.3 Summary

In summary, open banking in both Australia and the UK each has a strong focus on competition and innovation objectives, whilst the UK had an initial stronger focus on consumer protection, because of the influence of *PSD2*. Each of Australia and UK has

---

12. *Retail Banking Market Investigation Order 2017* (UK) ('*CMA Order*').
13. Competition and Markets Authority (n. 1).
14. *Directive 2015/2366/EU of the European Parliament and of the Council of 25 November 2015 on Payment Services in the Internal Market, amending Directives 2002/65/EC, 2009/110/EC, and 2013/36/EU and Regulation (EU) No 1093/2010 and repealing Directive 2007/64/EC* OJ L 337/35 ('*PSD2*') recital 5.
15. *Ibid.* recital 28.
16. Competition and Markets Authority (n. 1) 55.
17. HM Treasury et al., 'Joint Statement on the Future of Open Banking' (Policy Paper, 25 March 2022).

an emerging financial inclusion objective. These are illustrated in Figure 2.1, using the same representation explained in Chapter 1.

*Figure 2.1 Objectives of Open Banking in Australia and the UK*

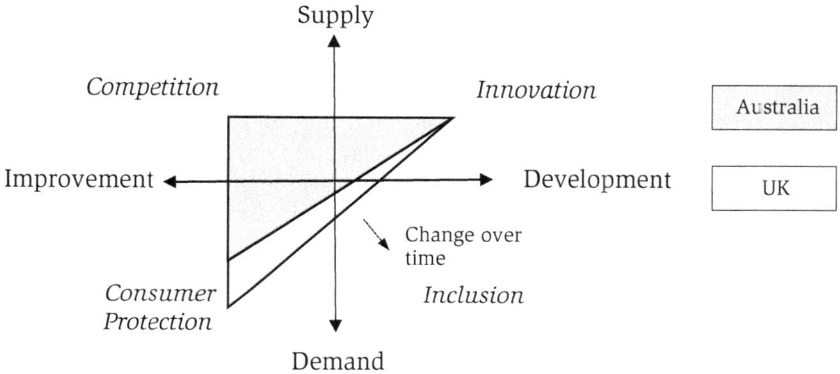


In addition, each of Australian and UK open banking systems emphasised the role of customer autonomy in achieving those objectives. These similarities in objectives and functions are important to the comparative analysis in later chapters as they mean that differences in the legal foundations of the two systems should not be attributed to the systems having different objectives.

## 2.3 HOW SIMILAR IS THE EXTENSIVENESS OF THEIR FOUNDATIONS?

Chapter 1 described three foundations of open banking systems: standardised technology, enforceable rules and regulation of participation. These foundations are similarly extensive in the open banking systems of Australia and the UK.

### 2.3.1 Standardisation of Technology

The Australian and UK open banking systems are each supported by the mandatory adoption of a single set of specific standards which are applicable to the data which are shared and the means by which those data are shared. The specificity of the mandatory standards provides a comprehensiveness to each system which enables a substantive comparison.

### (a) Australian Standards

The standards of the Australian open banking system ('Australian Standards')[18] were created by the Data Standards Chair, a statutory position created under the legislative foundation of the CDR.[19] The Data Standards Chair is supported by the Data Standards Body (DSB, which is now part of the Australian Treasury) which conducts the technical work required for the development of the standards.[20] The legislative foundation of Australian system provides for the data standards to cover the format and description of customer data; the disclosure of customer data; the collection, use, accuracy, storage, security and deletion of customer data; and de-identification of customer data.[21] The legislative framework mandates the adoption of the Australian standards for Australian open banking by requiring that requests for customer data, requests for the customer to authorise the disclosure of customer data, and the disclosure of customer data in response to a request, must all be made in accordance with them.[22]

### (b) UK Standards

The creation of the standards of the UK open banking system ('UK Standards') was a fundamental element of the *CMA Order*. It required that an Open Banking Implementation Entity (OBIE) be established to create standards which covered open APIs, data formats and security as well as governance arrangements and customer redress mechanisms.[23] Also, they were required to have the features necessary for banks to comply with the open banking requirements of the UK's implementation of *PSD2*.[24]

The mandatory nature of the UK Standards is more obscure than the Australian Standards. *PSD2* requires the adherence to standards,[25] but does not prescribe any particular data standard for use. Accordingly, the UK's implementation of *PSD2* does not impose obligations to use the UK Standards in the same way as Australian open banking does for the Australian Standards. However, the *CMA Order* does require that the CMA9 banks adhere to the UK Standards and, as Chapter 6 explains, for various reasons the use of the UK Standards has become widespread to the extent that the application of those standards is the core element of UK open banking.

18. Data Standards Body, 'Consumer Data Standards v 1.22.0', https://consumerdatastandards.org.au.
19. *Competition and Consumer Act* 2010 (Cth) ('*CCA*') s. 56FF.
20. *Ibid.* s. 56FK. The Data Standards Body was a function originally supported by Data61, part of Australia's national science research agency, Commonwealth Science and Industrial Research Organisation (CSIRO).
21. *Ibid.* s. 56FA.
22. *Competition and Consumer (Consumer Data Right) Rules 2020* ('*CDR Rules*') rr. 4.4(3), 4.5, 4.6. This is explained further in Chapter 5.
23. *CMA Order* (n. 12) Art. 10.2.
24. *Ibid.* Art. 10.1.2.
25. *Commission Delegated Regulation (EU) 2018/389 Supplementing Directive (EU) 2015/2366 of the European Parliament and of the Council with regard to Regulatory Technical Standards tor Strong Customer Authentication and Common and Secure Open Standards of Communication* OJ L69/23 Art. 30 ('*SCA-RTS*').

### 2.3.2 Enforceability of Rules

The Australian and UK open banking systems are each supported by the legal enforceability of rules which underpin the operation of their standards, and which apply over and above them. This distinguishes the two systems from open banking in those other jurisdictions where it is comprised only of voluntary standards, or individually negotiated contracts. The presence of enforceable rules enables the analysis of consistent legal rights, responsibilities and relationships established under the systems. The same analysis cannot be conducted on voluntary frameworks which are not supported by laws and regulations as they do not provide a consistent legal framework for all bank customers to share their data. Despite both jurisdictions having extensive foundations of legally enforceable rules, the structure and substance of the enforceable rules differs between them as explained in section 3 of this chapter below and the analysis in the later chapters of this book.

### 2.3.3 Regulation of Participation

Australian and UK open banking are designed to establish an 'ecosystem' of participation. This is regarded as being critical for achieving the benefits of open banking, for people, businesses and the wider economy in both Australia and the UK. Indeed, the CMA has defined the success of open banking so far in the UK by reference to the growth of the 'Open Banking ecosystem' and has stated that it is critical to future success:[26]

> Moving forward, it will be critical that this vibrant ecosystem and the benefits it generates for people, businesses and the wider economy in helping to open up competition and forge the way for new services to be offered, continues to thrive and develop.[27]

In Australia, the intention of open banking to create an ecosystem of participation has been clearly expressed, so that it can:

> connect more customers, data holders and data recipients, linked by their participation in a system with set rules and standards. Customers will develop relationships with both data holders and data recipients. Sometimes these connections will be strengthened by some parties performing more than one role. The connections and network effects should increase ... [and] [a]s the connections increase, a data ecosystem should naturally grow in a similar way to the ecosystems in other markets where unique functions may be performed by specialist service providers, enabling a wider range of higher quality and more cost-effective services. Specialisation may manifest in the regime in a number of different ways

26. Competition and Markets Authority, 'Update on Open Banking,' (Corporate report, 5 November 2021).
27. *Ibid.*

> including through the presence of software providers, software-as-a-service, outsourced service providers, arm's length businesses working cooperatively and arm's length businesses operating independently but in complementary ways.[28]

In both Australia and the UK, these open banking ecosystems are supported by extensive regulation of participation which requires both the participation of banks to enable customers to share their data, and the authorisation of recipients of those customer data, and enables the supervision of those participants. The extent of this regulation enables a meaningful analysis to be made of the legal support provided for participation in each system.

### *(a) Regulation of Participation in Australian Open Banking*

As explained in Chapter 5, Australian open banking subjects all Australian banks to open banking. Also, it requires that recipients of customer data be accredited, as explained in Chapter 9. As participants in open banking, both banks and recipients are subject to regulation.

The primary regulator of the Australian open banking system is the Australian Competition and Consumer Commission (ACCC). The ACCC is the primary competition regulator in Australia and is responsible for monitoring compliance and enforcement of the *Competition and Consumer Act 2010* (*CCA*) including, as noted in section 3 of this chapter below, the legislative provisions which establish the CDR and Australian open banking. In addition, the ACCC is responsible for the accreditation of recipients and acts 'Accreditation Register' to keep the 'Register of Accredited Persons',[29] as well as a database of data holders containing identification and other relevant details.[30] The ACCC is supported in the regulation of the CDR by the Office of the Australian Information Commissioner (OAIC), which is responsible for regulating privacy and confidentiality under the CDR and handles complaints and notifications of breaches.

### *(b) Regulation of Participation in UK Open Banking*

Chapters 5 and 9 also explain that UK open banking requires the participation of particular banks and the authorisation of recipients of customer data. Like the Australian system, the UK open banking system also subjects banks and recipients to regulation.

There are also multiple regulators involved in UK open banking. The implementation of the *CMA* Order, and OBIE's execution of the arrangements required, was subject to the oversight of the *CMA*. However, the OBIE does not act as authorising regulator for UK open banking, as this role is performed by the FCA, which was the

---

28. Australian Treasury, 'Inquiry into Future Directions for the Consumer Data Right: Giving Consumers Choice, Convenience and Confidence' (Report, October 2020) 106.
29. *CCA* (n. 19) ss 4(1) (definition of 'Accreditation Registrar'), 56E.
30. *CDR Rules* (n. 22) r. 5.25.

'competent authority' under the UK's implementation of *PSD2*.[31] In this role, the FCA is responsible for the authorisation, supervision and regulation of the participants in UK open banking. The FCA maintains the register of regulated participants in order to perform its functions,[32] and to perform its obligations under the *CMA Order* the OBIE maintains a directory of participants. In addition to the CMA and the FCA, the Information Commissioner's Office has regulatory responsibilities relating to data protection obligations in connection with open banking in the UK.

Changes to the regulatory structure of UK open banking were flagged in 2022 with the CMA stating that oversight in the future should be jointly led by the FCA and the Payment System Regulator, being the economic regulator for payment systems in the UK.[33]

### 2.3.4 Summary

Australian and UK open banking systems have similarly extensive foundations of standardisation of technology, enforceability of rules and regulation of participation. Although the substance of these foundations differs, their extent means that there is a comprehensive depth of content in these systems which is not available for legal analysis in systems which have narrower foundations, such as voluntary systems. This is illustrated in Figure 2.2, which compares the extent of the foundations of open banking in Australia and the UK with those of Singapore and Hong Kong, which are voluntary systems having a similar extent of standardisation but with limited regulation of participation (the regulation being more limited in Singapore than Hong Kong).

*Figure 2.2 Comparison of Foundations of Selected Systems*

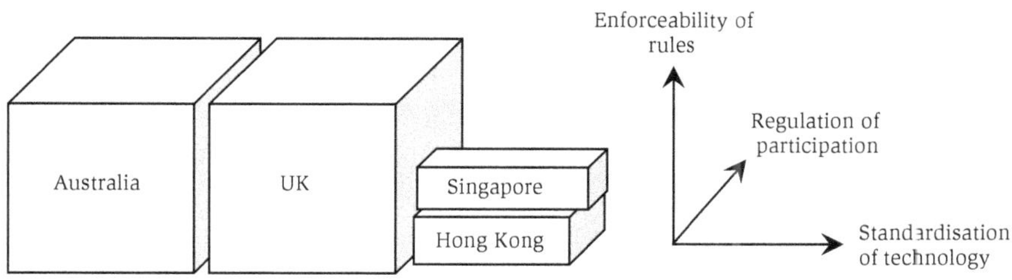


The extent of legal and regulatory foundations of Australian and UK open banking enables a comprehensive analysis of the legal rights, responsibilities and relationships in this book to be meaningfully undertaken.

31. The FCA is designated as the 'competent authority' for the purposes of *PSD2*: *Payment Services Regulation 2017* (UK) ('*PSR*') reg. 106.
32. *Ibid.* reg. 4.
33. HM Treasury et al. (n. 17).

## 2.4 HOW ARE THEIR LEGAL FOUNDATIONS DIFFERENT?

Despite the similarities described in the parts above, there are significant differences in the structure and substance of the legal foundations of open banking in Australia and the UK.

### 2.4.1 Differences in Structure of Legal Foundations

#### *(a) Structure of Legal Foundation of Open Banking in Australia*

The CDR was established by the *Treasury Laws (Consumer Data Right) Act 2019* (Cth).[34] This Act created a new Part IVD of the *CCA*,[35] which is economy-wide legislation intended to 'enhance the welfare of Australians through the promotion of competition and fair trading and provision for consumer protection'.[36] The new Part IVD creates the CDR and the architecture of standards, rules and regulation at its foundation. It applies to sectors of the Australian economy by designation of the Australian Treasurer through legislative instrument.[37] The *Consumer Data Right (Authorised Deposit Taking Institutions) Designation 2019* (Cth) ('*Open Banking Designation*')[38] made such a designation for the banking sector. Another designation has subsequently been made for the energy sector and a draft designation has been issued for the telecommunications sector.

Following the designation, the ACCC issued the *Competition and Consumer (Consumer Data Right) Rules 2020* ('*CDR Rules*'). The *CDR Rules* deal with disclosure, collection, use accuracy, storage, security or deletion of customer data, and the accreditation of recipients. They apply broadly to all sectors to which the CDR applies, although there are separate schedules with provisions for particular sectors. They have been updated on a number of occasions to address changes needed to facilitate the development of Australian open banking in the CDR.

The *CCA*, the *Open Banking Designation* and the *CDR Rules* are the legislative instruments at the foundation of the Australian open banking system. The *Privacy Act*, Australia's privacy legislation, does not apply to Australian open banking as the *CCA* contains its own privacy safeguards.[39]

#### *(b) Structure of Legal Foundation of Open Banking in the UK*

The two processes which led to open banking being established in the UK resulted in two separate legislative instruments at its foundation:

34. *Treasury Laws Amendment (Consumer Data Right) Act 2019* (Cth) ('*CDR Act*').
35. *CCA* (n. 19) s. 2.
36. *Ibid.*
37. *Ibid.* s. 56AC.
38. *Consumer Data Right (Authorised Deposit Taking Institutions) Designation 2019* (Cth) ('*Open Banking Designation*').
39. *CCA* (n. 19) s. 56EC.

- Part 2 of the *CMA Order* issued by the CMA under the *Enterprise Act (2002)* UK, which implemented the recommendations of the CMA's retail banking market investigation, and
- Part 7 of the *Payment Services Regulation 2017* (UK) (*PSR*), which translated *PSD2* into UK legislation.

The *CMA Order* is very limited with respect to the rights and responsibilities in sharing customer data as its primary function was to govern the establishment and operation of the OBIE which created the UK standards for the sharing of data.[40] Most of the substantive legal rights and responsibilities for UK open banking are in the *PSR*. These relate to the use of the shared data, the requirements for consent, and the storage of the shared data as well as authorisation of participants.[41] The *PSR* also requires compliance with particular Regulatory Technical Standards of the EU, including the Regulatory Technical Standard for Strong Customer Authentication and Secure Open Standards of Communication (*SCA-RTS*).[42] The *SCA-RTS* also provides the basis on which the UK Standards are approved for compliance with the *PSR* for a UK bank.[43]

Unlike the *CCA*, neither the *CMA Order* nor *PSR* contains a privacy regime for shared open banking data. Accordingly, when it was established, UK open banking relied on *GDPR* to apply to customer data which is 'personal data' for the purpose of *GDPR*,[44] being information relating to an identified or identifiable natural person. Although *GDPR* effectively became part of the domestic law of the UK as the 'UK GDPR' following the withdrawal of the UK from the EU,[45] for simplicity this book refers to it as the *GDPR*. Together, the *CMA Order*, *PSR*, and *GDPR* form the legislative foundation of UK open banking.

### 2.4.2 Differences in Substance of Legal Foundations

That there are significant differences in the substance of the legal foundations of open banking in Australia and the UK is evident from the analysis undertaken in Chapters 5 to 11 of this book. These include:

- *Differences in legal rights*: Australian open banking grants rights to customers to share data from a broader range of banks, other data holders, bank accounts

40. *CMA Order* (n. 12) Art. 14.
41. *PSR* (n. 31) reg. 70.
42. *SCA-RTS* (n. 25). *See also PSR* (n. 31) reg. 70(2)(a).
43. *SCA-RTS* (n. 25) Art. 30.
44. *See* Financial Conduct Authority, 'Payment Services and Electronic Money – Our Approach' (Approach Document, June 2019) 91. *See also* Information Commissioners Office, 'The Information Commissioner's Response to the HM Treasury Consultation on the Implementation of the Revised EU Payment Services Directive II' (Consultation Response, 17 March 2017). The connection between *GDPR* and *PSD2* is recognised in *PSD2*: *PSD2* (n. 14) recital 89, Art. 94(1). Although *PSR* contains neither that recital, nor that wording, it is clear that *GDPR* still applies to the personal data held under the UK system.
45. *See European Withdrawal Act 2018 2018* (UK) s. 3 ('*European Withdrawal Act 2018*'). *See also Data Protection, Privacy and Electronic Communications (Amendments etc) (EU Exit) Regulations 2019* (UK) ('*EU Exit Regulations*').

and accounts beyond banking whilst UK open banking grants customers the rights to initiate payments through open banking.

- *Differences in legal responsibilities*: Australian and UK open banking impose different responsibilities on recipients of customer data in relation to data minimisation and the treatment of customer data when a recipient defaults.
- *Differences in legal relationships*: Australian and UK open banking have different requirements for authorisation to participate in open banking, different arrangements for the use of intermediaries by authorised recipients and very different bases for allocating liability between participants.

From these differences in the legal substance between the systems arise different features of scope, scale and functionality. This is explained throughout this book and illustrated in Figure 2.3.

*Figure 2.3 Differences in Legal Features of Australian and UK Open Banking*

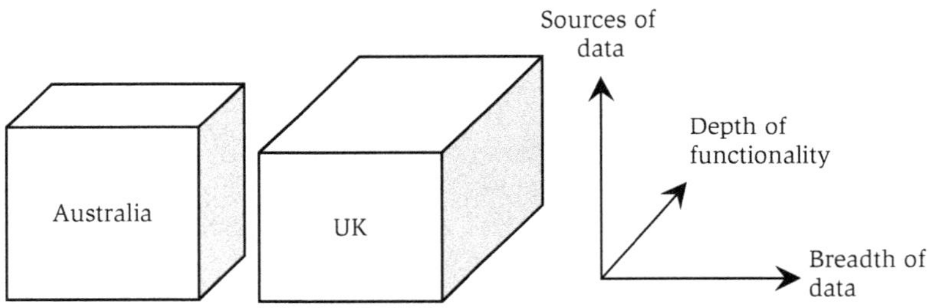


### 2.4.3 Summary

The legal foundations of open banking in Australia and the UK are very different. Australia has a hierarchy of legislative instruments on which the Australian Standards rest, whilst the UK standards rest on a combination of legislative instruments applying in a less hierarchical way. This is illustrated in Figure 2.4.

*Figure 2.4 Legal Foundations of Australian and UK Open Banking*

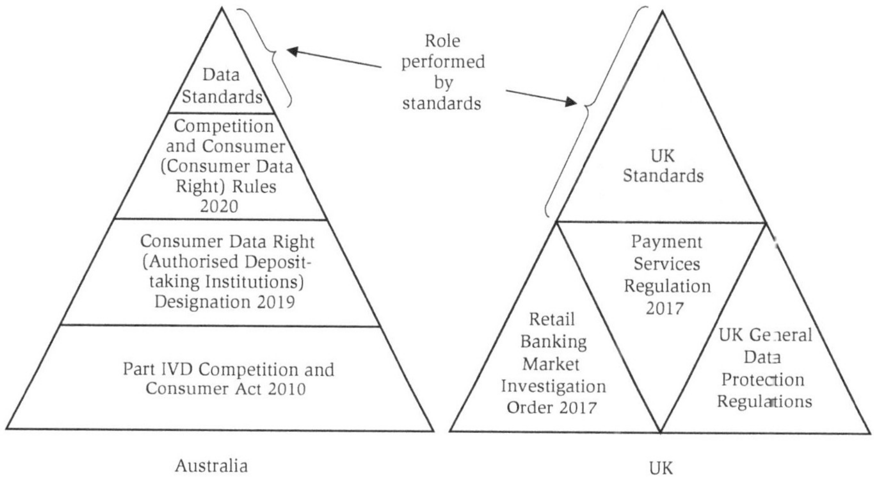


This difference in legislative foundation of Australian and UK open banking, when combined with the similarity in their purpose and the extensiveness of their foundations enables a meaningful analysis of the effect of those differences. This is enhanced by the commonalities in their banking laws which permit an evaluation against the legal foundation of banking payment systems.

## 2.5 HOW MUCH DO THEIR BANKING LAWS HAVE IN COMMON?

The analysis of the legal foundations of Australian and UK open banking in this book is not only a comparison between them to identify their similarities and differences. An evaluation against the functionally equivalent legal foundations of banking payment systems is also conducted. This is made possible by the commonality of the banking laws at the foundation of banking payment systems in Australia and the UK.

The laws of banking in both Australia and the UK primarily relate to the relationship between banker and customer, which is based on the common law of contract and agency. These differ little between the two jurisdictions as they are both common-law jurisdictions with a shared legal heritage. Much of banking law in both jurisdictions is based on case law rather than statute and English cases have been a primary source in Australian courts. For example, the principal English cases which form the basis of the banker-customer relationship, *Foley v. Hill,*[46] *Joachimson v. Swiss Bank Corporation*[47] and *Tournier v. National Provincial and Union Bank of England*[48]

46. *Foley v. Hill* (1848) 2 HL Cas 28 ('*Foley v. Hill*').
47. *Joachimson v. Swiss Bank Corporation* [1921] 3 KB 110 ('*Joachimson v. Swiss Bank Corporation*').
48. *Tournier v. National Provincial and Union Bank of England* [1924] 1 KB 461 ('*Tournier's case*').

have been followed and approved by Australian courts.[49] This is demonstrated by the analysis in later chapters of this book.

In addition, there have historically been strong similarities in the principles applicable to the regulation of their banking and payment systems.[50] Both jurisdictions adhere to international standards such as those applicable to bank and payment system regulation issued by the Financial Stability Board (FSB), the Basel Committee on Banking Supervision (BCBS), the BIS and the Committee on Payment and Settlement Systems (CPSS).

This commonality in the banking laws means that the same benchmark of the legal features of banking payment systems can be used to evaluate the open banking systems of Australia and the UK. When combined with the similarity in the objectives of the systems and the extensiveness of their foundations in technology, rules and participation, this enables meaningful conclusions to be drawn and attributed to each system's legal design. The basis on which this evaluation can take place is explained in the next two chapters.

49. *Laing v. Bank of NSW* (1952) 69 WN (NSW) 318 ('*Laing v. Bank of NSW*'); *Re ANZ Savings Bank Ltd* [1972] VR 690 ('*Re ANZ Savings Bank Ltd*'); *Smorgan v. Australia and New Zealand Banking Group Limited* (1976) 134 CLR 475 ('*Smorgan v. Australia and New Zealand Banking Group Limited*').

50. *See, e.g.*, Julia Black, 'The Development of Risk Based Regulation in Financial Services: Canada, the UK and Australia' (Research Report, ESRC Centre for the Analysis of Risk and Regulation, January 2004).

CHAPTER 3

# Data, Funds and Networks

Chapter 1 introduced the equivalence of the functions performed by open banking for customer data and those performed in banking payment systems for customer funds. This chapter develops this in more detail. It explains the nature of customer banking data as valuable information and how customer funds also constitute valuable information. It also explains the communication of information under both open banking and banking payment systems. It concludes by showing how open banking systems and banking payment systems are both networks for the communication of valuable information.

## 3.1 CUSTOMER BANKING DATA AS VALUABLE INFORMATION

Customer banking data can be described as comprising valuable information. This can be seen from consideration of the data shared in open banking, the information received in open banking, and the value of data and information.

### 3.1.1 Data Shared in Open Banking Systems

Legal research relating to data rarely defines what 'data' are, at a conceptual level. Laws and regulations are more concerned with the meaning derived *from data*, than the meaning *of data* as a concept. For example, what data are, conceptually, is not relevant to the legal protection granted to the personal information which can be derived from data, nor is it relevant to the legal issues associated with the competitive effects which control of that information can have. Indeed, beyond the law, information is the focus of more analysis than data as a concept itself. The analysis of data is often focussed on 'how they can be leveraged into insights and value, rather than to consider the nature of data from a more conceptual and philosophical perspective'.[1]

Conceptually, data are abstractions of the real world, which could be persons, objects or events.[2] The abstraction could be described as an attribute, a feature or a variable. For something to be able to be abstracted in this way, implies that it can be distinguished from its surroundings. For this reason, a datum is 'reducible to a *lack of uniformity*' meaning that it is a distinction which is being made.[3] The process of abstraction and distinction, or categorisation, is the foundation of conceptual descriptions of data.

To describe the data relevant to open banking systems, it is useful to use Kitchin's description of the five broad ways in which data may vary: form, structure, source, producer and type.[4] These are summarised in Table 3.1, with examples of the relevant customer banking data.

*Table 3.1 Data Characteristics (Adapted from Kitchin)*

| *Characteristic* | *Variation* | *Description* | *Open Banking Examples* |
|---|---|---|---|
| Form | Quantitative | Numerical records | Bank account numbers<br>Bank account balances |
| | Qualitative | Non-numerical | Customer address<br>Payee details |
| Structure | Structured | Organised in a defined data model | Open banking data sets |
| | Semi-structured | Loosely structured but no defined data model | Bank's own bank account records |
| | Unstructured | No structure | Copies of bank statements |
| Source | Captured | Produced through direct measurement | Banking transaction data from customer's perspective |
| | Exhaust | By-product of the main function of data generation | Banking transaction data when used to assess customer creditworthiness |
| | Derived | Produced through additional processing and analysis | Assessments of customer creditworthiness |
| Producer | Primary | Generated for observer's purpose | Banking transactional data from bank's perspective |
| | Secondary | Made available to others | Banking transactional data from data recipient's perspective |

1. Rob Kitchin, *The Data Revolution: Big Data, Open Data, Data Infrastructures and Their Consequences* (Sage, 2014).
2. John D Kelleher and Brendan Tierney, *Data Science* (MIT Press, 2018) 34.
3. Luciano Floridi, *Information: A Very Short Introduction* (Oxford University Press, 2010) 22.
4. Kitchin (n. 1).

| *Characteristic* | *Variation* | *Description* | *Open Banking Examples* |
|---|---|---|---|
| | Tertiary | Derived secondary data | Statistical analysis of all of the shared open banking data |
| Type | Indexical | Enables identification and linkages | Bank account numbers<br>Customer identification numbers |
| | Attribute | Non-indexical data | Type of bank account<br>Transaction types |
| | Metadata | Data about data | Descriptions of the data fields used in open banking |

The most typical of these characteristics to open banking data is structure. This is because, as explained in Chapter 1, a key foundation of open banking systems is standardised technology. The standards set out a consistent format for the data which are shared. For example, they prescribe the attributes to be used to describe the identification of the account, the identification of the transaction, the transaction type, the status of the transaction, the description of the transaction, when it was posted, at what date was the transaction's value determined, when the transaction was executed, the amount of the transaction, the currency, the name of the relevant merchant, the categorisation of the merchant, the biller code and biller name, and the payee.[5]

This standardisation means that open banking data are characterised as *structured data*. They differ from the ordinary bank account transaction data held by a bank which, although they may have their own internal structure, do not share their structure with the transaction data held by other banks. Also, they differ from copies of bank statements given to a customer which, because they are not digitised, have no internal data structure. The structuring of open banking data using common standards makes them intelligible as the data are clearly defined and separate and also means that they can be built into sets. Data which are structured like this:

> can be processed, searched, queried, combined, and analysed relatively straightforwardly using calculus and algorithms and can be visualised using various forms of graphs and maps, and easily processed by computers.[6]

In summary, it is the structuring of open banking data which enables them to be meaningful and readily usable by the recipient for the benefit of the customer. It enables open banking data to be received as *information*.

5. *See* Data Standards Body, 'Consumer Data Standards v 1.22.0', https://consumerdatastandards.org.au.
6. Kitchin (n. 1) 5.

### 3.1.2 Information Received Through Open Banking Systems

Information has different meanings. As noted by Claude Shannon, the founder of information theory, '[i]t is hardly to be expected that a single concept of information would satisfactorily account for the numerous possible applications of this general field'.[7] Some possible meanings of information include the result of accumulating associated data, the signal in the noise of data, the reworking of primary data into analytical form, or the organisation of zeros and ones into distinct patterns. However, this book uses the 'broadly adopted' definition of information as the combination of well-formed data with meaning. Floridi refers to the *General Definition of Information* (GDI) in explaining this definition of information, set out in Figure 3.1.[8]

*Figure 3.1 General Definition of Information (from Floridi)*

GDI) $\sigma$ is an instance of information, understood as semantic content, if and only if:
GDI.1) $\sigma$ consists of n *data* (d), for $n \geq 1$;
GDI.2) the data are *well-formed* (wfd);
GDI.3) the wfd are *meaningful* (mwfd = $\delta$).

For this purpose, data are:

- well-formed if they are grouped according to the rules (syntax) that govern the chosen system, code or language, and
- meaningful if they comply with the meanings (semantics) of the chosen system, code or language.

Open banking data satisfy these requirements. They are organised using consistent and agreed categories (such as the amount, the payee and the date of transaction) prescribed by the standards applicable to open banking systems. Because of this, open banking data are not mere 'abstractions' or 'distinctions' in the world, and the description which they provide of events which have occurred, results in a contextualisation which is meaningful. They are not mere data but information. Nevertheless, for consistency throughout this book they will continue to be referred to as customer data, as well as customer account information, as context requires.

A broader perspective on open banking data as information is provided by the 'knowledge pyramid', which conceptualises the relationship between data, information, knowledge and wisdom. The base of this pyramid is formed by data, on which rests information, on which rests knowledge and on top is wisdom. *See* Figure 3.2.

7. Claude Shannon, *Claude Ellwood Shannon: Collected Papers* (IEEE Press, 1993) 180.
8. Luciano Floridi, 'Philosophical Conceptions of Information', *Formal Theories of Information* (Springer, 2009) 13-53, 16.

*Figure 3.2 Knowledge Pyramid (Adapted from Kitchin)*[9]

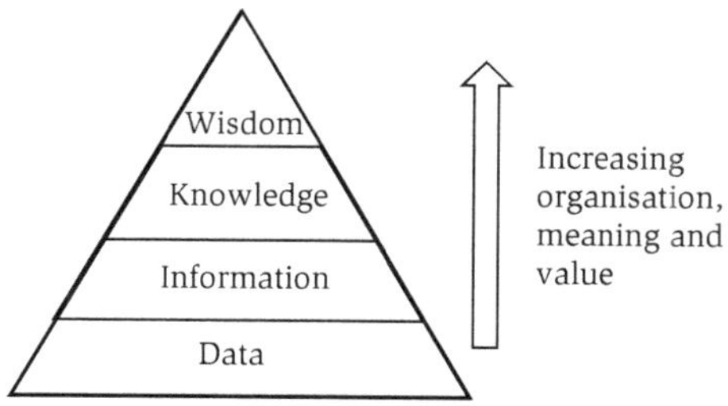


Each layer of the pyramid has more organisation, more meaning and, as a result, more value than the layer below it. As explained above, information is data that has been structured so that it is meaningful: 'Information is to data what wine is to a vineyard: the delicious extract and distillate'.[10] Knowledge is produced from information using cognitive processes such as perception and reasoning and it can be thought of as a way of knowing how to undertake a task, or a system of thought that links information together. Wisdom, at the apex of the pyramid, is often referred to as applied knowledge, or 'acting on knowledge in an appropriate way'.[11]

Applying this in the context of open banking systems, raw account transaction records held by a bank on its systems are data. When they are structured using open banking standards, they become information. The assessment of that information, for example to determine the creditworthiness of the customer, is knowledge. The application of that knowledge to make a further decision, for example the decision to make a loan based on that creditworthiness, could be described (using the terminology described above) as wisdom. This is shown in Figure 3.3.

*Figure 3.3 Knowledge Pyramid with Open Banking Examples*

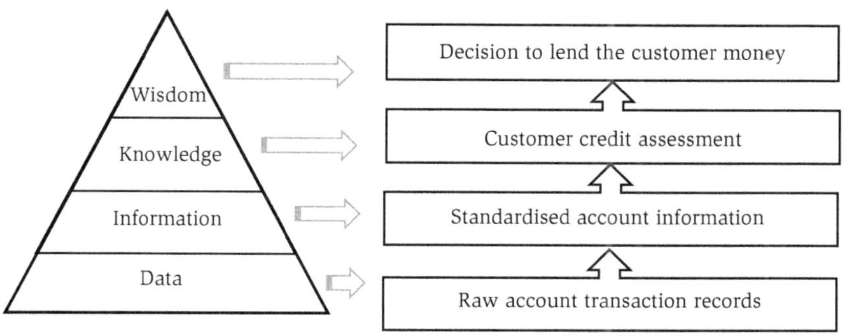


9. Kitchin (n. 1) 10.
10. David Weinberger, *Too Big to Know: Rethinking Knowledge Now That the Facts Aren't the Facts, Experts Are Everywhere, and the Smartest Person in the Room Is the Room* (Basic Books, 2011) 2.
11. Kelleher and Tierney (n. 2) 44.

Like data, information can be characterised in different ways. Floridi, for example, classifies information as 'factual' or 'instructional'.[12] Factual (or declarative) information is *about* some other fact, event or circumstance and is able to be qualified as being true or false. Instructional information *brings about* some fact, event or circumstance and cannot be qualified as true or false. In an open banking context, the balance of a bank account is an example of factual information and the instructions to make a payment from a bank account is an example of instructional information. As noted in Chapter 1, both of these can be shared under some open banking systems and in the context of UK open banking they are known as 'Read Access' and 'Write Access' respectively. Under Australian open banking, they are known as data sharing and action initiation respectively.[13]

### 3.1.3 Value of Data and Information

The value of data and information is widely accepted in an economic context. Data are becoming crucial to business success, either as a valuable asset either in understanding the behaviours of customers or as a resource which can be monetised in digital markets. Data are also recognised as a critical resource for the economy and the data economy is seen to complement the financial economy such that handling data is considered to be critical to economic success.[14]

Law also recognises the economic value of data and information. Although privacy as a fundamental human right is the basis of privacy laws, this has been complemented by an understanding that the legal rights to data have an economic nature. The recognition of this economic aspect of data has led to the understanding of data as a valuable tradeable commodity,[15] or even, 'the equivalent of the coin of the realm'.[16] The concept of information is also shared by competition law scholars who, particularly when considering data-related services provided at no monetary cost, consider that personal information 'serves as a form of currency, taking the place of money'.[17]

The general recognition of the value of data and information has given rise to work in measuring that value, for example by the Organisation for Economic Co-operation and Development (OECD)[18] and HM Treasury in the United Kingdom.[19]

12. Floridi, 'Philosophical Conceptions of Information' (n. 8) 35.
13. This is explained further in Chapter 5.
14. *See* Productivity Commission, Data Availability and Use (Report No. 82, 2017).
15. *See* Robert Walters, Leon E. Trakman and Bruno Zeller, *Data Protection Law: A Comparative Analysis of Asia-Pacific and European Approaches* (Springer, 2019) [12.2.2], [14.1].
16. *Securities and Exchange Comission v. Matiera*, 745 F 2d 197, [1] (Kaufman J) (1984) ('*Securities and Exchange Comission v. Matiera*').
17. *See* John M Newman, 'Antitrust in Zero-Price Markets: Foundations' (2015) *University of Pennsylvania Law Review* 149-206, 167. *See also* Michal S Gal and Daniel L Rubinfeld, 'The Hidden Costs of Free Goods: Implications for Antitrust Enforcement' (2016) 80(3) *Antitrust Law Journal* 521-562.
18. Organisation for Economic Co-operation and Development, *Exploring the Economics of Personal Data: A Survey of Methodologies for Measuring Monetary Value* (OECD Publishing, 2013).
19. HM Treasury, 'The Economic Value of Data: Discussion Paper' (Discussion Paper, 2018) www.gov.uk/government/publications.

However, despite this work, the value is difficult to determine and there is no obvious way to value data or information.[20] Possible methods of valuing data include measuring the benefit to business, the cost of replacing data if lost, data's impact on decisions in business, how much others will pay for data and the value of the new opportunities that data creates. Difficulty in valuing data emerges from complications arising from the effect of data's use, nature and markets.

### *(a) Use-Dependency and Subjectivity of*

It is the semantic character, or meaning, of information that provides value. Value is not inherent in data, but arises because of its usefulness, or what value can be created with the data. This usefulness and value comes from allowing:

> agents to take courses of actions (consider options, avoid errors, make choices, take rational decisions, and so forth) that normally yield higher expected payoffs (expected utility) than the agents would obtain in the absence of such information.[21]

The dependence of data's value on their use means that the same set of data might have different value to different people, or to the same person when used in different ways. In other words, data's value is subjective and use dependent.

This can be seen in the significant value ascribed to large amounts of data in the hands of entities for which it is highly useful where there is also a lack of value of the data attributed to a single person:

> Consider that, according to the Financial Times, in 2013 most people's profile information (an aggregate of age, gender, employment history, personal ailments, credit scores, income details, shopping history, locations, entertainment choices, address, and so forth) sold for less than $1 in total per person.[22]

This is because data relating to a single person may not have much incremental value to entities which already hold significant amounts of data on many people because the attributes and behaviours of another person do not add any additional insights to those already represented. This aspect of data's value is explained further in Chapter 7.

### *(b) Non-rivalrous and Non-excludable*

Determining the value of data is complicated by their 'non-rivalrous' nature in that data can be used repeatedly by more than one person without reducing its functional value to its holder. Data are also 'non-excludable' in the sense that they are easily shared and

20. *See* Viktor Mayer-Schönberger and Kenneth Cukier, *Big Data: The Essential Guide to Work, Life and Learning in the Age of Insight* (John Murray, 2nd ed., 2017) 121.
21. Floridi, *Information: A Very Short Introduction* (n. 3) 90.
22. Luciano Floridi, *The 4th Revolution: How the Infosphere Is Reshaping Human Reality* (Oxford University Press, 2014) 98.

limiting sharing requires deliberate effort. These factors mean that it is possible for data to have greater value through secondary and tertiary uses than they might in the use for which the data were originally collected:

> [d]ata's true value is like an iceberg floating in the ocean. Only a tiny part of it is visible at first sight, while much of it is hidden beneath the surface.[23]

Legally, this is reflected in the difficulty in articulating ownership of data. Australian and UK courts have been reluctant to ascribe property rights to information in the absence of statutory schemes which expressly do so, like intellectual property regimes. 'In general, information is not property at all. It is normally open to all who have eyes to read and ears to hear'.[24] This aspect of data's value is explained further in Chapter 8.

#### *(c) Markets for Data and Non-Fungibility*

Determining data's value is also complicated because of the absence of any liquid, efficient and accessible markets for data. In its report, the OECD did not recognise any market for data that an individual can access.[25] Also, there can be positive and negative externalities which arise with data, so that any type of market price does not reflect the true value. This can be due to the social impact of using, or misusing, data, especially personal data.[26] The complications in markets for data also arise because, as noted above, the value of data can differ depending on whether it is the value to the individual to whom it relates, or to someone else who is intending to use the data.

Determining a market value for data is also complicated because data are not fungible. The information derived from one customer's data is not the same as that which can be derived from another's. Accordingly, data relating to one person cannot replace data relating to another. Although customer data can be measured in bits, this is a measure of the *amount* of information, not its *meaning* or, as a result, its *value*. These aspects are explained further in Chapter 7.

### 3.1.4 Value of Open Banking Information

The previous section explained that data and information are valuable, although that value is difficult to measure. Similarly, data and information shared under open banking are valuable. Considering the complications in valuing data described above,

23. Viktor Mayer-Schönberger and Thomas Ramge, *Reinventing Capitalism in the Age of Big Data* (Basic Books, 2018) 105. *See also* Mayer-Schönberger and Cukier (n. 20) 106.
24. *Phipps v. Boardman* [1967] AC 46, 81 (Lord Upjohn) ('*Phipps v. Boardman*'). *See also Your Response Ltd v. Datateam Business Media Ltd* [2015] QB 41, [42] ('*Your Response v. Datateam Business Media*').
25. Organisation for Economic Co-operation and Development, *Exploring the Economics of Personal Data: A Survey of Methodologies for Measuring Monetary Value* (OECD Publishing, 2013).
26. *Ibid. See also* HM Treasury, 'The Economic Value of Data: Discussion Paper' (Discussion Paper, 2018) www.gov.uk/government/publications.

this value of customer data shared under open banking can be best seen from the potential gain from their use, and from the potential loss caused by their misuse.

### *(a) Economic Gain from Use*

The value of customer data through potential economic *gain* is shown by the 'use cases' developed for using open banking, and in this respect the data's value can be seen through their use to achieve open banking's objectives. For example, one primary use of open banking information is to identify alternative banking products which would save money for a customer. This information is valuable because of the economic benefit which its use can provide to the customer and also to the provider of the alternative banking products. A gain from open banking information may also come from the combination of the shared information with other information to provide greater insights (or knowledge) with respect to the customer's needs or wants. The use of algorithms and other sophisticated tools can enable service providers to target particular products at particular customers. A further basis for the economic value of open banking information is that the standardisation makes it more accessible for use as does the increase in interaction between businesses and customers.

### *(b) Economic Loss from Misuse*

The value through potential economic *loss* is shown by the behaviours which the safeguards built into open banking systems are intended to prevent, such as identity theft, unauthorised transactions on bank accounts and the sale of inappropriate financial services. Each of the customer and the recipient of the shared information can suffer loss in these circumstances. This value is also shown by the legal protection which has been given to customer account information under banking law. These include the laws relating to the duty of secrecy, the provision of banker's references and opinions, access to customers' passbooks and production of bankers' books as evidence.[27] These laws prevent unauthorised access to information such as the balance of a customer's account and the banking transactions which the customer has entered into with their bank – information shared under open banking systems. Unauthorised disclosure of this information can cause considerable damage to the customer particularly because '[t]he credit of the customer depends very largely upon the strict observance of that confidence'.[28] This protection is recognition of the potential economic loss suffered by the information's disclosure – demonstrating the value of customer data.

27. John Odgers, *Paget's Law of Banking* (LexisNexis, 15th ed., 2018) Ch. 3 pts 7-11.

28. *Tournier v. National Provincial and Union Bank of England* [1924] 1 KB 461, 474 ('*Tournier's case*').

## 3.2 CUSTOMER BANK FUNDS AS VALUABLE INFORMATION

Customer bank funds are also valuable information. This can be seen from consideration of money's informational function, information's monetary function and the relationship between money and information.

### 3.2.1 Money's Informational Function: The Unit of Account

Although money is often economically and legally described by three functions: a medium of exchange, a store of economic value and a unit of account,[29] it is the last of these which most clearly enables money to perform its informational function. This abstract function of money is not often the focus of legal analysis,[30] but it is important because it allows money to serve as 'a universal denominator of value'.[31] The unit of account enables the value of assets and obligations held, owed and paid to be measured, recorded and communicated in a standardised way. This informational function is one of money's earliest functions, traceable back to third millennium Babylon,[32] and is not dependent on modern information technology: '[e]ven when money seemed to be material treasure, heavy in pockets and ships' holds and bank vaults, it always was information'.[33]

Despite the importance of the unit of account to measuring value with money, it is difficult to ascribe value to that unit of account. Defining the value of a dollar or a pound for example, is problematic without comparison to something else. When money had a direct linkage with the amounts of precious metals such as gold or silver then those metals could define its value as it was a representation of that commodity.[34] However, once this linkage was severed, the value of the unit of account itself became obscure and effectively the unit of account is now an independent concept. It can be used as the relative measure for the valuation of other things but does not have any absolute value itself. The absence of inherent value means that on their own, units of account like 'dollar' or 'pound' are not meaningful:

29. Ewan McKendrick, *Goode and McKendrick on Commercial Law* (LexisNexis, 6th ed., 2020) 532; Charles Proctor et al., *Mann on the Legal Aspect of Money* (Oxford University Press, 7th ed., 2012) [1.07]; David Fox, *Property Rights in Money* (Oxford University Press, 2008) [1.19].
30. *See* David Fox, Francois Velde and Wolfgang Ernst, 'Monetary History Between Law and Economics' in David Fox and Wolfgang Ernst (eds), *Money in the Western Legal Tradition: Middle Ages to Bretton Woods* (Oxford University Press, 2016), 15.
31. Fox (n. 29) [1.25].
32. *Ibid.* [1.143]. Geva also notes that this function is supported by ancient texts 'ahead of its emergence in concrete form as a universal medium of exchange': Benjamin Geva, *The Payment Order of Antiquity and the Middle Ages: A Legal History* (Hart Publishing, 2011).
33. James Gleick, *The Information: A History, a Theory, a Flood* (Vintage, 2011) 8.
34. However, this was not always as clear as it might seem. For example, the economist Adam Smith notes that although the English pound sterling 'contained a pound, Tower weight, of silver of a known fineness' at the time of Edward I, by the time of his writing in 1776, it contained only a third of that: Adam Smith, *The Wealth of Nations: An Inquiry into the Nature and Causes of the Wealth of Nations* (Wordsworth Editions, 2012) 30.

> The dollar concept existing at any given time is as little susceptible of definition as, say the concept of 'blue'. No more can be said than that the dollar is the name for a value which, at any definite moment, is understood in the same sense throughout the community, and since goods and services are evaluated in terms of the dollar that unit is a standard or measure of value.[35]

For this reason, when it is not measuring the value of something else, the unit of account is more like data than information.

The information function of money enabled by the unit of account is critical to the operation of markets and the prices that they establish. This information relates both to events happening outside of the market and also the transactions which occur inside the market. Knowing the price at which others are, or have been, willing to buy and sell goods and services (price discovery) is fundamental to an efficient market's operation. That price is information, and it is expressed in money using the unit of account. Through price, using the unit of account, money denominates the value of goods and services and condenses the intentions of a large number of people down into a single figure which can be easily communicated. This highly informational role of money makes it 'the language in which market transactions are being conducted'.[36] Indeed, Mayer-Schönberger and Ramge have argued that data-driven markets will result in price no longer constituting the sole element of standardised information. Instead, other standardised data will contribute to this role as they can describe a greater range of information. Open banking is an example of this trend.

The informational function of money also enables monetary transactions, such as payments, to be performed. The unit of account facilitates the calculation of the amount to be paid, and the payment itself, because a debt is discharged by the payment of the specified number of units of account in the specified currency, regardless of the value of those units:

> It is not a question of what amount of coins or other currency has the debtor contracted to pay. A debt is not incurred in terms of currency, but in terms of units of account.[37]

Instructions to make payments are also enabled by the informational function of money, as they are expressed in the unit of account.

Money's informational function enabled by the unit of account permits the measurement of the value of other economic relationships too, such as assets and liabilities. A particularly relevant example is the bank account, which also demonstrates information's monetary function.

35. Arthur Nussbaum, *Money in the Law: National and International: A Comparative Study in the Borderline of Law and Economics* (Foundation Press, 1950) 6.
36. Mayer-Schönberger and Ramge (n. 23) 48.
37. *Adelaide Electric Supply Ltd v. Prudential Assurance Co. Ltd* [1934] AC 122 ('*Adelaide Electric*').

### 3.2.2 Information's Monetary Function: Bank Funds as Records

Money is not limited to legal tender. In fact, from an economics perspective, bank liabilities are a large component of money, and it is common to include deposits with commercial banks as money. This is referred to as 'bank money',[38] or 'commercial bank money',[39] and it represents nearly all of the money circulating in the economy.[40]

Although bank accounts were not always considered to be money from a legal perspective, as that characterisation was reserved for legal tender circulating as currency, accounts with commercial banks are now commonly considered to be money from a legal perspective.[41] One reason for this is that legal tender is now rarely used for anything other than payments of insubstantial sums of money and is rarely utilised in commercial dealings. In the context of monetary dealings, the money represented by the balance of a bank account is often referred to as 'funds'. Despite the common usage, a precise legal definition of the word 'funds' used in this way is surprisingly difficult to find. One reference can be found in the decision in *Visa International v. RBA*,[42] which implies that the money represented by the balance of bank accounts is included in 'funds.'[43] This is consistent with its dictionary definition as 'money in hand; pecuniary resources'.[44] This usage of the term 'funds' is particularly relevant to the discussion of payment by way of funds transfers in section 3.3.2 below.

The performance by bank funds of the three economic functions of money demonstrates the informational function of money.

- *Bank funds as a unit of account:* Bank funds are maintained through bank records by using units of account to measure the amount owed by the bank to customer. Historically, these bank records were made by hand but now are made in computer databases, so that money is recorded like other data. In fact, it 'may well be just a pile of digits', which emphasises the informational role of money.[45] However, bank funds also represent information's monetary role. This is shown by their function as a store of value.
- *Bank funds as a store of value*: The informational meaning of bank funds is closely related to the way in which they perform the monetary function of a

38. Benjamin Geva, '"Bank Money": The Rise, Fall and Metamorphosis of the "Transferable Deposit"' in David Fox and Wolfgang Ernst (eds), *Money in the Western Legal Tradition: Middle Ages to Bretton Woods* (Oxford University Press, 2016), 359.
39. Geva, *The Payment Order of Antiquity and the Middle Ages: A Legal History* (n. 32) 524.
40. Michael McLeay, Amar Radia and Ryland Thomas, 'Money Creation in the Modern Economy' (2014) *Bank of England Quarterly Bulletin* Q1.
41. *See* McKendrick (n. 29) 533. *See also* FrancisA Mann, *The Legal Aspect of Money* (Oxford University Press, 1938), Victoria Dixon (ed.), *Goode on Payment Obligations in Commercial and Financial Transactions* (Sweet & Maxwell, 4th ed., 2020) [1.03].
42. *Visa International Service Association v. Reserve Bank of Australia* [2003] FCA 977 ('*Visa International v. RBA*').
43. *Ibid*. 81.
44. Arthur Delbridge, John RL Bernard and David Blair, *The Macquarie Dictionary* (Macquarie Library Sydney, 1981).
45. Floridi, *The 4th Revolution: How the Infosphere Is Reshaping Human Reality* (n. 22) 46. *See also* Gottfried Leibbrandt and Natasha De Teran, *The Pay Off: How Changing the Way We Pay Changes Everything* (Elliot & Thompson, 2020) 157.

store of value. Value is stored in bank funds through the legal obligation of the bank to repay the amounts deposited with it to their customer. It is fundamental to the legal relationship between a bank and its customer that money given to the custody of the bank belongs to the bank and the bank 'undertakes to repay' money received for its customer.[46] Because the money given to the bank's custody becomes the bank's money, there is only the right to demand payment of a certain sum, denominated in the unit of account, to represent the value which is stored. Without this legal obligation, the information represented by the funds held in a bank account could not represent a store of value and, consequently, money.

- *Bank funds as a means of exchange*: However, the repayment obligation of the bank to its customer described above is more than a promise 'to repay at the branch of the bank where the account is kept and during banking hours.'[47] It also includes 'a promise to repay any part of the amount due, against the written order of the customer.'[48] The legal obligation of a bank to pay its customer's money to others at the customer's direction enables customers to use the funds in their bank account to make payments. This is how bank funds perform the medium of exchange function of money.

The store of value and medium of exchange functions described above outline two core functions of banking payment systems: the custody of customer's funds and the transfer of those funds on demand. These are the functions of storage and liquidity and the 'essence of what banks promise to their depositors',[49] and a 'primary economic function of commercial banks'.[50] These are analysed further in the next chapter.

### 3.2.3 Relationship Between Money and Information

This part of the chapter has shown that money and information are interrelated. Money has an informational function and information has a monetary function.

Money's informational function can be declarative, meaning that money is providing factual information, as it is with bank accounts and prices. Also, it can be non-declarative, where there is no factual content, as it is with the unit of account itself and an instruction to make payments. Information's monetary function can relate to the very meaning of money, as it does in constituting both bank accounts and the unit of account. Also, information's monetary function can be expressed in money, as it does with prices and payment instructions. Table 3.2 shows this using four examples used in the previous section.

46. *Foley v. Hill* (1848) 2 HL Cas 28, 36 ('*Foley v. Hill*'); *Joachimson v. Swiss Bank Corporation* [1921] 3 KB 110, 127 ('*Joachimson v. Swiss Bank Corporation*').
47. *Joachimson v. Swiss Bank Corporation* (n. 46) 127.
48. *Ibid.*
49. Dan Awrey and Kristin van Zwieten, 'The Shadow Payment System' (2017-2018) 43 *Journal of Competition Law* 775, 783.
50. Benjamin Geva, *Bank Collections and Payment Transactions: A Comparative Study of Legal Aspects* (Oxford University Press, 2001) 7.

*Table 3.2 Interrelationship Between Information and Money*

| *Information* / *Money* | *Declarative (Factual Content)* | *Non-declarative (Other Content)* |
|---|---|---|
| **Meaning of money** | **Bank Account**<br>– A form of money<br>– Declarative information about monetary obligation | **Units of account**<br>– A function of money<br>– Measures monetary obligations |
| **Measured in money** | **Price of exchange**<br>– Expressed in money<br>– Declarative information about a monetary transaction | **Payment instructions**<br>– Relates to money<br>– Instructional information about a monetary transaction |

Whilst the complexity of this interaction could be analysed further, it is not necessary to do so for the purposes of this book. Instead, it is sufficient that the funds in a customer's bank account are a form of money and represent information and a store of value. Accordingly, this most common form of money can be characterised as valuable information.

## 3.3 COMMUNICATION AND PAYMENTS

Open banking systems and banking payment systems are both based on communication of the valuable information comprised in customer data and customer funds. This can be seen from consideration of the communication in open banking and the communication in banking payment systems.

### 3.3.1 Communication in Open Banking

In information science, the transfer of information is comprised of a number of activities, such as networking, distributing, accessing, retrieving and transmitting.[51] For this book, the most relevant is how they are considered together as 'communication'. The seminal work of this theory is *A Mathematical Theory of Communication* by Claude Shannon. Information theory, as proposed by Shannon, aims to encode and transfer efficiently. Two concepts emerge from this which are particularly relevant: the problem of communication and the communication system.

#### *(a) Levels of the Problem of Communication*

According to Shannon, 'the fundamental problem of communication is that of reproducing at one point either exactly or approximately a message selected at another

51. Floridi, *Information: A Very Short Introduction* (n. 3) 4.

point'.[52] Weaver, in his introduction to Shannon's work, describes communication to be 'all of the procedures by which one mind may affect another'[53] and articulates three levels of the communications problem: technical, semantic and effectiveness problems.[54] These are described in Table 3.3.

*Table 3.3 Adaptation of Shannon's Communication Problem to Open Banking*[55]

| *Problem* | *Information Theory* | *Open Banking Adaptation* |
|---|---|---|
| Technical | How accurately can the symbols of communication be transmitted? | How accurately can the data relating to a customers' banking transactions be shared? |
| Semantic | How precisely do the transmitted symbols convey the desired meaning? | How precisely does that convey the meaning of the customer's banking relationships? |
| Effectiveness | How effectively does the received meaning affect conduct in the desired way? | How does that meaning, when received, result in conduct desired by the customer? |

Open banking systems also face this communication problem. They are designed to enable customer banking information to be shared so that it can be used for a purpose desired by the customer. The third column of Table 3.3 describes how the different levels of the communication problem can be applied to open banking systems. The relevant standards relating to the operation of APIs are intended to address the technical problem, as these determine how the information is transferred and in what form. The standards which determine the data fields able to be shared is intended to address the semantic problem, as they determine the meaning which is provided about the customer's banking relationship. The rules requiring the customer's consent to the way in which the information is to be used, are intended to address the effectiveness problem, as these determine how the customer benefits from the sharing of the information. Chapters 5 and 6 analyse all three aspects of the communication problem for open banking.

### *(b) Communication Systems*

Shannon described a communication system to have five parts (as shown in Figure 3.4):

52. Claude E Shannon, 'A Mathematical Theory of Communication' (1948) 27(3) *The Bell System Technical Journal* 379-423, 379.
53. Warren Weaver, 'Recent Contributions to the Mathematical Theory of Communication' (1953) *ETC: A Review of General Semantics* 261-281.
54. Shannon's information theory focuses on the technical problem only, through analysis of data encoding and transmission, uncertainty and probability. It does not deal with the semantic or effectiveness problem. For this reason, as a matter of information theory, 'the "meaning" of a message is generally irrelevant': Shannon (n. 52) 380.
55. Weaver (n. 53).

- an *information source* which produces the message;
- a *transmitter* which produces a signal for transmission using the message;
- a *channel*, which is the medium used to transmit the signal;
- a *receiver* who reconstructs the message from the signal; and
- the *destination* which is the person for whom the message is intended.[56]

*Figure 3.4 Communication System (Adapted from Shannon)*

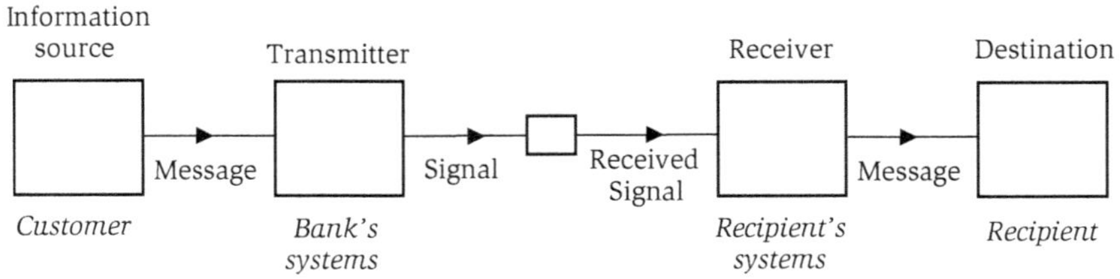


The italicised text in Figure 3.4 shows how, at a conceptual level, this can be applied to open banking systems, by treating the customer as the information source, the customer's bank's systems as the transmitter, the recipient's systems which process the information as the receiver and the recipient as the destination.[57]

This representation of an open banking system as a simple communication system is useful as it will be seen to have a significant level of similarity with funds transfer mechanisms, which show how payments are made by communication.

### 3.3.2 Payments as Communication

Economic definitions of payments tend to focus on the transfer of value between agents.[58] Alternative meanings can have a different emphasis, focussing on the transfer of monetary value,[59] or a monetary claim.[60] Payment is given a more precise definition at law.[61] Payment does not necessarily require the delivery of money if other value is provided, but legal definitions clarify that the obligation discharged must be a money

56. Shannon (n. 52). This does not include the noise source included in Shannon's original.
57. This is not an exact representation under the open banking systems as the requests for sharing customer data are communicated to the customer's bank through the data recipient. *See* Chapter 6.
58. Mark Manning, Erlend Nier and Jochen Schanz, *The Economics of Large-Value Payments and Settlement: Theory and Policy Issues for Central Banks* (Oxford University Press, 2009) 2.
59. Stephen Millard and Victoria Saporta, 'Past, Present and Future' in Stephen Millard, Andrew Haldane and Victoria Saporta (eds), *The Future of Payment Systems* (Routledge, 2008).
60. Committee on Payment and Settlement Systems, 'A Glossary of Terms Used in Payments and Settlement Systems' (Report, March 2003).
61. Geva quotes *Black's Law Dictionary* in defining payment as the 'performance of an obligation by the delivery of money or some other valuable thing accepted in partial or full discharge of the obligation': Geva, *The Payment Order of Antiquity and the Middle Ages: A Legal History* (n. 32) 25 quoting Bryan A Garner, *Black's Law Dictionary – Ninth Edition, West, St* (2009).

obligation.[62] *Goode on Commercial Law* defines there to be, in practice, five types of payment: delivery of physical money, acceptance of goods in part exchange, transfer of funds to the transferee's bank account, replacement of the existing contract with a new contract and set-off.[63] As most money is in the form of bank account funds, the transfer of funds between bank accounts is the most commonly used. This close linkage between banking and payments is fundamental to understanding the form in which most payments are made.

### *(a) Funds Transfers as Messages*

Funds transfers are not made through a legal process such as assignment or novation of the contractual rights against their bank by the payer to the payee, instead they are made by reducing the balance of the payer's account with their bank and increasing the balance of the payee's account with theirs.[64] They are initiated by a payment instruction being given to the payer's bank. In fact, '[t]ransfer may be a somewhat misleading word' with respect to what is happening to the money as nothing is actually transferred.[65] Instead, messages, or transfers of *information*, cause the change in the account balances, and rules which govern them are the equivalent of delivery and possession in legal tender. This communication of information does not effect a change in property rights, instead 'it is more accurate to speak in terms of the transfer of value from payer to payee'.[66] This communication of information to transfer value is an important connection between payments and transfers of information under open banking.

### *(b) Legal Relationships in Funds Transfers*

Funds transfers differ depending on the relationship between the banks of the payer and the payee. The two most relevant to this book have been judicially described as correspondent transfers (which are used if the payer and the payee's accounts are at different banks who themselves have accounts with each other) and complex transfers (which are used if the payer's bank and the payee's bank do not have accounts with each other).[67]

62. Michael Brindle and Raymond Cox, *Law of Bank Payments* (Sweet & Maxwell, Thomson Reuters, 5th ed., 2018) [1-002].
63. McKendrick (n. 29) 556.
64. Brindle and Cox (n. 62) [3-002]. The reduction in the balance represents the banks claim to reimbursement of the expenses incurred by the bank in effecting the transfer on their customer's behalf: David Fox and Sarah Green, *Cryptocurrencies in Public and Private Law* (Oxford University Press, 2019) [4.69].
65. *Libyan Arab Foreign Bank v. Bankers Trust Co* [1989] QB 728, 750 ('*Libyan Arab Foreign Bank v. Bankers Trust*').
66. Odgers (n. 27) [22.20].
67. *See Libyan Arab Foreign Bank v. Bankers Trust* (n. 65).

In a correspondent transfer, the payment is made by the adjustments across the accounts that the payer's and payee's banks have with each other.[68] It depends on a series of communications:

- the payer gives an instruction to their bank requesting payment be made to the payee;
- the payer's bank communicates with the payee's bank about the payment; and
- the payee's bank confirms to the payee that the money has been received into their account.

The banks involved adjust their accounts accordingly. This is shown in Figure 3.5.[69]

*Figure 3.5 Funds Transfer (Adapted from Geva)*

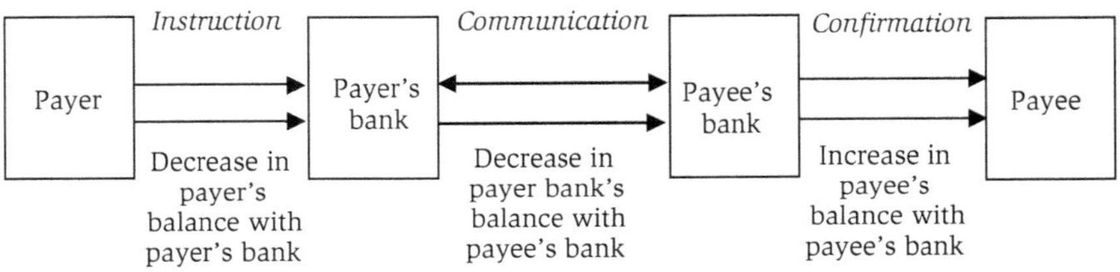


The similarity with Shannon's diagram of a communication system set out in Figure 3.4 is clear. Both involve the communication of information from customer to recipient. In fact, '[b]anks from this perspective, are specialized institutions for facilitating the transmission and recording of relevant payment information'.[70]

Complex systems are more complicated and require consideration of networks.

## 3.4 OPEN BANKING AND PAYMENT SYSTEMS AS NETWORKS

Open banking systems and banking payment systems form networks for the communication of valuable information. This can be seen from consideration of the nature of communication networks and how open banking systems and banking payment systems form those networks.

68. Although in some countries, like the UK and Australia, correspondent relationships are with banks overseas, they exist within other countries, such as the United States: McKendrick (n. 29) 569. Also, smaller banks can gain access to payment systems through the accounts which they hold with larger banks: Manning, Nier and Schanz (n. 58) 171.
69. Geva, *The Payment Order of Antiquity and the Middle Ages: A Legal History* (n. 32) 651.
70. Jeffrey Lacker, 'Payment Economics and the Role of Central Banks' in Stephen Millard, Andrew Haldane and Victoria Saporta (eds), *The Future of Payment Systems* (Routledge, 2008), 68.

### 3.4.1 Communication Networks

Section 3.2 above explained simple model of a communication system developed in information theory involving communication of a message from a source to a destination. However Shannon, the founder of that theory, also noted that communication can be more complex than that simple description of a communication system and instead it may require use of a 'network which consists of a number of branches',[71] or as Floridi describes, 'multiagent and distributed systems interacting in parallel, rather than individual agents related by simple, sequential channels of communication'.[72]

Networks of interconnected entities commonly arise in communication, for example in relation to the internet, wireless computer connectivity and mobile telephony. They also arise in other circumstances, such as in transport (e.g., a railway network) and in the supply of goods and services (e.g., the supply of energy). These networks involve the participation of multiple individual components connected by mutual dependence on performance. The systems that give rise to these networks are characterised as 'complex systems' because the interdependence of their component parts results in them exhibiting indirect effects and behaviours which differ from those parts. The consequence of this complexity is explained in the next chapter.

### 3.4.2 Open Banking Systems as Networks

The previous part of this chapter explained how a simple communication system can be represented in an open banking context, involving a customer, their bank and the recipient of the customer data. However, achievement of the objectives of open banking requires communication of customer data at scale, beyond small numbers of bilateral exchanges, involving many customers, many banks and many recipients. For example, such broad participation encourages competition by increasing the contestability of banking services, improves innovation by enabling collaboration in the development of banking products, fosters inclusion by facilitating increased access to trusted intermediaries for vulnerable customers, and enhances consumer protection by increasing the number of participants who can identify safety issues in open banking as they arise.

However, participation in open banking is not limited to the direct participation of customers, banks, and data recipients. To provide data-driven innovations, recipients use agents, intermediaries, and service providers. Further, different participants can perform multiple roles. This results in specialised and differentiated participants each relying on the services and data being provided by others. Through these developments, open banking systems can become more than merely entities connected by sequential communication channels, but multilateral networks and complex systems comprised of entities interacting through parallel and distributed connections.

71. Peter Elias, Amiel Feinstein and Claude Shannon, 'A Note on the Maximum Flow Through a Network' (1956) 2(4) *IRE Transactions on Information Theory* 117-119, 117.
72. Floridi, *Information: A Very Short Introduction* (n. 3) 53.

The development of these ecosystems is encouraged by the design of open banking systems. They allow participants to join progressively and do not prescribe the connections which participants establish with each other. There is no restriction on those who offer the most competitive and innovative data-driven services from connecting with more participants than others. Some participants, such as those who offer technology-based services to other participants as well as customers, could develop an extraordinary number of connections. Indeed, evidence of this concentration of connectivity is already emerging in UK open banking. The OBIE announced that the most common use of UK open banking by small- to medium-sized enterprises in the UK is in relation to online accounting services (of which there are a few large providers), and a single recipient in the UK system already claims that one-half of all open banking traffic in the UK system flows through their platform.

The development of these networks is also supported in these two jurisdictions by the mandatory use of a single standard explained in Chapter 2. This reduces transaction costs for all participants and enables participants to specialise with the assurance that any intermediate products or services can be incorporated into the broader system.

This development of open banking systems into networks and ecosystems is critical to realising data portability at sufficient scale to achieve open banking's objectives.

### 3.4.3 Banking Payment Systems as Networks

Banking payment systems also establish networks. They have done so for many centuries, as can be seen from the network of relationships in the system used by goldsmiths in seventeenth century England to clear and settle payments between them.[73] This is most readily seen in the multilateral settlement arrangements which are used if the payer's bank and the payee's bank do not have accounts with each other (these are the 'complex systems' in relation to funds transfers referred to in the previous part of this chapter). Many modern payment systems are of this type, with the central bank holding the accounts across which interbank payments are settled. In order to enable these arrangements, a communications network or clearing house can be established to facilitate interbank communication of payment instructions and other messages, and a facility for settling of the dealings which result, usually across the books of the central bank. Key elements of this are shown in Figure 3.6.

73. *See* Dan Awrey and Kristin van Zwieten, 'The Shadow Payment System' (2017-2018) 43 *J. Corp. L* 775.

*Figure 3.6 Payment System (Adapted from Brindle and Cox)*[74]

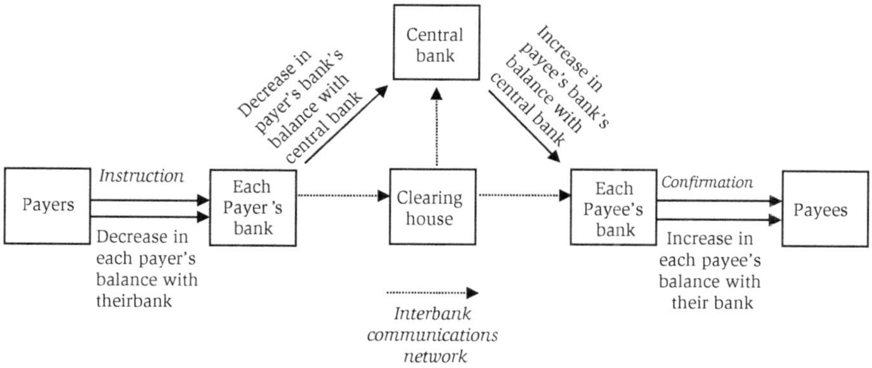


The essential feature of transfer of value by communication of information remains in the use of a payment system. The key difference with simple correspondent arrangements described earlier in this chapter is the organisational and institution arrangements required for the multilateral participation. This reduces costs through streamlining processes and standardising relationships and avoids the need for every bank or agent to have an account with each other. Consequently, the use of payment systems, rather than combinations of bilateral account arrangements, is less costly and presents less operational risk. Further efficiencies arise by reducing the liquidity that banks need to make payments, and by allowing banks to reallocate their resources to assets which produce a greater return. The result is:

> a network of interconnecting entities that facilitates the exchange of data required to initiate, authorize, clear, and settle cash or credit claims between payors and payees.[75]

This is an example of a complex network,[76] which represents a significant contribution to the efficiency goals of banking payment systems.

### 3.4.4 Open Banking and Banking Payment Systems as Valuable Information Networks

This chapter has shown how open banking systems and banking payment systems are networks for the transfer of valuable customer information. This similarity between

74. Brindle and Cox (n. 29).
75. Hal S Scott, 'The Importance of the Retail Payment System' (Article, Retail Payment Systems Conference; Harvard Law School Program on International Financial Systems, 26 Feruary 2015) 5.
76. Kimmo Soramäki et al., 'The Topology of Interbank Payment Flows' (2007) 379(1) *Physica A: Statistical Mechanics and Its Applications* 317-333, 317. *See also* Christopher Becher, Stephen Millard and Kimmo Soramaki, 'The Network Topology of CHAPS Sterling' (Working Paper No. 355, Bank of England, 24 November 2008).

banking payment systems and open banking systems as networks is not surprising, given the centrality of information to the operation of both. Indeed, the economic description of a payment system as 'any organized arrangement for transferring value between parties,'[77] would include open banking systems on the basis that data being transferred are valuable. This linkage is not new and 'each is essentially a different branch of the same network family tree'.[78] From this connection, the functional equivalence can be developed further into functions, foundations and risks, in the next chapter.

77. Manning, Nier and Schanz (n. 58) 3.
78. Andrew G Haldane, 'Rethinking the Financial Network', *Fragile stabilität–stabile fragilität* (Springer, 2013) 243-278, 244.

# CHAPTER 4
# Functions, Foundations and Risks

This chapter completes the explanation of the functional equivalence between open banking systems and banking payment systems. Using the foundation of open banking systems and banking payment systems both comprising networks for the communication of valuable information developed in the previous chapter, it identifies the comparable functions performed by each with respect to moving and storing value and the legal foundations which support that performance. It concludes by developing a framework to categorise the risks which arise in open banking systems.

## 4.1 FUNCTIONS AND LEGAL FOUNDATIONS FOR MOVING VALUE

Both banking payment systems and open banking systems perform functions relating to the movement of value. In banking payment systems this is referred to as liquidity, whilst in open banking systems they are the functions of customer autonomy and data portability.

### 4.1.1 Liquidity of Customer Funds in Banking Payment Systems

The economic driver of the development of banking payment systems is efficiency and the linkage which has developed between banking and modern payment systems is 'economically rationalized by the quest for efficiency gains'.[1]

One source of these efficiency gains is in reducing the use of legal tender, or cash. Without banking payment systems, cash would be needed for all transactions in which consumers and businesses participate. Economically, the holding of cash is an unproductive asset and the alternative, which is to engage in fewer transactions, results in a reduction in welfare. Also, cash is particularly exposed to theft and there can be

1. Benjamin Geva, *Bank Collections and Payment Transactions: A Comparative Study of Legal Aspects* (Oxford University Press, 2001) 8.

difficulty in verifying its true value. Consequently, cash cannot always perform the functions of money and, by enabling money to be paid without the use of cash, the banking payment system enables the functions of money to be more effectively and efficiently performed. This *liquidity function*, provided by enabling customers to direct funds transfers be made and providing the means to make them safely, enables payment systems to reduce transaction frictions and support the flow of money and, as a result, to form a fundamental part of the financial system. This provision of access to customers to money of a known value to be useable immediately for transaction purposes is the foundation of 'liquidity transformation' in banking.

### 4.1.2 Autonomy and Portability of Customer Data in Open Banking Systems

The functions enabling customers to make movements of value and providing the means to make them safely, are also performed in open banking systems, with respect to customer data instead of customer funds. These functions were identified in Chapter 1 as *autonomy* and *portability*. This comparison is shown in Table 4.1.

*Table 4.1 Movement of Value Functions in Banking and Open Banking*

| *Function* | *Banking Payment System* | *Open Banking System* | *Function* |
|---|---|---|---|
| Liquidity | Customer's *funds* able to be safely *transferred* at customer's direction. | Customer's *data* able to be safely *shared* at customer's direction. | Autonomy<br>Portability |

The italicised text in Table 4.1 shows a key difference between banking payment systems and open banking systems. Funds are *transferred* and received whilst data is *shared*. This is a consequence of the non-rivalrous nature of data referred to in section 3.1.3. This difference is analysed further in the following chapters.

As explained in Chapter 1, the performance of these functions is crucial for the effectiveness of open banking systems in achieving their objectives, just as it is for the efficiency of banking payment systems. They are supported by comparable legal foundations of banking payment systems and open banking systems.

### 4.1.3 Comparable Legal Foundations for Movement of Value Functions

The achievement of the efficiency objectives arising out of the liquidity function performed by a banking payment system relies on the legal foundations of the system. These foundations, or the 'rules of the game' amongst the participants, underpin 'the efficiency, reliability, safety and stability of the payment system, and the protection of participants and users from unfair rights allocation and criminal abuse'.[2]

2. Biagio Bossone and Massimo Cirasino, 'The Oversight of the Payments Systems: A Framework for the Development and Governance of Payment Systems in Emerging Economies' (Research Series, The World Bank, July 2001) 17.

The legal foundation which primarily supports the liquidity function is the customer's legal rights to require the transfer of their funds. These legal rights are, as explained in the following chapters, established under the common-law principles which define the banker-customer relationship. Comparable legal foundations support the performance of the autonomy and portability functions performed in open banking systems. As Chapter 1 explained, these functions are supported by the customer's legal rights to require their data to be shared. When combined with the functional similarity between banking payment systems and open banking systems, it follows that these legal rights support equivalent functions. This is shown in Table 4.2.

*Table 4.2 Comparable Legal Foundations for Movement of Value*

| *Banking Payment Systems* | | *Open Banking Systems* | |
|---|---|---|---|
| *Function* | *Legal Foundation* | *Legal Foundation* | *Function* |
| Liquidity | Customer's legal rights to require that their bank *transfer* their *funds* to others at their direction. | Customer's legal rights to require that their bank *share* their *data* with others at their direction. | Autonomy<br>Portability |

The italics identify the same differences between funds transfers and data sharing as in Table 4.1. In each of banking payment systems and open banking systems, support is also provided by the legal relationships between participants which enable the customers' instructions to be acted upon. These are explained in section 4.3 below.

## 4.2 FUNCTIONS AND LEGAL FOUNDATIONS FOR STORING VALUE

Each of banking payment systems and open banking systems performs functions relating to storing the value which has been moved. In banking payment systems this is custody of funds received by a bank for its customer, whilst in open banking systems it is the function performed by recipient accountability.

### 4.2.1 Custody of Customer Funds in Banking Payment Systems

Related to the efficiency derived from the liquidity of customer funds is the efficiency which comes from the storage of funds by banks for customers. Part of this efficiency is derived from customers not needing to ensure the safekeeping of cash. However, a much greater efficiency is generated from the ability of the bank to use the funds which it holds for customers by lending or otherwise investing them with others. This *custody function*, which combines safe storage and economic use of funds, is the core of fractional reserve banking and the process of credit creation by commercial banks. Its economic benefits are significant as it enables the savings of many to be collectively pooled to fund productive activities of others, whilst still maintaining access to those savings when needed. The use of these pooled deposits by banks to make investments which have a longer maturity and different creditworthiness than the deposits themselves is the foundation of the 'maturity transformation' and 'credit transformation' in banking.

### 4.2.2 Accountability for Customer Data in Open Banking Systems

The storage of value function is also performed in open banking systems, with respect to customer data instead of customer funds. Open banking systems provide for shared customer data to be safely stored and used. This function was identified and named in Chapter 1 as *accountability*. This comparison is shown in Table 4.3.

*Table 4.3 Storage of Value Functions in Banking and Open Banking*

| *Function* | *Banking Payment System* | *Open Banking System* | *Function* |
|---|---|---|---|
| Custody | *Funds received* for customer are safely stored and *economically* used. | *Data shared* for customer are safely stored and *appropriately* used. | Accountability |

The italicised text in Table 4.3 shows another key difference between banking payment systems and open banking systems. Funds are *economically* used by on-lending them as part of fractional reserve banking whilst data are *appropriately* used in accordance with the customer's directions. This is also a consequence of the non-rivalrous nature of data referred to in section 3.1.3.

As explained in Chapter 1, the performance of this function is crucial for the effectiveness of open banking systems in achieving their objectives, just as they are for the efficiency of banking payment systems. These functions are also supported by comparable legal foundations of banking payment systems and open banking systems.

### 4.2.3 Comparable Legal Foundations for Storage of Value Functions

The achievement of the efficiency objectives arising out of the custody functions performed by a banking payment system relies on the legal foundations of the system.

The legal foundation which supports this function is the bank's responsibilities in dealing with funds received for their customers. These legal responsibilities are established under the common-law principles which define the banker-customer relationship, the legal and regulatory principles which govern the manner in which money can be held for another, and the regulatory principles which are commonly applied to payment systems and are incorporated into the design and rules of payment systems.

Comparable legal foundations support the performance of the accountability function performed in open banking systems. As Chapter 1 explained, this function is supported by the legal responsibilities of the recipient of shared customer data. When combined with the functional similarity between banking payment systems and open banking systems, it follows that these legal responsibilities support equivalent functions. This is shown in Table 4.4.

*Table 4.4 Comparable Legal Foundations for Storage of Value*

| *Banking Payment Systems* | | *Open Banking Systems* | |
|---|---|---|---|
| *Function* | *Legal Foundation* | *Legal Foundation* | *Function* |
| Custody | Bank's legal responsibilities in dealing with funds *received by it* for its customer. | Recipient's legal responsibilities in dealing with data *shared with it* for its customer. | Accountability |

The italicised text in Table 4.4 shows another difference between banking payment systems and open banking systems due to the non-rivalrous nature of data. Funds are *received by* banks whilst data are *shared with* data recipients.

## 4.3 FUNCTIONS AND LEGAL FOUNDATIONS FOR PARTICIPATION

The previous chapter explained that both banking payment systems and open banking systems are networks for the communication of valuable information. It was shown that in order for data portability to achieve open banking's objectives there needed to be participation of banks and recipients at scale and a significant level of connections between participants, which was described as the function of participant connectivity in Chapter 1. This part applies this in determining the comparable factors which contribute to effective participation in banking payment systems and open banking systems and the legal foundations which support them.

### 4.3.1 Factors in Participation in Banking Payment Systems

There are two key factors in determining the participation of a banking payment system, the access to participation and the stability of participation.

#### *(a) Access to Participation*

It was noted earlier that participation in banking payment systems is critical in achieving their efficiency objective. Banking payment systems are not always efficient, and an inefficient banking payment system has the opposite effect to an efficient one, reducing the development of an economy and causing poor use of financial resources and inequitable risk sharing. Inefficiencies in banking payment systems can develop from economies of scale and network externalities inherent in payment services which can cause monopolistic practices and restrictions on participation.

A critical factor in the efficiency of banking payment systems is access to participation. Direct participation in significant payment systems in both Australia and the UK is governed by conditions placed on those who desire access.[3] A key purpose performed by these conditions is to manage the legal, financial and operational risks which could be caused by the failure of a participant to perform its obligations due to the complexity and interconnectedness created by the network. Whilst these conditions are imposed to protect the safety of a banking payment system, the requirements imposed can be prohibitive for some entities whose participation would improve the efficiency of the system. The investment required in hardware, software and procedures as well as risk management measures means that flexibility in allowing indirect participation can be more efficient by encouraging competition between the providers of payment services and enabling participation indirectly by those who cannot do so directly. As a result, a balance is required and regulators now commonly require that conditions to access payment systems reduce competition as little as possible and 'be justified in terms of safety and efficiency'.[4] Accordingly, enabling *access* to participation in banking payment systems is a critical factor in their efficiency.

### *(b) Stability of Participation*

As noted above, the 'other side of the coin' to the benefits delivered by multilateral participation in payment systems are the risks which can emerge from complexity and interconnectedness. The development of this complexity has been identified in the flows of funds between commercial banks over Fedwire in the US and the CHAPS system in the UK, although a different type of complexity arises in each due to the different number of banks which directly participate in the core system.[5] A consequence of this complexity is that the resulting interconnected systems can be both robust and fragile, depending on whether an event impacts a highly connected participant:

> Just as electricity is delivered through a network for which the failure of a single power station can be disastrous, the vast majority of modern money is provided and operated by a network of banks in which the failure of one can disrupt the system as a whole'.[6]

As with other complex systems, unless appropriately managed, the interdependence created in banking payment systems by multilateral participation could lead to 'cascading failures' or 'domino effects' or 'systemic failure'. Through the connectivity provided, the system itself can amplify the spreading of risk. This risk, known as

3. Such as the Reserve Bank Information and Transfer System (RITS) in Australia and Clearing House Automated Payment System (CHAPS) in the UK.
4. Committee on Payment and Settlement Systems and International Organization of Securities Commissions, 'Principles for Financial Markets Infrastructures' (Standards, Bank for International Settlements, April 2012) 101.
5. *See* Kimmo Soramäki et al., 'The Topology of Interbank Payment Flows' (2007) 379(1) *Physica A: Statistical Mechanics and Its Applications* 317-333, 317. *See also* Christopher Becher, Stephen Millard and Kimmo Soramaki, 'The Network Topology of CHAPS Sterling' (Working Paper No. 355, Bank of England, 24 November 2008) 24.
6. Felix Martin, *Money: The Unauthorised Biography from Coinage to Cryptocurrencies* (New York: Vintage, 2015) at 435.

systemic risk, can be tremendously significant if it occurs in a banking payment system because it undermines the ability of money to perform its functions:

> We'd always thought that if you wanted to cripple the US economy, you'd take out the payment systems. Banks would be forced to fall back on inefficient physical transfers of money. Businesses would resort to barter and IOUs; the level of economic activity across the country could drop like a rock.[7]

For this reason, the *stability* of participation in banking payment systems is a critical factor in their safety. Over time, an understanding of the efficiency and risk in these systems has developed, together with the role that legal rights, responsibilities and relationships perform in their management, and in their resilience. As economies have become more dependent on the stability of banking payment systems, central banks and banking regulators have developed international standards to identify and manage this risk, and components of it.[8] The initial set, the Core Principles for Systemically Important Payment Systems ('Core Principles'),[9] were prepared in 2001 in response the Asian financial crisis and the increasing focus on payments. These were followed by the Principles for Financial Market Infrastructures (PFMIs), which were prepared in 2012 to incorporate the lessons learned in the previous 10 years, including from the global financial crisis of 2007-2009.[10] A key objective of these standards is to ensure the stability of these systems, particularly through their design and operation.

### 4.3.2 Factors in Participation in Open Banking Systems

Similarly, there are two key factors in achieving the participant connectivity in an open banking system, providing a facility for participation and establishing credibility.

#### *(a) Facility for Participation*

As explained in Chapter 1, in order for open banking to deliver value to customers from their data and be effective in achieving its broader objectives, customer data must be shared with recipients who will *use* the shared data. The scale at which this sharing is conducted, or the scale of the data portability enabled, or the connectivity enabled by the system, is critical to achieving these objectives. Accordingly, the *facility* for participation provided by the open banking system is a critical factor in its effectiveness. Without the facilitation of such participation, the data portability required for open banking to achieve its objectives will be impaired.

---

7. Alan Greenspan, *The Age of Turbulence: Adventures in a New World* (London: Penguin, 2008) at 2.
8. These standards contributed to stability during the 2008 global financial crisis: Daniela Russo, 'CPSS-IOSCO Principles for Financial Market Infrastructures: Vectors of International Convergence' (2013) (17) *Financial Stability Review* 69-78.
9. Committee on Payment and Settlement Systems, 'Core Principles for Systemically Important Payment Systems' (Core Principles, Bank for International Settlements, January 2001).
10. Committee on Payment and Settlement Systems and International Organization of Securities Commissions (n. 4).

However, the accountability of those who receive customers' valuable banking data for the data's appropriate use is also critical. To provide confidence that the data-related obligations of recipients can be performed, open banking systems require those who receive data directly be authorised, and conditions are placed on that authorisation to ensure that those in whom customers are placing their trust are worthy of that trust. This need for authorisation balances the need for portability against the need for accountability. Even so, meeting these requirements is still prohibitive for smaller entities who do not need to participate fully in the open banking ecosystem but who could contribute significantly to the system's achievement of its competition and innovation goals. Facilitating participation for these entities requires facilitation of indirect participation. Also, many of those who do participate are likely to retain and rely on intermediaries and third parties who provide technological and other support services. Accordingly, in order to provide the participation required to achieve open banking's objectives, systems need to provide the facility for direct participation, indirect participation and outsourcing arrangements. These arrangements are examined in Chapter 9.

### *(b) Establishing Credibility*

The previous chapter showed how open banking systems are designed to develop into networks and become 'complex systems' of interdependencies where some participants are highly connected whilst others are not. Just like banking payment systems, the complexity circulated can be both robust and fragile, depending on the connectivity of a participant that fails. If a highly connected participant were to suddenly cease to provide open banking services, then not only might their customers suffer an interruption in their own business (which might provide services to others too), but also other data recipients may not be able to provide their own open banking services. Also, if such a participant were to be subject to a cyber-attack which spread from their systems to others, then they could cause widespread damage due to their connectivity.

Chapter 1 introduced the importance of trust and confidence as core features in the design of open banking and recognised crucial factors in its success. As that introduction explained, this extends beyond the trust which customers place in particular participants to include the confidence which customers and participants place in the system itself. This 'institutional', 'impersonal' or 'systemic' trust is based on confident reliance on the performance of the system, and it was described in Chapter 1 as the *credibility* of the system. As open banking develops into the innovative ecosystem required to achieve its objectives, it needs to establish and maintain credibility as an ecosystem, so that customers and participants participate based not only on the trust in which they hold in those with whom they transact, but also on the integrity and dependability of the system which they use for those transactions. This is also critical in banking payment systems:

> As in all past crises, the root of the problem is the loss of confidence by investors and the public in the strength of key institutions and markets.[11]

In banking payment systems, this arises from the safe provision of services to customers from the interaction of intermediaries and participants performing different tasks, many of whom are not known to those customers, within a framework of governing rules, standards and systems. Similarly, it can develop in open banking from the involvement of a series of banks, recipients and intermediaries interacting within the governance of the system to provide goods and services to customers through the safe sharing of their data. In other words, the credibility of the ecosystem can emerge from its success in developing as a safe multilateral network.

However, systems can lose their credibility quickly because the foundation is past performance and an expectation of the effectiveness of constraints on future performance. If an open banking system fails to perform as expected, for example by the failure of a participant to perform its obligations to many customers, then an 'essential condition' of their trustworthiness is eroded. In financial systems, this has been described as an informational source of systemic risk, in contrast to the sources of risk spread through the impact of falling asset prices or counterparty default.[12] It was seen in the global financial crisis in the market response to the lack of information on the derivative exposures of AIG and the risk aversion following the collapse of Lehman Brothers. This 'information contagion',[13] can cause system-wide risks even in systems which otherwise would not be considered to give rise to systemic risks, such as retail payment systems. Open banking systems are particularly exposed to information contagion as a loss of customer data by some customers could cause many others to lose confidence that the system is trustworthy and withdraw from using it for data sharing. Credibility can be lost quickly in network failures and open banking systems could be particularly susceptible to a spreading loss of confidence if it is not easy for non-defaulting participants to prove that they are complying with their data-related obligations. As Botsman puts it:

> What should we believe in if the system has failed us? Who, or what, can be relied upon? We begin to fear what else could go wrong. What other shortcomings we don't yet know about might lurk in the system? Fear, suspicion and disenchantment are deadly viruses that spread fast.[14]

---

11. Ben S Bernanke, 'Stabilizing the Financial Markets and the Economy' (Presentation, Economic Club of New York, New York, 15 October 2008).
12. *See, e.g.*, Nicole Gillespie and Robert Hurley, 'Trust and the Global Financial Crisis', *Handbook of Advances in Trust Research* (Edward Elgar Publishing, 2013); Felix Roth, 'The Effect of the Financial Crisis On Systemic Trust' (2009) 44(4) *Intereconomics* 203-208; Timothy C Earle, 'Trust, Confidence, and the 2008 Global Financial Crisis' (2009) 29(6) *Risk Analysis: An International Journal* 785-792.
13. *See* Viral V Acharya and Tanju Yorulmazer, 'Information Contagion and Inter-bank Correlation in a Theory of Systemic Risk' (Discussion Paper No. 3743, Centre for Economic Policy Research, February 2003).
14. Rachel Botsman, *Who can You Trust?: How Technology Brought Us Together–And Why It Could Drive Us Apart* (Penguin UK, 2017) 18.

The increasing awareness of, and aversion to, risks presented by the use of the system could quickly lead to it ceasing to be used, as the foundations of trust in open banking are eroded. Analysis of this is the focus of Chapter 11.

### 4.3.3 Balancing Participation Factors in Banking and Open Banking

Balancing access and stability is critical in ensuring the efficiency and safety of banking payment systems. Similarly, balancing facility and credibility in open banking systems is critical to ensuring the efficacy of, and trust in, open banking systems.

These needs for balance are functionally equivalent. This can be seen in the similarity between balance required in open banking systems design to the cost-risk trade-off in the provision of payment services, where the cost of risk reduction for a participant needs to be balanced against the impact of the risk not only on the participant but on the society more broadly, because of the externalities created by payment system failure. This is shown in Figure 4.1.

*Figure 4.1 Illustrations of Balance in Banking Payment Systems and Open Banking Systems*

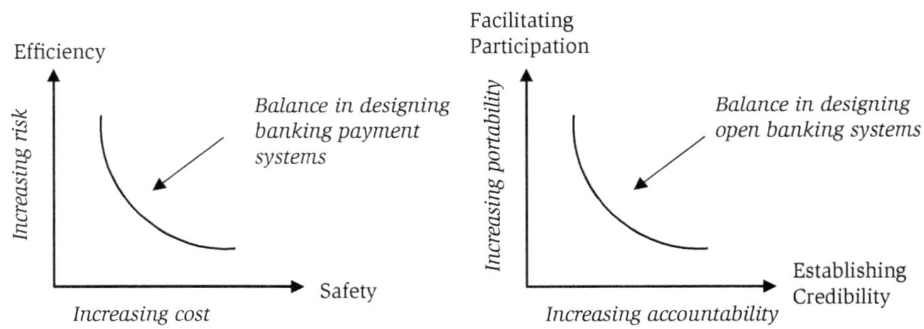


Table 4.5 shows the comparison of these balancing factors.

*Table 4.5 Factors in Participation in Banking Payment Systems and Open Banking Systems*

| *Factors* | *Banking Payment System* | *Open Banking System* | *Factors* |
|---|---|---|---|
| Access | Enable *access* for competitive participation to achieve system *efficiency*. | Providing *facility* for participation needed for system *efficacy*. | Facility |
| Stability | Preserve *stability* of system by ensuring that participant failure does not cause *system failure*. | Establishing *credibility* by ensuring that participant failure does not cause loss of *trust in the system*. | Credibility |

The italicised text shows differences between banking payment systems and open banking systems. First, the aim of access in banking payment systems is to achieve *efficiency*, whereas the broader aim of *efficacy* in achieving open banking's objectives is the aim of facilitating participation in open banking. Second, preventing *failure of the system* is the aim of the stability sought in banking payment systems, whilst maintaining *trust in the system* is the aim of ensuring its credibility in open banking.

Just as with the functions of banking payment systems and open banking systems explained in the previous chapter, these factors in participation are supported by the legal foundations of banking payment systems and open banking systems.

### 4.3.4 Comparable Legal Foundations for Participation Functions

The legal foundation which supports participation in banking payment systems is the legal relationships between the participants and regulators, primarily the conditions to establishing the legal relationships needed to participate, the terms of that relationship whilst they are participating, and the basis on which that relationship can be terminated if needed to protect the stability of the system if the participant fails. Comparable legal foundations support participation in open banking systems, based on establishing, maintaining, and terminating legal relationships which enable participation. This is shown in Table 4.6.

*Table 4.6 Comparable Legal Features of Participation*

<table>
<tr><th colspan="2">Banking Payment Systems</th><th colspan="2">Open Banking Systems</th></tr>
<tr><th>Factor</th><th>Legal Foundation</th><th>Legal Foundation</th><th>Factor</th></tr>
<tr><td>Access</td><td rowspan="2">Legal relationships between participants and with regulators which enable participation in the banking payment system, including the terms under which participation is permitted, governed, and terminated.</td><td rowspan="2">Legal relationships between participants and with regulators which enable participation in the open banking system, including the terms under which participation is permitted, governed, and terminated.</td><td>Facility</td></tr>
<tr><td>Stability</td><td>Credibility</td></tr>
</table>

Together with the legal rights and responsibilities described in previous parts of this chapter, these legal relationships form the legal foundations of banking payment systems used for the evaluation of open banking systems conducted in the following chapters of this book.

## 4.4 RISK CLASSIFICATION FOR OPEN BANKING SYSTEMS

In addition to comparing the legal foundations of the Australian and UK open banking systems and evaluating them against the legal foundations of banking payment systems, the following chapters also analyse the risks which arise from the legal design. To enable this, this part develops a risk classification for open banking systems from the classification of risks arising in communication problems and from risks customarily analysed in banking payment systems.

### 4.4.1 Classification Using Aspects of Communication Problems

It was noted in Chapter 3 that, in information theory, there are three aspects of problems in communication: how accurately symbols can be communicated (*technical*), how precisely the symbols convey meaning (*semantic*), and how effectively the communicated meaning affects conduct (*effectiveness*). As open banking systems are communication systems, these were adapted for an open banking context and the result was set out in Table 3.3 in Chapter 3.

These technical, semantic and effectiveness aspects of communication could be used as the basis of a risk classification for open banking systems. For example:

- something which could inhibit the accurate sharing of customer data under the system, such as a cyber-attack on the APIs used by a bank, would be a risk in addressing the *technical* aspect of communication;
- something which could affect the meaning conveyed by the data which is shared under the system, such as a cyber-attack on the customer data held by a recipient, would be a risk in addressing the *semantic* aspect of communication; and
- something which could affect the conduct resulting from the communication of the data, such as a failure by the recipient to use the shared data only as consented to by the customer, would be a risk addressing the *effectiveness* aspect of communication.

However, these three aspects of communication cannot explain all of the risks which could arise under an open banking system. This is because the concept of 'communication' contemplated, namely 'all of the procedures by which one mind may affect another',[15] assumes that the information is available to be communicated by the sender,[16] does not consider externalities generated when a communications system is part of a communications network, and does not contemplate the extent to which legal

15. Warren Weaver, 'Recent Contributions to the Mathematical Theory of Communication' (1953) *ETC: A Review of General Semantics* 261-281, 261.
16. Information theory assumes the availability of the message to be sent. This is because information 'relates not so much to what you do say, as to what you could say': *ibid*. 269. *See also* Claude E Shannon, 'A Mathematical Theory of Communication' (1948) 27(3) *The Bell System Technical Journal* 379-423, 379.

issues can interfere in the achievement of the desired effect of the communication.[17] Accordingly, in analysing the risks created by the deficiencies in the frameworks, it is necessary to develop a classification beyond the three aspects of communication problems.

### 4.4.2 Classification Using Risks Assessed in Banking Payment Systems

The earlier parts of this chapter and Chapter 3 showed that both open banking systems and banking payment systems are communication networks. This provides a basis for applying banking payment system risk assessment methodology to open banking systems which extends beyond that which could be developed from information theory. For example:

- *operational risk*, or 'the risk that deficiencies in information systems or internal processes, human errors, management failures, or disruptions from external events will result in the reduction, deterioration, or breakdown of services provided'.[18] This is the risk most customarily associated with information services, and could correspond with risks related to the integrity and security of shared data;
- *custody risk* or 'the risk of loss on assets held in custody in the event of a custodian's (or subcustodian's) insolvency, negligence, fraud, poor administration, or inadequate recordkeeping'.[19] This risk could correspond with reliance on the recipient to ensure that shared data will not be misused or improperly disclosed;
- *systemic* risk or 'the risk that the inability of one or more participants to perform as expected will cause other participants to be unable to meet their obligations when due'.[20] This risk could relate to the impact of the failure of a participant on other participants or on the system itself; and
- *legal* risk, or 'the risk of the unexpected application of a law or regulation' and the risk 'if the application of relevant laws and regulations is uncertain.'[21] This risk could correspond with deficiencies in legal foundations of an open banking system in supporting the system's functions.

However, the customary classification of risks in banking payment systems struggles in classifying information-related risks where the information itself is valuable. The key performance-related risks in banking payment systems, credit risk and liquidity risk, are not applied to information-related performance obligations. For example, although risks arising from the use of the derivative trade repositories (TRs)

17. As it is a mathematical theory for solving an 'engineering problem', there is no legal aspect to communication problems in information theory: *See* Shannon (n. 16) 410.
18. Committee on Payment and Settlement Systems and International Organization of Securities Commissions (n. 4) [2.9].
19. *Ibid.* [2.8].
20. *Ibid.* 178.
21. *Ibid.* [2.4].

which were established following the global financial crisis of 2007-2009 to receive and share information are now part of customary risk analysis, this is limited to operational risk.[22] Also, although SWIFT ('Society for Worldwide Interbank Financial Telecommunication'), whose information messages underpin many cross-border payments, is subject to regulatory oversight by the National Bank of Belgium (cooperating with the central banks of the G10 countries), the regulatory treatment is not based on the core principles applicable to payment systems, because it is not a payment system.[23]

Accordingly, in analysing the risks arising in open banking, it is necessary to develop a classification beyond that used in banking payment systems.

### 4.4.3 Developing an Open Banking Risk Classification

Instead of using either the classification of communication problems, or of risks in banking payment systems, it is preferable to develop a new classification by reference to the functions performed in open banking systems. That is, a classification of risks which takes account of the functional similarity between open banking systems and banking payment systems as networks for the communication of valuable information and the functions performed by them. This classification should be comprised of availability risk, communication risk, performance risk, value risk, network risk, and validity risk.

#### *(a) Availability Risk*

Chapter 1 establishes that a core function of open banking systems is to enable a customer's data to be safely shared at the customer's direction (the autonomy function). If the data required to be shared in order to provide the good or service requested by the customer are not available through the open banking system, then this *availability risk* could impair the system's performance of this function.

Availability risk corresponds most closely with liquidity risk in banking payment systems in the sense that each represents the risk that the information needing to be communicated (such as the balance of the relevant account) is insufficiently available for the purpose to be served. Availability risk is considered further in Chapter 5.

#### *(b) Communication Risk*

Another risk in enabling the customer's data to be safely shared at their direction is the inability to accurately communicate the data and ensure receipt of the related information. If the data cannot be accurately sent, or their meaning cannot be accurately

22. *Ibid.*
23. The result is five high-level expectations based on operational risk management, relating to risk identification and management, information security, reliability and resilience, technology planning and communication with users: National Bank of Belgium, 'Financial Stability Review' (Review, 2007) 97.

received and understood, then this *communication risk* could also impair the framework's performance of its portability function.

Communication risk corresponds with the technical and semantic aspects of communication problems and with operational risk under banking payment systems. Communication risk is considered further in Chapter 6.

### *(c) Performance Risk*

Chapter 1 establishes that another core function of open banking systems is to ensure that the shared data are safely stored and appropriately used (the accountability function). If either the bank or the recipient does not perform its data-related obligations, such as the obligations to share and use data through the framework only in accordance with its rules, then this *performance risk* can impair the framework's execution of its accountability function.

Performance risk corresponds with the effectiveness aspects of communication problems (in that any improper use of data is not conduct which is intended to result from the sharing of data) and with credit risk under banking payment systems (in that it is the risk that a participant does not perform the obligations which they promised to perform). Performance risk is considered further in Chapter 7.

### *(d) Value Risk*

Another risk in ensuring that shared data are safely stored and appropriately used is that the recipient does not protect the value of the customer's data by maintaining their confidentiality, quality and integrity. If this protection is not present, including in the insolvency of the data recipient, then this *value risk* can also impair the ability of the framework to perform its accountability function.

Value risk corresponds with the effectiveness aspects of communication problems (in that any improper use of data is not conduct which is intended to result from the sharing of data) and with custody risk under banking payment systems (in that it is the risk that a participant does not preserve the value of what has been placed in their custody). Value risk is considered further in Chapter 8.

### *(e) Network Risk*

Chapter 1 articulated that another function of open banking systems was to provide the participant connectivity required for effective participation in the sharing and use of customer data. Chapter 4 explained that the accessibility which enables this participation results in interdependence which can cause a participant's failure to result in the collapse of trust to other participants in the communication network and the network as a whole. If this occurs, then this *network risk* can impair the ability of the system to perform its participant connectivity function.

Network risk corresponds with systemic risk in banking payment systems. Network risk is considered further in Chapters 9 and 11.

### (f) *Validity Risk*

Chapter 1 explained that open banking systems have both technological and legal foundations, and the effectiveness of communication under a system can be impaired if the law requires that the participants interrupt, ignore or delete it. Each of the functions to be performed by an open banking system is subject to this risk that the law will not support or recognise the validity of its performance, for example, because the obligations are legally uncertain or unenforceable. If this occurs, then this *validity risk* can impair the ability of the system to perform any of its functions.

Validity risk corresponds with the concept of 'noise' in communication system, as it can be considered to be 'changes in the transmitted signal' which were not intended by the information source, such as distortions or errors in transmission.[24] Validity risk corresponds with legal risk in banking payment systems. Validity risk is considered further in Chapters 6 and 10.

## 4.5 COMPARABLE RIGHTS, RESPONSIBILITIES, RELATIONSHIPS AND RISKS

This and the previous chapter have shown that the functions which are important for the efficiency and safety of banking payment systems are comparable with the functions which are important for the efficacy and trustworthiness of open banking systems. They have combined this with the functional similarity between banking payment systems and open banking systems, showing that the legal rights, responsibilities and relationships which underpin those functions in banking payment systems should also support open banking systems, applying to customer data rather than customer funds. This is shown together in Table 4.7.

*Table 4.7 Comparable Legal Rights, Responsibilities and Relationships*

| *Function* | *Banking Payment Systems* | *Open Banking Systems* | *Function* |
|---|---|---|---|
| Liquidity | Customer's legal *rights* to require that their bank transfer their funds to others at their direction. | Customer's legal *rights* to require that their bank share their data with others at their direction. | Autonomy |
| Custody | Bank's legal *responsibilities* in dealing with funds received by it for its customer. | Recipient's legal *responsibilities* in dealing with data shared with it for its customer. | Accountability |

24. Weaver (n. 15) 269. Noise can also be 'semantic', meaning 'perturbations or distortions of meaning which are not intended by the source but which inescapably affect the destination': *ibid*. 286.

| *Function* | *Banking Payment Systems* | *Open Banking Systems* | *Function* |
|---|---|---|---|
| Participation | Legal *relationships* between participants and regulators which enable participation in the banking payment system. | Legal *relationships* between participants and regulators which enable participation in the open banking system. | Connectivity (enabling Portability) |

In addition, this chapter has established a risk framework for open banking systems, which corresponds to risks which arise in banking payment systems, as set out in Table 4.8.

*Table 4.8 Comparable Risks Between Open Banking Systems and Banking Payment Systems*

| *Open Banking Risk* | *Primary Open Banking Function Impaired* | *Banking Payment System Equivalent* |
|---|---|---|
| Availability Risk | Customer Autonomy | Liquidity risk |
| Communication Risk | Data Portability | Operational risk |
| Performance Risk | Recipient Accountability | Credit risk |
| Value Risk | Recipient Accountability | Custody risk |
| Network Risk | Participant Connectivity | Systemic risk |
| Validity Risk | All functions | Legal risk |

As the rights, responsibilities and relationships set out in Table 4.7 underpin the performance of the functions required to achieve the objectives of open banking, they can form the basis of a comparison between them. The extent to which an open banking system includes these legal features to enable these functions can inform an assessment as to whether its legal design supports its efficacy and trustworthiness and the potential risks created. Also, due to the functional equivalence established in this chapter, the equivalent rights, responsibilities, relationships and risks in the banking payment system can serve as a benchmark against which those of the open banking systems can be evaluated. The relationships between the Objectives, Functions, Foundations and Risks developed in the previous chapters is illustrated in Figure 4.2.

*Figure 4.2 Objectives, Functions, Foundations and Risks of Open Banking Systems*

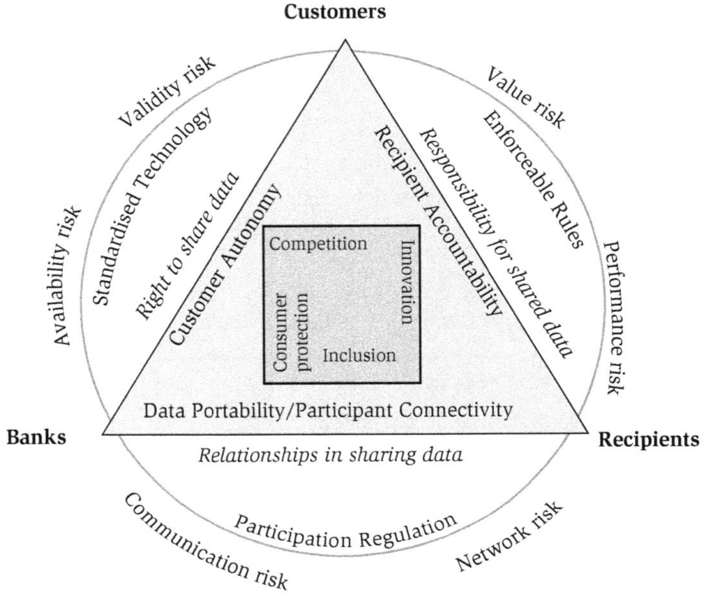


Moving from the centre outwards, the objectives of open banking are within the square, the functions which enable them to be achieved are within the triangle, the foundations for performing those functions within the circle, and the risks which arise from them outside of the circle.

# CHAPTER 5
# Supplying Customer Data for Sharing

This chapter commences the analysis of the legal foundations of open banking systems by examining the legal rights which support making data available for customers to share. It compares those legal rights under the Australian and UK open banking systems and evaluates them against the equivalent legal rights of banking payment systems. The analysis addresses two questions:

- What data should customers have rights to share?
- Who should be required to share customer data?

The answers to these questions are fundamental to an open banking system's performance of its *autonomy* and *portability* functions.

## 5.1 WHAT DATA SHOULD CUSTOMERS HAVE RIGHTS TO SHARE?

The scope of the data which are able to be shared and the sources from which customers may share their data are fundamental to achieving open banking's objectives. Without the sufficient breadth and depth of data being shared and used, an open banking system will not generate the insights and choices needed to improve competition, encourage innovation and foster inclusion. Also, if the open banking system cannot be used to share a particular set of data, then a less secure method is likely to be used, defeating open banking's consumer protection objectives.

The legal rights which form the foundation of two key features of the extent of customer data able to be shared, the accounts from which data may be shared and the data which may be shared from those accounts, are comparatively analysed below, followed by an evaluation against the rights which customers have in banking payment systems to share data, and to transfer funds, from their accounts.

### 5.1.1 Comparison of Data Able to Be Shared under Open Banking Systems

#### *(a) Customer Accounts from Which Data May Be Shared*

The right to share data under Australian open banking applies to 'CDR data' as defined in the *CCA*.[1] This requires that the data be 'within a class of information' designated in the *Open Banking Designation*.[2] The *Open Banking Designation* designates information by reference to a 'product' – a very broad definition based on the definition of 'banking business' in the *Banking Act 1959* (Cth) ('*Australian Banking Act*').[3] This encompasses goods and services offered or supplied to a person in connection with taking money on deposit, making advances of money, or other financial activities which are included in the definition of 'banking business' in the *Australian Banking Act*.[4] The *CDR Rules* refines this broad reference to 29 different bank accounts. These encompass savings, current, cheque and transaction accounts, debit, charge and credit card accounts, home loan, mortgage and personal loan accounts, and business financing accounts, such as lines of credit, overdrafts, and asset finance accounts.[5] This breadth of coverage was designed to ensure that the Australian system applied to banking products which are 'widely available to the general public' but not 'banking products especially designed for individual customers'.[6]

There are fewer accounts from which data may be shared under UK open banking. The *CMA Order*, through its description of the 'Read/Write Data Standard', requires access to be provided to transaction information for personal current account products, which includes personal current accounts (with or without an overdraft facility), basic bank accounts, packaged accounts, reward accounts, student or graduate accounts and youth accounts,[7] and business current account products, which includes business current accounts and 'standard tariff unsecured business overdrafts'.[8] The *PSR* complements this coverage by providing for access to data from a 'payment account', which is 'an account held in the name of one or more payment service users which is used for the execution of payment transactions'.[9] In the view of the FCA, payment accounts include 'current accounts, e-money accounts, flexible savings accounts, credit card accounts and current account mortgages'.[10] Mortgage

1. *Competition and Consumer Act 2010* (Cth) s. 56FF ('*CCA*') s. 56AI.
2. The definition of CDR data also includes data which is 'wholly or partly' derived from such information: *ibid.* s. 56A(1)(b). However, this cannot be required to be shared under the *CDR Rules*: *ibid.* s. 56BD(1)(a). However, the privacy safeguards can apply to this data.
3. *Consumer Data Right (Authorised Deposit Taking Institutions) Designation 2019* (Cth) ('*Open Banking Designation*') s. 4(2) (definition of 'product'). *See Banking Act 1959* (Cth) s. 5 (definition of 'banking business') ('*Australian Banking Act*').
4. *Open Banking Designation* (n. 3).
5. *Competition and Consumer (Consumer Data Right) Rules 2020* ('*CDR Rules*') sch. 3 cl. 1.4.
6. Australian Treasury, 'Inquiry into Future Directions for Consumer Data Right: Giving Consumers Choice, Convenience and Confidence' (Report, October 2020) 36.
7. *Retail Banking Market Investigation Order 2017* (UK) ('*CMA Order*') Art. 12.4.1.
8. *Ibid.* 12.4.2.
9. *Payment Services Regulation 2017* (UK) ('*PSR*') r. 2.
10. Financial Conduct Authority, 'Payment Services and Electronic Money – Our Approach' (Approach Document, June 2019) 213.

and loan accounts, fixed term deposit accounts and cash savings accounts are not subject to UK open banking.[11]

The narrower scope of UK open banking reflects the constraints imposed by its dual legislative lineage.[12] The CMA's Retail Market Investigation limited the products and parties within the scope of the *CMA Order*,[13] and the scope of the *PSR* was limited by *PSD2*.[14] The result is that important customer banking services, such as those provided through mortgage accounts, are not covered by the UK system. This limits the visibility of the state of a customer's finances which can be given by UK open banking, and it cannot assist with the evaluation of, and switching between, different mortgages. Further, the lack of coverage of savings accounts means that some use cases are constrained, such as sweeping funds between current accounts and savings accounts when needed. The inability of UK open banking to cover these products restricts the scope of the data which customers can share, and the functions which UK open banking can perform.

Australian open banking is not subject to any similar legislative constraint on its account coverage. It includes those accounts which are notably absent from the UK, such as mortgage accounts and savings accounts. Indeed, its coverage includes those types of accounts which are expected to be added to UK open banking in its proposed extension for 'Open Finance'.[15] The more extensive scope of data which a customer can share under Australian open banking enhances the autonomy provided to Australian customers. Competition for a greater range of banking products is enhanced by data for those products being able to be shared, and innovation is encouraged by more data being available to be used in designing new products and services.

It is also worth noting that the Australian system can also apply to other accounts of the customer, such as their energy accounts, and soon telecommunication accounts, as it is part of the broader CDR. Due to the single legislative structure and accreditation system, the data are able to be shared by customers across sector boundaries and are not 'siloed' in a particular sector. This is intended to enable the combination of complementary data sets allowing the development of new insights and value to the customer. For example, a customer could choose to share their energy data with their bank to facilitate assessment and monitoring of the affordability of their current energy arrangements, or their banking data with their energy company to verify creditworthiness. The extended scope of data able to be shared under the Australian system

11. *Ibid. See also* Financial Conduct Authority, *FCA Handbook* (Financial Conduct Authority, 2013) PERG [15.3].
12. *See* Chapter 2.
13. *See* Explanatory Note, Retail Banking Market Investigation Order 2017 (UK) [38] ('Explanatory Note, Retail Banking Market Investigation Order'). *See also* Competition and Markets Authority, 'Retail Banking Market Investigation' (Terms of Reference, 6 November 2014) https://assets.publishing.service.gov.uk/media/545a981c40f0b6130e000011/Terms_of_reference_retail_banking.pdf.
14. *Directive 2015/2366/EU of the European Parliament and of the Council of 25 November 2015 on Payment Services in the Internal Market, amending Directives 2002/65/EC, 2009/110/EC, and 2013/36/EU and Regulation (EU) No 1093/2010 and repealing Directive 2007/64/EC* OJ L 337/35 ('*PSD2*') Art. 115. *See also* HM Treasury and Financial Conduct Authority, 'Expectations for the Third Party Access Provisions in the Payment Services Directive II' (Statement, July 2017) 228.
15. *See* Chapter 2.

supports the achievement of inclusion objectives as a bank's use of customer data from those accounts can complement assessments of creditworthiness, as has been shown by its use in other jurisdictions such as India. It is intended that the design of UK open banking will be extended in a similar way as part of the 'Smart Data' proposals.[16]

### *(b) Data Able to Be Shared from Customer Accounts*

Under Australian open banking, information about the product,[17] information about the user of the product,[18] and information about the use of the product,[19] are all able to be shared by the customer. The last of these includes information which identifies an account associated with the product, the balance of such an account, information about a transaction made by the customer in connection with the product and information about an authorisation given by the customer in connection with such an account, including who can use, access or view the account and third party authorisations to make payments.[20] The account number and account name are included, as are direct debit authorisations, scheduled payments and payee authorisations.[21] The Australian Standards supplement this by specifying 'Enumerated Values' of the accounts from which data can be shared and the data fields from those accounts.[22]

Under UK open banking, the *CMA Order* requires that the 'Read/Write Data Standard' provides access to transaction information on the accounts covered and to initiate payments on behalf of customers on those accounts.[23] The detail of the data to be shared, including the data fields for each of the accounts, is provided by the UK Standards.[24] Although the *PSR* does not define what data may be shared, it contains an obligation on an account servicing payment service provider (ASPSP) to:

16. *See* Chapter 2.
17. This is information about a product, including its identification, description, price, fees, charges, interest rates, features and benefits, terms and conditions and eligibility criteria: *Open Banking Designation* (n. 3) s. 8(1).
18. This is information about a person to whom the product is supplied (or their associate if the product has also been, or is being supplied to that associate) which has been either provided by that person (or their associate) in connection with the person's acquisition or use of the product, or was otherwise obtained by or on behalf of the entity that holds the information, or on whose behalf the information is held: *ibid.* s. 6(1).
19. *Ibid.* s. 7(1).
20. *Ibid.* s. 7(2).
21. *Ibid.* s. 7 (Examples 1, 2).
22. The twelve 'Enumerated Values' are business loans, credit and charge cards, leases, margin loans, overdrafts, personal loans, regulated trust accounts, residential mortgages, term deposits, trade finance, travel cards and transaction and savings accounts. The data fields to be shared include account balances, account identifiers, transaction information, direct debits, scheduled payments, payees and product details: Data Standards Body, 'Consumer Data Standards v 1.22.0', https://consumerdatastandards.org.au.
23. *CMA Order* (n. 7) Art. 10.1.2.
24. For example, the description of each of the data fields covered for transaction data can be found in the 'Data Dictionary' section of the 'Account and Transaction API' sections of the Open Banking API specifications: Open Banking Implementation Entity, 'Open Banking API Specifications ' (Standard, v3.1.10) https://standards.openbanking.org.uk. These are also described as

treat a data request from the account information service provider (AISP) in the same way as a data request received directly from the payer unless the ASPSP has objective reasons for treating the request differently.[25]

The *SCA-RTS* adds to this, specifying that banks:

shall provide account information service providers with the same information from designated payment accounts and associated payment transactions made available to the payment service user when directly requesting access to the account information, provided that this information does not include sensitive payment data.[26]

The FCA has provided further clarity by stating that banks 'should make available the maximum amount of information that would be available to the customer across the channels the customer uses to access their payment account'.[27] The FCA also gives the examples of account information, such as the name of the account holder and the account number, and of transaction data, which should be at the same level of granularity as is available to the customer when they access their account directly.[28] The *PSR* relies on the UK Standards to provide further detail of the information which is able to be shared.

### *(i) Exclusion of Bank's Own Analysis*

Broadly speaking, the data able to be shared from an account are comparable between the systems. Importantly, neither Australian nor UK open banking requires the bank's own analysis or opinion to be shared. Under Australian open banking, this is excluded by the *Open Banking Designation* as 'materially enhanced information' which was 'wholly or partly derived through the application of insight or analysis'.[29] Examples of this information include:

the outcome of an income, expense or asset verification assessment; a categorisation of transactions as being related to groceries or rent; significantly improved descriptions of transactions utilising geolocation or business name information from external sources; assessments of a customer's ability to meet loan repayments (also known as loan serviceability); or inferences that a customer has recently experienced a life event, such as a house purchase.[30]

---

'data clusters' in the Open Banking Customer Experience Guidelines: Open Banking Implementation Entity, 'Customer Experience Guidelines' (Standard, v3.1.10) https://standards.openbanking.org.uk.

25. *PSR* (n. 9) reg. 70(2)(b).
26. *Commission Delegated Regulation (EU) 2018/389 Supplementing Directive (EU) 2015/2366 of the European Parliament and of the Council with regard to Regulatory Technical Standards for Strong Customer Authentication and Common and Secure Open Standards of Communication* OJ L69/23 Art. 36(1)(a) ('SCA-RTS').
27. Financial Conduct Authority, 'Payment Services and Electronic Money – Our Approach' (n. 10) 216.
28. *Ibid.* 217.
29. *Open Banking Designation* (n. 3) ss 7(3), 10(1).
30. Explanatory Statement, Consumer Data Right (Authorised Deposit taking Institutions Designation) 2019 (Cth) 11 ('Open Banking Designation Explanatory Statement'). This data may become CDR data, and subject to the privacy safeguards, if it is derived data: *see* n. 2.

However, account balances, the interest earned or charged, fees, charges, reference numbers or identification information are not materially enhanced information and are shareable under the Australian system.[31] The equivalent exclusion of a bank's own analysis is more obscure in UK open banking as it is made by implication, through the articulation that only information already available to the customer can be shared.[32] The position of Australian and UK open banking in not requiring the banks to share their own analysis is sensible, even though such information would be useful to competitors. Requiring a bank to make its own analysis of customer data (as opposed to the customer data itself) freely available to others under open banking could interfere with intellectual property rights and commercial arrangements in relation to the use of data and data technologies. In addition, making such data freely available to others could discourage investment in data and data technologies as any competitive advantage obtained from such investment would become easily available to competitors. Further, requiring banks to share their own opinions on customers with others could expose them to potential legal liability should those opinions be negligent or not be accurate.[33] For these reasons, the exclusion of 'value-added' information is an important design feature of the Australian and UK open banking systems.

#### *(ii) Initiation of Payments*

The most significant difference between the data able to be shared under each system is that UK open banking enables customers to authorise data recipients to give payment instructions on their accounts to the customer's bank, which is the 'write' element of the UK Standards and a 'payment initiation service' under *PSR*.[34] As explained in Chapter 3, this can be described as instructional information. Payment initiation enables data recipients to enhance any advice which they provide to customers using their data by putting that advice into effect, for example by transferring funds between the customer's accounts. Also, it overcomes customer inertia in switching between products. The additional functionality which payment initiation provides supports the competition and innovation objectives of open banking:

> For example, when a customer receives a personalized mortgage offer from a third party that has collated their data, the customer can initiate payment without leaving the mortgage site. ... Including payment initiation in an open banking scheme is important for ensuring its successful adoption.[35]

31. *Open Banking Designation* (n. 3) s. 10(3).
32. *See* nn. 25-27 above and accompanying text. The FCA has stated that the information shared should not include analysis of transaction data which a bank makes available to its customers: Financial Conduct Authority, 'Payment Services and Electronic Money – Our Approach' (n. 10) 217.
33. *See Hedley Byrne & Co Ltd v. Heller & Partners Ltd* [1964] AC 465 ('*Hedley Byrney v. Heller*'); *Commercial Banking Company of Sydney Ltd v. R H Brown & Co* [1972] HCA 24 ('*Commercial Banking Company of Sydney Ltd v. R H Brown & Co*').
34. *PSR* (n. 9) reg. 2 (definition of 'payment initiation service').
35. Ariadne Plaitakis and Stefan Staschen, 'Open Banking: How to Design for Financial Inclusion' (Working Paper, CGAP, 2020) 18.

This is not currently possible under Australian open banking, as none of the *CCA*, the *Open Banking Designation*, the *CDR Rules* or the Australian Standards enable payment initiation on the customer's accounts. However, draft amendments to the *CCA* have been released to enable payment initiation, as well as the initiation of broader actions on behalf of customers with respect to banking and the other sectors to which the CDR applies.[36] Nevertheless, until these amendments are made, together with the necessary additions to the *CDR Rules* and Australian Standards, the lack of a right for customers to share this instructional information in relation to their accounts constrains the customer autonomy provided by Australian open banking.

### 5.1.2 Evaluation Against Rights in Accounts under Banking Payment Systems

#### *(a) Rights to Customer Data under Banking Law*

Before evaluating the legal rights to share customer data under Australian and UK open banking against the customer's rights to transfer their funds, it useful to consider whether the scope of existing rights to customer data provided under banking law could be relevant. Two aspects of banking law are pertinent, the bank's duty of confidentiality and the practice of bankers' references.

##### *(i) Duty of Confidentiality*

One of the difficulties in implementing open banking is that that information technology systems of banks have been designed for many years to keep customer data secret and secure. The legal foundation for this is the duty of confidentiality which a bank owes their customer, which arises out of the contract between a bank and its customer, and which extends to all of the transactions through the account.[37] This duty is taken very seriously by banks, and it has resulted in customer banking data being less widely used than other sources of personal information. It also provides banks with a commercial advantage, and it serves as a barrier to entry and competition. The competitive position provided to banks by this duty is reinforced by the fact that it does not enable the customer to require the bank to share data about their account, and it does not prevent the bank from using the customer data as it wishes provided that it is

36. *See* 'Consumer Data Right – Exposure Draft Legislation to Enable Action Initiation', *Australian Government, The Treasury* (Exposure Draft Legislation, 26 September 2022) https://treasury.gov.au/consultation/c2022-317468. For the reasoning for this, *see* Australian Treasury, 'Inquiry into Future Directions for the Consumer Data Right: Giving Consumers Choice, Convenience and Confidence' (n. 6).

37. *Tournier v. National Provincial and Union Bank of England* [1924] 1 KB 461 ('*Tournier's case*'). The duty has also been applied in Australian courts: *see Brighton v. Australia and New Zealand Banking Group Ltd* [2011] NSWCA 152 ('*Brighton v. Australia and New Zealand Banking Group Ltd*'). For a comparison of the duty with privacy law *see* Graham Greenleaf and Alan Tyree, 'Bankers' Duties and Data Privacy Principles: Global Trends, and Asia-Pacific Comparisons' in Sandra Booysen and Dora Neo (eds), *Can Banks Still Keep a Secret* (Cambridge University Press, 2017) 31-61.

not disclosed. In fact, the bank's legal duty of confidentiality locks-in the bank's exclusive use of the data from their customer's account. Accordingly, in the context of the functions performed by open banking, the bank's duty of confidentiality does not support data portability and provides only limited recipient accountability.

Sometimes, banks can seek to use the duty of secrecy as a basis for resisting the implementation of open banking. However, it is important to note that the bank's legal duty is subject to qualifications. Two of these are where the disclosure is required by law and where the disclosure is made with the express or implied consent of the customer.[38] As both the Australian and UK open banking systems contain legal obligations on banks to share customer data, and require the customer's consent to data sharing, compliance by a bank with data sharing requests made under Australian and UK open banking does not breach a bank's duty to keep its customer information confidential.

### *(ii) Bankers' References*

An historical banking practice enables customers to request that their banks share data in the context of references to the customers financial standing.[39] This practice, which has been described judicially to be a 'very wholesome and useful habit' usually takes place at the request and with the knowledge of the customer.[40] On a superficial level, this practice bears some similarity to data sharing under open banking systems. However, there are two fundamental differences:

- *No obligation to respond*: Under the customary practice, the bank is not obliged to respond to the request for a reference and it does so at its own discretion, whereas a bank is obliged to respond to a request made under Australian and UK open banking. This right to share data under open banking is essential to the customer autonomy required to achieve open banking's objectives.
- *Sharing opinion not data*: In supplying a reference on a customer, a bank does not share the customer's account data, but instead provides an opinion derived from that data. As noted above, such an opinion would not be required to be shared under either the Australian or UK system even though the practice of bankers' references shows that sharing 'value-added' information can be beneficial.

Accordingly, in the context of the functions performed by open banking, the practice of bankers' references provides little customer autonomy and limited data portability. Having shown that the legal rights associated with the bank's duty of confidentiality do not share functional equivalence with the rights to share data under

38. *Tournier's case* (n. 37) 471 (Banks L.J.)
39. *See Parsons v. Barclay & Co. Ltd.* (1910) 2 LDB 248 ('*Parsons v. Barclay & Co. Ltd.*'). *See also Turner v. Royal Bank of Scotland plc* [1999] 2 All ER (Comm) 664 ('*Turner v. Royal Bank of Scotland plc*').
40. *Parsons v. Barclay & Co. Ltd.* (n. 39) 132.

open banking, it is preferable to evaluate those rights under open banking against the customer's right to transfer their funds.

### (b) *Rights to Transfer Customer Funds from Bank Accounts*

A fundamental term implied into the contract between a bank and its customer is that the bank promises to repay the customer's funds.[41] This 'includes a promise to repay any part of the amount due against the written order of the customer, addressed to the bank at the branch'.[42] This right of the customer to direct payment of the funds from their account is an important part of the value of the account to the customer, and the primary method for the customer to use those funds. As shown in Chapter 4, this right to transfer funds from an account can be used as a benchmark against which the rights to share data from an account can be evaluated.

The comparison of Australian and UK open banking in the previous part of this chapter showed that UK open banking has a more limited range of accounts from which customers can share their data because UK open banking applies to payment accounts only and not to mortgage accounts and savings accounts. These are also accounts from which a customer does not have the right to transfer their funds. On a superficial level, this would appear to indicate that the scope of customers' rights to share their data under UK open banking is aligned with customers' rights to transfer their funds under banking payment systems. However, this conclusion represents a fundamental misunderstanding of the functional equivalence between customer data and customer funds. The analysis in Chapter 3 established that customer data and customer funds each represents valuable information to the customer, and that open banking systems and banking payment systems each represent networks for the transfer of that valuable information. Data about a customer's account can be valuable whether or not payments of money can be made from the account. For example, important insights about a customer's financial affairs can be obtained from the customer's mortgage or savings account even if the customer cannot transfer their funds from the account. The functional equivalence of information and money does not mean that there is value in sharing information about money only if the money can be transferred. That would be to confuse the value of particular information with particular informational value.

A more insightful evaluation focusses on what is customarily provided to customers in exchange for deposited funds which they are not able to transfer, such as funds in term deposit accounts. The conditions of these term deposit accounts usually provide that the customer is paid a higher interest rate on those funds in compensation for their loss of use of their funds cannot be used by them, as an 'illiquidity premium'.[43] In an open banking context, these accounts are conceptually similar to the bank

41. *Joachimson v. Swiss Bank Corporation* [1921] 3 KB 110, 127 ('*Joachimson v. Swiss Bank Corporation*').
42. *Ibid*.
43. *See* Yakov Amihud and Haim Mendelson, 'The Pricing of Illiquidity as a Characteristic and as a Risk' (2015) 19(3) *Multinational Finance Journal* 149-168, 150.

accounts from which a customer cannot share their data under UK open banking. There is no equivalent compensation offered to customers for the loss of use of their data from these accounts. It is true that, unlike their funds in a term deposit, the data are still available to the customer. However, unlike the bank, very few customers would have the technological ability to derive much value from their own data and the customer is likely to need to share the data in order to use the data effectively and to realise their value. The customer could still share the data by sending a copy of their account statement, but an analogue representation of the account data, as opposed to a standardised digital form, is not able to deliver the same customer benefits, particularly at scale.

Accordingly, when evaluated against the rights of customers to transfer their funds, the limitations on the accounts from which the customer may share data represent an uncompensated loss to the customer of the value which they might have derived from sharing that data. Just as the inability of a customer to withdraw their funds from a bank account impairs the liquidity of the customer with respect to their funds, so does the inability to share data from a bank account impair the autonomy and portability of the customer with respect to their data. It follows that the narrower scope of accounts from which customers have the legal right to share data under UK open banking impairs its ability to perform these functions and, as a result, to achieve its objectives.

## 5.2 WHO SHOULD BE REQUIRED TO SHARE CUSTOMER DATA?

A further determinant of the customer data which can be shared under open banking systems is the entities which are required to respond to customer data sharing requests. Whilst banks are the initial focus of open banking, they are not the only financial service providers that hold customer account data and equivalent financial data are held by others, such as non-bank lenders. Accordingly, an open banking system's performance of their customer autonomy function, and the achievement of its objectives, can be enhanced by enabling customers to require these entities to share their customer account data too.

The rights relating to two key features of who should be required to share data, which banks are required to share data and which data recipients are required to share data, are comparatively analysed below, followed by an evaluation against asymmetry in rights to transfer funds, and rights against banks in transferring customer funds, in banking payment systems.

### 5.2.1 Comparison of Who Must Share Data in Open Banking Systems

#### *(a) Banks Required to Share Customer Data*

The obligation under the Australian system to disclose CDR data requested by, or on behalf of, a CDR customer applies to 'data holders'.[44] That definition, contained in the

44. *CDR Rules* (n. 5) r. 4.6.

*CCA*[45] and the *Open Banking Designation*,[46] comprises authorised deposit-taking institutions (ADIs) which are authorised to conduct banking business in Australia by the Australian Prudential Regulation Authority (APRA) under the *Australian Banking Act*.[47] This includes all banks, building societies and credit unions authorised to conduct banking business in Australia.[48] The operative definition of data holder is affected by the banking sector-specific provisions contained in the *CDR Rules*.[49] These set out a 'staged application' of the obligation, which started with the four largest ADIs in July 2020 and then expanded to the others by July 2021.[50] As noted in Chapter 2, as of July 2022, Australian open banking applied to 76 different Australian banks.

The application of the legal obligation to share data under the UK system is complicated by its legislative foundation. Under the *PSR*, compliance is required by 'ASPSP'.[51] These are 'payment service providers' who provide and maintain a 'payment account' for a payer. The term 'payment service provider' has a broad meaning, including banks and building societies in the UK,[52] as well as other authorised payment institutions, such as authorised electronic money institutions (such as online wallet providers) and authorised payment institutions (such as money remitters, non-bank credit card issuers and merchant acquiring firms).[53] However, under the *CMA Order*, only the nine specified banks and building societies are required to comply (known as the 'CMA9').[54] These were the largest banks operating in Great Britain and Northern Ireland at the time that the CMA conducted its Retail Banking Market Investigation and those for which the CMA determined that open banking was an appropriate remedy for competition concerns. Although the CMA had no legal power to impose open banking on other providers (or other products), it saw clear benefits in broader adherence to the UK Standards, particularly for providers who are subject to the *PSR*.[55] Accordingly, as a result of a range of measures described in Chapter 6, adherence to the UK Standards is the central component of the UK system.

As noted in Chapter 2, as of March 2022, 90 account providers in the UK were participating. Consequently, although the breadth of the regulatory obligation is clearer under the Australian system, the resulting coverage of banks under both systems is similar.[56] However, despite this, the sources from which a customer can share their

45. *CCA* (n. 1) s. 56AJ.
46. *Open Banking Designation* (n. 3) s. 5(2).
47. *See Banking Act 1959* (Cth) s. 9(3) ('*Australian Banking Act*').
48. *See* Australian Prudential Regulation Authority, 'Register of Authorised Deposit-Taking Institutions', 30 November 2020) https://www.apra.gov.au/register-of-authorised-deposit-taking-institutions.
49. *CDR Rules* (n. 5) sch. 3.
50. *Ibid*. sch. 3 div 6.2. These provisions exclude ADIs which are foreign companies operating as a branch in Australia.
51. *PSR* (n. 9) reg. 70(2).
52. However, the *PSR* does not apply to credit unions, municipal banks and The National Savings Bank: *ibid*. reg. 3.
53. *Ibid*. reg. 2 (definition of 'payment service provider'). *See also* Financial Conduct Authority, 'Payment Services and Electronic Money – Our Approach' (n. 10) 14.
54. *CMA Order* (n. 7) Art. 3.1.1.
55. *See* Explanatory Note, Retail Banking Market Investigation Order (n. 13) [38].
56. Noting that compliance with the UK Standards for banks other than the CMA9 does not result in a requirement to comply with other aspects of the *CMA Order*.

data are on a broader scale under the Australian system because data recipients are also required to respond to customers' data sharing requests.

### *(b) Reciprocity: Data Recipients Required to Share Customer Data*

As noted in Chapter 2, each of Australian and UK open banking imposes a requirement that the recipients of customer data are authorised.[57] A further requirement imposed on recipients by some open banking systems is that they must respond to their own customers' requests to share data with other authorised recipients. This is known as 'reciprocity', and it is incorporated into the open banking systems of Mexico, India and Brazil.[58] It is also part of open banking (and the CDR) in Australia.

Australian open banking incorporates reciprocity by extending the scope of those who must respond to a request to share data beyond banks. The *CCA* contemplates that the *CDR Rules* may contain requirements for a 'CDR participant' to disclose CDR data,[59] which includes both a data holder and an accredited data recipient.[60] This reciprocity under the Australian system could arise in three ways. First, if a bank became accredited as a data recipient before their obligation to share data had commenced (due to the staged application of data sharing obligations under the Australian system), then the obligation to respond to data sharing requests was brought forward to match the ability for them to receive customer data.[61] Second, accredited data recipients who hold designated CDR data which were not obtained through the CDR can be required to share that data.[62] This would, for example, impose the obligation to share data on a non-bank lender that is an accredited data recipient for data about transactions which they have conducted with their customer. Third, the *CDR Rules* can require accredited data recipients to transfer data which they received through the CDR at their customer's request.[63]

There is no equivalent reciprocity in the UK system. The *CMA Order* requires only the CMA9 banks to share data. There is a limited form of reciprocity in the *PSR* in that a bank could also provide an account information service (AIS) and receive customer data from other banks. However, this is not a reciprocal obligation to share data imposed on data recipients. Instead, the obligation to share data remains on banks alone, but does not exclude banks from also receiving data. It does not provide customers with any further sources of their data to share.

The reciprocity included in Australian open banking is aimed at improving its effectiveness by increasing the scope of the data sets to which the customers have

57. *See* Chapter 9 for further explanation.
58. Ariadne Plaitakis and Stefan Staschen, 'Open Banking: How to Design for Financial Inclusion' (Working Paper, CGAP, 2020).
59. *CCA* (n. 1) s. 56BC(1).
60. *Ibid.* s. 56AL(1).
61. *CDR Rules* (n. 5) sch. 3 r. 6.6.
62. *CCA* (n. 1) s. 56AJ(3).
63. Explanatory Memorandum, Treasury Laws Amendment (Consumer Data Right) Bill 2018 (Cth) ('CDR Bill EM') [1.130]

access,[64] increasing the fairness of the system for those required to share data,[65] and encouraging the full participation of eligible entities:

> A CDR system in which eligible entities participate fully – both as data holders and data recipients – will be more vibrant and dynamic than one in which accredited data recipients are solely receivers of data, and data holders are largely only transmitters of data.[66]

On the other hand, reciprocity has been argued to discourage data recipients from participating either because of the increased costs to participate or because of the cost of having to share valuable customer data. Further, if imposed too broadly it may interfere with achieving the overall competition goals of the framework if, for example, it impedes the flow of customer data from banks to new competitors.

The lack of reciprocity in the design of UK's open banking limits customer autonomy because it enables customers to share their account data only if they are held by banks and not if they are held by non-bank providers of equivalent services. This might be defended on the basis that the UK system's narrow account coverage (which excludes loans) means that there should not be non-bank providers of covered accounts. However, this is using one limitation on customer autonomy to justify another. The consequences is asymmetry in UK open banking in that some entities are required to share data but not entitled to receive data, whilst others can receive data but are not obliged to share data. The impact of this asymmetry is evaluated against banking payment systems next.

### 5.2.2 Evaluation Against Banking Payment Systems

#### *(a) Lack of Asymmetry in Banking Payment Systems*

Banking payment systems are not designed to enable a bank to either make payments but not receive them or receive payments but not make them. The former bank would run out of liquidity and cause a risk to the system, the latter bank (also known as a 'liquidity sink') would drain the liquidity from others and also cause a risk to the system. Further, the customers of the latter bank would be disadvantaged in not being able to make payments from their accounts. Accordingly, there is no inherent asymmetry built into the funds transfer obligations between banks in banking payment systems. This would indicate that, when evaluated against a customer's rights to transfer their funds, the lack of reciprocity in the UK system is a limitation on customer autonomy. However, it is necessary to address two contrary arguments, relating to the comparability of transfer and use of customer data and funds and the necessity for asymmetry in open banking.

64. *Ibid.* [1.123]. Due to its cross-sector coverage it goes further, by imposing reciprocity on all accredited entities, regardless of the industry sector in which they operate. However, this is limited in application until the data to which the reciprocal sharing obligation applies is subject to designation under the *CCA* and appropriate data standards to enable its transfer: *ibid.* [1.131].
65. *Ibid.* [1.123].
66. *Ibid.* [1.124].

### (i) *Comparability of Use of Customer Data and Funds*

Chapter 2 showed that there are some differences in the nature of funds and data. Because data are non-rivalrous, a bank that shares but does not receive data does not 'run out' of data, and a recipient that receives but does not share data will not 'drain' the data from banks, as banks will still have the data which they have shared. This would appear to contradict the evaluation of the lack of reciprocity under open banking by reference to rights to make funds transfers.

However, such an evaluation is valid when the *use* of data is considered. Chapter 2 also showed that the value of data is derived from their use. A recipient of customer data that is not required to share customer data has a comparative advantage in use of data over another entity that needs to share, but cannot receive, customer data. Although it does not 'drain' data from the bank which shared them, it does enjoy unparalleled use and value of the combination of the data shared and data held. Further, as sharing contributes to customers realising the value in their data, the asymmetry created by restricting their ability to share data held by some data holders deprives them of that value. On this basis, by restricting the amount of data that a customer may use and the scale of the system, the lack of reciprocity in the UK system remains a limit on the customer autonomy which it provides. However, it could still be justified by the purpose of asymmetry in open banking.

### (ii) *Purpose of Asymmetry in Open Banking*

This asymmetry built into the design of open banking is intended to encourage competition and innovation by requiring banks to share data with new competitors such as fintechs. It is a direct response to the gatekeeper role which banks have established for themselves with respect to their customers' data described in Chapter 1. To this extent, it is necessary for the effectiveness of open banking systems.

However, a deeper analysis of the focus of open banking is needed. If the focus is the provision of banking services by banks, and only banks, then the regulatory asymmetry's purpose of challenging the market power of incumbent banks is well served by the asymmetry of requiring only those banks to share data. However, if the focus is the use of customer banking data for the benefit of the customer, then the comparison with the lack of asymmetry with respect to funds in banking payment systems is more meaningful, and the restriction of the data sharing rights to only one source of that data limits the effectiveness of open banking. To provide a simple example, if a customer has accounts with both banks and non-bank lenders, preventing the customer from sharing the data held by the non-bank lenders does not improve competitiveness, innovation, inclusion and consumer protection as much as permitting the customer to share all of their data. Indeed, such regulatory asymmetry serves to protect the non-bank lenders from competition and creates the opportunity for new data bottlenecks to arise.

The unintended consequences of this asymmetry are most acute where the recipient already has an established and networked relationship with customers, together with significant other data sets relating to those customers. This is the case where the data recipient is a 'big tech' company,[67] such as a large technology or social media firm. In these circumstances, it could have a long-term impact on competition:

> Although open banking regimes effectively allow third parties access to customer data from traditional incumbents such as banks, solving one type of data asymmetry, they inadvertently may create a different type of data asymmetry. A lack of reciprocity in the open banking scheme may greatly increase the power of BigTech platforms (e.g., Amazon, Facebook, Google), that can tap into this data by becoming accredited [data recipients] in order to enter and strengthen their financial services offerings.[68]

The result could be a concentration of data-driven services in the hands of a few technology firms and the dis-intermediation of banking more generally. According to the BIS, by taking advantage of open banking systems 'big techs have the potential to loom large very quickly as systemically relevant financial institutions'.[69] Accordingly, the need to relieve the asymmetry created by banks' holding of customer data does not justify the lack of the same reciprocity which exists in banking payment systems with respect to a customer's right to transfer their funds. Indeed, it shows that the departure from that reciprocity in the design of an open banking system could conflict with the objectives of the framework, as it would if reciprocity did not apply in a banking payment system.

### *(b) Rights Against Banks as Agent in Paying Customer Funds*

A further area of banking payments law against which the customer's right to share data should be evaluated is the duties of a bank in the payment of their customer's funds. As these differ from the duties of ordinary debtors, it is important to determine whether they would justify limiting data sharing obligations to banks. In this regard, the bank's duties as agent of the customer are particularly relevant.

Although a bank acts as principal (and not as agent) with respect to its obligation to repay the balance of a customer's account,[70] it acts as the customer's agent in making payments on their behalf.[71] This dual nature of the bank's role as principal and agent underpins the banker-customer relationship,[72] and it establishes key duties and responsibilities of the bank when acting as agent, including the obligation to use due

67. Adopting the term used by the BIS: Bank for International Settlements, 'Big Tech in Finance: Opportunities and Risks' (Annual Report part III, June 2019) www.bis.org/publ/arpdf/ar2019e.htm.
68. Plaitakis and Staschen (n. 35) 16.
69. Bank for International Settlements, 'Big Tech in Finance: Opportunities and Risks' (Annual Report part III, June 2019) 55 www.bis.org/publ/arpdf/ar2019e.htm.
70. *Foley v. Hill* (1848) 2 HL Cas 28. ('*Foley v. Hill*').
71. *See Royal Products Ltd v. Midland Bank Ltd* [1981] 2 Lloyd's Rep. 194 ('*Royal Products v. Midland Bank*'). *See also* Michael Brindle and Raymond Cox, *Law of Bank Payments* (Sweet & Maxwell, Thomson Reuters, 5th ed., 2018) [3-082].
72. *See* Brindle and Cox (n. 71) [3-081].

care and skill.[73] This duty, for example, requires that a bank does not carry out its customer's payment instruction where the bank is 'put on inquiry' in having reasonable grounds for believing that the instructions are the subject of fraud or dishonesty.[74]

Neither Australian or UK open banking's legislative instruments make any reference to the bank acting as agent for, or otherwise on behalf of, its customer when it responds to the customer's request to share data. This raises the issue of whether, as a result of the introduction of open banking, it should be implied into the contract between bank and customer that the bank shares customer data as the customer's agent, and therefore owes a similar duty to its customer. Curiously, UK open banking appears to accommodate this duty. The *PSR* gives the bank the right to deny an AISP access to customer data in circumstances where the bank has reasonably justified and duly evidenced reasons relating to unauthorised or fraudulent access to the payment account by the AISP, including the unauthorised or fraudulent initiation of a payment transaction.[75] These circumstances are very similar to those in which a bank's duty as the customer's agent requires it not to follow a payment instruction. Further, because of the general nature of the obligation to share data under the *PSR*, namely to 'treat a data request from the account information service provider in the same way as a data request received directly from the payer',[76] a bank under the UK system may also refuse information requests 'for legitimate reasons which would have led them to refuse those orders or requests from the customer themselves'.[77] These rights of a bank under UK open banking would accommodate the exercise of a duty to use due care and skill by an agent to deny a request to share data. Australian open banking is not similarly aligned in that a bank is not given the right to deny a request to share data based on suspected fraud or dishonesty. Instead, the bank can deny a request if the bank considers it necessary to prevent physical harm or abuse, or if the bank has reasonable grounds to believe that disclosure would adversely impact the security, integrity, or stability of the register of accredited persons or the bank's own information and communication technology systems.[78]

It might be argued the lack of alignment of the Australian system with the bank's duties in the payment of funds represents a limitation on its effectiveness with respect to consumer protection in comparison with the UK system. However, there is no certainty that such a duty arises under UK open banking either. Consistency of the bank's duty to refuse payment instructions with its rights to refuse data requests under UK open banking is an insufficient basis to imply that a bank is acting as the customer's agent in sharing customer data. If the imposition of such a duty on the bank were intended, then it could have been included in the legislation with the right to refuse

73. *See Royal Products v. Midland Bank* (n. 71). *See also Barclays Bank plc v. Quincecare Ltd and another* [1992] 4 All ER 363 ('*Quincecare*'). This duty is based in contract and not in tort: *see National Australia Bank Ltd v. Nemur Varity Pty Ltd* [2002] VSCA 18, [45] ('*National Australia Bank v. Nemur Varity*').
74. *Quincecare* (n. 73) 376.
75. *PSR* (n. 9) reg. 71(7).
76. *Ibid.* reg. 70(2)(b).
77. Financial Conduct Authority, 'Payment Services and Electronic Money – Our Approach' (n. 10) [17.143].
78. *CDR Rules* (n. 5) r. 4.7.

access. Further, unlike an instruction to pay customer funds, an instruction to share customer data cannot be characterised as 'an ordinary banking operation' which attracts the duty to use reasonable care and skill.[79] Indeed, as analysed in section 3.1 above, the disclosure of customer data by a bank is contrary to the 'ordinary' duty of a bank to maintain the confidentiality of its customer's affairs.

Nevertheless, this begs the question as to whether the same duty *should* apply to the bank in sharing the customer's data as when the bank pays the customer's funds, such that its absence from *each* system represents a flaw in its design when evaluated against banking payment systems. Both instances are transfers of valuable information and the customer can be harmed by a lack of due care and skill in sharing data from their account. However, the duty of a bank to use due care and skill in paying a customer's funds only arises because it performs this task as the customer's agent. It is not part of a more general duty of care such as that which is owed by 'professional persons'.[80] To extend this duty to the sharing of data would require that the customer data belongs to the customer, like their funds. For two reasons, this is not the case. First, as noted in Chapter 3, Australian and UK courts have been reluctant to ascribe property rights to information in the absence of statutory schemes which expressly do so, like intellectual property regimes. None of the legislative instruments of either open banking system attempt to establish property rights in, or 'ownership' of, customer data. Second, also as explained in Chapter 3, data is non-rivalrous, meaning that both the bank and the customer can use and share customer data at the same time. The analysis of the bank's duty of confidentiality with respect to customer data above showed that the bank is able to use customer information as it thinks fit. This ability of the bank to use customer information as its own is inconsistent with the bank holding that information in the capacity as the customer's agent.[81] Accordingly, the bank is not sharing data which is 'owned' by the customer, it is sharing data which it holds and controls itself.

Consequently, under both systems the bank should not be seen as agent of the customer in sharing customer data in the same way as it does in transferring the customer's funds. Further, the absence of this agency relationship should not of itself be regarded as a flaw in open banking's design when evaluated against the rights of a customer to transfer their funds, because it arises from the inherent difference in the nature of customer funds and customer data. This is an important conclusion because if the bank were acting as agent due to its banker-customer relationship, then its duties under open banking would differ from those of other holders of data under the same system, creating asymmetry between them.

79. *See Royal Products v. Midland Bank* (n. 71) 198.
80. '[I]n this area of discourse a banker is not a professional person': *National Australia Bank v. Nemur Varity* (n. 73) [47].
81. *See Regal (Hastings) Ltd v. Gulliver* [1967] 2 AC 134 ('*Regal (Hastings) Ltd v. Gulliver*'). 'Thus irrespective of its source, information derived by an agent in the course of the agency cannot be used for the benefit of the agent but for the sole benefit of the principal': Gino Dal Pont, *Law of Agency* (Butterworths, 4th ed., 2020) [12.5].

## 5.3 HOW CAN LEGAL FOUNDATIONS SUPPORT SUPPLYING DATA?

### 5.3.1 Summary of Comparison and Evaluation

This chapter has examined the implications of the legal foundations of Australian and UK open banking for supplying customer data for sharing, through a comparison of their legal features relating to what data customers should have rights to share and who should be required to share customer data, and an evaluation against equivalent legal features of banking payment systems relating to customer funds.

The analysis has shown that the scope of the data customers have rights to share under UK open banking is more constrained than under Australian open banking, due to the limitations on the account coverage in the UK system. This limitation on the supply of data able to be shared is exacerbated by limitations on the sources of data due to the limitation of the banks covered by the UK system, and the lack of reciprocity to include recipients who themselves hold customer data. However, the analysis has also shown that the functionality under Australian open banking is more constrained then under UK open banking due to the inability to share instructional information to enable payment initiation.

The consequence is that whilst the legal foundations of both Australian and UK open banking support customer autonomy, they do so in different ways and the support is weaker in the UK system for the sharing of data due to reduced scope and scale. This has the effect of also reducing data portability. This is illustrated in Figure 5.1.

*Figure 5.1 Illustration of Evaluation and Comparison Relating to Supplying Data*

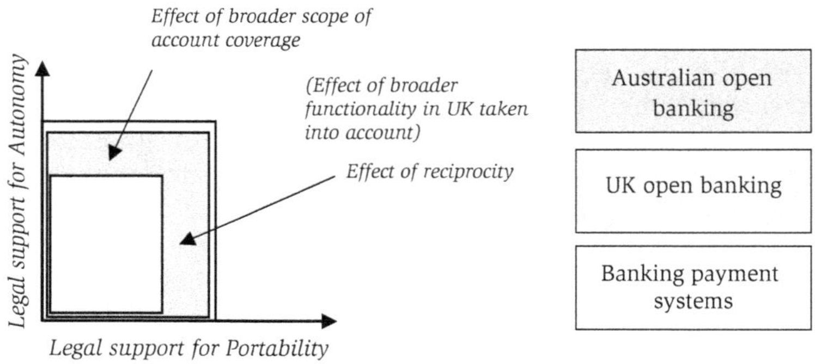


The analysis has shown how the different legal foundations result in different support being provided for customer autonomy and, as a result, data portability. It also demonstrates the need to manage availability risk. This risk is explained next, followed by an illustration of the comparable liquidity risk in banking payment systems, and a discussion of how liquidity risk management methods could be applied in the legal design of open banking systems.

### 5.3.2 Availability Risk in Open Banking Systems

Availability risk arises in open banking if data that customers need to share to obtain the goods or services they want are not available through open banking. A critical element in understanding this risk is that open banking is not the only method which customers can use to share their data. Whilst open banking is designed to be more effective than these other methods, customers retain the choice to share their data using other technological and legal frameworks. Open banking *complements* these other methods, it does not *replace* them. Accordingly, in assessing the impact of availability risk, it cannot be assumed that customers will use open banking. Indeed, if customers cannot use the open banking systems to share data needed for a good or service they desire, then it is likely that customers will choose another way to share these data, even if that other way is not as safe or reliable as open banking. The experience with customer behaviour in sharing data more generally demonstrates that consumers may choose a more convenient method to share their data over one which is more trustworthy.

Further, if more data than those available through open banking are needed for a good or service desired by a customer, for example for a full view of a customer's finances, then there is likely to be a preference by customers for all of the data to be shared using a single method, rather than partly through open banking and partly through other methods. This would result in screen scraping being preferred even for the data which could be shared through open banking. The consequence of this would be the impairment of the framework's achievement of its consumer protection objectives.

Accordingly, one result of availability risk is that customers are likely to use screen scraping to share data. A prohibition on screen scraping without the development of a comprehensive open banking system seeks to address the symptoms rather than the cause of this risk. If customers cannot use either open banking or screen scraping to share the data needed for the goods or services they want, then the customers will either not receive those goods or services, or the goods or services they receive will be adversely affected due to the deficiencies in data needed. Neither of these results satisfies the objectives of open banking. In fact, where screen scraping is prohibited for sharing data which are not available through open banking, arguably the result is anti-competitive as it reinforces the bank's role as the sole gateway for the sharing of the data which is not able to be otherwise shared. Accordingly, whilst a prohibition on screen scraping may appear to address the consumer protection objective of the framework, it can amplify the effect of availability risk which impacts the ability to achieve the competition and innovation objectives of the framework.[82]

To further explain this aspect of availability risk, the next section sets out an illustration of the comparable risk in banking payment systems, *liquidity risk*.

82. *See* Select Committee on Financial Technology and Regulatory Technology (Australia), Senate, Interim Report (Report, September 2020) 220.

### 5.3.3 Illustration of Liquidity Risk in Banking Payment Systems: Icelandic Banks

Liquidity risk in banking payment systems is:

> the risk that a party within the system will have insufficient funds to meet financial obligations within the system as and when expected, although it may be able to do so at some time in the future.[83]

Liquidity risk is comparable with availability risk in open banking systems. However, this alignment between availability risk in open banking systems and liquidity risk in banking payment systems is subtle. If 'liquidity' in open banking is limited to those data which are *able to be shared* under open banking, then the liquidity risks are really communication risks as they relate only to the risk of the transfer not being able to be made. However, if 'liquidity' is determined by reference to those data which the customer *needs to share* to obtain the good or service that they desire, then availability risk in open banking systems and liquidity risk in banking payment systems are closely aligned. From this perspective, the limits on the scope of the data which may be shared under open banking represents a liquidity problem for the system, as the liquidity of data needed by customers is absent, even though it is in existence.

Consequences of liquidity risk in banking payment systems are were evident in the collapse of Iceland's three main banks, Glitner, Kaupthing, and Landsbanki ('Icelandic banks'), which accounted for 95% of Iceland's banking system, in October 2008.[84] A key factor in their collapse was that the Icelandic banks could not find the funds in the foreign currencies which they needed to repay their extensive offshore funding.[85] This was in large part due to the impact on the liquidity of markets of the global financial crisis and the collapse of Lehman Brothers.[86] However, the liquidity position for the Icelandic banks was exacerbated by orders made by the UK's Financial Supervisory Authority under the *Anti-terrorism, Crime and Security Act 2001 (UK)* which froze the assets of the Landsbanki branch in the UK,[87] and prevented the processing of transfers for Icelandic owned banks in the UK.[88] The consequence was a severe disruption of access to the international payment system for payments in and out of Iceland. The contraction of liquidity in international markets, the withdrawal of

83. Committee on Payment and Settlement Systems, 'Core Principles for Systemically Important Payment Systems' (Core Principles, Bank for International Settlements, January 2001) 5.
84. *See* Ingimundur Fridriksson, 'The Banking Crisis in Iceland in 2008' (2009) *The Central Bank of Iceland*. *See also* Mark J Flannery, 'Iceland's failed Banks: A Post-Mortem' (Report, Special Investigation Commission, Annex 3, November 2009) 91.
85. *See* Patrizia Baudino, Jon Thor Sturluson and Jean-Philippe Svoronos, 'The Banking Crisis in Iceland' (FSI Crisis Management Series Paper No. 1, Bank for International Settlements, March 2020).
86. *See* Chapters 6 and 11 for further explanation.
87. *Landsbanki Freezing Order 2008* (UK) Art. 4 ('*Landsbanki Freezing Order*'). The *Landsbanki Freezing Order* was given under the *Anti-terrorism, Crime and Security Act 2001* (UK) ('*Anti-terrorism, Crime and Security Act*').
88. *See Du Preez Ltd (formerly Habana Ltd) v. Kaupthing Singer and Friedlander (Isle of Man) Ltd* (2010) 12 IETLR 943 ('*Du Preez Ltd (formerly Habana Ltd) v. Kaupthing Singer and Friedlander (Isle of Man) Ltd*').

foreign currency deposits and the restriction of access to the international payment system, caused a foreign currency liquidity crisis for the Icelandic banks with catastrophic consequences:

> At home and abroad, Icelanders experienced their country's 'terrorist entity' label as the final tremor that brought down the house. The nation's international payment system collapsed. Funds sent to other countries were held up at some banks, or simply disappeared. Money could not be sent outside the island. Most banks simply refused either to send or to receive Icelandic payments. Icelanders throughout the world often found to their horror that their credit cards no longer worked and that they could not transfer funds from home. Foreign trade became next to impossible, since payments could not be cleared.[89]

One cause of the collapse was banks seeking an alternative source of liquidity by borrowing offshore because there was a lack of sufficient available funds onshore. This source proved not to be reliable when needed. From the perspective of the payment system as a communication system, the information required for the messages to be sent which would discharge the obligations of the Icelandic banks was not available to them.

Similarly, if the customer data needed for the data-driven supply of goods or services desired by customers are not available through an open banking system, then it is to be expected that they will be shared through another method, such as screen scraping. Just as offshore foreign currency funding proved not to be as reliable as domestic funding, screen scraping is not as reliable as data sharing through the open banking systems, as they are more vulnerable to information security failures and customer data loss. The consequence of this reliance on screen scraping could be that the data needed ceases to be effectively shared resulting in the cessation of the supply of the desired goods and services, even though the data needed is still available to the customer. This would be exacerbated if a prohibition on screen scraping were imposed where there was no ability to use open banking to share the same data.

Although there were additional factors which led to the Icelandic bank's collapse, and hopefully availability risks in open banking systems will not arise at the same catastrophic scale, it serves as an illustration of how risks can eventuate if there are constraints placed on the availability of data which customers need an open banking system to enable them to share. Just as the Icelandic Banks sought different sources of funding beyond the scope of their regulators' control, so could customers seek to share their data beyond the scope of open banking. On this basis, the legal features of banking payment systems which are designed to manage liquidity risk deserve consideration for incorporation into the legal foundations of open banking systems.

### 5.3.4 Incorporating Liquidity Risk Management Features in Open Banking

Although liquidity risk in banking payment systems is comparable to availability risk in open banking systems, some of the key liquidity risk management methods are not able

89. Ásgeir Jónsson and Guillaume Cannat, *Why Iceland?* (McGraw-Hill New York, 2009) 187.

to be readily adapted for use in open banking. Liquidity risk can be managed by providing for replacement assets to replenish missing liquidity when needed, through mechanisms such as cross-currency swap lines or repo facilities. However, as explained in Chapter 3, data are not fungible and there are no replacement assets for data not able to be shared. Also, as open banking is a peer-to-peer system, it has no equivalent to 'payment queues' or 'position limits' which can be managed in order to mitigate liquidity risks in banking payment systems.

A further method of managing liquidity risk in banking payment systems is to facilitate alternative transfer mechanisms or to 'reroute' payments which cannot otherwise be made. The equivalent to this in open banking is to permit screen scraping for the sharing of data which are unavailable through the system which, as noted in the next chapter, is the approach taken in Australia and other jurisdictions.[90] However, a preferrable method of managing availability risk in open banking systems is to enable the sharing of all of the data (factual and instructional) required by the customer through open banking. To do this, the legal design of open banking systems should enable customers to share the scope of data which a customer can already access and enable customers to authorise others to perform the functions which the customer can perform from their online access to their accounts. Without this, the design of the system might not only constrain the sharing of data by customers, limiting the performance of its autonomy and portability functions, but it might also cause customers to use alternative mechanisms to share their data, limiting the achievement of its consumer protection objectives too.

90. *PSD2* expressly contemplates this approach in the ability to use a modified customer interface in the absence of a suitable dedicated interface. *See* section 6.1.1.

CHAPTER 6

# Sharing Customer Data

This chapter examines the legal foundations for sharing customer data under open banking systems. It compares the legal rights supporting the sharing of those data under the Australian and UK open banking systems and evaluates them against the equivalent legal rights under banking payment systems. The analysis addresses two questions:

- How should customer data be shared?
- How should rights to share data be established?

The answers to these questions are fundamental to an open banking system's performance of its *autonomy* and *portability* functions.

## 6.1 HOW SHOULD CUSTOMER DATA BE SHARED?

How customer data are shared under open banking is fundamental to the customers' rights to share their data. Both Australian and UK open banking utilise APIs which serve as a technological foundation for the data portability essential to open banking. However, there is also a legal foundation of this data portability which warrants examination.

The legal rights which form the foundation of two key features of the method of sharing customer data, namely that requests are made through data recipients and the use of APIs, are comparatively analysed below, followed by an evaluation against the rights against banks in receiving customer funds, and the authentication of customer instructions, in banking payment systems.

### 6.1.1 Comparison of How Data Must Be Shared in the Open Banking Systems

#### *(a) Requests for Sharing Data Made Only Through Data Recipients*

In Australian open banking, the *CCA* provides for the request for the transfer of data to be given by, or on behalf of, a person who is a 'CDR consumer' in respect of CDR data. For a person to be a CDR consumer in respect of CDR data it requires that:

- the CDR data relates to the person because of the supply of a good or service to the person or their associates;
- the CDR data is held by, or on behalf of, another person who is a data holder or an accredited data recipient of the CDR data; and
- the person is identifiable, or reasonably identifiable from the CDR data or other information held by that person.[1]

A CDR consumer is different from a 'consumer' as used in the other parts of the *CCA* and it includes businesses,[2] because the rights to share data are exercisable by businesses as well as consumers.[3] The actual right for CDR consumers to request that their CDR data be shared is contained in the *CDR Rules*.[4] They provide that a CDR consumer may request the disclosure of their CDR data,[5] or request that an 'accredited person' access their CDR data in order to provide goods and services to the CDR consumer.[6] However, whilst there are requirements set out in the *CDR Rules* for the CDR consumer to request disclosure of CDR data to themselves,[7] at this stage, the Australian Standards do not include the standards necessary for CDR consumers to make direct requests for their customer data. Accordingly, despite its being a stated object of Part IVD of the *CCA* to enable consumers' data to be disclosed to themselves 'for use as they see fit' this has not been enabled under the Australian system.[8]

In UK open banking, the *PSR* provides the right to access the customer's data to the 'AISP' which is being used by the 'payment service user'. The definition of payment service user is straightforward (a person when making use of a payment service as payer, payee or both),[9] and an AISP is an entity which is authorised to provide 'an online service to provide consolidated information on one or more payment accounts held by the payment service user'.[10] Like Australian open banking, the *PSR* does not

1. *Competition and Consumer Act 2010* (Cth) s. 56AI ('*CCA*').
2. *Ibid.* s. 56AI(4).
3. There is flexibility in the legislative structure to change the definition of CDR consumer for different sectors: Explanatory Memorandum, Treasury Laws Amendment (Consumer Data Right) Bill 2018 (Cth) ('CDR Bill EM') [1.112].
4. *CCA* (n. 1) s. 56BE.
5. *Competition and Consumer (Consumer Data Right) Rules 2020* ('*CDR Rules*') r. 3.3.
6. *Ibid.* r. 4.3. An 'accredited person' is a person who is accredited to receive data: *CCA* (n. 1) s. 4 (definition of 'accredited person').
7. *Ibid.* pt 3.
8. *CCA* (n. 1) s. 56AA(a)(i).
9. *Payment Services Regulation 2017* (UK) ('*PSR*') r. 2 (definition of 'payment service user').
10. *Ibid.* r. 2 (definition of 'account information service').

include any right of the payment service user to access their data themselves. However, the definition of 'AIS' requires that the consolidated information produced using the shared customer data is provided to the payment service user.[11]

Neither Australian nor UK open banking currently provides the customer with a right to request that the customer data held by the bank be shared directly with themselves in the same form in which it can be shared with recipients. There is a consumer protection reason for this because most customers would not have the technical capability to collect, classify and analyse the standardised data, or to access the data through the API through which it is provided. By requiring that the requests are made and received by an authorised data recipient, each system ensures that the appropriate security requirements will be met by those requesting data and mitigates against others taking advantage of a customer's lack of technical understanding.[12] However, it raises three concerns:

- *Impairs customer autonomy.* The autonomy which the customer gains with respect to their data from open banking is diminished if they cannot access or use those data themselves. It would be a common expectation that a customer's right to share their data with others would include a right to share data 'with oneself' in a digital, rather than an analogue, form.
- *Restricts innovation.* Some customers would have the technical expertise to be able to use their data and others could obtain software that could receive and interpret that data for them. Enabling customers to engage in such 'self-service' capabilities would further encourage competition and innovation in open banking services.
- *Reduces transparency.* The confidence of customers in using open banking will be important for the success of open banking systems, and that confidence will be supported by customers both knowing what data they are sharing and being able to correct that data when necessary. Whilst each system has protections for the integrity of customer data, these require an element of transparency to be effective.[13]

On this basis, despite a consumer protection justification, the inability of customers to make requests to receive their own data in the same form as it can be shared with others impairs the portability of data under both systems and the autonomy which they provide to customers. This is evaluated further by reference to banking payment systems in section below.

### *(b) Customer Data Shared Using APIs*

Requests by an accredited person for access to a CDR consumer's data under Australian open banking are made using the data holder's 'accredited person request service'. This is:

11. *Ibid.*
12. *See* Australian Treasury, 'Statutory Review of the Consumer Data Right' (Report, 2022) 25.
13. *See* Chapter 8 below.

an online service that:

(i) can be used by accredited persons to make consumer data requests, on behalf of eligible CDR consumers, to the data holder; and
(ii) enables requested data to be disclosed in machine-readable form; and
(iii) conforms with the data standards.[14]

Although not specified in the legislative instruments, requests made by accredited persons are to be made through the use of APIs.[15] This is given effect by the Australian Standards which provide only for requests and disclosures to be made through APIs.[16] If an accredited person uses this service to make a valid request (meaning that the CDR consumer is eligible,[17] and has consented to the disclosure) then the data holder must disclose the data requested through their accredited person request service and in accordance with the Australian Standards.[18] A data holder is not permitted to charge for fulfilling the requests made by accredited persons.[19]

The *PSR* is not as clear as the *CDR Rules* in its requirements as to how a request to share data under open banking is made, although the result is similar. It requires that the 'ASPSP' (this includes banks) must 'communicate securely with the AISP' in accordance with the regulatory technical standards adopted under Article 98 of *PSD2*.[20] These standards are the *SCA-RTS* referred earlier, which covers strong customer authentication and common secure communication.[21] It permits banks to provide access using one of two methods:

(1) *Modified customer interface* – access is provided through the customer interfaces modified to meet the requirements of the *SCA-RTS*. This is similar to screen scraping except that the secure communications and identification requirements of the *SCA-RTS* mean that the data recipient must identify itself to the bank.

14. *CDR Rules* (n. 5) r. 1.13(b).
15. Explanatory Statement, Competition and Consumer (Consumer Data Right) Rules 2020 (Cth) [80] ('CDR Rules Explanatory Statement').
16. Data Standards Body, 'Consumer Data Standards v 1.22.0', https://consumerdatastandards.or g.au. Three of the five operational principles, and all of the eight technical principles which form the basis of the Australian Standards expressly concern APIs.
17. They are eligible if they are an individual of at least 18 years of age holding an open account with the bank that can be accessed online: *CDR Rules* (n. 5) r. 1.10B, sch. 3 r. 2.1.
18. *Ibid*. r. 4.6.
19. *CCA* (n. 1) ss 56AM, 56BD, 56B, *Consumer Data Right (Authorised Deposit Taking Institutions) Designation 2019* (Cth) ('Open Banking Designation') s. 5(1).
20. *Payment Services Regulation 2017* (UK) ('*PSR*') reg. 70(2)(a).
21. *Commission Delegated Regulation (EU) 2018/389 Supplementing Directive (EU) 2015/2366 of the European Parliament and of the Council with regard to Regulatory Technical Standards tor Strong Customer Authentication and Common and Secure Open Standards of Communication* OJ L69/23 ('SCA-RTS'). Strong Customer Authentication (SCA) 'means authentication based on the use of two or more elements that are independent ... with the elements falling into two or more of the following categories: (a) something known only by the payment service user ("knowledge"); (b) something held only by the payment service user ("possession"); and (c) something inherent to the payment service user ("inherence")': *PSR* (n. 20) reg. 2 (definition of 'strong customer authentication').

(2) *Dedicated interface* – access is provided through a 'dedicated interface', such as through APIs. If a bank chooses to take this approach, then it must develop a fallback mechanism so that access can continue if the dedicated interface does not perform to the required standard. The fallback mechanism would use the modified customer interface described above. However, a bank can be exempted from the requirement to provide a fallback mechanism by the FCA if specified service and testing requirements are met by the dedicated interface.

Under the *SCA-RTS*, banks must be free to decide which form of access is provided 'to ensure technology and business-model neutrality'.[22] However, it does require that they must ensure that they follow communication standards 'issued by international or European standardisation organisations'.[23] This includes the UK Standards, which require the use of APIs.[24] The *CMA Order* requires that the CMA9 banks provide access without charge to the transaction data sets under the Read/Write Data Standard.[25]

Australian and UK open banking are aligned in that their standards neither require, nor permit, the use of screen scraping to meet obligations to share customer data under the system and the APIs used by each do not require that the login credentials of the customer are shared with anyone other than the bank. However, none of the *CCA, CDR Rules, CMA Order* or the *PSR* prohibit use of screen scraping beyond the scope of the Australian or UK systems. The UK system goes further than the Australian system by requiring strong customer authentication (which prevents screen scraping) on the payment accounts covered by *PSR*.[26] The Australian system has no equivalent comprehensive prohibition on screen scraping for accounts covered by open banking.[27] Whilst this difference could be regarded as a current flaw in the design of Australian open banking, it is conceptually consistent with the UK approach of not prohibiting screen scraping beyond the operation of the system, for as long as payment initiation is not available under Australian open banking. It is also consistent with the approach taken in other jurisdictions.[28] It should also be noted that the prohibition of

22. *SCA-RTS* (n. 21) Ch. 1 para. 20.
23. *Ibid.* Art. 30(3).
24. Open Banking Implementation Entity, 'Open Banking API Specifications ' (Standard, v3.1.10) https://standards.openbanking.org.uk.
25. *Retail Banking Market Investigation Order 2017* (UK) ('*CMA Order*') Art. 14.1.
26. Some UK banks have introduced the 'strong customer authentication' for accounts not covered by *PSR* and, as a result, prohibited screen scraping for all accounts despite the limitations on *PSR's* scope: Financial Conduct Authority, 'Approach to Final Regulatory Technical Standards and EBA Guidelines under the Revised Payment Services Directive (PSD2)' (Policy Statement No. PS18/24, December 2018) 23.
27. It was recommended that the use of the open banking system should not be the only method available to share banking data whilst it was being established: Australian Treasury, 'Review into Open Banking: Giving Customers Choice, Convenience and Confidence' (Report, December 2017) 10.
28. Bank for International Settlements, 'Report on Open Banking and Application Programming Interfaces' (Report, November 2019) 7.

screen scraping once payment initiation commences in Australian open banking has been recommended by two government reports.[29]

### 6.1.2 Evaluation Against Method of Transferring Customer Funds

#### *(a) Contrast with Credit and Debit Transfers of Funds*

The instruction to a customer's bank to pay the customer's funds can come from either the customer (a credit transfer) or the payee (a debit transfer). The analysis above shows that the Australian and UK systems do not offer the same flexibility in that they do not permit customers to make direct requests to share data and instead they can only be made by data recipients on their behalf. When evaluated against the right of customers to directly request transfers of their funds, the lack of an equivalent right under the open banking systems is similar to a customer not being able to make credit transfers from their account. This would be a significant impairment in the efficiency provided to customers by a banking payment system and a restriction in the customer's fundamental rights to their funds. However, this comparison is not perfect because a 'credit transfer' under open banking would involve the customer communicating directly with the bank to instruct it to share data with the recipient. This is not the same as the customer instructing the bank to share the data with the customer. A closer analogy might be if a customer could not withdraw cash from their bank account. Indeed, the risks might be thought similar in that there are no controls over what the customer might do with their money once it is withdrawn. Nevertheless, a restriction on withdrawals from a bank account would be considered an unacceptable constraint on customer autonomy with respect to their funds.

The arguments for not permitting customers to require their data be shared with themselves outlined in section 6.1.1 would not be accepted as a basis for not permitting customers to direct a transfer of their funds or withdraw their cash. Further, there is no obvious difference in the nature of customer data and customer funds which justifies customers being able to directly request transfers of their funds but not their data. Accordingly, when evaluated against the customer's rights with respect to their funds, the inability of customers to request their own data under the Australian and UK systems limits the communication of data under open banking and the autonomy provided to customers under both systems.

#### *(b) Contrast with Bank's Agency Duties in Receiving Customer Funds*

The role and duties of the bank in receiving payments also warrants examination. A bank acts as the customer's agent in receiving payments on their behalf,[30] although the

29. *See* Australian Treasury, 'Inquiry into Future Directions for Consumer Data Right: Giving Consumers Choice, Convenience and Confidence' (Report, October 2020); Australian Treasury, 'Statutory Review of the Consumer Data Right' (n. 12).
30. *See The Brimnes* [1975] QB 929 ('*The Brimnes*'); *Mardorf Peach & Co v. Attica Sea Carriers Corp. of Liberia, The Laconia* [1976] 2 All ER 249 ('*The Laconia*'). *See also* Benjamin Geva, *Bank*

bank holds the received funds as principal rather than as agent.[31] The nature of the agency relationship is more complicated in the case of debit transfers because the payer's bank is not receiving instructions directly from its customer, the payer. Instead, the instruction to pay is communicated to the payer's bank by either the payee or the payee's bank, but it remains a mandate of the payer, as the payer's bank's customer.[32] Nevertheless, in receiving its customer's funds, the payee's bank acts as its customer's agent.[33] This agency results in the payee's bank owing duties to its customer which are similar in nature to those which a payer's bank owes to its customer, namely a duty of due care and skill. This includes a duty to exercise reasonable care and skill in maintaining its equipment so that it can receive payments for the customer,[34] and a responsibility for delay or loss occurring at the beneficiary's bank.[35]

Although the flow of instructions in the Australian and UK open banking systems for the sharing of data is similar to that which takes place in the banking payment system for fund transfers,[36] neither framework's legislative instruments create an express agency relationship between a customer and the recipient who requests the customer's data. The *CMA Order* makes a reference to a third party being able to access account information or initiate a payment 'on behalf of the customer' but goes no further.[37] Neither *PSR* nor the *SCA-RTS* makes any references to agency or the data recipient acting on behalf of the customer. Accordingly, the legislative instruments of UK open banking give no basis for implying an agency relationship between customer and data recipient, absent a separate agreement between the two.

In contrast, the Australian legislative instruments leave room for agency to be implied. The *CDR Rules* define a consumer data request made by an accredited person as being made 'on behalf of a CDR consumer',[38] and it is referred to in this way in the relevant operative provisions.[39] This leaves open the possibility of an agency relationship arising between the customer and recipient under the Australian system. An express agreement using the words of agency is not required to establish an agency

---

*Collections and Payment Transactions: A Comparative Study of Legal Aspects* (Oxford University Press, 2001) 296.

31. *See Royal Products Ltd v. Midland Bank Ltd* [1981] 2 Lloyd's Rep. 194 ('*Royal Products v. Midland Bank*'). *See also* Geva, *Bank Collections and Payment Transactions: A Comparative Study of Legal Aspects* (n. 30) 295; John Odgers, *Paget's Law of Banking* (LexisNexis, 15th ed., 2018) [22.69]. The bank is taken to immediately borrow the money back from the payee: Michael Brindle and Raymond Cox, *Law of Bank Payments* (Sweet & Maxwell, Thomson Reuters, 5th ed., 2018) [3-118].
32. *See Mercedez-Benz Finance Ltd v. Clydesdale Bank Plc* [1997] CLC 81 ('*Mercedez-Benz Finance Ltd v. Clydesdale Bank Plc*'); *Esso Petroleum v. Milton* [1997] 1 WLR 938 ('*Esso Petroleum v. Milton*'). Where it is the payee's bank that communicates the instruction, it gives that communication as agent for the payer: *See* Odgers (n. 31) [22.70].
33. Odgers (n. 31) [22.69].
34. *Ibid.*
35. *See* Geva, *Bank Collections and Payment Transactions: A Comparative Study of Legal Aspects* (n. 30) 295.
36. *See* Figures 2.1, 2.2.
37. *CMA Order* (n. 25) Art. 10.1.2. It is not clear whether the 'on behalf of' reference applies to both account access and payment initiation.
38. *CDR Rules* (n. 5) r. 1.7 (definition of 'consumer data request').
39. *Ibid.* r. 4.4(2).

relationship if the principal's knowledge and approval can be inferred.[40] Whilst agency does require consent, this could be to the circumstances on which the law imposes agency and not to the legal relationship itself.[41] However, in other parts of the *CDR Rules* where agency is clearly intended there are express references to acting on behalf of 'the principal'.[42] More substantively, other incidents of agency are not present. The Australian system does not require the data recipient to hold the benefit of its use of the customer data solely for the customer, nor does it seek to make the customer responsible, as principal, for the actions of the data recipient.[43] On the other hand, these two broader incidents of agency are also lacking in the relationship between a customer and a bank receiving a payment on their behalf. As noted above, the agency of the payee's bank is limited to receiving funds for the customer and then immediately borrowing them. The same limited agency could apply to the recipient under the Australian system, so that it acts as the customer's agent in making the request to the bank 'on behalf of the customer' for the sharing of the customer's data, but then receives and holds that data as principal. If this is the case, it would imply that the duties of a payee's bank when receiving a payment for its customer also apply to this activity, such as the duty to use due care and skill, and to ensure that the equipment used can receive the information to be shared. Arguably, this alignment with the customer's rights under banking payment systems could render the Australian system more effective in achieving the consumer protection objectives through the additional duties imposed on the data recipient. However, before reaching this conclusion, it is necessary to examine the process for authenticating the customer's instructions to determine its consistency with such an agency relationship.

### *(c) Authentication of the Customer's Instructions*

One clear indicator of agency between the data recipient and the customer would be if the customer is able to authorise the data recipient to use the customer's login credentials on the customer's behalf. This would be similar to the agent using an electronic door key, or affixing an electronic seal, on behalf of their principal.[44] However, as section 6.1.1(b) above showed, neither framework permits this approach, also known as screen scraping, to be taken. Instead, each framework uses APIs to establish a 'redirection' authentication process where, once the request of the customer to share data is conveyed by the data recipient to the bank, customers are digitally redirected to their bank to authenticate themselves, and to authorise the sharing of

40. *Bonette v. Woolworths Ltd* (1937) 37 SR (NSW) 142, 150 ('*Bonette v. Woolworths Ltd*').
41. *Branthwaite v. Worcester Works Finance Ltd* [1969] 1 A.C. 552, 587 ('*Branthwaite v. Worcester Works Finance Ltd*').
42. For example, in references to 'CDR outsourcing arrangement': *CDR Rules* (n. 5) r. 1.10.
43. *See* Peter Watts and Fred MB Reynolds, *Bowstead and Reynolds on Agency* (Sweet & Maxwell, 22nd ed., 2020) [6-077], [8-002]. Gino Dal Pont, *Law of Agency* (Butterworths, 4th ed., 2020) [12.5], [19.1].
44. *See* Geva, *Bank Collections and Payment Transactions: A Comparative Study of Legal Aspects* (n. 30) 395.

their data, directly with their bank.[45] Whilst this process is not inconsistent with an agency relationship being established between customer and data recipient, it would significantly limit its scope. Once the instructions to share data are given directly by the customer to their bank through the redirection process, agency of the data recipient is no longer relevant. Accordingly, if there were any agency of the data recipient under the Australian open banking system, it would subsist only for as long as the data recipient conveys the customer's request as part of the redirection process. This is narrower in scope than the agency of the payee's bank since the data recipient does not receive the customer data as the customer's agent. It means that any duties arising out of this agency would be very limited and would apply only to the act of redirecting the customer to their bank.

The analysis shows that neither Australian nor UK open banking imposes agency duties on recipients to the same extent as those imposed on the payee's bank in banking payment systems. However, this should not be evaluated as a flaw in their design. In open banking, the customer of the bank and the customer of the recipient are the same and the customer directly confirms their authority to their bank through the redirection process. This differs from most bank payments. Instead, this is similar to the position under a debit transfer if the payer confirms the validity of the mandate directly with their bank. In these circumstances, the protection offered by granting customers rights against the recipient as their agent is limited.

## 6.2 WHERE SHOULD RIGHTS TO SHARE DATA BE ESTABLISHED?

Standardisation in data formats and data processing procedures enhances the effectiveness of data sharing and distinguishes open banking from data access and portability provisions in privacy laws. The use of standards performs a fundamental role in the sharing of customer data in open banking systems and their performance of their data portability function. However, although technological standards can complement legal rights and obligations, they do not perform the same function. Accordingly, the role of standards in the rights to share data under open banking systems deserves analysis.

The rights relating to two key features of the role of standards, the use of a single set of mandatory standards and the interaction between those standards and legal obligations, are comparatively analysed below, followed by an evaluation against the clarity, certainty, and enforceability of rights which customers have to transfer funds from their account in banking payment systems.

45. *See* Data Standards Body (n. 22) ('Security Profile' / 'Authentication Flows'). *See also* Data Standards Body, 'Consumer Experience Guidelines' (Guidelines, v 1.4.0 17 July 2020). In the UK Standards, a 'decoupled approach' is also permitted: Open Banking Implementation Entity, 'Customer Experience Guidelines' (Standard, v3.1.10) https://standards.openbanking.org.uk. However, like redirection, this also involves the customer's authentication data being exchanged directly between the bank and customer: European Banking Authority, 'Opinion of the European Banking Authority on the Implementation of the RTS on SCA and CSC' (EBA Opinion No EBA-Op-2018-04, 13 June 2018) [48].

### 6.2.1 Comparison of the Role of Standards in the Open Banking Systems

#### *(a) Single Set of Mandatory Standards*

As noted in Chapter 2, each of Australian and UK open banking relies on the mandatory use of a single set of standards: the Australian Standards, and the UK Standards respectively.

The mandatory nature of the Australian Standards is set out in the *CDR Rules*. These require that requests by accredited persons for customer data,[46] requests for the customer to authorise the disclosure of customer data,[47] and the disclosure of customer data in response to a request,[48] must all be made in accordance with the Australian Standards. Further, the *CCA* provides that the Australian Standards are given legal effect through the contract which is taken to be in force between a data holder and each accredited person.[49] However, unlike the *CDR Rules*, the Australian Standards are not a legislative instrument.[50]

As noted in Chapter 2, the mandatory nature of the UK Standards is not as clear. *PSD2* requires the adherence to standards,[51] but does not prescribe any particular data standard for use even though it requires standards to be complied with. In implementing *PSD2* through *PSR*, the UK was prevented from mandating any particular data standard.[52] Accordingly, *PSR* imposes no obligations to use the UK Standards in the same way as the *CDR Rules* do for the Australian Standards. However, other account providers are able to participate voluntarily in the UK system by adopting the UK Standards as the basis for their adherence to *PSR*. The combination of requiring the largest banks to use the UK Standards, clarification of the regulatory 'expectations' to use the UK Standards,[53] establishing the OBIE to oversee and encourage their adoption and implementation and shaping them as an efficient means to meet the requirements of the *PSR*, has resulted in adherence to the UK Standards being the central element of the UK system.[54]

This mandatory nature of the standards used in the Australian and UK systems replaces the need for bilateral contracts between the bank and the data recipient for the sharing of data, which is difficult for smaller recipients.[55] It also avoids the interoperability concerns where banks can choose different standards with which to comply, such as in the EU. Whilst it can be argued that a choice of standards assists innovation

---

46. *CDR Rules* (n. 5) r. 4.4(3).
47. *Ibid.* r. 4.5.
48. *Ibid.* r. 4.6.
49. *CCA* (n. 1) s. 56FD.
50. *Ibid.* s. 56FA(4).
51. *SCA-RTS* (n. 42) Art. 30.
52. *PSD2* prevents HM Treasury or the FCA from mandating any particular data standard: also HM Treasury and Financial Conduct Authority, 'Expectations for the Third Party Access Provisions in the Payment Services Directive II' (Statement, July 2017) [1.7].
53. *See* HM Treasury and Financial Conduct Authority (n. 14).
54. *See ibid.* [1.8].
55. The *PSR* prohibits an ASPSP from requiring an AISP to enter into a contract before access is provided: *PSR* (n. 20) reg. 70(2)(c).

to experiment on their own, more effective interfaces, the result of this choice is that the data able to be transferred by a customer will depend on the bank where the payment account is held.[56] The lack of a specific and uniform mandatory standard in the EU has attracted significant criticism in relation to the constraints it imposes on the effectiveness on open banking in the EU, as well as legal certainty in the detail of data portability. In contrast, the rules-based approach of Australian and UK open banking avoids fragmentation in data transfer rights and obligations.

Using a common standard improves the effectiveness of the data sharing through open banking, as each participant is using the same technological 'language' for that communication. It improves the effectiveness of the transformation of that data into information, as the meaning of the data is more easily understood. It provides 'a specific baseline for implementation' to be consistent across the open banking systems and, in the case of the Australian system, across all sectors to which the CDR applies.[57] The interoperability which it enables facilitates the open banking systems to achieve their objectives more easily. Accordingly, the use by each system of a single set of mandatory standards enhances their performance of their data portability function and their effectiveness in achieving their objectives.

### *(b) Interaction of Standards with Legal Rights*

The use of standards is common in information and communication technologies. The common technical language that they represent can, through interoperability and reliability, support innovation. They also represent a method of dealing with the difficulty of law keeping up to date with rapidly changing technology. The delegation of operational rules to an agency of technical experts is an effective way of managing the interaction between rapidly changing technology and law. It permits the involvement of technical experts in setting, maintaining and updating the detail required in technical areas whilst the legislature concerns itself with higher-level rules and principles. Both the Australian and UK open banking systems use data standards to serve this purpose, in order to specify technological requirements for the sharing of data.

Whilst matters of technological implementation may need to be expressed in technical terms to achieve the desired precision, legal issues arise if substantive legal rights are accessible only by those with an appropriate technical background to find them and understand what they mean. In other words, if they go beyond the regulation of form, and regulate behaviour like legal rules. In this circumstance, they could not only *supplement* legal rules, but they could *supplant* them.[58] Transparency of substantive legal rights is critical for important systems and its absence could result in reduced comprehension and a divergence between their expression and the intended legal

56. European Banking Authority (n. 45) 18.
57. Data Standards Body, 'Consumer Data Standards v 1.22.0' (n. 22) ('Introduction' and 'Principles').
58. *See* Daniel Benoliel, 'Technological Standards, Inc.: Rethinking Cyberspace Regulatory Epistemology' (2004) 92 *Calif. L. Rev.* 1069, 1075.

outcome.[59] Moreover, it leads to incorporation of regulation into the technological process potentially without any opportunity to challenge the regulation for those affected.[60]

The design of the Australian system addresses these concerns by limiting the Australian Standards to be operative rather than substantive. They 'only describe how the CDR must be implemented in accordance with the rules which will set out the substantive rights and obligations of participants'.[61] In other words, they are supposed to be more like 'technical standards' rather than legal rules. This is in contrast to the role performed by UK Standards, which cover not only open APIs, data formats and security but also governance arrangements and customer redress mechanisms.[62] The difference can be seen from the extent of coverage of the right to share data in the legislative instruments of each framework: in UK open banking, the right is contained in one regulation of *PSR*,[63] whilst in Australian open banking, there are 20 pages in the *CDR Rules*.[64] This reliance on the standards to provide substantive, rather than operational, detail in the UK system is due to a combination of the principles-based approach of the *PSR* and the use of the UK Standards as a framework for agreeing the detail between participants. The result is that the UK Standards are not only performing the function of the Australian Standards under the Australian system, but also that of the *CDR Rules*, which is a legislative instrument.

This extensive use of standards in UK open banking creates concerns relating to both the clarity and enforceability of those rights. This is particularly apparent when evaluated against the rights of customers to transfer their funds under banking payment systems.

### 6.2.2 Evaluation Against Rights of Customer to Transfer Funds

#### *(a) Clarity and Certainty in the Customer's Right to Transfer Funds*

The evaluation against the clarity and certainty in the customer's right to transfer funds has two components, the need for customers to engage with complexity to understand their rights in banking payment systems, and the balancing of complexity with certainty in open banking systems.

##### *(i) Clarity Despite Complexity in Banking Payment Systems*

Technical standards play an important role in payments. For example, the shift to the ISO 20022 messaging standard in payment systems over the last decade which allows

59. *See* Committee on Payment and Settlement Systems, 'General Guidance for National Payment System Development' (Report, Bank for International Settlements, January 2006) 40.
60. *See* Michael Kirby, 'The Fundamental Problem of Regulating Technology' (2009) 5 *Indian Journal of Law & Technology* 1, 28. *See also* Lawrence Lessig, *Code Version 2.0* (Basic Books, 2006) Ch. 5.
61. CDR Bill EM (n. 3) [1.263].
62. *CMA Order* (n. 25) Art. 10.2.
63. *PSR* (n. 20) reg. 70.
64. *CDR Rules* (n. 5) pt 4.

more data to be included with each payment. However, the use of standards in payments does not displace the need for independent clarity and transparency of legal rights which is fundamental in banking payment systems. A 'well-founded, clear, transparent and enforceable legal basis' is a foundational requirement in the regulation of payment systems.[65] If the legal foundations are 'inadequate, uncertain or opaque' then the risks of the system increase, and the potential benefits decrease.[66]

The implied right of customers to transfer the funds in their account is fundamental to the contract between bank and customer.[67] Further, bank customers also have clarity as to what they can transfer – the balance of their account.[68] This too is at the heart of the banker-customer relationship,[69] and is clearly communicated by the bank to the customer. Chapter 3 showed that the arrangements which banks use to transfer customer funds can be complicated, either because of the need for correspondent banking facilities or multilateral payment systems. Customers are not party to those arrangements. If the rules of those systems are part of the 'ordinary usage and practice of bankers' then the customer can rely on them against their own bank as being implied into the contract between bank and customer.[70] However, if those rules derogate from the customer's rights then the rules do not bind the customer without their consent.[71] Accordingly, the technical detail of the operation of the banking payment system is not an essential component of the legal rights of the customer to transfer their funds. The clarity and certainty which this provides to customers is an important component of the effectiveness of those rights and the confidence in banking payment systems.

### *(ii) Balancing Complexity with Certainty in Open Banking*

As shown in the previous section, the UK Standards and the Australian Standards are both essential components of the legal right to share data under their respective systems. Whilst the use of standards avoids the need to incorporate dynamic and technical concepts into static legislation, a by-product is that the standards can be difficult to understand for a person from a non-technical background such as a customer, lawyer, regulator or a court. For example, the data to be shared under UK open banking for a personal current account is described in the 'Open Banking

65. *See* Committee on Payment and Settlement Systems and International Organization of Securities Commissions, 'Principles for Financial Markets Infrastructures' (Standards, Bank for International Settlements, April 2012) 1.
66. Committee on Payment and Settlement Systems and International Organization of Securities Commissions (n. 65) 21.
67. *Joachimson v. Swiss Bank Corporation* [1921] 3 KB 110, 127 ('*Joachimson v. Swiss Bank Corporation*') 127.
68. *Croton v. R* (1967) 41 ALJ 289 ('*Croton v. R*').
69. *See Foley v. Hill* (1848) 2 HL Cas 28. ('*Foley v. Hill*'). *See also Laing v. Bank of NSW* (1952) 69 WN (NSW) 318 ('*Laing v. Bank of NSW*').
70. *Tayeb v. HSBC Bank plc* [2004] 4 All ER 1024 ('*Tayeb v. HSBC Bank plc* '). *See also Tidal Energy Ltd v. Bank of Scotland Plc* [2015] 2 All ER 15 ('*Tidal Energy Ltd v. Bank of Scotland Plc*').
71. *Barclays Bank Plc v. Bank of England* [1985] 1 All ER 385 ('*Barclays Bank Plc v. Bank of England*').

Read-Write API' part of the 'API Specification' section of the UK Standards in the 'Data Dictionary' which is comprised in the Data Model part of the Accounts section.[72] Navigating the path to this, and then interpreting the descriptive column (entitled 'EnhancedDefinition') is not a simple task. Access to the equivalent Australian Standard is simpler as it requires fewer steps and the 'Description' column in the 'Banking APIs' section of the Consumer Data Standards is also simpler to understand for someone from a non-technical background.[73]

Arguably, the need for this detail to understand the customer's right to share their data represents an issue in the design of each open banking system, more so in the UK due to the increased complexity. However, the technical complexity of the standards is sought to be managed in each system by government oversight of the standard setting process, involvement of a broad cross-section of interested parties and transparency in the process and the outcomes. For example, the Australian Standards are required to be published on the internet and available for free.[74] The *CDR Rules* also require the Data Standards Chair to establish an advisory committee which is required to have a consumer and a privacy representative, and provides the ACCC, the Australian Office of the Information Commissioner and the Department of Treasury with the right to join as observers.[75] In addition, the *CDR Rules* require the Data Standards Chair to engage in public consultation before making or amending a data standard.[76] The *CMA Order* requires that the OBIE comprise UK financial industry specialists 'and other stakeholders, such as HM Treasury and the FCA', that it take into account 'views of a wide range of stakeholders, including fintechs, banks/building societies, consumer and small- and medium-sized enterprises (SME) groups, price-comparison websites, credit reference agencies, regulators and other interested third parties' and that it ensures transparency of decision making.[77]

This is not a complete solution because transparency in the process of setting standards does not necessarily deliver clarity in the rights which the standards articulate. To address this, Australian open banking uses the *CDR Rules*, a legislative instrument, to provide a greater description of the legal rights and to confine the role of the standards with respect to those rights.[78] UK open banking takes a different approach, providing only a principles-based description in its legislative instruments, and leaving the rest to standards. It might be argued that a principles-based description is more comprehensible for non-lawyers than more detailed regulation. However, comprehensibility to the general public does not necessarily mean legal clarity. A principles-based description only improves clarity if it is coextensive with the actual legal rights which are created. This cannot be the case under UK open banking, given that the principles-based description which it uses for the information able to be shared accommodates not only the data shared under the UK Standards, but also the data

72. Open Banking Implementation Entity, 'Open Banking API Specifications ' (n. 24).
73. Data Standards Body, 'Consumer Data Standards v 1.22.0' (n. 16).
74. *CCA* (n. 1) s. 56FC.
75. *CDR Rules* (n. 5) div 8.2.
76. *Ibid.* div 8.3.
77. *CMA Order* (n. 25) sch. 1.
78. *See, e.g., CCA* (n. 1) s. 56FA(2).

shared under different standards used in the EU for the purpose of *PSD2*. Accordingly, although neither open banking system provides the same clarity in the right to share data as is provided in the customer's right to transfer funds, Australian open banking provides more clarity than its UK counterpart. This comparative lack of clarity constrains the effectiveness of the UK system and the reliance on standards rather than legal rules to provide substantive rights to customers restricts the legal support of customer autonomy in its legal design when evaluated against banking payment systems.

### *(b) Enforcement of Customer's Rights to Transfer Funds*

A customer's right to transfer their funds is enforceable as a term of their account contract with their bank.[79] Other, regulatory-based, enforcement mechanisms are also provided by the ePayments Code[80] in Australia and by the *PSR*[81] in the UK.

An equivalent ability to legally enforce the right to compel the bank to share data is important to support consumer protection and confidence in open banking. Without this, the systems are merely voluntary standards with which the bank can choose whether or not to comply. As noted in the previous section, the use of mandatory standards in the Australian and the UK systems removes the need for bilateral contracts to be negotiated between banks and recipients, and as a result, enforceability of the rights to share data between them is provided through their legislative instruments.

The obligations for banks to share data under the Australian system are contained in 'civil penalty provisions',[82] meaning that a court can impose significant penalties for breach of these requirements, in addition to the substantive enforcement rights granted to the ACCC. It also means that there is a statutory right for a customer to take direct action against a bank for the damages caused by the bank's non-compliance with these rules.[83] Further, a failure to comply with a binding data standard by a bank or data recipient, is enforceable by application to the court by the ACCC or 'a person aggrieved by the failure'.[84] The court may make an order giving directions against the person in breach (or its directors) about compliance with, or enforcement of, the binding data standard.[85] These rights to enforce are available to individuals and businesses alike.

79. *Joachimson v. Swiss Bank Corporation* (n. 67) 127.
80. Australian Securities & Investments Commission, 'ePayments Code' (Code of Conduct, 29 March 2016) https://download.asic.gov.au/media/3798542/epayments-code-published-29-march-2016.pdf.
81. *PSR* (n. 20).
82. *CDR Rules* (n. 5) r. 9.8. This is in accordance with s. 56BL of the *CCA*.
83. *CCA* (n. 1) s. 82(1)(d).
84. *Ibid.* s. 56FE(1). A 'person aggrieved' by the failure is not defined in the *CCA*. In the *Administrative Decisions (Judicial Review) Act 1977* it is defined to include a person whose interests are adversely affected: *Administrative Decisions (Judicial Review) Act 1977* (Cth) s. 3(4) ('*ADJR Act*'). It has been subject to judicial consideration in other contexts. *See Argos Pty Ltd v. Corbell, Minister for the Environment and Sustainable Development* [2014] HCA 50, 62 ('*Argos v. Corbell*').
85. *CCA* (n. 1) s. 56FE(2).

In UK open banking, the duties of the banks required to comply with the *CMA Order* are 'owed to any person who may be affected by a contravention'.[86] In addition to this, the CMA can enforce those duties by giving directions,[87] and take civil proceedings to enforce them.[88] The *PSR* provides substantive enforcement rights to the FCA with respect to failures to comply.[89] Further, the *PSR* provides that a contravention of these requirements is 'actionable at the suit of a private person who suffers loss as a result of the contravention'.[90] However, this excludes individuals who incurred a loss in carrying on a business of providing payment services and it excludes any non-individuals who carry on a business of any kind.[91] Unless such businesses are dealing with a bank to which the *CMA Order* applies, the legislative design of the UK system does not supply an ability to enforce any right to share their data. There is no equivalent to the direct enforceability of the Australian Standards under the UK system.

The gap in the enforcement rights under the UK system for business customers represents a significant difference from the rights of a business customer under banking payment systems and the Australian system. Whilst there are dispute resolution processes required in both frameworks,[92] these do not perform the same role as an ability to take legal action. The result is that, whilst the UK system facilitates the sharing of data through its design, it does not provide a legal right to share data to business customers, unless they are customers of the nine banks specified in the *CMA Order*. When compared to both the Australian system and when evaluated against the rights of customers to transfer their funds, this represents significantly less legal support for customer autonomy under UK open banking.

## 6.3 HOW CAN LEGAL FOUNDATIONS SUPPORT SHARING DATA?

### 6.3.1 Summary of Comparison and Evaluation

This chapter has examined the implications of the legal foundations of Australian and UK open banking for sharing customer data through a comparison of their legal features relating to how customer data should be shared and where should the rights to share data be established, and an evaluation against equivalent legal features of banking payment systems.

The analysis has shown that each of Australian and UK open banking benefits from the use of APIs instead of screen scraping to share customer data, and a form of customer authentication based on that used for payments of customer funds. It has also shown that whilst each system enables authorised recipients to request data be shared on behalf of customers, neither permits the customer to request the data be shared with themselves. The potential consequences of this are considered further in Chapter 8.

86. *Enterprise Act 2002* (UK) s. 167 ('*Enterprise Act*').
87. *CMA Order* (n. 25) Art. 57.
88. *Enterprise Act* (n. 86) s. 167(3).
89. *PSR* (n. 20) pt 9.
90. *Ibid.* reg. 148(1).
91. *Ibid.* reg. 148(3).
92. *See CDR Rules* (n. 5) pt 6 and *PSR* (n. 20) reg. 101.

This chapter has also shown how each of Australian and UK open banking benefits from the consistency provided by mandatory compliance with a single set of data standards. However, due to the absence of detailed rules in its legislative structure, the UK system relies on data standards to comprise more of the substance of the data sharing rights than Australian open banking. This provides less clarity and certainty to the customers who are intended to use open banking to share their data. When evaluated against a customer's rights to transfer their funds, the discrepancy is more noticeable. This is due to the complicated legislative structure of the UK system, which also results in a lack of enforceable rights to share data for business customers.

The consequences of these differences are that whilst the legal foundations of both Australian and UK open banking support data portability, the support is weaker than that provided in banking payment systems. Also, the lesser clarity of the legal rights to share data means that the legal foundations of both provide less support for customer autonomy than that provided in banking payment systems, and the UK system provides less support than the Australian system. This is illustrated in Figure 6.1.

*Figure 6.1 Illustration of Evaluation and Comparison Relating to Sharing Data*

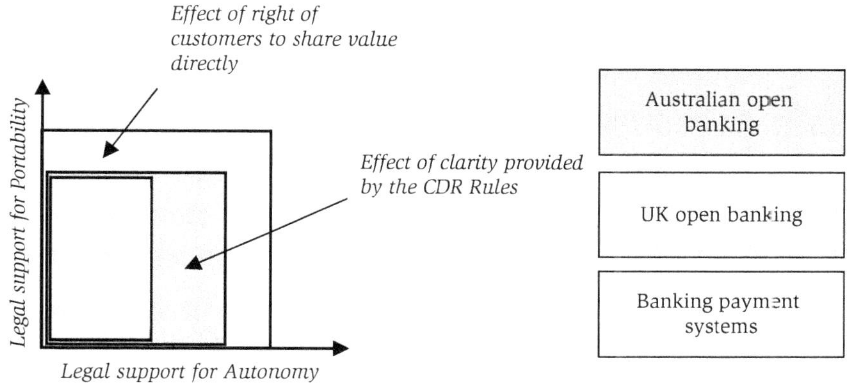


This analysis has shown the necessity of both technological and legal support for sharing customer data for an open banking system to perform its portability and autonomy functions. It has shown the importance of the certainty provided by the use of a single set of standards and the challenge presented to provide legal clarity with respect to those standards. The first of these demonstrates the importance of management of communication risk, whilst the second is a demonstration of validity risk. These risks are explained next, followed by an illustration of the comparable operational and legal risks in banking payment systems, and a discussion of how operational and legal risk management methods could be applied in the legal design of open banking systems.

### 6.3.2 Communication and Validity Risks in Open Banking Systems

Communication risk in open banking arises when customer data cannot be accurately sent, or their meaning cannot be accurately received and understood, so that the data cannot be used as desired by the customer. A critical element in understanding this risk is that there are both technical and semantic elements, in that it could be a consequence of the message not being able to be effectively sent or its meaning not effectively understood. Accordingly, it can arise when there is a failure in the technological means of transmitting a message or in the basis on which a message for communication is formed. As explained in Chapter 3, the technical and semantic elements of the communication problem in open banking are dealt with by the relevant standards, particularly those relating to the use of APIs to share data and the data fields and formats for expressing those data. If there is insufficient coordination for participants in an open banking system to use the same standards, or if the standards are insufficiently precise so that adherence still does not result in sufficient coordination, then the resulting communication risk obstructs the system's performance of its portability function and the achievement of its objectives.

Validity risk arises from a lack of certainty and clarity in the legal rights to share customer data if the functions to be performed by open banking are not legally recognised such that there is no ability to legally compel, or legally manage non-performance of those functions. A critical element in understanding this risk is that there are both technological and legal foundations of open banking systems and that validity risk usually only becomes evident when technological functions of an open banking system are not performed as expected. In these circumstances, validity risk becomes evident and impairs the effectiveness and credibility of the open banking system.

The communication of customer data might be considered to be only a technological function in respect of which a technological articulation is sufficient. However, it is still underpinned by legal rights and obligations which need to be clear and enforceable. If they are not, then there will be no legal accountability for a failure to meet the technological expectations. The consequences of this would be significant for an open banking system. For example, if customers found that there were no legal consequences for a failure to perform the responsibilities and duties with respect to the communication of their data then the resulting conflict between the technological processes and legal obligations would cause uncertainty in the treatment of customer data and the outcomes for customers. There would be likely to be a serious and potentially fatal impact on the system's credibility and, as a result, its effectiveness in performing any of its functions. This chapter has shown that this can arise if substantive rights are contained in complicated technological standards, rather than legislative instruments, such that they are inaccessible, unclear and uncertain in their operation.

To further explain these aspects of communication and validity risks, the next section sets out an illustration of the comparable risks in banking payment systems, *operational risks,* and *legal risks.*

### 6.3.3 Illustration of Operational and Legal Risks in Financial Systems

#### *(a) Illustration of Operational Risks: World Trade Centre*

Operational risk in banking payment systems is:

> the risk that operational factors such as technical malfunctions or operational mistakes will cause or exacerbate credit or liquidity risks.[93]

In a broader context of financial market infrastructure, operational risks can cause the 'reduction, deterioration or breakdown of services' provided by the infrastructure, and is considered to be the primary risk for information-based infrastructures, such as derivative TRs.[94]

The consequences of operational risks relating to communication failure is shown by the impact of the terrorist attacks on the World Trade Centre in New York on 11 September 2001. In addition to the horrific loss of life caused:

> [t]he destructive force of the attacks themselves caused severe disruptions to the U.S. banking system, particularly in banks' abilities to send payments. The physical disruptions caused by the attacks included outages of telephone switching equipment in Lower Manhattan's financial district, impaired records processing and communications systems at individual banks, the evacuation of buildings that were the sites for the payments operations of large banks, and the suspended delivery of checks by air couriers.[95]

The consequences of this included some banks experiencing difficulties in making payments and others receiving fewer payments than expected. Failures in settlement occurred and payment messages were lost. The normal coordination of payments broke down, banks required greater liquid funds as a precaution in the ensuing uncertainty and liquidity shortages developed in banks. Balance sheets in the banking system were inflated by the increase in assets not able to be transferred and bank capital ratios fell. However, there were no runs on banks, extraordinary demands for funds from the public, or a fear of that a bank would fail, or cause the failure of others. Nevertheless, the interdependencies between banks in the system still caused liquidity dislocation. To restore the coordination, the Federal Reserve responded by supplying an additional $100 billion in liquidity through discount window loans. Liquidity coordination was restored within days. The event demonstrated how a localised problem in communication can affect an entire system and the critical nature of coordination in the transfer of value through a network.

The consequences of the attack on the banking payment systems have implications for the technical and semantic aspects of communication under open banking. For example, it is possible that similar disruptions in communication infrastructure

93. Committee on Payment and Settlement Systems, 'Core Principles for Systemically Important Payment Systems' (Core Principles, Bank for International Settlements, January 2001) 5.
94. Committee on Payment and Settlement Systems and International Organization of Securities Commissions (n. 65) 20.
95. James McAndrews and Simon Potter, 'Liquidity Effects of the Events of September 11, 2001' (2002) *FRBNY Economic Policy Review* 59.

could cause communication failure in open banking systems. However, the more fundamental lesson for open banking design relates to the need to re-establish the coordination of payments following the attack so that the banking payment system could function normally. In open banking systems, a key foundation for this coordination is the standards which ensure that customer data has the same meaning for the recipient as it has for the customer and the bank. The purpose of mandatory and precise standards is to avoid the confusion which existed in the banking payment system following the September 11 attacks. For this reason, the legal features of banking payment systems which are designed to manage this aspect of operational risk deserve consideration for incorporation into the legal foundations of open banking systems. This is explained in the next section.

### *(b) Illustration of Legal Risk: Lehman Brothers*

Legal risk in banking payment systems is:

> the risk that a poor legal framework or legal uncertainties will cause or exacerbate credit or liquidity risks.[96]

The consequences of legal risk in financial systems is shown by aspects of the resolution of the collapse of Lehman Brothers ('Lehman'),[97] in the global financial crisis of 2007-2009. Lehman had been a global investment banking firm and was widely considered to be 'too big to fail' and, in the words of the Financial Crisis Inquiry Commission of the United States, with Lehman's collapse 'the financial crisis reached cataclysmic proportions'.[98] Relevantly:

> Lehman, like other large OTC derivatives dealers, experienced runs on its derivatives operations that played a role in its failure. Its massive derivatives positions greatly complicated its bankruptcy, and the impact of its bankruptcy through interconnections with derivatives counterparties and other financial institutions contributed significantly to the severity and depth of the financial crisis.[99]

The complexity of Lehman's financial arrangements, especially those relating to derivatives and other financial market transactions, resulted in a lack of clarity as to its financial position which complicated attempts to avoid its collapse:

> there was no way to know who would be owed how much and when payments would have to be made – information that would be critically important to analyse

96. Committee on Payment and Settlement Systems, 'Core Principles for Systemically Important Payment Systems' (n. 93) 5.
97. Many entities in the Lehman Brothers corporate group globally entered insolvency proceedings, including Lehman Brothers Holdings Inc., Lehman Brothers International (Europe) and Lehman Brothers Inc. These are collectively referred to as 'Lehman' unless specificity is required.
98. Financial Crisis Inquiry Commission, United States, *The Financial Crisis Inquiry Report: The Final Report of the National Commission on the Causes of the Financial and Economic Crisis in the United States Including Dissenting Views* (Final Report, 1 May 2011) 342.
99. *Ibid.*

> the possible impact of a Lehman bankruptcy on derivatives counterparties and the financial markets.[100]

A consequence of Lehman's collapse was that many complicated legal and financial structures were considered for the first time by the courts. This judicial consideration revealed some results which market participants found surprising and the complexity of arrangements was not always upheld, particularly where there was a lack of clarity in the understanding of the legal rights and obligations. This is demonstrated by two legal cases: *Wingecarribee Shire Council v. Lehman*[101] and *Pearson v. Lehman Brothers Finance SA.*[102]

*Wingecarribee v. Lehman* concerned a challenge to the terms of synthetic collateralised debt obligations (known as 'synthetic CDOs') arranged by Lehman affiliates and offered to local councils in Australia. These were extremely complicated investments structured to use derivatives to link the investment to the performance of a notional portfolio of assets. Despite being set out in transaction documents, the terms of the investments were found to be of a 'byzantine' complexity',[103] and too complex for the councils to understand.[104] Further, it was found that the risks arising from the effect of those terms were not reflected in the credit ratings provided on the investments.[105] Accordingly, the investors were not found to be legally bound by the technical operation of the complex terms.

*Pearson v. Lehman Brothers Finance SA*,[106] concerned the treatment of repurchase transactions ('repos') executed automatically, without the need for any human intervention, between two Lehman entities. These automated transactions did not cease on the commencement of the insolvency administration of one entity, despite the instruction from the administrators that no further transactions were to be entered into:[107]

> The computer automated process bizarrely continued on its sweet way, doing thousands more repos every day for a further ten days until someone from the administrators asked what the flashing light on the relevant computer was about, found out, and then ordered it to be switched off.[108]

The court found that, despite the creation of technological records of automatic transactions recorded after the commencement of the administration, the outcome of the transactions should be decided on the basis of the last repo which was authorised, being the final one completed before the administration's commencement.[109]

100. *Ibid.*
101. *Wingecarribee Shire Council v. Lehman* [2012] FCS 1028 ('*Wingecarribee v. Lehman*').
102. *Pearson v. Lehman Brothers Finance S.A.* [2011] EWCA Civ 1544 ('*Pearson v. Lehman*').
103. *Wingecarribee v. Lehman* (n. 101) [115].
104. *Ibid.* [313], [892].
105. *Ibid.* [64].
106. *Pearson v. Lehman* (n. 102).
107. *Ibid.* [32].
108. Lord Justice Briggs, 'How Has English Law Coped With the Lehman Collapse?' in Dennis Faber and Niels Vermunt (eds), *Bank Failure: Lessons from Lehman Brothers* (Oxford University Press, 2017). [6.17].
109. Consideration of which the court considered to be 'a somewhat metaphysical exercise': *Pearson v. Lehman* (n. 102) [158].

Accordingly, the parties were not legally bound by the technological arrangements purported to be entered into beyond the time at which legal authority to transact ceased.

Each of these two cases show that courts are not constrained by the complexity of difficult to understand arrangements or the technological governance of arrangements where they are inconsistent with law. In each case, the expected outcome of the parties designing the arrangements was overridden in Lehman's collapse. This lack of enforceability represents legal risk, and it can also be found in the judicial decisions which found that customers are not bound by provisions of payment systems or complex contracts the terms of which are not easily available, accessible or understandable,[110] and judicial decisions which did not recognise the result of accounting, clearing or technological processes which were inconsistent with the operation of insolvency laws.[111]

Similar risks of legal invalidity could arise in open banking systems which rely on complicated technical standards, which might also be described to be of 'byzantine complexity', to set out substantive legal rights and responsibilities. It is entirely plausible that customers and some participants may not understand the legal rights and obligations which are 'built into' such standards. Just as the commercial complexity of Lehman's financial arrangements and the automatically executing repos led to lengthy litigation which resulted in the commercially intended outcome not being upheld, so could the legal rights and responsibilities contained only in the technological complexity of the open banking standards not be upheld at law. For this reason, the legal features of banking payment systems which are designed to manage legal risk deserve consideration for incorporation into the legal foundations of open banking systems.

### 6.3.4 Incorporating Operational and Legal Risk Management Features in Open Banking

#### *(a) Operational Risk Management*

The first example above illustrates two aspects of operational risk. The first was the risk to the technical aspects of communication, meaning the technology used to share messages. Risks of this nature are managed in open banking by the requirements for authorisation to participate explained in Chapter 9. The second aspect was the risk to the semantic aspects of communication, meaning the coordination required to ensure that the communications were not only occurring but also that they provided the meaning intended. Banking payment systems do this by requiring participants to adhere to the same messaging standards. There is little flexibility in this regard in banking payment systems as there is no allowance made for misunderstanding messages. From a risk management perspective, it is difficult to argue that the same

110. *See Tayeb v. HSBC Bank plc* [2004] 4 All ER 1024 (*'Tayeb v. HSBC Bank plc'*); *Tidal Energy Ltd v. Bank of Scotland Plc* [2015] 2 All ER 15 (*'Tidal Energy Ltd v. Bank of Scotland Plc'*).

111. *See Pearson v. Lehman* (n. 102). *See also British Eagle International Air Lines Ltd v. Cie Nationale Air France* [1975] 1 WLR 758 (*'British Eagle'*); *International Air Transport Association v. Ansett Australia Holdings Limited* [2008] HCA 3 (*'IATA v. Ansett'*).

approach should not be taken in open banking, as it is in both the Australian and UK systems with the adoption of a single, specific and mandatory set of standards under each.

### *(b) Legal Risk Management*

Because of its foundational nature, the management of legal risks in a banking payment system is 'critical to its overall soundness',[112] and is the first principle of risk management in systemically important payment systems.[113] The management of legal risks in banking payment systems requires that there are rules and procedures which are 'clear, understandable, and consistent with relevant laws and regulations', and which 'provide a high degree of legal certainty'.[114]

It could be argued that the same approach of providing clarity and certainty cannot be taken in the design of open banking because of the inherently complicated nature of data-related activities. This argument would suggest that because these activities are technological, the legal rights with respect to them can never be as clear and certain as those which apply to banking payment systems. This is incorrect for two reasons. First, as the analysis in Chapter 4 shows, banking payment systems are also communication networks and their participants have been using and improving technology from the time that money was coins of precious metal to it being comprised of computer records. Second, through its legal design, the Australian system has implemented an integrated technological, legal and governance framework. The critical feature in Australian open banking which enables this is the *CDR Rules*, which were included to 'complement the principle-based legislative provisions' and determine the rights and obligations of participants, as well as the 'requirements for data standard setting governance and processes'.[115] UK open banking seeks, but fails, to cover these elements in the UK Standards.[116] The *CDR Rules* succeed in this role because they have the benefits of flexibility and legal certainty, and serve to connect the inflexible high-level *CCA* and the flexible technological Australian Standards. Accordingly, in order to manage validity risk in open banking it is important to have a legal structure which enables legal certainty and clarity *as well as* flexibility. Without it, there is significant risk that the legal basis for many activities is 'inadequate, uncertain or opaque',[117] and the resulting validity risk in the design of the open banking systems could challenge their credibility and their ability to perform any of their functions.

112. Committee on Payment and Settlement Systems, 'Core Principles for Systemically Important Payment Systems' (n. 93) [7.1.1].
113. *See ibid. See also* Committee on Payment and Settlement Systems and International Organization of Securities Commissions (n. 65) 1.
114. Committee on Payment and Settlement Systems and International Organization of Securities Commissions (n. 65) 21.
115. Australian Treasury, 'Consumer Data Right' (Explanatory Guide, 9 May 2018) 12.
116. *See* section 3.5.
117. Committee on Payment and Settlement Systems and International Organization of Securities Commissions (n. 65) 21.

CHAPTER 7

# Utilising Shared Customer Data

This chapter examines the legal foundations for the governance of the use of shared customer data under open banking systems. It compares the legal responsibilities supporting utilising data under Australian and UK open banking and evaluates them against the equivalent legal responsibilities under banking payment systems. This analysis addresses two questions:

- Should there be limits on requests for customer data?
- How should shared customer data be used?

The answers to these questions are fundamental to an open banking system's performance of its *accountability* and *autonomy* functions.

## 7.1 SHOULD THERE BE LIMITS ON REQUESTS FOR CUSTOMER DATA?

The EU's *GDPR* is used widely as a benchmark of privacy law. One of the six core principles of processing personal data under *GDPR* is that personal data must be 'adequate, relevant and limited to what is necessary in relation to the purposes for which they are processed'.[1] This is known as the 'data minimisation' principle. This has been incorporated into the legal design of Australian and UK open banking to limit the requests which can be made for sharing customer data and it is fundamental to their effectiveness in performing their accountability function.

1. *Regulation (EU) 2016/679 of the European Parliament and of the Council of 27 April 2016 on the Protection Of Natural Persons with regard to the Processing Of Personal Data and on the Free Movement of such Data, and repealing Directive 95/46/EC (General Data Protection Regulation)* OJ L119/1 ('*GDPR*') Art. 5(1)(c). The others are the principles of: lawfulness, fairness and transparency; purpose limitation; accuracy; storage limitation; and integrity and confidentiality: *ibid.* Art. 5(1)(a), (b), (d)-(f).

The legal responsibilities which form the foundation for two key features of data minimisation under the Australian and UK systems, namely scope of data minimisation and its effect on data sharing relationships, are comparatively analysed below, followed by evaluation against limits on requests to transfer funds and the value of the funds transferred in banking payment systems.

### 7.1.1 Comparison of Data Minimisation in Open Banking Systems

#### *(a) Scope of Data Minimisation*

Data minimisation is incorporated into the Australian system through the *CDR Rules*.[2] They prohibit an accredited recipient from using CDR data beyond what is reasonably required to provide goods or services which have been requested by the customer.[3] It is supported by a separate requirement in the *CDR Rules* that an accredited recipient can only request CDR data which it needs to provide those goods or services.[4] This means that, for example, an accredited recipient must not request ongoing access to transaction data in order to assess eligibility for loans at a single point in time, and must not use data supplied for the provision of an account aggregation service to create a profile of customers' spending habits.[5]

The *PSR* incorporates a conceptually similar limitation into UK open banking. An AISP must not use, access or store any information except for the purpose of the AIS explicitly requested by the payment service user.[6] The AIS is:

> [a]n online service to provide consolidated information on one or more payment accounts held by the payment service user with another payment service provider or with more than one payment service provider, and includes such a service whether information is provided –
>
> (a) in its original form or after processing;
> (b) only to the payment service user or to the payment service user and to another person in accordance with the payment service user's instructions.[7]

An AISP is not permitted to use data shared with it under the *PSR* for the provision of services other than an AIS. As a result, the scope of the data use permitted in the UK system initially appears very limited and would not permit use for purposes such as assessing credit or completing loan applications. However, flexibility is provided through the inclusion in the definition of AIS of the ability to provide the consolidated information to another person, in addition to the customer, on the customer's

2. *Competition and Consumer (Consumer Data Right) Rules 2020* ('*CDR Rules*') r. 1.8.
3. *Ibid.* rr. 1.8, 4.4.
4. *Ibid.* rr. 4.3(1), (2).
5. *See* Explanatory Statement, Competition and Consumer (Consumer Data Right) Rules 2020 (Cth) 10 ('CDR Rules Explanatory Statement').
6. *Payment Services Regulation 2017* (UK) ('*PSR*') reg. 70(3)(f).
7. *Ibid.* reg. 2(1) (definition of 'account information service').

instructions. This other person could be, for example, a third party that provides credit scoring services and makes loan applications.[8]

These requirements of the *PSR* are complemented by the data minimisation principle in *GDPR* which also applies to personal data shared using UK open banking. This means that a recipient under UK open banking must not collect personal data beyond those required to supply the specific AIS requested by the customer and access to the personal data should be limited to what is necessary for that purpose.[9] For example, an AISP is not permitted to process the description of transactions in open banking data if it is not necessary for the AIS which the AISP provides.[10]

The primary difference in data minimisation between the two open banking systems is in their scope. Australian open banking requires that the data is needed for a good or service requested by the customer, but there is no limit on the good or service which may be requested. This is in contrast to UK open banking where the service requested by the customer must be an AIS.[11] As data portability is essential to the effectiveness of open banking, the narrowness of the permitted service could limit the benefit of the UK system. However, as noted above, there is further flexibility through the ability to provide the consolidated account information to a third party which can enable other services to be provided. In these circumstances, the requirements of *GDPR*, including its less restrictive data minimisation principle, would apply to the third party.[12] This should enable a similar breadth of potential uses to be requested by the customer under the UK system as are available under the Australian system. Accordingly, with the appropriate use of third parties, the design of UK open banking with respect to data minimisation should not significantly reduce the data which a customer may share in comparison to Australian open banking. The need to use those third parties could itself be regarded as an unnecessary source of complexity but this could be managed through agency and outsourcing arrangements by recipients, as explained in Chapter 9.

### *(b) Effect of Data Minimisation on Data Sharing Relationships*

The incorporation of data minimisation into open banking shapes the nature of the relationship between customer and recipient. Under the UK system, this transaction is required to be established in a contract between the customer and the data recipient for the AIS.[13] There is no similar requirement for a pre-existing contract specified in the legislative instruments of the Australian system, although the *CDR Rules* do refer to the

8. *See* Financial Conduct Authority, 'AISP Models under PSD2', (Guidance, 21 January 2020) https://www.fca.org.uk/firms/agency-models-under-psd2.
9. European Data Protection Board, 'Guidelines 06/2020 on the Interplay of the Second Payment Services Directive and the GDPR' (Guidelines, 17 July 2020) 61.
10. *Ibid.* 63.
11. *PSR* (n. 6) reg. 70.
12. *See* Financial Conduct Authority, 'AISP Models under PSD2' (n. 8).
13. 'Payment services [under *PSD2*] are always provided on a contractual basis between the payment services user and the payment services provider': European Data Protection Board (n. 9) [14]. This is reflected in recital 87 of *Directive 2015/2366/EU of the European Parliament and of the Council of 25 November 2015 on Payment Services in the Internal Market, amending*

'relevant contract' between the accredited person and the CDR consumer relating to the requested supply in its provisions for revocation or suspension of a person's accreditation.[14] However, the foundations of contract formation should be present if the customer has requested the supply of the good or service and the data recipient has agreed to provide it in exchange for the receipt of the customer's data, assuming contractual capacity is present.

Data minimisation means that that data shared under open banking are more than something of value exchanged by the customer in return for the good or service. Instead, the data are an essential requirement which the customer contributes for the provision of the good or service which they have requested. Because of data minimisation, customers in open banking do not share their data to 'purchase' the supply which they have requested.[15] This differs from other data sharing arrangements where the customer receives a 'free' service in exchange for their data, which the recipient uses to gain knowledge about the customer's preferences and behaviour for their own economic gain. By confining the data shared to what is needed, data minimisation seeks to balance the exchange between customer and data recipient. This relationship, enabled by data minimisation, enhances the ability of open banking to perform its accountability function with respect to the data shared by enabling the data to be used only in accordance with the customer's direction. In effect, data minimisation balances the autonomy and accountability functions of open banking by constraining the data shared to what are needed to be used. In this regard, the differences between the systems identified above are not as relevant as they do not affect the need for the data requested to be linked to their use. However, to analyse this further, it is necessary to evaluate it against the use of customer funds by a bank.

### 7.1.2 Evaluation Against Bank's Responsibilities in Use of Customer Funds

#### *(a) No Similar Limits on Use of Customer Funds*

The legal design of banking payment systems does not incorporate responsibilities in relation to transfers of customer funds which are equivalent to data minimisation. There is no legal requirement that a bank may only apply funds received on behalf of its customer to the extent needed for the bank to provide another service which has been requested by the customer. Instead, once money is credited to the customer's account by the bank, it:

*Directives 2002/65/EC, 2009/110/EC, and 2013/36/EU and Regulation (EU) No 1093/2010 and repealing Directive 2007/64/EC* OJ L 337/35 ('*PSD2*')

14. *CDR Rules* (n. 2) r. 5.17.
15. *See Directive (EU) 2019/770 of the European Parliament and of The Council of 20 May 2019 on Certain Aspects Concerning Contracts for the Supply of Digital Content and Digital Services* OJ L 136 ('*Directive (EU) 2019/770 of the European Parliament and of The Council of 20 May 2019 on Certain Aspects Concerning Contracts for the Supply of Digital Content and Digital Services*').

> is then the banker's money; he is known to deal with it as his own; he makes what profit of it he can, which profit he retains himself.[16]

In taking custody of its customer's funds, the bank offers its customers the benefits of storage and liquidity described in Chapter 4 by agreeing to repay the amount received at the customer's request. It is possible for this to be provided in connection with another service requested by the customer, such as the custody of the customer's securities or the safekeeping of the customer's other property, but the bank's responsibilities for the customer's funds are not dependent on, and the bank's rights to use the funds received are not limited by, any such additional service. Accordingly, data minimisation represents a significant difference between the legal design of the open banking systems and banking payment systems.

There would be a significant adverse impact on the effectiveness of the banking payment system if data minimisation were to apply to funds received for a customer by their bank. It would mean that a bank could only use those funds to the extent they are needed to provide another service which the customer had requested. This might arise in some circumstances, for example if the funds are needed as collateral for financing made available for the customer. However, it would not arise where the customer just wanted to keep their funds at their bank. Accordingly, key benefits provided by the banking payment system – the bank being able to on-lend the funds as its own and the customer not having to hold and use cash – would be severely constrained.

Nevertheless, before seeking to derive any conclusion from this with respect to the legal design of open banking systems, it is necessary to analyse whether there are relevant differences in the nature of customer data and customer funds. One particular feature of customer data is important, namely that the value of data depends on their use.

### *(b) Use-Dependency of the Value of Customer Data*

As explained in Chapter 2, data are not inherently valuable, and value is derived from data through use. Customer data produces value for the customer when they are used for the customer's benefit and different uses of the same data produce different value. For example, a customer's banking data produces more value for a customer when it is used to move the customer's money to the account which, at that time, is paying the highest interest rate than when used to inform a customer of their account balance. This dependency of value on use does not apply to customer funds. Due to money's functions as a store of value and a unit of account, customer funds in a bank account maintain their value whilst they are stored and when being used.

#### *(i) Data Minimisation and Accountability*

This difference challenges the argument that data minimisation imposes a constraint on the effectiveness of open banking systems. Data minimisation means that a

16. *Foley v. Hill* (1848) 2 HL Cas 28, 36 ('*Foley v. Hill*').

customer exchanges data in return for a good or service from the recipient which requires those data. For the exchange between the customer and recipient to be fair, both customer and recipient need to understand the value of what they are exchanging. If the customer does not understand the use to which their data are to be put, then the customer cannot understand the value of what they are providing, or the 'price' which they are paying. The recipient is not in the same position as it knows the use to which it is intending to put the customer's data. This information asymmetry as to the use of the customer's data creates an imbalance between customer and recipient and potential unfairness in the exchange of which the data forms part. A similar balance would arise in a banking payment system if a bank were able to choose the term and interest rate for the investment of a customer's funds in a term deposit without having to inform, or consult with, the customer.

The incorporation of data minimisation in the open banking systems addresses this asymmetry in the relationship between the customer and recipient by requiring that the data can be used only for the purpose of providing the good or service which the customer has requested. This results in the use of the shared data being in accordance with the customer's direction. Accordingly, data minimisation should not be considered a flaw in the design of open banking when evaluated against banking payment systems, but a feature which is intended to improve the effectiveness of the systems in achieving their accountability function.

### *(ii) Data Minimisation and Compliance*

However, an open banking system's ability to achieve that effectiveness is dependent on the data recipient complying with its data minimisation responsibilities. Similar reliance on data controller compliance has been identified as a weakness in data protection regimes. This is not solely because of willing non-compliance with obligations, but because data-related rules are often difficult to comprehend due to their complexity, and difficult to apply in practice because they are often not 'workable, sector-specific, and context-specific'.[17] Further, compliance often takes the form of ensuring that tasks on a checklist are completed for the purpose of showing supervisors and auditors, rather than achieving the purpose of the regulation.[18] Of particular practical concern is the potential for customer data transferred under open banking to be commingled with data which is not subject to the same obligations such that it becomes impossible to comply with the open banking responsibilities. The design of Australian and UK open banking manages this to some extent by allowing for the responsibilities under the respective data protection regimes to apply in place of those under the open banking systems. For example, under the Australian system, an ADI that receives data under open banking is treated as a data holder and not a data recipient for that data if the customer has acquired a product from them, the ADI

17. Bert-Jaap Koops, 'The Trouble with European Data Protection Law' (2014) 4(4) *International Data Privacy Law* 250-261, 254.
18. *Ibid. See also* Neil Robinson et al., 'Review of the European Data Protection Directive' (Technical Report, Information Commissioner's Office, May 2009).

reasonably believes that the data is relevant to the product and has obtained the customer's consent.[19] This reduces the complexity in managing the transferred data because the data, and the other data held by the ADI in respect of that customer and product, becomes subject to the *Privacy Act* instead of many of the privacy safeguards under the *CCA*. A similar effect is achieved under the UK system, in that *GDPR* and not the *PSR* applies to the treatment of the consolidated account information which is provided to a third party.

These mechanisms are not perfect and will not remove all potential difficulty in complying with responsibilities for transferred data in the context of the holding of large amounts of customer data from different sources. Also, they will not remove the risk that a recipient does not comply with its obligations even though it could. These risks apply also to the use of customer's consent in Australian and UK open banking and are analysed further in that context in the next section of this chapter.

## 7.2 HOW SHOULD SHARED CUSTOMER DATA BE USED?

Consent is at the foundation of effective data sharing. The need for a customer's consent is incorporated into both the Australian and UK systems, as it is critical to the appropriate use of customer data and the accountability function to be performed in open banking. For example, in Australia:

> [c]onsumer consent for the collection and use of their data is the bedrock of the CDR regime. Consent enables consumers to be the decision makers in the CDR regime, ensuring that they can direct where their data goes in order to obtain the most value from it.[20]

This need for consent is in addition to the requirements of data minimisation.[21] The responsibilities relating to two key features of consent, its nature, and criticisms of reliance on it, are comparatively analysed below, followed by evaluation against control of the use of funds and the value of what is transferred in banking payment systems.

### 7.2.1 Comparison of the Role of Consent in the Open Banking Systems

#### *(a) Express, Clear, and Specific Consent*

Both Australian and UK open banking rely on customer consent to authorise and control the use of customer data. Neither system provides an alternative basis on which a recipient may obtain or use customer data. This differs from each jurisdiction's

19. *Competition and Consumer Act 2010* (Cth) ('*CCA*') s. 56AJ(4), *CDR Rules* (n. 2) r. 7.2.
20. Office of the Australian Information Commissioner, 'Consumer Data Right Privacy Safeguard Guidelines' (Guidelines, July 2020) Ch. 3.
21. This is more complicated for the purpose of applying the *GDPR* because consent under *PSD2* is not recognised as the consent needed to process information under *GDPR*: European Data Protection Board (n. 9).

respective privacy laws, *GDPR* and the *Privacy Act*, which provide other bases on which data may be used.[22]

Under Australian open banking, the privacy safeguards in the *CCA* provide that CDR data may not be used by an accredited data recipient unless the use is authorised under the *CDR Rules*.[23] The *CDR Rules* permit the data to be used if it is in accordance with both the data minimisation principle and a current consent of the customer.[24] Further permitted uses include deriving data from the data for that same purpose and de-identifying the data for general research or disclosure (with consent) and disclosure to specified support providers.[25]

Under UK open banking, the *PSR* also relies on consent. It requires that the AISP that receives data of a payment service user:

- not provide AISs without the payment service user's explicit consent, and
- not use, access, or store any information for any purpose except for the provision of the AIS explicitly requested by the payment service user.[26]

Further, the *PSR* requires that an AISP must not access, process, or retain any personal data for the provision of payment services by it, unless it has the explicit consent of the payment services user to do so.[27]

The *CDR Rules* require that a consent be voluntary, express, informed, specific as to purpose, time limited and easily withdrawn.[28] They further require that the consent:

- be obtained in accordance with the CDR data standards, including the consumer experience standards, and have regard to the consumer experience guidelines,[29]
- not include or refer to other documents so as to reduce comprehensibility or be bundled with other directions, permissions, consents, or agreements,[30]

22. Under *GDPR* contractual necessity, legal compliance, protection of vital interests, public interest and legitimate interests are also lawful bases for the processing of personal information: *GDPR* (n. 1) Art. 6(1). Under the *Privacy Act* personal information can be collected if the information is reasonably necessary for one or more of the entity's functions or activities and used for the purpose for which it was collected, or a secondary purpose which is related to it, if such a use would be reasonably expected: *Privacy Act 1998* (Cth) ('*Privacy Act*') sch. 1 APPs 3 and 6.
23. *CCA* (n. 19) s. 56EI(1)(b). Use which is otherwise required or authorised by Australian law or a court or tribunal is also permitted: *ibid.* s. 56EI(1)(c).
24. *CDR Rules* (n. 2) r. 7.5(1)(a). Neither the *CCA* nor the *CDR Rules* define 'use'. The Australian Office of the Information Commissioner has defined an entity to use CDR data when it 'handles and manages that data within its effective control', for example by accessing, reading and searching the data, making a decision base on it, passing it from one part of the entity to another, deriving data from it or de-identifying the data: Office of the Australian Information Commissioner (n. 20) [B.149].
25. *CDR Rules* (n. 2) r. 7.5. There are specific restrictions on the use of the CDR data for direct marketing: *ibid.*
26. *PSR* (n. 6) regs 70(3)(a), (f).
27. *Ibid.* r. 97.
28. *CDR Rules* (n. 2) r. 4.9.
29. *Ibid.* r. 4.10(1)(a).
30. *Ibid.* r. 4.10(1)(b).

- enable the customer to choose the types of CDR data to which the consent applies and the specific uses to which they are consenting,[31] and
- allow the customer to choose whether the consent applies to a single occasion or over a specified period of time.[32]

A consent expires if it is withdrawn, its period has expired or 12 months has passed since it was given.[33] Further, an accredited data recipient must only seek a consent in compliance with the data minimisation principle and must not seek a consent for the purpose of identifying, compiling insights on, or building a profile in relation to, any identifiable person who is not the CDR consumer who made the consumer data request.[34]

The requirements for consent under UK open banking are similar. As noted above, the consent is required to be 'explicit'.[35] In the view of the FCA, explicit consent under the *PSR* requires that the AISP:

> should make available to customers the information needed to make an informed decision and understand what they are consenting to (e.g., they must be able to understand the nature of the service being provided to them) and the consent should be clear and specific. For AISPs, aside from any requirements of data protection legislation, we consider this to include information about how the customer's payment account information will be used and whether any other parties will have access to that information.[36]

This means, for example, that the customer's consent must be obtained for any analytics to be performed on the information as part of an AIS. This use of the phrase 'explicit consent' causes some complication in the UK system because it does not have the same meaning as it does in *GDPR*.[37] In fact, under *GDPR*, the processing of personal data under UK open banking is not authorised on the basis of consent, but on the basis of it being 'necessary for the performance of a contract to which the data subject is party or in order to take steps at the request of the data subject prior to entering into a contract'.[38] This requires that an AISP needs to be able to demonstrate that the data being used is objectively necessary for its provision of the AIS.[39] It also requires that the contract with the payment service users makes them fully aware of the specific categories of data that will be used and the purpose to which they will be put.[40]

31. *Ibid.* r. 4.11(1)(a).
32. *Ibid.* r. 4.11(1)(b).
33. *Ibid.* r. 4.14.
34. *Ibid.* r. 4.12.
35. *PSR* (n. 6) reg. 70(3)(a).
36. Financial Conduct Authority, 'Payment Services and Electronic Money - Our Approach' (Approach Document, June 2019) [17.55].
37. *See* European Data Protection Board (n. 9). Explicit consent is required under *GDPR* only for personal data revealing racial or ethnic origin, political opinions, religious or philosophical beliefs, trade union membership as well as data concerning health or a person's sex life or sexual orientation, or genetic or biometric data: *GDPR* (n. 1) Art. 9.
38. European Data Protection Board (n. 9) 8. *See also GDPR* (n. 1) Art. 6(1)(b).
39. European Data Protection Board (n. 9) [19].
40. *Ibid.* [36].

The standards under each system provide further guidance on the form of consent. The Australian Standards require that the consent process should be easy to understand, each customer must be presented with an active choice to give consent, consent should be a genuine choice and should not be a precondition of service.[41] Further, for the purpose of understanding consents, statements as to the purpose and use of data should be specific, refer to the broader uses and relate to the goods or services provided.[42] Similarly, the UK Standards provide that 'an AISP must make it very clear why it's needed, what's being shared and for how long'.[43] This includes language for purpose statements, provision of enough information to make informed decisions, and use of the recommended structure and language.

This shows that the requirements for consent and its form are similar in each of Australian and UK open banking. Consent is needed under both, and it needs to be voluntary, express, specific, informed, and clear – more so than under the respective privacy laws.[44] This enhances the effectiveness of both systems in performing their accountability functions by ensuring that the data shared is appropriately used.

However, the reliance on consent by those privacy law regimes is subject to criticism, which needs to be analysed in the context of open banking.

### *(b) Response to Criticisms of Reliance on Consent*

In the context of privacy law, consent has been criticised as a method of authorising the processing of personal information and providing control to data subjects.[45] The reasons for this criticism include that the large quantity of information given to a person in order to obtain their informed consent places too much of a cognitive load on them for the consent to be truly informed,[46] it is often given on a 'non-negotiable, non-informed, and pressurized basis' which with the result that consent is 'largely theoretical and has no practical meaning'.[47]

The design of both the Australian and UK systems seeks to manage these shortcomings of consent through two features standardisation and consent management.

41. Data Standards Body, 'Consumer Experience Guidelines' (Guidelines, v 1.4.0 17 July 2020).
42. *Ibid.*
43. Open Banking Implementation Entity, 'Customer Experience Guidelines' (Standard, v3.1.10) https://standards.openbanking.org.uk.
44. Implied consent is permitted under the *Privacy Act* (n. 22) s. 6(1) (definition of 'consent') and explicit consent is required only for particular types of personal data under *GDPR*: *GDPR* (n. 1) Art. 9(2)(a).
45. *See* especially Koops (n. 17). 'It is remarkably easy to get consumers to consent to anything on the internet': Fracassi and Magnuson (n. 20).
46. *See* Yoan Hermstruwer, 'Contracting Around Privacy: The (Behavioral) Law and Economics of Consent and Big Data' (2017) 8 *Journal of Intellectual Property, Information Technology and Electronic Commerce Law* 9. *See also* Santiago Ramirez Lopez, 'Informing Consent' (2018) 9 *Journal of Intellectual Property, Information Technology and Electronic Commerce Law* 35.
47. Koops (n. 17) 251.

### *(i) Standardisation of Consent*

Each system seeks to standardise the consent process through the application of customer experience standards and guidelines based on consumer experience testing.[48] These are intended to create a consistent experience for customers in providing their consent, so that the process can become familiar regardless of the data recipient with whom they are dealing, and so that 'consent fatigue' can be reduced. This standardisation includes language used in describing the data which can be used and, in the UK, allocation of the data into 'clusters' which can be grouped together for better comprehension. It has been recommended that this standardisation is to be taken further in Australia, so that a 'CDR dictionary' is to be created for particular words to have standardised meanings and for those words to be drafted in a 'formulaic way' so that they could be more readily codified for use with data technologies.[49] Codification of consent so that it can be attached to data has also been recommended for UK open banking.

### *(ii) Consent Management*

Each system provides access to customers to the consents which they have provided, so that they can be understood, managed, and withdrawn. Consumer 'dashboards' are required to be provided by banks under both the Australian Standards and the UK Standards,[50] in Australian open banking (unlike UK open banking), they need to be provided by the recipient too.[51] It has also been recommended that this concept be taken further in the Australia to enable centralised consent management services to be offered to customers by providing for the customer's consents themselves to be sharable under the Australian system.[52]

It is too early to assess if these strategies for the management of the shortcomings of consent will be successful. A lot depends on the technologies being both effective and easily used by customers. If they are not successful, customers could become overwhelmed with the complexity of having to understand and manage the consents which they have provided for the use of their data. This would reduce the customers' ability to understand the use to which their data are being put, the value of the data

48. For Australia, *see* the 'consent flow': Data Standards Body, 'Consumer Experience Guidelines' (n. 41). For the UK, *see* the 'customer journey': Open Banking Implementation Entity, 'Customer Experience Guidelines' (n. 43).
49. Australian Treasury, 'Inquiry into Future Directions for Consumer Data Right: Giving Consumers Choice, Convenience and Confidence' (Report, October 2020) 133. *See also* Australian Treasury, 'Government Response to the Inquiry into Future Directions for the Consumer Data Right' (Report, December 2021) 23.
50. For Australia, *see* 'manage and withdraw': Data Standards Body, 'Consumer Experience Guidelines' (n. 41). For the UK, *see* 'AIS access dashboard and revocation': Open Banking Implementation Entity, 'Customer Experience Guidelines' (n. 43).
51. *CDR Rules* (n. 2) rr. 1.14-1.15.
52. Australian Treasury, 'Inquiry into Future Directions for the Consumer Data Right: Giving Consumers Choice, Convenience and Confidence' (n. 49) 142. *See* Australian Treasury, 'Government Response to the Inquiry into Future Directions for the Consumer Data Right' (Report, December 2021).

which they are sharing and, as a result, the 'price' which they are paying for the goods or services which they have requested. This would render the sharing of data less beneficial and less safe for customers and cause the reliance on consent to impair the functions performed by the open banking systems. To understand its functions further, the reliance on consent needs to be evaluated against customers' rights in controlling their funds.

### 7.2.2 Evaluation Against Customer Rights in Controlling Customer Funds

#### *(a) No Customer Control over Bank's Use of Funds*

As noted in the earlier part of this chapter, a customer does not control their bank's use of the funds received by the bank on the customer's behalf. Although a bank receives a funds transfer as its customer's agent, this does not grant control of the funds to the customer because the bank's authority in that agency is limited to receiving the payment and crediting the payment to the customer's account.[53] Once the funds are credited to the customer's account, the funds are owned by the bank as principal, not as trustee or agent, and the bank owes a debt to the customer for the amount credited to the customer's account.[54] The bank:

> is not bound to keep it or deal with it as the property of the customer, but he is, of course, answerable for the amount, because he has contracted, having received that money, to repay to the customer, when demanded, a sum equivalent to that paid into his hands.[55]

The right to repayment of that 'sum equivalent' represents the 'money' of the customer comprised in the balance of their bank account and the bank's responsibilities to its customer for the transferred funds are encompassed in its promise to repay that amount. The funds actually 'received' belong to the bank, may be dealt with by the bank as its own funds, and are not subject to the customer's control or consent.[56] This enables the bank to on-lend those funds, creating credit and generating value and benefit in the banking payment system.

Consequently, the requirement for consent represents a significant difference between open banking systems and banking payment systems. If a data recipient had the same freedom to use customer data as the bank does to use customer funds, then the open banking systems would be more like 'open data' arrangements, where the data are widely shareable with anyone. Neither Australian nor UK open banking has

53. For the UK *see Royal Products Ltd v. Midland Bank Ltd* [1981] 2 Lloyd's Rep. 194 ('*Royal Products v. Midland Bank*'); *The Laconia* [1976] 2 All ER 249 ('*The Laconia*'). For Australia *see ANZ Banking Group v. Westpac Banking Corporation* (1988) 78 ALR 157 ('*ANZ v. Westpac*'). *See* section 3.4.2(a) above.
54. For the UK *see Joachimson v. Swiss Bank Corporation* [1921] 3 KB 110 ('*Joachimson v. Swiss Bank Corporation*'); *Foley v. Hill* (n. 16). For Australia *see Laing v. Bank of NSW* (1952) 69 WN (NSW) 318 ('*Laing v. Bank of NSW*').
55. *Foley v. Hill* (n. 16) 36.
56. *Ibid.*

taken this approach and each only allows data to be shared when authorised by the customer.

As with data minimisation, there would be a significant adverse impact on the benefits provided by banking payment systems if a bank required the consent of its customer to use the funds which it receives for the customer. The bank could no longer lend or otherwise invest those funds as it chose and the bank's ability to create credit and generate gains using those funds, would be limited. It would also change the nature of the bank's business by placing the management of its assets into the control of individual customers. In doing so, it would likely threaten the bank's viability as its functions of liquidity transformation, maturity transformation and credit transformation need to be managed on a portfolio basis rather than on an individual asset and liability basis.

This would seem to support the argument that, when evaluated against banking payment systems, the requirement for consent in the open banking systems is a constraint on their effectiveness. However, just as with data minimisation, it is necessary to analyse whether there is a relevant difference between customer data and customer funds. In this case, the difference which justifies the use of consent is the subjectivity in the value of customer data.[57]

### *(b) Using Consent to Manage Subjectivity of Data's Value*

Although, as established in Chapter 2, customer data and customer funds are both types of information, the nature of the information and value is different. For customer funds, the information is the measure of the funds in the unit of account – for example, the balance is $100. Because of this measurement, the value of the customer funds is objectively ascertainable and an amount of money in one customer's account with a bank is fungible with the same amount of money in the same type of account of another customer with the same bank. This means that if the customer's funds are lost because of an unauthorised transaction on their account then the customer can be compensated by the payment of an amount equal to the value of the lost funds.[58]

As Chapter 1 explained, there is no precise way to value data or information, but two methods are through the potential gain from its use and the potential loss from its misuse. A customer should value their data because of the gain which their use could provide them (e.g., by identifying better products or services for them) and because of the loss which they could cause them (e.g., by enabling unauthorised transactions to be made on their account). However, a different customer may place no value on the first customer's data because their use will not provide them with any gain, and their misuse will not cause them any loss. The value of customer data is subjective, it differs depending on the subject's relationship to the information which the data can express. This subjectivity is why, for example, a customer cannot be compensated for a loss of their data by sharing another customer's data, or the bank's own data, with them.

57. Use-dependency of data's value is also a valid basis for consent. *See* Chapter 6.
58. Other amounts might also be payable such as interest.

This subjectivity in the value of customer data creates further asymmetry in the relationship between customer and recipient. Although the customer's data are valuable to them, they are not as valuable to the recipient. A recipient is not going to generate as much subjective value from the use of one customer's data as the customer could themselves. Instead, the recipient's economic gain from customer data is generated by the use of many customers' data at scale and no particular customer's data are likely to be significantly more valuable than any others. This imbalance does not arise with customers' money, where the objective value is the same to the bank and the customer.[59] On a purely economic basis, this means that a recipient has less economic incentive to take care of a particular customer's data than the customer would themselves. This represents an increased risk for the customer in the recipient's use of their data.

Requiring the customer's consent to the use of their data seeks to manage the risk of loss caused to the customer by the loss or misuse of their data. It is needed because there is no easy way to compensate a customer for the loss of their data and also because the data are not as objectively valuable to the recipient as they are to the customer. Requiring consent seeks to impose control on the recipient to manage this risk and to make sharing the data safer. Without that control, the customer's position would be similar to its bank being permitted to make withdrawals or transfers from the customer's account without the customer's permission.[60] Accordingly, the reliance on consent should not be considered a flaw in open banking's design when evaluated against banking payment systems but a feature which is intended to improve the risk management in the data sharing. In doing so, it enhances the effectiveness of the systems in performing their accountability function by enabling the data which are shared to be appropriately used.

However, as with data minimisation, the benefits of using consent in open banking rely on compliance by the recipient with the responsibilities imposed. Under both Australian and UK open banking, customers take risk on the performance by the recipient of its obligations. The consent management mechanisms considered above assist in providing some transparency, but they are unable to ensure compliance. The risks which arise from this are analysed further in the next part.

59. It could be that a bank does not care as much about a particular some of money as a customer, because of the difference between the amount of money that each has but this is not a difference in the valuation of the money itself.
60. This would be contrary to the bank's mandate. Arguably, the information on the balance of their account is a better analogy to customer data than the funds actually received by the bank. Once the customer's funds are received by the bank, the customer's value is in the 'sum equivalent' recorded in their bank account. On this argument, the requirement for consent to use customer data is aligned with the requirement for consent to change the balance of the customer's account.

## 7.3 HOW CAN LEGAL FOUNDATIONS SUPPORT UTILISING SHARED DATA?

### 7.3.1 Summary of Comparison and Evaluation

This chapter has examined the implications of the legal foundations of Australian and UK open banking for governing the use of shared customer data through a comparison of their legal features relating to limitations on data requests and how shared data can be used, and an evaluation against equivalent legal features of banking payment systems.

It has shown that although the data minimisation principle is framed differently in each of the Australian and UK systems, in practice, the difference should not be meaningful for their effectiveness in performing their accountability functions. It has also shown that although data minimisation would reduce the benefit for customers and banks if it were imposed on customer funds in a banking payment system, its use in open banking systems is justified because it addresses the information asymmetry which would otherwise be present relating to how the customer's data are to be used.

The chapter has also shown that the requirement for consent is similar in each of Australian and UK open banking and that this supports the effectiveness of the systems in performing their accountability function. Although there are criticisms of the use of consent in privacy laws, each system has incorporated features intended to address these issues. The analysis has also shown that there is no similar requirement imposed on a bank to obtain their customer's consent for the bank's use of their customer's funds, but this difference is justified by the subjective nature of the value of customer data. For this reason, the requirement for consent is needed to balance an asymmetry between the customer and recipient which would otherwise potentially decrease the fairness of the data sharing.

The consequence is that the legal foundations of both Australian and UK open banking support accountability to an extent beyond that provided in banking payment systems because of the controls placed on shared data's use by consent. However, their support for autonomy is weaker than that provided in banking payment systems, due to the constraints on sharing of data created by data minimisation. This is illustrated in Figure 7.1.

*Figure 7.1 Illustration of Evaluation and Comparison Relating to Utilisation of Shared Data*

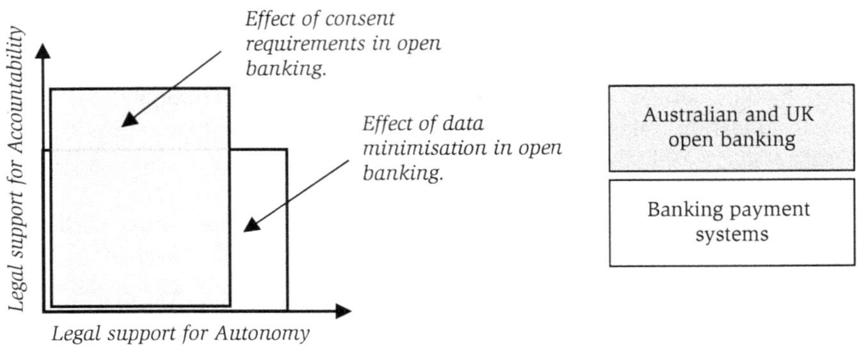


The analysis demonstrates the need to balance accountability and autonomy in designing the legal foundations for utilising shared customer data. It also demonstrates the reliance placed on the recipient to comply with its data-related compliance obligations, and the importance of managing performance risk. This risk is explained next, followed by an illustration of the comparable credit risk in banking payment systems, and a discussion of the how credit risk management methods could be applied in the legal design of open banking systems.

### 7.3.2 Performance Risk in Open Banking Systems

Performance risk arises in open banking when participants do not perform their obligations under an open banking system. An element of performance risk is inherent in open banking. As noted above, an open banking system relies on the compliance by the recipient with the constraints of data minimisation and of the customer's consent, as well as other obligations explained in later chapters. This results in customers taking risk on the recipient's non-compliance. A critical element in understanding this risk is its duration. Although data are often referred to as being 'consumed', due to their non-rivalrous nature they remain in the custody of the recipient with whom they have been shared after they have been used and they cannot be 'repaid' like money. Accordingly a customer has no way of verifying the ultimate performance of its obligations of the recipient of their data and remains exposed to the risk on its performance.

The consequence of this performance risk is that the customer needs to trust in the performance by the recipient of its obligations. This is complicated by difficulties in customers being able to verify that participants are worthy of that trust through their performance only after their trust has been conferred. To assist in establishing trustworthiness, open banking systems impose authorisation requirements, explained in Chapter 9.

However, the impact of performance risk is not limited to the relationships between a customer and its recipient. As explained in Chapter 4, a failure of a recipient to meet the trust placed in it could affect other recipients too. If it emerged that a significant recipient had failed to perform, then other recipients would find it difficult to prove to their customers that they too have not breached their obligations where there is insufficient transparency as to whether their obligations are discharged. This would cause the trust and confidence of customers in the system, its participants and regulators to fail and a reduction in the use of the system to share data. A collapse in confidence in an open banking system could happen rapidly if a large recipient were to fail to perform its obligations. This is considered further in Chapter 11.

To further explain this aspect of performance risk, the next section sets out an illustration of the comparable risk in banking payment systems, *credit risk*.

### 7.3.3 Illustration of Credit Risks in Banking Payment Systems: Bankhaus Herstatt

Credit risk in banking payment systems is:

> the risk that a party within the system will be unable fully to meet financial obligations within the system either when due or at any time in the future.[61]

Banks make promises to pay funds to customers to be performed at a later time and, as a result, customers take risk on the credit of the bank in performing those obligations. Banks also build up credit risk in banking payment systems when they hold claims on each other due to their customers' transactions which are not yet settled.

The consequences of credit risk created by the timing of obligations is shown by aspects of the failure in 1974 of Bankhaus Herstatt ('Herstatt'), a relatively small German private bank active in the foreign exchange (FX) market.[62] Due to significant losses incurred in forward FX contracts, on the afternoon of 26 June 1974 (Frankfurt time) the banking licence of Herstatt was withdrawn and Herstatt's New York correspondent bank suspended outgoing payments from Herstatt's account. Critically, the timing was such that the German interbank system was closed, but the payment system in the US had just opened. The result of the time difference was that counterparties to Herstatt under were 'caught between two sides' of FX transactions, having made payments to Herstatt in Frankfurt in Deutsche Marks but not having received payments from Herstatt in New York in United States dollars under the same transactions. The resulting credit risk which causes one party to take principal risk on the other due to different timing of their obligations, became known as 'Herstatt risk':

61. Committee on Payment and Settlement Systems, 'Core Principles for Systemically Important Payment Systems' (Core Principles, Bank for International Settlements, January 2001) 5.
62. Committee on Payment and Settlement Systems, 'Settlement Risk in Foreign Exchange Transactions' (Report, Bank for International Settlements, March 1996) [2.2.1].

> Bankhaus Herstatt's closure was the first and most dramatic case of a bank failure where incomplete settlement of foreign exchange transactions caused severe problems in payment and settlement systems.[63]

The consequences of Herstatt's default were particularly significant because of the mistrust it caused between banks, causing a 60% fall in interbank payments and a significant increase in interbank interest rates. It led to court cases in the United Kingdom,[64] and the United States,[65] and resulted in changes in the rules of the relevant US payment system. It also led to the creation of three fundamental components of the international banking payments infrastructure: the BCBS at the BIS, to address the gaps in supervisory oversight for international banks, the Continuous Linked Settlement (CLS) Bank, which enables the different legs of FX transactions to be settled simultaneously, and legislation which ensures settlement finality in critical payment and security systems.

The failure of Herstatt is illustrative as to the potential consequences of performance risk in open banking. Whilst the period during which credit risk was being taken on Herstatt was short (within a single day), its failure to perform during that period exposed a weakness in risk management which had disastrous consequences. Similarly, the delay between when a recipient is required to perform its obligations and when customers become aware of a failure to perform could have significant consequences for an open banking system if the recipient has a large number of customers. Like obligations to make payments in a foreign currency, data-related performance obligations cannot be discharged simply by payment in an amount of domestic currency. However, unlike obligations to make payments in a foreign currency, data-related performance obligations cannot be discharged simply by performance of the unperformed obligation, as damage may have already been caused to the customer by the misuse of the data. Accordingly, the legal features used in banking payment systems to manage credit risk deserve consideration for incorporation into the legal foundations of open banking.

### 7.3.4 Incorporating Credit Risk Management Features into Open Banking

The need to manage credit risk is a key foundation of the regulation of banking payment systems. However, some of the primary methods rely on money's fungibility and objective value. For example, the payment of amounts which are due can be verified, the obligation to pay can be collateralised by other amounts of the same value, and the payment obligations between parties can be simplified by clearing and settlement. As data are neither fungible nor have an objective value, the customer has no way of verifying that the recipient has 'finally settled' its obligations and there is no

63. Gabriele Galati, 'Settlement Risk In Foreign Exchange Markets and CLS Bank' (2002) 4 *BIS Quarterly Review* 55-65, 55.
64. *Momm and Others v. Barclays Bank International Ltd.* [1977] QB 790 ('*Momm v. Barclays Bank*').
65. *Delbrueck & Co v. Manufacturers Hanover Trust Co*, 609 F 2d 1047 (1979) ('*Delbrueck & Co v. Manufacturers Hanover Trust Co*').

'settlement asset' which can be delivered to the customer which will discharge the risk being taken, these approaches cannot be adopted in open banking. Other methods of managing credit risk rely on changing the time or means of settling the obligations so that they can be discharged together. This too is not an available option for open banking systems unless data are deleted after their first use.

Nevertheless, other aspects of the management of credit risk in banking payment systems could be adapted to manage the performance risks in open banking systems. First, participants could be required to monitor and report the level of performance obligations which they are incurring, similar in concept (but not method) to how credit risk is monitored in banking payment systems.[66] This would allow regulators to determine how much risk is being taken, particularly if a participant is showing signs of non-compliance.[67] Second, compensation should be available for customers who have suffered loss because of the failure of their recipient to perform, as explained in Chapter 10. Third, the development of technological means of enabling performance to be verified should be encouraged, so that a function comparable to that of a settlement asset can be performed. One aspect of this is to standardise the nature of the legal obligations being incurred so that they can be incorporated into technological processes. Another is enabling the data shared to be technologically traced in a way which verifies performance. There is potential for this process to be assisted by tokenisation, so as to render the open banking system more like a payment system based on transferrable stores of value rather than the maintenance of accounts. Whilst these might not be possible to implement in the short term, any increase in transparency which they could provide would support the trust placed in the participants in the system by customers. If steps such as these are not taken to manage this performance risk, then the system's design might not only impair its effectiveness in performing its accountability function, but it could damage its credibility.

66. *See* Committee on Payment and Settlement Systems and International Organization of Securities Commissions, 'Principles for Financial Markets Infrastructures' (Standards, Bank for International Settlements, April 2012).
67. This concept is not dissimilar to the monitoring of credit risk taken by a clearing house in relation to its open positions, *see ibid.* 42.

## CHAPTER 8
# Preserving Value of Shared Customer Data

This chapter examines the legal foundations for the preservation of the value of customer data shared under open banking systems. It compares the legal responsibilities supporting that value under Australian and UK open banking and evaluates them against the equivalent legal responsibilities under banking payment systems. This analysis addresses two questions:

- How should the quality of shared data be maintained?
- How should the security of shared data be managed?

The answers to these questions are fundamental to an open banking system's performance of its *accountability* and *autonomy* functions.

### 8.1 HOW SHOULD QUALITY OF SHARED DATA BE MANAGED?

The value of data is dependent on its quality. For information to have value:

> it must have some features that are value-adding and value-preserving, such as timeliness, relevance, and updateness. Nobody pays for yesterday's newspaper or the wrong kind of information. Such features go under the general term of information quality.[1]

Similarly, the quality of customer data is fundamental to the effectiveness of open banking. The use of incorrect customer data in relation to the customer's funds, expenditure, or income, would produce incorrect results potentially both negating the benefits of sharing that data and causing significant loss to the customer or others who rely on the data.

The legal responsibilities for three key features of data quality, the accuracy, deletion, and de-identification of the shared data, are comparatively analysed below

1. Luciano Floridi, *Information: A Very Short Introduction* (Oxford University Press, 2010) 90.

and followed by an evaluation against the legal responsibilities for the integrity of account information and the bank's obligation to repay in banking payment systems.

### 8.1.1 Comparison of Data Integrity in the Open Banking Systems

#### *(a) Accuracy of Data*

The responsibilities in Australian open banking for the accuracy of CDR data are found in the requirement in the privacy safeguards to take reasonable steps to ensure that the data are 'accurate, up to date and complete' having regard to the purpose for which they are held.[2] This obligation applies to both banks and recipients each time that they are required or authorised to disclose the CDR data under the *CDR Rules*.[3] What steps are reasonable are determined having regard to the nature of the entity (including its size, resources and complexity of its operations), the sensitivity of the CDR data and adverse consequences to the consumer and the practicability of taking action, including time and cost involved.[4] 'In some circumstances, it will be reasonable for an accredited data recipient to take no steps to ensure the quality of CDR data', the OAIC has noted, '[f]or example, where an accredited data recipient collects CDR data from a data holder known to be reliable'.[5] The result is that recipients have only a limited legal responsibility for the accuracy of a customer's CDR data, as the obligation arises only if they are required or authorised to share the data and, in any case, it should be reasonable for the recipient to rely on the correctness of the data. However, if either a bank or a recipient becomes aware that data which it has disclosed were incorrect when they disclosed the data, because they were not accurate, up to date and complete at that time, then they must notify the CDR consumer.[6] The CDR consumer can then request that the data be corrected,[7] and that the corrected data be disclosed to the recipient of the earlier disclosure.[8]

*GDPR* contains the equivalent obligations of accuracy for UK open banking, requiring that personal data are:

> accurate and, where necessary, kept up to date; every reasonable step must be taken to ensure that personal data that are inaccurate, having regard to the purposes for which they are processed, are erased or rectified without delay.[9]

---

2. *Competition and Consumer Act 2010* (Cth) ('*CCA*') s. 56EN.
3. *Ibid.* s. 56EN(1), (2).
4. Office of the Australian Information Commissioner, 'Consumer Data Right Privacy Safeguard Guidelines' (Guidelines, July 2020) [11.31].
5. *Ibid.* [11.32].
6. *CCA* (n. 2) s. 56EN(3).
7. *Ibid.* s. 56EP. The *CDR Rules* require that the data be corrected at no charge: *Competition and Consumer (Consumer Data Right) Rules 2020* ('*CDR Rules*') rr. 7.14, 7.15.
8. The *CDR Rules* set out notice requirements to the CDR consumer: *ibid.* r. 7.10.
9. *Regulation (EU) 2016/679 of the European Parliament and of the Council of 27 April 2016 on the Protection Of Natural Persons with regard to the Processing Of Personal Data and on the Free Movement of such Data, and repealing Directive 95/46/EC (General Data Protection Regulation)* OJ L119/1 ('*GDPR*') Art. 5(1)(d).

This is combined with a right for a person to rectify 'without undue delay' inaccurate personal data concerning them and to complete such data which are incomplete.[10] Unlike the equivalent principles in the Australian system, this is not specific to the time of disclosure and instead is dependent on the purpose for which the data are being used. For example, if they are being used for a purpose that relies on the data being current, then the data should be kept up to date, particularly if the information could have serious implications for an individual.[11] The reasonable steps are not prescribed as they depend on the purpose for which the data will be used and the significance to an individual of the decisions made using the data.[12] However, it is recognised that it can be impractical to check the accuracy of information which someone else provides and that it is reasonable to assume the accuracy of information provided by a source which is known to be reliable or 'a well-known organisation', unless inaccuracy could have serious consequences or 'if common sense suggests there may be a mistake'.[13]

This comparison shows that the legal responsibilities for accuracy of shared data are similar in both Australian and UK open banking, although they only apply to personal data under the UK system because of the limitation in the scope of *GDPR*. Under each, a data recipient should have no responsibility to independently verify the correctness of the customer data received from a bank if they have no reason to suspect it is not correct. Also, under each system the recipient's responsibility is to take 'reasonable steps' to ensure accuracy, rather than guaranteeing correctness. This is justifiable because, as a matter of practice, the recipient is not in a position to verify the accuracy of the customer data transferred to it from the customer's bank – the bank is in the best position, and it owes the obligation to ensure accuracy at the time that it shares the customer data with the recipient.

However, the customer is also in a position to verify the correctness of the customer data. Whilst each of Australian and UK open banking enables a customer to correct their customer data, it is important that there are transparency mechanisms which permit the customer to do so. As noted in Chapter 6, neither framework currently enables the customer to request the customer data be shared with themselves in the form in which it is shared with others. Although, whilst each system requires that 'dashboards' are made available to the customer, these provide transparency on the consents granted, not the information to which they relate. That being said, the privacy safeguards in Australian open banking require a data recipient to have a policy on how a customer can access their data and seek their correction,[14] and *GDPR* grants individual customers the right to access their personal data.[15] However, it is not clear how the customer will exercise their right to correct the customer data in the Australian

10. *Ibid.* Art. 16. The term 'inaccurate' is not defined in GDPR but is taken to mean incorrect or misleading as to any matter or fact: Information Commissioner's Office, 'Guide to the General Data Protection Regulation' (Guide, 1 January 2021) 33.
11. *Ibid.* 36.
12. *Ibid.* 37.
13. *Ibid.*
14. *CCA* (n. 2) s. 56ED(5)(c).
15. *GDPR* (n. 9) Art. 15.

system or how a business customer under the UK system can do so. This lack of clarity is not helpful to customers and for as long as customers cannot make their own requests for customer data, it represents a constraint on the ability of the shared data to be appropriately used and the accountability performed by the systems.

### *(b) Deletion of Redundant Data*

The quality of data is impacted by the redundancy of the data as well as its accuracy. This is because '[m]ost data loses some of its utility over time. In such circumstances, continuing to rely on old data doesn't just fail to add value; it actually destroys the value of fresher data'.[16] Accordingly, it is important to analyse how redundant data are removed from each system as the use of redundant data impairs their effectiveness.

In Australian open banking, if an accredited data recipient is holding CDR data which it no longer needs for the purpose permitted under the *CDR Rules* or the *CCA* (defined as 'redundant data'), then it is required to take the steps set out in the *CDR Rules* to destroy or de-identify that data.[17] Redundant data includes CDR data for which the consent to their use has expired.[18] The *CDR Rules* set out a 'CDR data deletion process' which requires that a person deletes the CDR data and any copies of it, to the extent reasonably practical and direct any other person to whom the person has disclosed the CDR data to also do so.[19] If deletion is not possible, for example, because irretrievable destruction from backup systems is not achievable, then it is sufficient for the data to be put 'beyond use' such that the accredited data recipient is not able to use or disclose the CDR data, cannot give any other entity access to the CDR data, surrounds the CDR data with appropriate technical, physical and organisational security and commits to reasonable steps to 'irretrievably destroy' CDR data when it becomes possible.[20]

*GDPR* also sets out a right to erasure of personal data, which can also apply to personal data shared under UK open banking. This requires the recipient to erase the customer's personal data 'without undue delay' if, most relevantly, the data are 'no longer necessary in relation to the purposes for which they were collected or otherwise processed'.[21] The *GDPR* process also applies to all backup systems which record those data. Similarly, where deletion in the backup systems takes time (because, for example, it needs to be overwritten by new data) the data must be put 'beyond use' and

16. Viktor Mayer-Schönberger and Kenneth Cukier, *Big Data: The Essential Guide to Work, Life and Learning in the Age of Insight* (John Murray, 2nd ed., 2017) 112. *See also* Gianclaudio Malgieri and Bart Custers, 'Pricing Privacy: The Right to Know the Value of Your Personal Data' (2018) 34(2) *Computer Law & Security Review* 289.
17. *CCA* (n. 2) s. 56EO(2).
18. Office of the Australian Information Commissioner (n. 4) [12.78].
19. *CDR Rules* (n. 7) r. 1.18. In determining what is reasonably practical, the amount of CDR data, the nature of the accredited data recipient and its information handling practices, the possible adverse consequences for a consumer and the practicability, including the time and cost involved, are all to be taken into account: Office of the Australian Information Commissioner (n. 20) [12.105].
20. Office of the Australian Information Commissioner (n. 4) [12.107].
21. *GDPR* (n. 9) Art. 17(1)(a).

not used for any other purpose.[22] Because *GDPR* is limited to personal data, the right of erasure does not apply to business account data under the UK system. The requirements of *PSR* still apply and, as analysed in Chapter 7, the data are not able to be used for any other purpose, even though there is no right to require deletion. However, the risk profile of business customers whose data has been deleted and whose data has not been deleted are not the same, even if the retained data cannot be used by the holder. Retained data can still be the subject of unauthorised disclosure, as cyber-attacks on holders of large historical data sets have shown.

### *(c) De-identification of Data*

Other than the limited application of deletion obligations in the UK system to personal data, because of its reliance on *GDPR*, the requirements for deletion of redundant data are broadly comparable under each framework. Where they differ is in the ability to de-identify and reuse redundant data. The *CDR Rules* set out a 'CDR data de-identification process' which enables a de-identification technique to be used on redundant data instead of deletion.[23] This can be used by a data recipient if it ensures that no person is any longer identifiable, or reasonably identifiable, from the data after de-identification taking into account any other information held by any other person.[24] Additionally, the CDR consumer needs to have consented to de-identification, the accredited person must have given the CDR consumer a statement of further information on de-identification, the CDR consumer must not have elected for the CDR data to be deleted and the accredited person must think it appropriate in the circumstances to de-identify rather than delete the CDR Data.[25] Redundant data which has been de-identified in accordance with this process may be disclosed to any person, including by sale.[26]

Whilst a similar concept exists under *GDPR* in that it ceases to apply to personal data which have been rendered anonymous in such a way that the data subject is no longer identifiable,[27] the *PSR* does not permit the information shared to be anonymised for use for another purpose. Also, although *GDPR* sets out conditions for the processing of personal data for purposes other than for which they have been collected,[28] such as where the customer has given their consent or where the processing is compatible with the initial purpose, these are not applicable to data shared under UK open banking.[29]

22. Information Commissioner's Office (n. 10).
23. *CDR Rules* (n. 7) r. 1.17.
24. *Ibid.* 1.17(2).
25. *Ibid.* rr. 4.11, 4.15-4.17, 7.12.
26. *Ibid.* r. 7.5(1).
27. Information Commissioners Office, 'Anonymisation: Managing Data Protection Risk Code of Practice' (Code of practice, November 2012).
28. *GDPR* (n. 9) Art. 6.
29. The European Data Protection Board (EDPB) has stated that, based on particular wording of *PSD2*, further use with consent, but not compatibility with initial purpose, is applicable to data received under *PSD2*: European Data Protection Board (n. 9) [22]. However, the wording relied on by the EDPB, 'in accordance with the data protection rules' in *PSD2* Art. 67(2)(f), is not included in *PSR* reg. 70(3)(f). Accordingly, the information received under the UK system cannot

Accordingly, the reuse of redundant data is not facilitated under the UK system, even if anonymised.

The ability to de-identify and reuse shared data represents a potentially significant difference between Australian and UK open banking. Following the analysis in Chapter 2, the ability to reuse information increases its value and 'data's full value is much greater than the value from its first use'.[30] One way in which this increase in value occurs is through combining the data with other data sets, to produce insights not otherwise available. From an economic perspective, the option to reuse customer data is accretive in their value, and 'the data's worth is the sum of these choices'.[31] Accordingly, the inclusion of the ability to reuse customer data increases the potential benefits of the Australian system.[32]

However, the conditions for exercising the right to de-identify and reuse data under Australian open banking are not easily met. The requirement that is most difficult to meet is that 'no person would any longer be identifiable, or reasonably identifiable, from ... other information that would be held, following the completion of the de-identification process, by *any person*'.[33] This implies no risk of re-identification assuming an 'open release environment' even if open release is not intended.[34] It is doubtful that this standard can be currently met as a technological matter, particularly as OAIC and Data61 (part of the Australian government's national science agency) have previously stated that 'after de-identification, risk is still generally not zero'.[35] As a result, 'there is significant complexity and risk involved with attempting to de-identify unit record data derived from CDR data to the "required extent" as defined in the CDR Rules'.[36] Accordingly, it should not be expected that any significant benefits derived from de-identification under Australian open banking will be available unless further clarity is provided of what standard of de-identification is needed,[37] and the technical possibility of de-identification is currently not a meaningful difference between the frameworks. Nevertheless, the standard for de-identification to reuse customer data in the open banking systems should not be more restrictive than under privacy laws. Otherwise this could result in regulatory arbitrage with recipients preferring to collect data outside the open banking systems so that the data can be more

be used for any other purpose. Also *see* Financial Conduct Authority, 'Payment Services and Electronic Money – Our Approach' (Approach Document, June 2019) 222.

30. Mayer-Schönberger and Cukier (n. 16) 104.
31. *Ibid.* 105.
32. Although this is not likely to directly benefit the relevant customer.
33. *CDR Rules* (n. 7) r. 1.17 (emphasis added).
34. Office of the Australian Information Commissioner (n. 4) [12.96].
35. Office of the Australian Information Commissioner and Data 61, 'The De-Identification Decision-Making Framework' (Guidance, 18 September 2017) ix. The complexity of this issue is increased in that the *CDR Rules* require that a data-recipient has regard to this framework in making its determination that there is no risk of re-identification: *CDR Rules* (n. 7) r. 1.17(2)(a).
36. Office of the Australian Information Commissioner (n. 4) 12.99. In an earlier (October 2019) draft of these guidelines, the OAIC was even more negative, stating that 'even if some CDR data is able to be sufficiently de-identified to this required extent, the utility of that data for many intended uses would likely be compromised.'
37. The ACCC has further recommended that a data standard be produced for de-identification: Explanatory Statement, Competition and Consumer (Consumer Data Right) Rules 2020 (Cth) 10 ('CDR Rules Explanatory Statement') [59].

easily used.[38] This would deprive customers of the other benefits and protections of the open banking systems.

### 8.1.2 Evaluation Against Customer Rights in Bank Accounts

#### *(a) Nature of Responsibility for Account Information*

The promise of 'storage' of value is at the foundation of banks' relationships with their customers and, as the customer's funds are represented by the credit balance owing by the bank on their customer accounts, this is provided through the integrity of the records of those accounts. The account which represents that record is the core of the banker – customer relationship.[39] Although the method used to share this information with customers has changed over time, from passbook, to bank statements, to electronic access to bank accounts, customers have been granted an ability to rely on the correctness of the bank's records in good faith, even if the account had been over-credited by mistake.[40] Further, a bank customer has no implied duty to check bank statements relating to the customer's account, or notify the bank of any errors or unauthorised transactions.[41] Unauthorised changes to the customer's account are dealt with as a matter of the core functions and duties of a bank, and not as a failure of operational requirements.[42] This demonstrates that the bank's responsibility to ensure the integrity of the information constituting the customer's account is clear, unconditional and direct.

This is not the same under open banking. As the previous section shows, a recipient has little real responsibility to maintain accuracy of the shared data. It could be argued that this represents a weakness in open banking's design due to the importance of accuracy to the value of that data. It would follow from this argument that the data recipient should be responsible to the customer for the quality of the

38. For example, by reverting to screen scraping where that is permitted. Also, it provides an advantage to ADIs who can, for particular customer data which they receive under the Australian system, be treated as being subject to the *Privacy Act* rather than the *CCA* see section 7.1.1(b) above.
39. *See Hart v. Sangster* [1957] 1 Ch. 337 ('*Hart v. Sangster* '); *Ladbroke & Co v. Todd* [1914-15] All ER Rep 1134 ('*Ladbroke & Co v. Todd*').
40. *See* Gregory Burton et al., *The Law Relating to Banker and Customer in Australia* (Thomson Reuters, 2022) [3.840].
41. *See Tai Hing Cotton Mill Ltd v. Liu Chong Hing Bank Ltd* [1986] AC 80 ('*Tai Hing*'). This allows the customer to honestly take the benefit of an error in their account (such as an erroneous credit entry) if the customer alters their position in reliance on the entry in good faith: *See Holland v. Manchester and Liverpool District Banking Co Ltd* (1909) 25 TLR 386 ('*Holland v. Manchester and Liverpool District Banking Co Ltd*'); *Lloyds Bank Ltd. v. Brooks* (1950) 6 LDAB 161 ('*Lloyds Bank Ltd. v. Brooks*'). However, it does not permit a customer to knowingly take advantage of an error: *ibid.* 165.
42. For example, the case of *British and North European Bank v. Zalzstein* concerned the unauthorised amendment of the bank's customer's passbook to change the amount owing by bank to customer. Although this was a case of unauthorised alteration of information records, is was dealt with on the basis of the rights between bank and customer to recover funds: *British and North European Bank Ltd v. Zalzstein* [1927] 2 KB 91 ('*British and North European Bank Ltd v. Zalzstein*').

customer's account information in the same unqualified way that a bank is responsible for the integrity of the customer's account. However, this argument does not consider the difference in the legal relationship which each of the bank and recipient have with the customer account information as custodian for it.

- *For the bank*, the information measures and defines its obligation to repay the amount received on behalf of the customer. Its content, and as a result its accuracy, is fundamental to the bank's legal obligations.
- *For the recipient*, the information is something valuable which has been shared with it by the customer to be used for a particular purpose. The information's content is why it is valuable, but the recipient's obligations are not defined by that content. The responsibilities of the recipient to the customer are unchanged by the meaning of the information shared with it.

In banking payment systems, customer account information defines a bank's obligations with respect to customer funds, whilst in open banking systems customer account information is the subject of the recipient's obligations with respect to customer data. From a banking law perspective, the difference in obligation is similar to that which a bank would owe under a debenture which it issued to a customer, and the obligation which the bank would owe in respect of a debenture issued by someone else which it held in safe custody for a customer. Whilst the bank's obligations under its debenture are clear and direct, the bank does not have unqualified responsibility for any loss of value of what it holds in safe custody, as its liability is based in either negligence or conversion.[43] Consequently, it does not follow that the same unqualified obligation owed by the bank to maintain the correctness of the customer account records needs to be imposed on the recipient and instead the bank's safe custody obligations when it holds customer property are a better benchmark. Further, given that the recipient would find it nearly impossible to discharge that obligation, it would not enhance the efficacy of open banking to do so. For these reasons, the absence of an equivalent clear and direct obligation to ensure the information's integrity should not be regarded as a flaw in open banking's design when evaluated against banking payment systems.

### *(b) Comparing Repayment of Funds and Deletion of Data*

The most fundamental of a bank's responsibilities to its customer is to repay the amount of the customer's funds. The contract between bank and customer includes 'the promise to repay [the funds] ... at the branch of the bank where the account is kept' and 'a promise to repay any part of the amount due against the written order of the customer'.[44] Although repayment by the bank of the amount demanded by the customer is made from the bank's own funds rather than the actual funds received for

43. *See* John Odgers, *Paget's Law of Banking* (LexisNexis, 15th ed., 2018) Ch. 7.
44. *Joachimson v. Swiss Bank Corporation* [1921] 3 KB 110 ('*Joachimson v. Swiss Bank Corporation*') 127.

the customer, its effect is to reduce the bank's ability to use funds of an amount equal to those originally received. Repayment discharges the bank's responsibilities to the customer for those funds and discharges the bank's obligation to repay them.

Transfer of the data back to the customer by the recipient does not discharge the data recipient's obligations in the same way. As the analysis in Chapter 2 showed, data are non-rivalrous, meaning that both the bank and the customer can use and share the customer data at the same time. Accordingly, the transfer of the data back to the customer does not prevent the recipient's further use of the data. Instead, to prevent the recipient's use, the recipient must delete all of its copies of the data.

In one sense, the position of the customer in relation to the repayment of their funds is similar to the customer's position in relation to the deletion of their data. In both circumstances, the customer is exposed to risk of non-performance by the bank or recipient. However, the risk taken by a customer with respect to their funds lasts only until they are repaid.[45] This payment settles the bank's obligations because the client accepts the funds as a 'settlement asset', and the repayment can be verified by the customer by their receipt of the amount of their funds. As Chapter 7 explained, there is no equivalent in open banking as there is no settlement asset which the customer can accept in discharge of the recipient's obligations. Although the risk taken by a customer with respect to their data also should only last until they can verify that it has been deleted, the customer has no way of making that verification unless the recipient's systems are audited, and neither open banking system requires this to occur. Accordingly, the customer takes ongoing risk that the recipient has in fact performed its obligations and is not continuing to use, replicate and share the customer's data without the customer's knowledge. Non-compliance by the recipient could result in the customer's banking information being improperly used and, if at scale, could significantly impair the credibility of the system. This is a key difference between open banking systems and banking payment systems. Of itself, it is not a flaw in the design of open banking, as it is a direct consequence of the difference between customer data and customer funds. However, the absence of the verification mechanism required to manage the consequence of that difference should be regarded as an issue for the legal support provided for the systems' performance of their accountability functions when evaluated against banking payment systems.

## 8.2 HOW SHOULD THE SECURITY OF SHARED DATA BE MAINTAINED?

The security of data is fundamental to banking payment systems:

> A cyber-attack involving a breach of data integrity in the financial system could have the most severe financial stability implications. For example, an attack that had implications for the integrity of banks' record of their assets and liabilities could impede their ability to disburse funds to customers or collect on monies due.

45. Assuming that no insolvency-related 'clawback' provisions (such as those related to unfair preferences) subsequently applies.

> In the extreme, it could raise questions about the institution's solvency status. This could force directors to withdraw the bank from trading while investors may pull back on capital market funding.[46]

Similarly, the security of customer data is fundamental to the efficacy of open banking systems. If customer data is altered such that it no longer provides accurate information on the customer's accounts, then sharing it is rendered pointless, and potentially harmful to the customer. Also, just as in banking payment systems, a wide-ranging cyber-attack could impair the credibility of the open banking system as a whole. The legal responsibilities for two key features of data security, the information security protections of the shared data, and the treatment of shared data on participant departure are comparatively analysed below followed by an evaluation against the legal responsibilities for the information security of account information and the protection of customer value in participant withdrawal from banking payment systems.

### 8.2.1 Comparison of Data Security in the Open Banking Systems

#### *(a) Information Security Responsibilities*

Under Australian open banking, in order to be accredited, a data recipient must take prescribed steps to protect CDR data from misuse, interference and loss, unauthorised access, modification and disclosure.[47] The steps are operational in nature: to define and implement security governance, define the boundaries of the CDR data environment, have and maintain an information security capability, implement a formal controls assessment program and have plans to manage and report security incidents.[48] The *CDR Rules* also require there to be Australian Standards about the security of CDR data,[49] and the Australian Standards contain specific security profiles which are required to be met.[50]

---

46. Reserve Bank of Australia, 'Financial Stability Review' (Report, October 2018) 57.
47. *CCA* (n. 2) s. 56EO(1). This obligation is repeated in the *CDR Rules*: *CDR Rules* (n. 7) 5.12(1)(a). Whilst these terms are not defined, the OAIC gives them a comprehensive meaning, including the use of CDR data for a purpose not permitted by the CDR; attacks on CDR data that interferes with them but does not modify their content; the accidental or inadvertent loss of the CDR data where they are no longer accessible or useable for their purpose; access by someone who is not permitted to do so; the alteration of CDR data in a way which is not permitted; and where an accredited data recipient makes CDR data accessible to others outside the entity: Office of the Australian Information Commissioner (n. 4) [12.17].
48. *CDR Rules* (n. 7) r. 7.11, sch. 2. Similarly, the 'minimum information security controls' needed for the required information security capability are procedural – the data recipient must have processes in place to limit the risk of inappropriate or unauthorised access, take steps to secure their network and systems and to limit prevent and remove malware, implement formal programs on vulnerability management and information security training and 'securely manage' their information assets: *ibid.* sch. 2 pt 2.
49. *Ibid.* r. 8.11.
50. The 'Financial Grade API (FAPI) Profile' and the 'Client Initiated Backchannel Authentication Flow (CIBA) Profile': Data Standards Body, 'Consumer Data Standards v 1.22.0', https://consumerdatastandards.org.au. infosec profile 0.1.1.

The information security requirements under UK open banking are similar. The *CMA Order* requires that the UK Standards include security standards.[51] Accordingly, specific security profiles are included.[52] The *PSR* requires that data recipients must have a security policy and procedure for monitoring, handling and following up security incidents, and a statement of the applicant's security policy.[53] The *PSR* also requires an AISP to establish a risk management framework for operational and security risks.[54] In line with these,[55] the FCA has directed that AISPs comply with guidelines on security measures issued by the European Banking Authority in respect of *PSD2*.[56] An AISP is also required to notify the FCA of any major security incident, and its customers if it has, or may have, an impact on their financial interests.[57] In addition to the *PSR* requirements, *GDPR* has its own security obligations, requiring that open banking data which are personal data, are processed in a manner which ensures 'appropriate security', including through 'protection against unauthorised or unlawful processing and against accidental loss, destruction or damage' by means of appropriate technical and organisational measures.[58] No specific security measures are required by *GDPR* as the requirements depend on the particular context.[59]

Without going into the technical detail of the requirements, which are beyond the scope of this book, each system requires recipients to adhere to a security profile based on similar technical foundations.[60] Also, the breadth of coverage under each system is similar in that each addresses the broad information security concepts of confidentiality (preventing unauthorised disclosure), integrity (preventing unauthorised modification) and availability (ensuring that information is available to be processed and transmitted).

---

51. *Retail Banking Market Investigation Order 2017* (UK) ('*CMA Order*') [10.2.3].
52. The 'Financial Grade API (FAPI) Profile' and the 'Client Initiated Backchannel Authentication Flow (CIBA) Profile': Open Banking Implementation Entity, 'Open Banking Security Profiles' (Standard, 2018-2019) https://standards.openbanking.org.uk/security-profiles/.
53. *Payment Services Regulation 2017* (UK) ('*PSR*') regs 5(1), 17, sch. 2. Registration to provide AISs under the *PSR* requires a statement of the applicant's security policy, including a detailed risk assessment in relation to the payment services to be provided (such as risks of fraud and illegal use of sensitive and personal data), and a description of the applicant's security control and mitigation measures.
54. *Ibid.* reg. 98(1).
55. *See also* Financial Conduct Authority, *FCA Handbook* (Financial Conduct Authority, 2013) [SUP 16.13.12]. *See also* Financial Conduct Authority, 'Payment Services and Electronic Money – Our Approach' (n. 29) [18.3].
56. These cover operational matters such as governance, risk assessment, protection, detection, business continuity, testing, situational awareness and continuous learning and customer relationship management: European Banking Authority, 'Guidelines on the Security Measures for Operational and Security Risks of Payment Services under Directive (EU) 2015/2366 (PSD2)' (Final Report No EBA/GL/2017/17, 12/12/2017).
57. *PSR* (n. 53) reg. 99.
58. *GDPR* (n. 9) Art. 5(1)(f).
59. Information Commissioner's Office (n. 10) 217. The EDPB has noted the severity of the risks involved in financial personal data and concluded that, as a result, 'the security measures must be accordingly high': European Data Protection Board (n. 9) 20.
60. The 'Financial Grade API (FAPI) Profile' and the 'Client Initiated Backchannel Authentication Flow (CIBA) Profile': *see* n. 52.

It is noteworthy that neither Australian nor UK open banking imposes significant direct obligations on recipients to ensure the security of data even though, in the case of the Australian system, the expressed purpose of the information security privacy safeguard is 'to ensure that CDR data is protected from misuse, interference and loss as well as from unauthorised access, modification or disclosure',[61] and in the case of the UK system, the OBIE is to 'ensure that customers are fully protected against privacy and security risks'.[62] Instead, as noted above, the obligations are operational and procedural, and framed as being to take 'reasonable steps'. The UK system does contain one clear security-related obligation on AISPs, to ensure that the customer's personalised security credentials are 'not accessible to other parties'.[63] However, this is not a point of material difference between the systems as Australian open banking does not allow access to account data using the customer's security credentials so these should not be held by the data recipient. This absence of direct security obligations is evaluated further in the next section with respect to the equivalent obligations in banking payment systems.

### *(b) Protection of Customer Data on Participant Departure*

A further critical feature of the preservation of value of shared customer data is the requirements for its treatment when a recipient ceases to participate in an open banking system, either voluntarily or involuntarily.

Under Australian open banking, the *CDR Rules* set out detailed consequences for the treatment of shared data by a recipient whose authorisation to participate is to cease. They require that a person whose accreditation is surrendered, suspended or revoked:

- must not seek to collect any CDR data;[64]
- must notify each CDR consumer who has consented to their collection of CDR data of the surrender, suspension or revocation and that, in the case of a suspension, their consents to collect and use the CDR data may be withdrawn at any time.[65]

In the case of a suspension, the recipient remains accredited and continues to be subject to the obligations of an accredited person.[66] In the case of a surrender or revocation, the consents to collect and use CDR data, and the authorisations to disclose CDR data given to the data recipient, expire.[67] Also, the recipient must delete or de-identify the collected CDR data in accordance with the processes analysed above

61. Explanatory Memorandum, Treasury Laws Amendment (Consumer Data Right) Bill 2018 (Cth) [1.15] ('CDR Bill EM') [1.372].
62. Explanatory Note, Retail Banking Market Investigation Order 2017 (UK) [40] ('Explanatory Note, Retail Banking Market Investigation Order').
63. *PSR* (n. 53) reg. 70(3)(b).
64. *CDR Rules* (n. 7) r. 5.23(3)(a).
65. *Ibid.* r. 5.23(3)(b).
66. *Ibid.* r. 5.23(2).
67. *Ibid.* rr. 4.14(2), 4.26(2).

unless it is needed for legal or dispute resolution proceedings.[68] The recipient remains subject to the privacy safeguards relating to use and disclosure of CDR data, including for direct marketing, of CDR data continue to apply.[69]

There is nothing equivalent in UK banking which links these events to the collection, holding and use of data. The *PSR* contains no provisions relating to the use of the data shared, other than in relation to the requirement for consent.[70] Further, the complexities in the interaction between *PSR* and *GDPR* arise partly because *GDPR* contains no provisions relating to the authorisation under *PSD2*. An entity's loss of authorisation to receive customer data under *PSD2* will result in it no longer being able to provide the AIS and, as a result, no longer receive, use and share the data which that authorisation permitted.[71] However, the UK system does not provide the same clarity of obligations on the recipient, or the express protections of notification of customers and ability to withdraw consent as is provided to customers under the Australian system. This difference should be regarded as material for two reasons. First, as Chapter 7 shows, the customer is relying on the performance of the recipient in relation to the use, and deletion, of their data. Accordingly, notification of the customer and enabling them to withdraw consent to further use of data is important if the capacity for the data recipient to perform its obligations is reduced. Secondly, the clarity of the data recipient's obligations is important if the data recipient is insolvent, as explained in Chapter 11.

### 8.2.2 Evaluation Against Data Security in Banking Payment Systems

#### *(a) Information Security Responsibilities of Banks*

Information security has always been critical to banking payment systems. Banking data is required to 'be protected from loss and leakage, unauthorised access, and other processing risks, such as negligence, fraud, poor administration, and inadequate recordkeeping'.[72] According to both the Reserve Bank of Australia and the Bank of England, information security issues which compromise the core functions of the banking payment system affect the trust in which the system is held, and the confidence in the system as a whole.[73] In this context, the use of digital records has caused information integrity to be a central challenge in banking payment systems.

68. *Ibid.* r. 5.23(4).
69. *Ibid.* r. 5.23(2). These are privacy safeguards 6, 7 and 12 contained in *CCA* (n. 2) ss 56EI, 56EJ, 56EO.
70. *See* section 7.2.
71. *See* section 7.1.
72. Committee on Payment and Settlement Systems and International Organization of Securities Commissions, 'Principles for Financial Markets Infrastructures' (Standards, Bank for International Settlements, April 2012) [3.17.12].
73. *See* Reserve Bank of Australia (n. 46). *See also* Bank of England, Future of Finance: What it means for the UK Financial System (Report, June 2019) 3, 14.

The regulatory framework applicable to banks seeks to manage this risk by imposing information security obligations, such as the requirements of the APRA,[74] and the Prudential Regulation Authority of the UK.[75] These treat information security as part of operational risk management.[76] As a result, it is regulated through procedural requirements, governance arrangements and general duties which are broadly, and sometimes obscurely, described. This principles-based approach is intended to avoid both inflexibility in the face of changing technology, and over-regulation.[77]

The security requirements of the two open banking systems take a comparable approach, adopting an operational perspective, rather than imposing direct and positive obligations. This similarity is not surprising given the foundational role that banks perform in open banking and the desirability of not transferring customer data from a high information security environment to one with lower information security. However, it does raise the question as to whether positive and unqualified obligations to keep customer data secure should be imposed in open banking.[78] By comparison, a bank's obligation to repay its customer's funds is a direct and positive obligation, not qualified by any theft or cyber-security attack to which the bank has been subject. Taking a similar approach in open banking systems would impose an unconditional obligation on data recipients to ensure that customer data are 'not accessible' to other persons. However, for the reasons discussed in the previous section in relation to data quality, a bank's responsibility for the integrity of the balance of the customer's account is not the correct benchmark. Instead, the correct benchmark is the bank's responsibility for the safe custody of the customer's property. A bank is not liable for the theft of such assets if there is no negligence or conversion by the bank or its employees. Accordingly, the absence of an unqualified and direct obligation to keep the customer's data secure in the open banking systems should not be considered a flaw in open banking's design when evaluated against banking payment systems.

### *(b) Protection of Customer Value on Default by Segregation*

Protection of customer value from participant default is also critical in payment systems. When an authorised bank ceases to hold its authorisation to conduct banking business it is required to repay the customer funds held. The historical connection between banks and payment systems and the role of banks in holding customer value as creditor and not as bailee or trustee results in some confusion in analysing the legal support provided for this requirement, as the customer's value in a bank deposit is the

74. *APRA Prudential Standard CPS 234 Information Security* ('*CPS 234*').
75. Prudential Regulation Authority, 'CBEST Threat Intelligence-Led Assessments' (Implementation Guide, January 2021).
76. Committee on Payment and Settlement Systems and International Organization of Securities Commissions (n. 72) [2.9].
77. *See* European Banking Authority, 'Guidelines on the Security Measures for Operational and Security Risks of Payment Services under Directive (EU) 2015/2366 (PSD2)' (n. 56) 27. *See also* Anton Didenko, 'Cybersecurity Regulation in the Financial Sector: Prospects of Legal Harmonisation in the EU and Beyond' (2020) 25(1) *Uniform Law Review* 125.
78. The obligations to not disclose data do not cover the prevention of unauthorised access, *see* Office of the Australian Information Commissioner (n. 4) [B.114].

contractual promise of the bank to repay the amount deposited, and that value is preserved through depositor protection, as explained in Chapter 10. However, the evaluation becomes clearer when considering participants in payment systems who are not banks or clearing and settlement systems which involve the holding and delivery of obligations and property, rather than the payment of money. In these circumstances, segregation arrangements are often used to ensure the customer's assets being held by a participant for a customer are clearly identified, separately held from the assets available to the participant's creditors,[79] and able to be transferred to another participant so that the customer can continue to benefit from the system despite the participant's default.[80] These arrangements have proven instrumental in minimising the disruption caused by the default of participants in securities and futures clearing systems.

Neither Australian nor UK open banking seeks to protect customer value by segregating data held by a participant should it default. Australian open banking includes a data segregation requirement as part of its information security controls, but this requires customer data held or stored *on behalf of a data recipient* to be segregated from other customer data and not commingled.[81] It does not require the segregation of any customer's data by the data recipient itself. Nor does either system contain obligations for a defaulting recipient to transfer customer data to another participant in the open banking system, reflecting the 'portability' of positions in a clearing system. However, as explained in Chapter 1, unlike money data is 'non-rivalrous' in that it can be used repeatedly by more than one person without reducing its functional value to its holder. This means that the segregation and portability protections contained in financial systems may not be warranted, despite the value of the data which has been shared with the participant before it defaulted. The default of a data recipient does not mean that the data shared with it is lost to the customer in the same way as customer funds received by a defaulting bank, or customer property received by a defaulting broker, could be lost. Nor is it essential that the continued sharing or use of the data by the defaulting participant be enforced, or that the data shared with the defaulting participant be 'repaid'. Instead, the value of the data to the customer could be protected by a combination of enabling the customer to require their bank to share their data with another recipient and requiring the defaulting recipient deleted the customer data held by it. This enables the customer to continue to derive value from the appropriate use of their data by the performing recipient and to prevent any loss of value to the customer from the inappropriate use of their data by the defaulting recipient. This is consistent with the obligation to delete customer data which is imposed on a data recipient whose accreditation is revoked under the Australian system. However, as noted above, there is no equivalent obligation under UK open banking.

79. *See* the 'client money' regulations which require client funds to be segregated from a licensed entity's own assets: *Corporations Regulations 2001* (Cth) reg. 7.8.01 (*Corporations Regulations*). *See also* Financial Conduct Authority, *FCA Handbook* (Financial Conduct Authority, 2013), CASS 7.10.16.
80. Committee on Payment and Settlement Systems and International Organization of Securities Commissions (n. 72) 82. This is particularly relevant for central counterparties.
81. *CDR Rules* (n. 7) sch. 2 r. 2.2(2)(e).

## 8.3 HOW CAN LEGAL FOUNDATIONS SUPPORT PRESERVING VALUE?

### 8.3.1 Summary of Comparison and Evaluation

This chapter has examined the implications of the legal foundations of Australian and UK open banking for the preservation of value in shared customer data through a comparison of their legal features relating to the quality and security of shared data, and an evaluation against equivalent legal features of payment systems.

The analysis has shown that the legal responsibilities which support the preservation of the quality of shared data are similar in Australian and UK open banking, although the UK system supports this only for personal information. For good reasons, neither system provides the same unqualified obligations owed by a bank for the correctness of the records of the customer's account. However, the analysis has also highlighted the need for customers to have, and to exercise, the right to access the shared data so they are able to determine its accuracy and exercise their rights to correct the data. The chapter further shows that the legal foundations for obligations for data security are comparable between the Australian and UK open banking systems and are broadly aligned with those of banking payment systems.

This chapter has also shown that the requirements for the deletion of customer data when they are no longer needed are not significantly different between Australian and UK open banking, to the extent that personal information is involved, and that this legal foundation is conceptually similar to the bank's obligation to repay customer funds. However, the difference in the legal foundations is apparent when business customer data and the circumstance of a recipient which ceases to participate are considered. In these circumstances, the absence of any clear legal foundations for dealing with customer data impairs the support granted for the accountability provided by the UK system.

The consequence of these differences is that the legal foundations of neither open banking system provides the same support for autonomy or accountability as banking payment systems, and UK open banking supports accountability less than Australian open banking. This is illustrated in Figure 8.1.

*Figure 8.1 Illustration of Evaluation and Comparison Relating to Preservation of Data's Value*

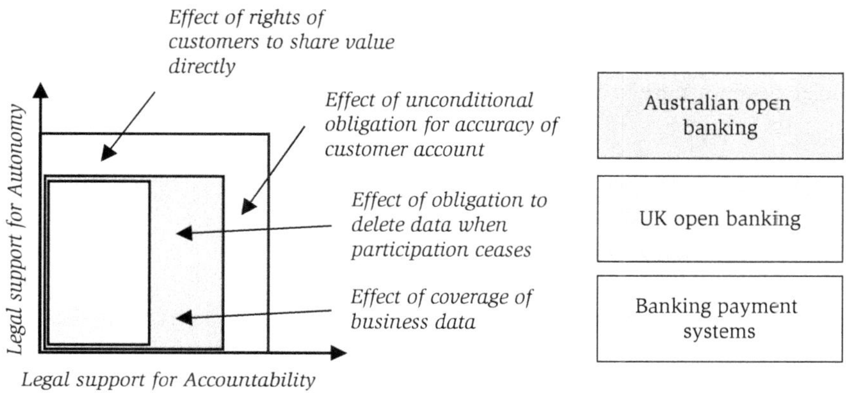


This analysis shows the need to balance autonomy and accountability in designing the legal foundations for preserving the value of shared customer data. It also demonstrates the need to manage value risk. This risk is explained next, followed by an illustration of the comparable operational and custody risks in banking payment systems, and a discussion of how operational and custody risk management methods could be applied in the legal design of open banking systems.

### 8.3.2 Value Risk in Open Banking Systems

Value risk arises in open banking if the value of shared customer data is not protected. A critical element in understanding this risk is that the value of customer data to the customer depends not only on the use of the data for the customer's benefit, but also on the absence of misuse of the data to the customer's detriment. Accordingly, sharing data could cause harm if the detriment suffered by the customer from the data's misuse exceeds the benefit to the customer from the data's use. This value risk can arise when the quality of data is reduced, or the data are subject to misuse or unauthorised disclosure or modification. This dependence of the value of customer data on use and misuse is fundamental in assessing value risk in open banking. It means that unauthorised modification of customer data is a risk to their value because it affects the ability to use those customer data for the benefit of the customer. It also means that unauthorised use of customer data is a risk to their value because it results in misuse of customer data. Accordingly, information security is fundamental to value risk in open banking systems.

As with the communication and performance risks analysed in previous chapters, value risk is not limited to the potential for loss caused to a particular customer. The risk also impacts the open banking system as a whole because of the increasing connectivity of participants as the system develops. A recipient that is the subject of a cyber-attack may hold the data of many customers and may be connected to many other recipients. Accordingly, many customers could be affected by one instance of value risk and, if the risk is realised, could suffer loss. This would damage the system's credibility.[82]

To further explain this aspect of value risk, the next section sets out an illustration of comparable risks: *operational risk* in banking payment systems, and *custody risk* in financial systems more broadly.

### 8.3.3 Illustration of Operational and Custody Risks in Banking Payment Systems

#### *(a) Operational Risk: Bank of Bangladesh*

As noted in Chapter 6, operational risk in banking payment systems is the risk arising from operational factors such as technical malfunctions or operational mistakes.

A relevant illustrative example of operational risk is the cyber-security fraud incident involving the Bank of Bangladesh and its connection with the SWIFT messaging system. This involved an attack being made on the internal network of a central bank to provide access to its gateway for international transfers:

> Using tailored malware, the group penetrated the payment gateway and eventually overrode the bank's required credentials. One February morning [the attacker] sent thirty-five fraudulent payment instructions over the Swift network, requesting the transfer of $951 million from Bangladesh Bank's account at the Federal Reserve Bank of New York, where (like many other central banks) it maintained an ample balance of dollar reserves.[83]

The resulting loss was approximately $81 million, although there was potential for far greater loss but for the crashing of a computer and suspicious matter reporting. Nevertheless, the incident caused significant concern through global banking payment systems. The then CEO of SWIFT noted that the fraud, which compromised the bank's payment generation credentials and allowed fraudulent messages to be sent 'gets to the heart of banking' because '[k]eeping money secure is core business for banks'.[84] As a consequence, he noted that 'banks that are compromised like this can be put out of business' and there is a problem because 'the financial system is hugely interconnected and it operates on trust'.[85] The consequence was a renewed regulatory focus on cyber-security risk, including on the security of endpoints in wholesale payment

82. For consideration of the broader confidence impact of cyber-security incidents, *see* U.S. Office of Financial Research, '2017 Financial Stability Report' (Report, 5 December 2017) Ch. 1 https://www.financialresearch.gov/financial-stability-reports/2017-financial-stability-report/.
83. Gottfried Leibbrandt and Natasha De Teran, *The Pay Off: How Changing the Way We Pay Changes Everything* (Elliot & Thompson, 2020) 103.
84. Gottfried Leibbrandt, 'Gottfried Leibbrandt on Cyber Security and Innovation' (Keynote Address, 14th Annual European Financial Services Conference, Brussels, 24 May 2016) https://www.swift.com/insights/press-releases/gottfried-leibbrandt-on-cyber-security-and-innovation.
85. *Ibid.*

systems.[86] In particular, an understanding rapidly grew that the security of each endpoint of a system could affect the whole:

> Given the interconnectedness of various stakeholders in the wholesale payment ecosystem, fraud may not only result in financial losses and reputational risk at the compromised endpoint but, in an extreme case and in the absence of appropriate arrangements within the ecosystem for preventing, detecting, responding to and communicating about fraud, may also undermine confidence in the integrity of the entire system.[87]

The Bank of Bangladesh cyber-attack is illustrative of the impact which value risk could have on an open banking system. A cyber-attack which causes a significant amount of customer data to be subject to unauthorised use or modification would also 'go to the heart of open banking' because it would conflict with the three functions of autonomy, portability and accountability. Also, just as was feared with the Bank of Bangladesh attack, the confidence in the system could quickly collapse as a result, particularly if the attack spread to other participants in the system.

### *(b) Custody Risk: MF Global*

Custody risk in financial systems can also be seen to be comparable to value risk. Custody risk is:

> the risk of loss on assets held in custody in the event of a custodian's (or subcustodian's) insolvency, negligence, fraud poor administration or inadequate recordkeeping.[88]

This risk is illustrated by the role played by data integrity in resolving the collapse of MF Global in 2011. MF Global was the largest failure of a financial services firm since Lehman Brothers and like Lehman, MF Global was a broker and held customer funds. However, unlike Lehman, there was a massive shortfall in customer funds amounting to $1.6 billion. This led to litigation over the remains. Relevantly, in Australia, that litigation resulted directly from a failure in the integrity of the data relating to customer records:

> [T]here is no document in the nature of a trust account, or a statement of trust account, for each client recording the contributions or withdrawals by that client' and the broker did not record the cash balances of each client.[89]

As a result, it was not possible to calculate how much of the remaining pool of customer funds was attributable to any particular client. This failure in record keeping

86. *See* Committee on Payment and Settlement Systems, 'Reducing the Risk of Wholesale Payments Fraud Related to Endpoint Security' (Report, Bank for International Settlements, May 2018).
87. *See ibid.* 2.
88. Committee on Payment and Settlement Systems and International Organization of Securities Commissions (n. 72) 175.
89. *In re MF Global Australia Ltd (in liq)* [2012] NSWSC 994, [50] ('*MF Global Australia*').

was found to not 'permit distribution by single account to fairly or sensibly occur'.[90] The significant detrimental impact of this failure in data integrity and quality led to regulatory reforms requiring increased reconciliation and reporting to ensure the quality of the recordkeeping. Just as the Bank of Bangladesh shows the potential for harm caused by a cyber-attack for an open banking system, so does the MF Global collapse show the impact of a failure of data quality. The obligations of MF Global to protect customer value were rendered meaningless by the failure to keep good records.

For these reasons, the legal features used in banking payment systems to manage operational and custody risk deserve consideration for incorporation into the legal foundations of open banking.

### 8.3.4 Incorporating Operational and Custody Risk Management in Open Banking

As explained earlier in this chapter, cyber-security risk is managed as part of operational risk in banking payment systems and is of particular focus due to the significant number of cyber security incidents in the financial services sector, and their potentially severe effect.

The analysis in the chapter has shown how information security requirements are already included in the conditions of authorisation to participate as a recipient in the Australian and UK open banking systems. These are aimed at addressing concerns similar to those relating to endpoint security which arise in the Bank of Bangladesh cyber-attack. However, there are other elements of information security operational risk management which can be adapted from financial systems which are of a more holistic nature. Such an approach is warranted because deficiencies in data integrity and the safeguarding of data will affect not only the relevant authorities and the participants that rely on that data but other infrastructures and service providers as well.[91] This can be most clearly seen with the approach taken to data market infrastructure such as derivative TRs:[92]

> Specific operational risks that a TR must manage include risks to data integrity, data security, and business continuity. Because the data recorded by a TR may be used as inputs to the activities of the TR's participants, relevant authorities, and other parties, including other FMIs and service providers, all trade data collected, stored, and disseminated by a TR should be protected from corruption, loss, leakage, unauthorised access, and other processing risks. In addition, a TR may be part of a network linking various entities (such as CCPs, dealers, custodians, and service providers) and could transmit risk or cause processing delays to such linked entities in the event of an operational disruption.

Although neither the Australian nor UK open banking systems operates using central infrastructure to receive, store and transfer open banking data, and the

90. *Ibid.* [52].
91. Committee on Payment and Settlement Systems and International Organization of Securities Commissions (n. 72) [3.17.3].
92. *Ibid.* 94.

minimisation of central infrastructure avoids the concentration of too much valuable information in one place, this does not mean that information security management for open banking should not incorporate assessment of the system as a whole, rather than just of its parts. The risks described in the *PFMIs* in relation to TRs could apply to open banking systems despite there being no single TR. Accordingly, to appropriately manage information security for an open banking system, a holistic perspective should be taken. This same approach can also be seen in the 'macroprudential' approach to bank regulation following the financial crisis which extended regulation beyond individual banks to the stability of the banking system as a whole. This was due to a recognition that firms which were individually stable could still be fragile collectively.

Whilst custody risk management methods are not customarily applied to information in banking payment systems, this should not prevent them from being applied in open banking systems. For example, managing this risk is considered particularly important for central securities depositories, even though most of their assets are dematerialised so that they 'exist only as accounting records'.[93] Custody risk management requires rules and procedures and robust internal controls consistent with a legal framework designed to ensure segregation of assets of the custodian from those of its clients. This would require that open banking systems are designed so that customer data to which maintenance and security obligations apply are identifiable and not comingled with other data such that it becomes impossible to perform the custody obligations, and to facilitate the data's deletion when necessary to preserve its value for the customer.

93. *Ibid.* 73.

CHAPTER 9

# Facilitating Participation in Open Banking

This chapter examines the legal foundations for facilitating participation in open banking systems. It compares the legal relationships established between participants and with regulators which enable access to the Australian and UK open banking systems and evaluates them against the equivalent legal relationships established under banking payment systems. The analysis addresses three questions:

- How should direct participation be authorised?
- How should indirect participation be authorised?
- How should outsourcing arrangements be authorised?

The answers to these questions are fundamental to an open banking system's performance of its *connectivity* and *accountability* functions.

## 9.1 HOW SHOULD DIRECT PARTICIPATION BE AUTHORISED?

Chapter 1 shows that achievement of an open banking system's objectives depends on its performance of the functions of customer autonomy, data portability and recipient accountability. This requires the participation of recipients to receive and use customer data. The previous two chapters have shown that this results in a significant amount of trust being placed in the performance of those recipients and a key element of establishing the trustworthiness of the open banking system is the authorisation for recipients to participate.

The legal requirements relating to the authorisation required to be a recipient are comparatively analysed below, followed by evaluation against authorisation to participate in banking payment systems.

### 9.1.1 Comparison of Authorisations to Participate under Open Banking Systems

#### *(a) Accreditation and Authorisation Requirements*

In Australian open banking, the *Competition and Consumer Act 2010* (Cth) (*CCA*),[1] defines a 'CDR participant' as being a data holder, or an accredited data recipient, for CDR data.[2] As explained in Chapter 5, data holders include all ADIs which are authorised to conduct banking business in Australia by the APRA under section 9(3) of the *Banking Act 1959* (Cth). An accredited data recipient is a person accredited by the Australian ACCC,[3] and who has received CDR data under the *Competition and Consumer (Consumer Data Right) Rules 2020* ('*CDR Rules*').[4]

Requirements for accreditation of data recipients are set out in the *CDR Rules*.[5] In addition to satisfying the information security requirements analysed in Chapter 8, and the compensation requirements analysed in Chapter 11, the person must have appropriate internal dispute resolution processes, be a member of a recognised external dispute resolution scheme,[6] and 'be, having regard to the fit and proper person criteria, a fit and proper person to be accredited at that level'.[7] These criteria require consideration of any convictions of serious criminal offences or offences of dishonesty, any contravention of law relevant to the management of CDR data,[8] any determinations of interference with privacy, any history of insolvency or bankruptcy, and the objects of Part IVD of the *CCA*.[9] ADIs are able to obtain 'streamlined accreditation' as a data recipient.[10]

The ACCC also performs the role of the 'Accreditation Registrar' and keeps the 'Register of Accredited Persons'.[11] The register includes, for each accredited person, identification details, the level of accreditation, the conditions on accreditation and whether the accreditation has been suspended or revoked.[12] In addition, the Accreditation Registrar must maintain a database of data holders containing identification and

1. *Competition and Consumer Act 2010* (Cth) ('*Competition and Consumer Act*')
2. *Ibid.* s. 56AL.
3. The ACCC is the Data Recipient Accreditor: *CCA* (n. 1) ss 56CA, 4(1) (definition of 'Data Recipient Accreditor').
4. *Competition and Consumer (Consumer Data Right) Rules 2020* ('*CDR Rules*'). *See also ibid.* s. 56AK.
5. *CCA* (n. 1) ss 56BB(d), 56BH.
6. *CDR Rules* (n. 4) rr. 5.12(1)(b), 5.12(1)(c).
7. *Ibid.* r. 5.12(2)(a).
8. This includes the *CCA*, any regulations under it, the *CDR Rules*, the *Corporations Act 2001* (Cth) and the *Corporations Regulations 2001* (Cth), the *Privacy Act 1998* (Cth) and the *Australian Securities and Investments Commission Act 2001* (Cth): *ibid.* r. 1.7 (definition of 'law relevant to the management of CDR data'), cl. 7.1 sch. 3.
9. *Ibid.* r. 1.9. *See also* Australian Competition and Consumer Commission, 'Accreditation Guidelines' (Guide, 9 December 2020) [5.2].
10. *Ibid.* sch. 3 cl. 7.3.
11. *CCA* (n. 1) ss 4(1) (definition of 'Accreditation Registrar'), 56CE.
12. *CDR Rules* (n. 4) r. 5.24.

other relevant details.[13] The information on accredited persons and data holders is required to be made publicly available.[14]

UK open banking does not have a formal concept of a 'participant' in its legislative instruments. The *CMA Order*,[15] which established the OBIE to create and administer the UK Standards, required nine banks to participate by complying with those standards,[16] and required those standards to include provisions relating to 'whitelisting as a system for approving third party providers fairly and quickly unless there is sufficient existing regulatory oversight'.[17] The OBIE provides operational support for data recipients seeking to join the UK system, but requires that the regulatory requirements must first be satisfied.[18]

Those regulatory requirements are provided by the *PSR*. As analysed in Chapters 5 and 6, the *PSR* requires that data be shared by ASPSP with AISPs.[19] ASPSPs are entities which are authorised to provide and maintain payment accounts for customers such as banks and building societies, electronic money institutions and other payment institutions.[20] AISPs are required to register with the FCA unless they already hold a broader authorisation under the *PSR*.[21] In addition to the information security requirements analysed in Chapter 8,[22] and the compensation requirements analysed in Chapter 11, an AISP is required to have a description of the applicant's procedure for monitoring, handling and following up security incidents and security-related customer complaints,[23] and to provide evidence that the directors and persons responsible for the management of the applicant are of good repute and that they possess appropriate knowledge and experience to perform payment services.[24]

To perform its obligations under the *CMA Order*, the OBIE maintains a directory of ASPSPs and AISPs, which is referred to as the 'Directory Of Open Banking Participants' or the 'Directory'.[25] The OBIE has published the 'Open Banking

13. *Ibid.* r. 5.25.
14. *Ibid.* r. 5.27.
15. *Retail Banking Market Investigation Order 2017* (UK) ('*CMA Order*').
16. *See* section 3.3.
17. *CMA Order* (n. 15) [10.2.3].
18. Open Banking Implementation Entity, 'How to Enrol with Open Banking', *Open Banking – Third Party Providers* (Guide, 2021) https://www.openbanking.org.uk/providers/third-party-providers/. Although the OBIE was established under an order of the Competition and Markets Authority, the order does not establish the OBIE as a regulator: *see CMA Order* (n. 15).
19. *Payment Services Regulation 2017* (UK) reg. 70 ('*PSR*').
20. *Ibid.* reg. 2 (definition of 'payment service provider'). *See also* Financial Conduct Authority, 'Payment Services and Electronic Money – Our Approach' (Approach Document, June 2019) 14. *See* section 3.3.1 above.
21. *PSR* (n. 19) regs 2(1) (definitions of 'payment service' and 'payment service provider'), 138. Other than an authorisation under *PSR* as a small payment institution: *ibid.* reg. 14(4). Authorisation as a small electronic money institution is also insufficient: Financial Conduct Authority, 'Payment Services and Electronic Money – Our Approach' (n. 20) [3.123].
22. *See* section 8.2.
23. *PSR* (n. 19) regs 17, sch. 2. Dispute resolution processes are also dealt with in regulation 101 of the *PSR*.
24. *Ibid.* reg. 17, sch. 2.
25. Open Banking Implementation Entity, 'Open Banking Guidelines for Read/Write Participants' (Guidelines, May 2018) https://www.openbanking.org.uk/wp-content/uploads/Guidelines-for-Read-Write-Participants.pdf 4.

Guidelines for Read/Write Participants' ('UK Guidelines') to 'describe and provide direction on the roles and responsibilities of the Participants' in the Directory.[26] The term 'Participant' is used, but not defined, in the UK Guidelines. However, it appears to mean both ASPSPs and AISPs.[27] The UK Guidelines describe the Directory as the 'key architectural component' which provides the necessary functional capabilities required for ASPSPs to provide whitelisted Participants with access to APIs, and for Participants that have been authorised or registered with their Competent Authority to enable them to identify and to facilitate on-boarding with ASPSPs so that they can use the APIs provided by the ASPSPs.[28]

Despite the significant difference in their legislative foundation, the eligibility requirements for data recipients to participate are similar in the frameworks, with each having requirements directed at good standing, access to dispute resolution processes, information security and compensation requirements. Further, there are similar technological requirements to be satisfied to be admitted to the relevant register under each framework in order to have operational access.[29] However, there is a conceptual difference in the nature of the authorisation required for each system, relating to the services provided with the data shared.

### *(b) Contrast in Conceptual Foundation of Authorisations*

Although accreditation under Australian open banking authorises a data recipient to request, receive, and use shared data, it does not authorise any particular service to be provided using the data. If an accredited data recipient uses shared data to provide a service which is subject to regulation beyond Part IVD of the *CCA*, then the data recipient will need to obtain the authorisations required by that other regulation. For example, an accredited data recipient that uses the shared data to provide a financial service regulated by the *Corporations Act 2001* (Cth) ('*Corporations Act*'), such as the provision of financial product advice,[30] is also required to obtain the licence required under the *Corporations Act* to provide that advice.[31] In contrast, nothing other than

---

26. *Ibid.* The legal status of this is unclear.
27. Open Banking Implementation Entity, 'Open Banking Guidelines for Read/Write Participants' (Guidelines, May 2018) 7, 17 https://www.openbanking.org.uk/wp-content/uploads/Guidelines-for-Read-Write-Participants.pdf.
28. *Ibid.* 8. 'At its core the Directory is an identity and access management service providing identity information supporting natural persons, organisations and software identity classes.': Open Banking Implementation Entity, 'Directory 2.0 Technical Overview v1.5', *Open Banking Develepor Zone* (Technical Specification, 29 December 2020) [2.1] https://openbanking.atlassian.net/wiki/spaces/DZ/pages/1150124033/Directory+2.0+Technical+Overview+v1.5.
29. *See* Australian Competition and Consumer Commission, 'Participant On-boarding Guide' (Guide, June 2021) https://www.cdr.gov.au/sites/default/files/2021-07/CDR_Participant%20On-boarding%20Guide_v1.3_6.pdf; Open Banking Implementation Entity, 'Enrolling onto the OBIE Directory' (Guide, November 2020) https://www.openbanking.org.uk/wp-content/uploads/Enrolling-Onto-Open-Banking-Guide.pdf.
30. *See Corporations Act 2001* (Cth) ('*Corporations Act*') s. 766B.
31. The licence required for carrying on a business of providing financial services in Australia is an Australian Financial Services Licence: *Corporations Act* s. 911A.

authorisation as an AISP is required under UK open banking to request, receive and use shared data to provide an AIS.[32]

This difference means that authorisation to participate in the Australian system is a necessary, but may not be a sufficient, condition to provide a service using shared data, whilst authorisation to participate in the UK system is necessary *and* sufficient to provide the AIS using shared data. This conceptual difference in approach to authorisation of recipients is also evident from:

- the different responsibilities of the regulators which authorise participation in each framework, being an economy-wide competition regulator in Australia (the ACCC) and the regulator of financial services, including payment services, in the UK (the FCA); and
- the different 'fit and proper' requirements applicable to authorisation under each system. The UK system requires that specified individuals have knowledge and experience to perform payment services.[33] In contrast, the Australian system looks to the purposes of Part IVD of the *CCA*, namely to 'enable consumers in certain sectors (currently banking) to require information about them to be shared safely, efficiently and conveniently'.[34] UK has a focus on a financial service and Australia has a focus on an information service.[35]

The simplicity and efficiency provided by the requirement for only a single authorisation assists in providing access to recipients in UK open banking. However, two further aspects need consideration. First, the authorisation to participate in the UK system permits only the provision of an AIS. No other authorisations are available which permit the use of the shared data to provide other services. This limits the flexibility of the AISP and the customer autonomy provided.[36] Second, the provision of an AIS alone should not require a further authorisation under Australian financial service licensing requirements,[37] or Australian credit licensing requirements.[38] Accordingly, if the service provided by the data recipient under the Australian system were

32. Namely 'to provide consolidated information on one or more payment accounts held by the payment service user with another payment service provider or with more than one payment service provider': *PSR* (n. 19) reg. 2(1) (definition of 'account information service').
33. *Ibid.* reg. 17, sch. 2.
34. Australian Competition and Consumer Commission, 'Accreditation Guidelines' (Guide, 9 December 2020) 10.
35. If a data recipient under the Australian system provided a regulated financial service then in order to obtain the requisite Australian Financial Services Licence they would need to demonstrate similar knowledge and experience to that required under the UK system: *Corporations Act 2001* (Cth) s. 912A(1) ('*Corporations Act*').
36. *See* section 9.2.1 below.
37. Unless it is financial product advice, by being a 'recommendation or a statement of opinion, or a report of either of those things' which 'is intended to influence a person or persons in making a decision about a particular financial product or class of financial products, or an interest in a particular financial product or class of financial products, or could reasonably be regarded as being intended to have such an influence': *Corporations Act* (n. 31) s. 766B.
38. Unless it is credit assistance, by suggesting that a consumer apply for, remain in, or increase, a particular credit contract: *National Consumer Credit Protection Act 2009* (Cth) s. 8 ('*NCCP Act*').

limited to the scope of an AIS, then only one authorisation is required, being accreditation from the ACCC to be a data recipient.

Conceptually, authorisation under Australian open banking only provides access to the data sharing network and the data shared through it, whilst authorisation under UK open banking combines access to the data sharing network and permission to provide a single service using the shared data. The Australian system enables greater flexibility in the services provided using the shared data, which is important for achieving its competition and innovation objectives but needs to be complemented by service-specific regulation (like financial services and credit regulation) where needed. The UK system provides greater regulatory simplicity, which could also enhance its achievement of competition and innovation objectives, but at the cost of the flexibility provided in the Australian system, which could also limit its effectiveness in achieving those same objectives. However, before reaching a conclusion on the effect of this difference, an assessment of the flexibility provided through the use of other participation arrangements is needed. This is set out in section 9.2 below.

### 9.1.2 Evaluation Against Authorisations to Participate in Banking Payment Systems

A bank's participation in banking payment systems in both Australia and the UK is governed by the regulatory authorisations required to conduct banking business (which enable customer funds to be received as deposits and loaned to other customers),[39] and the conditions for access to payment systems (which enable the funds to be paid and received on behalf of customers).[40]

#### *(a) Authorisation to Conduct Banking Business*

Banking business authorisation requires banks to meet initial requirements, governance obligations and prudential regulation. These are designed to ensure that their financial promises are met.[41] They are needed due to the potential 'fragility' created by banks' economic functions of liquidity transformation (providing access to liquid deposits whilst holding illiquid assets), maturity transformation (borrowing short term deposits and lending long-term loans) and credit transformation (taking on greater credit risks than those which they themselves create). Further, the role that banks' deposit obligations perform both as money and in the making of payments amplifies

39. For Australia *see Banking Act 1959* (Cth) ('*Australian Banking Act*') s. 9. For the UK *see PRA Rulebook: Notifications Instrument 2014* (UK) PRA 2014/20 Glossary (definition of 'bank') ('*PRA Rulebook: Notifications Instrument*'). *See also Regulation (EU) No 575/2013 of the European Parliament and of the Council of 26 June 2013 on Prudential Requirements for Credit Institutions and Investment Firms and Amending Regulation (EU) No 648/2012.* OJ L 176/18 Art. 4(1) ('*CRR*').
40. Such as the RITS in Australia and CHAPS in the UK.
41. The prudential framework ... is designed to ensure that 'under all reasonable circumstances, financial promises made by regulated entities are met': Australian Prudential Regulation Authority, 'APRA's Policy Priorities' (Information Paper, 1 February 2021) 4.

the impact that a bank's failure can have on other banks, banking payment systems and society more generally. These are systemic risks, as described in Chapter 4. Systemic risks also arise in payment systems. Misuse of, or a failure in, a payment system imposes 'costs on agents in the economy beyond the participants in the particular transaction'.[42] Therefore, conditions are imposed on access to payment systems 'to protect systems and their participants from participation in the system by institutions that would expose them to excessive legal, financial or operational risks'.[43]

### *(b) Conditions to Participate in Payment Systems*

Historically, there has been a preference to use authorisation as a bank as a requirement for permission to participate in important payment systems:

> Limiting membership to entities with high financial standing clearly increases the resilience of the system, as it reduces the probability that the net will be unwound due to member default. For instance, direct membership might be restricted to entities subject to close prudential supervision.[44]

In fact, analyses of payment systems 'often take for granted that the institutional structure of these systems is deeply intertwined with the conventional banking system'.[45] However, the use of authorisation to take deposits and lend money as a condition for access to payment systems conflates the storage and liquidity functions being performed. Also, limiting access to payment systems causes competition concerns arising out of the protected market position of those participants who control access. As a result, international standards now prefer that the conditions to participate be limited to those which are necessary to manage specific risks so that competition is impaired as little as possible. This can be seen from the changes made to permit electronic money institutions and payment institutions authorised under the *PSR* to seek direct access membership of the primary interbank payment systems of the UK.[46]

---

42. Charles Kahn, Stephen Quinn and Will Roberds, 'Central Banks and Payment Systems: The Evolving Trade-Off Between Cost and Risk' Norges Bank Conference on the Uses of Central Banks: Lessons from History, June, 5-6 June 2014) 11.
43. Committee on Payment and Settlement Systems, 'Core Principles for Systemically Important Payment Systems' (Core Principles, Bank for International Settlements, January 2001) [2.1], [3.9.1].
44. Mark Manning, Erlend Nier and Jochen Schanz, *The Economics of Large-Value Payments and Settlement: Theory and Policy Issues for Central Banks* (Oxford University Press, 2009) [3.2.3].
45. Dan Awrey and Kristin van Zwieten, 'The Shadow Payment System' (2017-2018) *43 J. Corp. L 775*, 815.
46. CHAPS, Faster Payments, Bacs and Image Clearing System: *see* Bank of England, Financial Conduct Authority and Pay.uk, 'Access to UK Payment Schemes for Non-Bank Payment Service Providers' (Information Paper, December 2019). The position in Australian interbank payment systems is not as advanced. For example, in addition to ADIs, only Australian licensed central counterparties or securities settlement facilities and other institutions that are 'an actual or prospective provider of third-party (customer) payment services with a need to settle clearing obligations' are able to hold an exchange settlement account allowing for direct settlement in the RITS: Reserve Bank of Australia, 'Exchange Settlement Account Policy', *Payments and Infrastructure* (Policy, 26 July 2019) https://www.rba.gov.au/payments-and-infrastructure/esa/.

The distinction between authorisations required to perform different functions is evident in Australian open banking through the separation of the authorisation required to participate in the network for sharing customer data from the authorisation needed to provide services using the shared data. In doing so, the Australian system enables the requirements to be tailored for the specific risks to be managed, which can be different for sharing customer data and the service provided with those data. In contrast, UK open banking uses the authorisation required for the service provided using the shared data as the basis for participation in the network for sharing the data. This does not permit the tailoring of the requirements to the risks to be managed from different services and, as a result, the UK system limits the services which can be provided. This is akin to the historical approach of using bank authorisation as a condition for admission to payment systems which combined the authorisation requirements for providing storage and liquidity functions in banking payment systems. Due to the limited requirements to obtain registration as an AISP, the impact is not a reduction in the availability of access to UK open banking, as it is in payment systems. Instead, due to the limited nature of the authorised services, there is a reduction in the breadth of the competitive participation which authorisation enables. However, as noted in the previous section, before reaching a conclusion on the effect of this difference, it is necessary to consider the other means of enabling participation in the UK system. These are analysed in section 9.2 below.

## 9.2 HOW SHOULD INDIRECT PARTICIPATION BE AUTHORISED?

Chapter 4 explained that the requirements to participate directly in banking payment systems can be prohibitive for some entities. The costs involved means that flexibility in allowing indirect participation can be more efficient and can encourage competition. However, such flexibility can also concentrate risks and increase the possibility of widespread disruptions, requiring careful balancing of its advantages and disadvantages. Chapter 4 also explained that similar concerns apply in facilitating participation and ensuring credibility in open banking systems.

The manner of authorising indirect participation in the open banking systems are comparatively analysed below, followed by evaluation against the authorisation of indirect participation in banking payment systems.

### 9.2.1 Comparison of Indirect Participation under Open Banking Systems

Initially, there were few options for indirect participation in Australian open banking. However, two years after its commencement, the Australian Government found that 'current barriers to enter the CDR (including the cost of accreditation) are deterring many businesses from participating'.[47] Amendments were made to the CDR Rules to address this deficiency and to:

47. Competition and Consumer (Consumer Data Right) Amendment (2021 Measures No. 1) Rules 2021 – Exposure Draft Explanatory Materials 2021 (Cth) 3 ('CDR Rules Version 3 EM').

> facilitate greater participation in the CDR regime by participants and consumers, provide greater control and choice to consumers in sharing their data; promote innovation of CDR offerings including intermediary services, and enable services to be more effectively and efficiently provided to customers.[48]

The changes which most affected indirect participation were the introduction of a 'sponsored' level of accreditation and the ability for a data recipient with unrestricted accreditation to appoint representatives. These are analysed below, followed by a comparison of the rights to share data beyond each open banking system.

### *(a) Different Levels of Authorisation*

The legislative design of the Australian system always contemplated different levels of accreditation 'to reflect the different risks associated with different data sets and data uses'.[49] The *CCA* specifically provides for different levels corresponding to the different risks of specified classes of CDR data, specified classes of activities and specified classes of applicants for accreditation.[50] Despite this, the Australian *CDR Rules* originally only provided for an 'unrestricted' level of accreditation.[51] Now, the *CDR Rules* permit a data recipient to seek accreditation at a new 'sponsored' level if they have arrangements with another data recipient (a 'sponsor') which has an unrestricted level of accreditation. These arrangements include a written sponsorship agreement with the sponsor and assistance and training on technical and compliance matters from the sponsor.[52] The sponsor is required to take reasonable steps to ensure that the sponsored participant complies with their obligations as an accredited person.[53] Consequently, the sponsored data recipient can become accredited in less costly manner.[54] However, the sponsored data recipient may only make requests for CDR data through their sponsor and may not make requests directly to a CDR consumer.[55] The result is that a sponsored participant could provide an AIS if it were sponsored by a bank, participate in a digital marketplace using CDR data if it were sponsored by the marketplace operator, use CDR data provided in a 'data enclave' by the sponsor and 'white-label' the CDR infrastructure services which the sponsor provides.[56]

Unlike the Australian system, the UK system does not contemplate different levels of authorisation to provide AISs. The *PSR* contemplates that payment institutions

48. *Ibid.* at 1.
49. Australian Treasury, 'Consumer Data Right Overview' (Explanatory Guide, 9 May 2018) 8.
50. *CCA* (n. 1) s. 56BH(1)(d). A lower level of accreditation might, for example, be required for access to the balance of a customer's account: CDR Bill EM (n. 6) [1.230].
51. Australian Competition and Consumer Commission, 'Accreditation Guidelines' (n. 9).
52. *CDR Rules* (n. 4) rr. 5.1A, 5.1B. *See also* Competition and Consumer (Consumer Data Right) Amendment (2021 Measures No. 1) Rules 2021 – Exposure Draft 2021 (Cth) sch. 1 ('CDR Rules Version 3').
53. *CDR Rules* (n. 4) r. [5.1B(8)].
54. The sponsored data recipient does not need to provide an independent third-party assurance report in relation to its information security requirements and instead it is required to provide a self-assessment and attestation: *ibid.* sch. 1 cl. 2.2.
55. *Ibid.* r. 5.1B(3).
56. CDR Rules Version 3 EM (n. 47) 7.

which have different authorisations can provide AISs but the different levels of these authorisations represent the different payment services which the payment institution is authorised to provide, not different levels of authorisation to provide the AIS.[57] There is only a single level of authorisation available, which is registration as an AISP.[58] However, the PSR provides flexibility through the use of agents.

### *(b) Agents and Representatives*

The *PSR* provides enables the use of agents and acting on behalf of an AISP in the provision of their AIS,[59] and who provides services on behalf of the AISP.[60] Although initially the *PSR* did not cover the use of agents by an AISP, it was found that the resulting inability of the FCA to require registration or removal of agents 'leaves a gap in the regulatory regime which could lead to consumer detriment' and agents are now required to be registered with the FCA.[61] The application for the agent's registration is not as extensive as that required to be registered as an AISP and requires identification information, evidence that directors and management are fit and proper persons,[62] and a description of the services for which the agent is appointed.[63] The AISP must ensure that its agents inform its customers of the agency arrangement.[64] The AISP is responsible for anything done by its agent in providing AISs on its behalf and must take all reasonable steps to ensure that the *PSR* is complied with by the agent.[65] For this purpose, the AISP is expected 'to have appropriate systems and controls in place to oversee their agents' activities effectively'.[66] An agent may be removed from the register by the FCA if the registration was obtained falsely, it is desirable in order to protect the interests of consumers or the agent's provision of service is unlawful.[67]

A function similar to that performed by agents of an AISP under UK open banking can now be performed by 'representatives' of an accredited data recipient (ADR) under Australian open banking. An ADR with unrestricted accreditation can appoint an unaccredited person as their representative to seek customer consent to receive data

57. *PSR* (n. 19) reg. 2 (definitions of 'account information service provider', 'payment service provider').
58. *Ibid.* reg. 17.
59. *Ibid.* reg. 2 (defintion of 'agent').
60. Financial Conduct Authority, 'AISP Models under PSD2', (Guidance, 21 January 2020) https://www.fca.org.uk/firms/agency-models-under-psd2.
61. *PSR* (n. 19) reg. 34. *See The Payment Systems and Services and Electronic Money (Miscellaneous Amendments) Regulations 2017* (UK) reg. 7 (*The Payment Systems and Services and Electronic Money (Miscellaneous Amendments) Regulations*). *See also Explanatory Memorandum to the Payment Systems and Services and Electronic Money (Miscellaneous Amendments) Regulations 2017 2017* (UK) at [7.7] (*Explanatory Memorandum to the Payment Systems and Services and Electronic Money (Miscellaneous Amendments) Regulations 2017*).
62. Where the agent is not itself a payment service provider under the *PSR*: Financial Conduct Authority, 'Payment Services and Electronic Money – Our Approach' (n. 20) [5.18].
63. *PSR* (n. 19) reg. 34(3).
64. *Ibid.* reg. 34(16).
65. *Ibid.* reg. 36.
66. Financial Conduct Authority, 'Payment Services and Electronic Money – Our Approach' (n. 20) [5.2].
67. *PSR* (n. 19) reg. 35(1).

and to use the data shared so that the representative can provide goods or services to the customer.[68] There must be a written contract between the data recipient and the representative containing prescribed terms relating to the use and treatment of the data and the data recipient is legally required to ensure that the representative complies with that contract and is responsible for breaches of the *CDR Rules* by its representative.[69] The CDR representatives of a data recipient are required to be notified to the ACCC and disclosed to customers.[70]

The result of the ability of AISPs to appoint agents and for ADRs to sponsor other data recipients and appoint representatives is that facilitation of indirect participation is broadly similar in Australia and the UK. In each jurisdiction, an authorised entity is responsible for the actions of the indirect participant and requirements for binding arrangements between them.

### *(c) Sharing Customer Data Beyond the Open Banking System*

The above analysis focusses on indirect participation from 'within' the open banking system. UK open banking offers even more flexibility for indirect participation through the use of 'third parties' or 'another person' who can receive customer data without being subject to regulation under the *PSR*. This is permitted by the definition of 'AIS' in the *PSR*, which allows for the consolidated information on the customer's payment accounts to be provided 'to another person in accordance with the payment service user's instructions'.[71] This enables an AISP to provide the information to another party who is not regulated under the *PSR*, with the customer's consent and permits the use of the shared data beyond the provision of the AIS for which the AISP is authorised, for example 'credit scoring, mortgage applications or loan applications' and the passing of that information to a loan company.[72] This use would not otherwise be permitted due to the limits on the services able to be offered by direct participation analysed in section 9.1 above. However, these third parties involved in the collection, processing and use of customer data, which are not AISPs or agents of them, are not subject to *PSR*. As noted by the FCA:

> More than one business may be involved in obtaining, processing and using payment account information to provide an online service to a customer. However, the business that requires authorisation or registration to provide the AIS is the one that provides consolidated account information to the payment service user (including through an agent) in line with the payment service user's request to that business.[73]

68. The accredited data recipient makes the request for the shared data and shares the data received with the representative: *CDR Rules* (n. 4) r. 1.10AA.
69. *Ibid*. rr. 1.10AA, 1.10A, 1.16A, 4.3A-4.3C, 7.3, 7.6, 7.8A, 7.10A, 7.11, 7.16.
70. *Ibid*. rr. 5.14, 7.2.
71. *PSR* (n. 19) reg. 2 (definition of 'account information service').
72. Financial Conduct Authority, 'AISP Models under PSD2' (n. 60).
73. Financial Conduct Authority, *FCA Handbook* (Financial Conduct Authority, 2013) [PERG 15.3 Q25A].

However they are subject to *GDPR* with respect to those data.[74] This is not the same as the responsibilities imposed on AISPs for the agents which they appoint to act on their behalf. If it were, then there would have been no need to amend the *PSR* to include agents appointed by an AISP within the scope of FCA regulation.[75]

Australian open banking does not offer similar flexibility in sharing customer data beyond the perimeter of its authorisation framework. Whilst the *CDR Rules* also permit some disclosures to those outside of the Australian system's regulatory architecture, they limit disclosures to specified classes of 'trusted advisors'[76] who:

> as members of a professional class ... are subject to existing professional or regulatory oversight, including obligations consistent with safeguarding consumer data (e.g. fiduciary or other duties to act in the best interests of their clients).[77]

Although, like the use of third parties under UK open banking, this enables shared data to be provided to someone beyond Australian open banking's regulatory perimeter with the customer's consent, it limits this to recipients who already owe professional duties to the customer, rather than merely being subject to generally applicable data protection legislation. The consequences of this difference are evaluated against indirect participation in payment systems next.

### 9.2.2 Evaluation Against Indirect Participation in Banking Payment Systems

#### *(a) Tiering of Participation*

The analysis in previous chapters shows that agency relationships are fundamental to banking payment systems. This occurs when banks appoint correspondent banks to make payments on their behalf, and when banks who are members of a payment system make payments on behalf of other banks who are not members. This provides those other banks with 'indirect participation' in the payment system, and results in 'tiering' of participation in the system.[78] Such tiering of participation provides benefits by avoiding the expense of direct membership for the indirectly participating banks, providing economies of scale in processing for the settlement bank and reducing liquidity demands through internalisation of payments and liquidity pooling amongst

74. Financial Conduct Authority, 'AISP Models under PSD2' (n. 60).
75. *See* n. 61 and accompanying text.
76. Including qualified accountants, practicing lawyers, registered tax agents and advisers, financial counselling agencies, regulated financial advisers and financial planners and mortgage brokers: *CDR Rules* (n. 4) r. 1.10C.
77. CDR Rules Version 3 EM (n. 47) 15.
78. *See* Committee on Payment and Settlement Systems and International Organization of Securities Commissions, 'Principles for Financial Markets Infrastructures' (Standards, Bank for International Settlements, April 2012) [3.19.1].

the customer banks.[79] However, in the context of payment systems, indirect participation can also increase the risk in the system, as the liquidity and credit risks of the customer banks are concentrated in the settlement bank and the customer banks take increased operational risk on the settlement bank. Also, the customer banks create risks for the settlement bank as the settlement bank is responsible to the payment system for their performance. This is particularly material where the number and size of indirect transactions is large in comparison to those of direct participation.[80] To manage these risks, a payment system:

> should ensure that its procedures, rules, and agreements with direct participants allow it to gather basic information about indirect participants in order to identify, monitor, and manage any material risks to the FMI arising from such tiered participation arrangements.[81]

The sponsored level of accreditation and the ability to appoint representatives under Australian open banking, and the ability to appoint agents under UK open banking, are consistent with approach taken to regulation of indirect participation in payment systems. In each case, the data recipient is responsible for the entity which it sponsors or which it has appointed as its representative or agent and the regulator is required to be notified of the sponsored recipient, representative or agent.

### *(b) Transfer of Value Beyond the System*

However, this alignment with payment systems does not extend to the ability for an AISP to use third parties without any registration or notification requirements, or responsibility to the customer, under UK open banking. As the money represented by bank funds is constituted by amounts owing by commercial banks, banks are always involved either for their customers or as customers themselves. Indeed, this is a fundamental purpose of the authorisations needed to conduct banking business. Commercial bank money needs to be converted to something else, such as cash, before being withdrawn from the banking payment system. From this perspective, the absence of any requirement under the UK system for AISP to register or notify the FCA of third parties with whom customer data are being shared, or to be responsible for those third parties, is not consistent with the requirements applied to indirect participants in payment systems. Third parties remain subject to data conduct requirements under *GDPR*, but this is not the same as the responsibilities imposed on AISPs for the agents which they appoint to act on their behalf. Essentially, the third party is beyond

79. Manning, Nier and Schanz (n. 44) 170. *See also* John Jackson and Mark Manning, 'Central Bank Intraday Collateral Policy and Implications for Tiering in RTGS Payment Systems' in Stephen Millard, Andrew Haldane and Victoria Saporta (eds), *The Future of Payment Systems* (Routledge, 2008).
80. Committee on Payment and Settlement Systems and International Organization of Securities Commissions (n. 78) [3.19.3].
81. *Ibid.* [3.19.5].

the UK system, and no one within the system has responsibilities to the customer for its conduct.[82]

The recent changes to the *CDR Rules* do not take the same approach, as disclosures to those outside of the Australian system's regulatory architecture are to be made to specified classes of regulated 'trusted advisors'. This is more aligned with banking payment systems as it ensures that there is still a regulated relationship between the recipient of the shared data and the customer which imposes duties in the customer's favour, beyond those under generally applicable law. It could be argued that the ability for customers to consent to their data being shared with others beyond UK open banking is no different to the customer sharing the information themselves by some other process. Whilst this is true from the customer's perspective, from a systemic perspective, this is different because of the impact of misuse of customer data on the credibility of the open banking system. If a customer suffers loss because of the misuse of their data which has been shared using open banking, and the open banking system provides no regulatory remedy because the data was shared with someone beyond its regulatory perimeter, then the trustworthiness of the system will be damaged. As the analysis in Chapter 4 shows, this loss of trust can affect the confidence in the open banking system as a whole, and its continued use by customers and participants. UK open banking relies on the *GDPR* to guard against that loss of trust. Australian open banking takes a more robust approach, not solely relying on Australia's privacy legislation, the *Privacy Act*,[83] but by ensuring that there is a regulated professional relationship with the customer protecting the use of the shared data. This difference means that UK open banking offers greater access to customer data than Australian open banking and that which payment system regulation offers in relation to customer funds. However, the trade-off for this is a reduction in the directness of accountability to the customer for the customers for the use and custody of customer data.

## 9.3 HOW SHOULD OUTSOURCING ARRANGEMENTS BE AUTHORISED?

An alternative to incurring all of the investment and costs to meet the requirements to participate in open banking is to enter into arrangements which other entities to supply the services to assist in meeting those requirements. These outsourcing arrangements are permitted under both Australian and UK open banking, as well as in banking payment systems. However, just as with indirect participation, this can also concentrate risks in the performance of outsourced service providers who supply services to many direct and indirect participants.

82. The FCA takes the view that regulation is only required for the provision of the consolidated account information to the customer: Financial Conduct Authority, *FCA Handbook* (Financial Conduct Authority, 2013) [PERG 15/6 Q25A].
83. *Privacy Act 1998* (Cth) (*Privacy Act*).

The manner of authorising arrangements with outsourced service providers in the open banking systems are comparatively analysed below, followed by evaluation against the authorisation of outsourced service providers in banking payment systems.

### 9.3.1 Authorising Outsourcing Arrangements in Open Banking

The *CDR Rules* offer some further flexibility in participation in Australian open banking by enabling CDR data to be disclosed under 'CDR outsourcing arrangements'.[84] These are written contracts between two persons under which one of them (the 'provider') will either:

- collect CDR data from a CDR participant on behalf of the principal; or
- provide goods and services to the other person (the 'principal') using the CDR data disclosed to it by the other person.[85]

Under the contract, the provider must, at the principal's direction, provide the principal with access to the CDR data, return or delete the CDR data, and direct any person to whom it has disclosed the CDR data to do the same.[86] The provider must take the same information security steps to protect any CDR data collected by it, or disclosed to it, as part of the arrangement, or which derives from that data.[87] Also, the provider must not disclose that data to another person, unless the disclosure is under another CDR outsourcing arrangement.[88] The principal must, if it is an accredited person, ensure that the provider complies with its obligations,[89] and any use or disclosure of the CDR data by the provider is taken to have been by the principal, whether or not the use or disclosure was in accordance with the outsourcing arrangement.[90] This prevents the CDR data from being used or disclosed by the provider to another person, unless such disclosure would be permitted by the data recipient. In addition to these obligations, the accredited person must provide to customers a list of the outsourced service providers used, the nature of services provided by each of them, and the CDR data that may be disclosed to each of them, as part of the accredited entity's CDR policy.[91]

This approach to outsourcing is the result of changes made to the design of the Australian system. Originally, outsourcing arrangements permitted the use of agents, but if the agent was not accredited at the unrestricted level, these only permitted goods or services to be provided to the data recipient. These constraints were recognised as a weakness in the accessibility of Australian open banking and *CDR Rules* were

84. *CDR Rules* (n. 4) r. 1.10.
85. *Ibid*. r. 1.10(2)(a).
86. *Ibid*. r. 1.10(2)(b).
87. *Ibid*. rr. 1.10(2)(a), 1.10(4).
88. *Ibid*. r. 1.10(2)(b).
89. *Ibid*. r. 1.16.
90. *Ibid*. r. 7.6(2).
91. *Ibid*. r. 7.2(4).

amended to permit unaccredited outsourced service providers to collect customer data on behalf of an accredited entity.[92]

UK open banking is more flexible in the use of outsourced service providers. An AISP is able to use 'technical service providers' which obtain and process customer information to support the AISP. Provided they do not have any direct relationship with the customer, technical service providers do not need to be authorised or registered by the FCA.[93] The AISP remains responsible for compliance with the *PSR* when a technical service provider is being used.[94] Complementing this are outsourcing arrangements with persons to perform operational functions for the AISP without accessing the customer's account on behalf of the AISP. These are required to be included in the description of the AISP's structural organisation as part of an application to register as an AISP,[95] and changes to them must not cause the AISP to cease meeting the conditions of their registration.[96] The AISP is responsible for the acts and omissions of someone to which its activities are outsourced in the same way as it is for its agent.[97] It is noteworthy that more detailed requirements are applicable under the *PSR* to the outsourcing by entities authorised as payment institutions, such as requirements for notification to the FCA, contracts with the outsourcing provider, and the arrangements must not impair the quality of the entity's internal control or the ability of the FCA to monitor compliance with the *PSR*.[98] However, these are not applicable to an entity which is only receiving customer data as an AISP and not dealing with customer funds.

Originally, the most significant difference between the systems in relation to outsourcing was that Australian open banking was very constrained by comparison with UK open banking. It did not enable an unaccredited entity to collect data directly from a customer to provide intermediary services to the data recipient like a technical service provider under the UK system. Outsourcing arrangements permitted the use of agents, but if the agent was not accredited at the unrestricted level, these only permitted goods or services to be provided to the data recipient. These constraints were recognised as a weakness in the Australian system and the *CDR Rules* were amended to permit unaccredited outsourced service providers to collect CDR data on behalf of an accredited entity.[99] However, there remains one area of difference in the systems with respect to outsourced service providers. The Australian system imposes more detailed regulation with respect to the provision of outsourced services, similar to those which are imposed under the *PSR* on authorised payment institutions. As noted above, they are subject to regulation under Australian open banking regardless of their relationship with the customer, and that regulation imposes responsibility and supervision requirements similar to those which are imposed under the *PSR* on authorised payment

92. CDR Rules Version 3 (n. 52) sch. 2.
93. Financial Conduct Authority, 'Guidance on the Scope of the Payment Services Regulations 2017' (Perimiter Guidance Manual, April 2021) [PERG 15.3].
94. *Ibid*.
95. Financial Conduct Authority, 'Payment Services and Electronic Money – Our Approach' (n. 20) [3.171].
96. *Ibid*. [4.58].
97. *PSR* (n. 19) reg. 36.
98. *See ibid*. reg. 25(2).
99. CDR Rules Version 3 (n. 52) sch. 2.

institutions but not on outsourcing by AISPs. This difference is evaluated against the arrangements in banking payment systems next.

### 9.3.2 Evaluation Against Regulation of Outsourcing by Banks

Banks use outsourcing to reduce costs, access new technology, permit a focus on the banks' core business, and to take the benefit of economies of scale.[100] According to the BIS, banks are 'increasingly using third parties to carry out activities that the [banks] themselves would normally have undertaken'.[101] In addition to benefits, outsourcing also brings risks, which can arise through failure to oversee the outsourced provider, poor service from the outsourced provider, misalignment of strategy and practices by the outsourced provider, failure of the outsourced provider to comply with the laws which apply to the bank, technology failures by the outsourced provider, fraud and default of the outsourced provider, impediments to access to information, and concentration risk on the outsourced provider.[102] These risks can affect the stability not only of the participants, but also others that depend on them and the system as a whole. As a result, in Australia and the UK, banks are required to adhere to regulations on material outsourcing.[103]

In recent years, there has been an increasing emphasis on outsourcing risks relating to technology providers, and in particular cloud computing.[104] Of particular relevance is the increasing recognition of the potential for concentration risk to develop where:

> a single service provider, or a small number of service providers which are very difficult to substitute may, in some cases dominate the provision of certain outsourced and third party services to large numbers of ... regulated firms. The failure of or a prolonged, significant disruption at a critical third party could have adverse consequences on financial stability'.[105]

This is particularly relevant for outsourcing information technology functions as they can be provided in a standardised, rather than tailored, form on a large scale and

100. Bank for International Settlements, 'Outsourcing in Financial Services' (Report, Joint Forum, February 2005) 6. *See also* Daniel Gozman and Leslie Willcocks, 'The Emerging Cloud Dilemma: Balancing Innovation with Cross-Border Privacy and Outsourcing Regulations' (2019) 97 *Journal of Business Research* 235-256.
101. Bank for International Settlements, 'Outsourcing in Financial Services' (n. 100) 1.
102. *Ibid*. 12.
103. *See APRA Prudential Standard CPS 231 Outsourcing* ('*CPS 231*'); Prudential Regulation Authority, 'Supervisory Statement SS2/21 Outsourcing and Third Party Risk Management' (Supervisory Statement, March 2021).
104. *See* Australian Prudential Regulation Authority, 'Outsourcing Involving Cloud Computing Services' (Information Paper, 24 September 2018); Financial Conduct Authority, 'Guidance for Firms Outsourcing to the "Cloud" and Other Third-Party IT Services' (Finalised Guidance No FG16, July 2016, updated September 2019).
105. Prudential Regulation Authority, 'Outsourcing and Third Party Risk Management' (Policy Statement No. PS7/21, March 2021) [12.1].

in an automated manner.[106] Regulated entities are not able to see all of the connections between their outsourced service providers and the other participants in the banking payment system or, as a result, all of the potential risks which could arise. Accordingly, the relevant regulators are required to supervise the participants' outsourcing arrangements 'identifying and monitoring risk concentrations at individual service providers and assessing whether or not such concentrations could pose a risk to the stability of the financial system'.[107] This is enabled by ensuring participants have comprehensive enforceable agreements with material outsourcing providers and that they notify regulators of their material outsourcing arrangements.

The regulatory requirements relating to outsourcing in Australian open banking, but not UK open banking, are comparable to those applying to banks in banking payment systems. Unlike the Australian system, the UK system does not require that a contract with particular provisions be in place with outsourced service providers, and it does not have a clear disclosure obligation in relation to the identity and role of outsourced service providers. Under the *PSR*, conditions of a nature similar to those required under the Australian system are needed only if the outsourcing relates to the payment of money, rather than the transfer of data.[108] Accordingly, the ability to properly identify and assess the risk that any concentration of service providers for data recipients could present to the UK system as a whole is impaired when evaluated against banking payment systems.

## 9.4 HOW CAN LEGAL FOUNDATIONS FACILITATE PARTICIPATION?

### 9.4.1 Summary of Comparison and Evaluation

This chapter has examined the implications of the legal foundations of Australian and UK open banking for facilitating participation, through a comparison of their legal features relating to direct and indirect participation and outsourcing arrangements, and an evaluation against equivalent legal features of payment systems.

The analysis has shown that although the requirements for authorisation as a recipient under Australian and UK open banking are broadly comparable, there is a conceptual difference between them. The Australian system imposes them as a condition of access to the data sharing network whilst the UK system imposes them as a condition of providing the service using data received through such a network. The analysis has also shown that the UK approach is not as aligned with developments in banking payment systems which seek to tailor access requirements to the risks being managed.

106. European Banking Authority, 'EBA Guidelines on Outsourcing Arrangements' (Final Report No EBA/GL/2019/02, 25 February 2019) 15.

107. *Ibid.* 5.

108. The Australian system includes a data segregation requirement as part of its information security controls, to ensure that CDR data held or stored on behalf of a data recipient is segregated from other CDR data and not commingled: *CDR Rules* (n. 4) sch. 2 r. 2.2(2)(e). This offers some protection in the case of the outsourced service provider's default.

The analysis has also shown that the legal foundations of UK open banking relating to indirect participation enable more use of customer data beyond its authorisation perimeter in a way which differs from Australian open banking and banking payment systems. This more relaxed approach is also seen in the outsourcing requirements applicable under UK open banking which are aligned with Australian open banking and banking payment systems only to the extent that payments are involved under the UK system.

The consequences of these differences is that the legal foundations of UK open banking support connectivity more than in Australian open banking or banking payment systems. The trade-off for this is that UK open banking's legal foundations provide less support for accountability than Australian open banking. This is illustrated in Figure 9.1.

*Figure 9.1 Illustration of Evaluation and Comparison Relating to Facilitation of Participation*

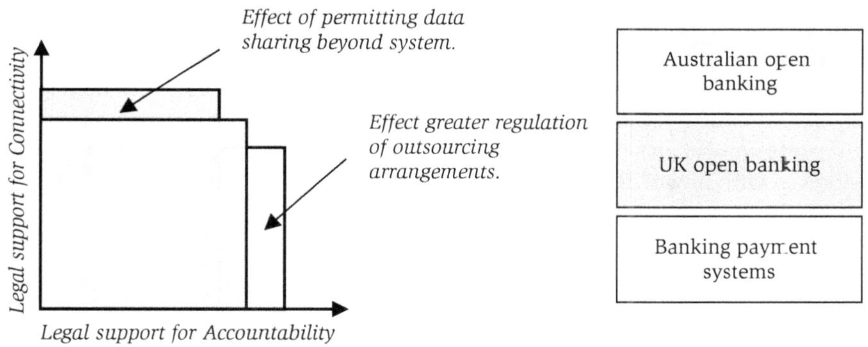


This analysis shows the need to balance connectivity and accountability in the legal foundations which facilitate participation. This also demonstrates the importance of managing network risk. This risk is explained next, followed by an illustration of the comparable concentration risk in banking payment systems, and a discussion of how concentration risk management methods could be applied in the legal foundations of open banking systems.

### 9.4.2 Network Risk in Open Banking Systems

Network risk arises in open banking systems when the interdependencies created between participants cause the default of one participant to result in other participants no longer being trusted with customer data. A critical element in understanding this risk is that these interdependencies are necessary for the efficacy of open banking systems. The technology requirements for participation in open banking as a bank or recipient, including with respect to information security, are extensive. Smaller fintechs or smaller banks who do not have the resources to develop these capabilities themselves will most likely retain and rely on service providers for this purpose. Due to the expansion of open banking systems as networks, and their reliance on standardised functions which can be scaled easily, it is plausible, if not probable, that a few such providers will provide these services to many participants. Further, the rapid expansion of open banking systems as highly connected networks and complex systems, means that a service provider, such as a cloud computing provider, could quickly become critical to the systems' operation. This results in these service providers potentially becoming 'single points of failure' for the system such that:

> an ostensibly large and diverse number of entities all dependent on just a few unregulated providers for critical services, creating a substantial concentration risk and increasing the threat of contagion in the event of a service failure.[109]

The sudden suspension or cessation of the services provided by a dominant service provider, for example because of their insolvency or a successful cyber-attack, would impact the ability of many other participants in the system to function, potentially severely impairing the communication of customer data and causing a severe loss of data. Further, due to the cost and risk involved in safely storing data, it is plausible that they could be responsible for the storage of a significant proportion, or even the majority, of the customer data shared with data recipients. Consequently, the failure of just one of these highly connected providers could not only damage the communication of customer data through much of the open banking system but also significantly impact the confidence of customers and the credibility of the system, causing the withdrawal of further services. This could mean that:

> [i]n a manner parallel to the policy debate following the 2008 financial crisis, policymakers might need to begin answering the question of whether other firms, particularly in tech and telecommunications, have become too big and too interconnected.[110]

To further explain this aspect of network risk, the next section sets out an illustration of the comparable risk in banking payment systems, a form of operational risk called *concentration risk*.

### 9.4.3 Illustration of Concentration Risk in Banking Payment Systems: Caldwell

Reliance on a few outsourced service providers is recognised as a significant risk in banking payment systems, where it can create 'concentration risk', which can affect

109. Wayne Byers, 'Peering into a Cloudy Future' (Speech, Curious Thinkers Conference, Sydney, 21 September 2018).
110. Jonathan William Welburn et al., 'Systemic Risk in the Broad Economy' (Report, Rand Corporation, 2020) 38 https://www.rand.org/pubs/research_reports/RR4185.html.

the stability of not only the participants, but others that depend on them too.[111] Concentration risk is defined to be a combination of operational and systemic risks:

> Concentration risks may arise when one regulated entity relies extensively on one service provider or when many regulated entities rely on one or very few service providers.[112]

Concentration risk is illustrated by aspects of the collapse of Caldwell and Company ('Caldwell') in 1930, which was fundamental to the first banking crisis of the Great Depression in the United States. The causes of Caldwell's collapse were many and its impact significant. Caldwell controlled the largest chain of banks in the southern United States, many of these being correspondent banks holding the deposits of smaller banks within their own group. When the smaller banks needed cash, they turned to their correspondent banks. In effect, the smaller banks outsourced the holding of their customer's funds. However, when Caldwell lost substantial funds in securities markets, it drained cash from the correspondent banks in the group, triggering the failures of 120 affiliated banks which relied upon it, so that bank runs 'radiated outwards' from these focal events.[113] The severing of the correspondent links with failed banks in turn contributed to the failure of other banks:

> The failures of [Caldwell and its affiliates] triggered a correspondent cascade that forced scores of commercial banks to suspend operations. In communities where these banks closed, depositors panicked and withdrew funds en masse from other banks. Panic spread from town to town. Within a few weeks, hundreds of banks suspended operations.[114]

The impact of the collapse of Caldwell on other banks is instructive as to the potential consequences of a lack of transparency with respect to the connections between participants and outsourcing providers, such as cloud computing providers. As noted above, many participants in a successful open banking system could be relying on a handful of key cloud computing or cyber-security providers for services which are critical to the functions which they perform. This dependence on those service providers by open banking participants is not dissimilar to the dependence which customer banks in a correspondent network have on their settlement banks. This is now recognised in banking payment systems, where the reliance placed on outsourced service providers, such as cloud computing platforms, is of particular focus in the management of concentration risk.

---

111. *See* Financial Stability Board, 'Regulatory and Supervisory Issues Relating to Outsourcing and Third-Party Relationships' (Discussion Paper, 9 November 2020) 14. *See also* International Organization of Securities Commissions, 'Principles of Outsourcing' (Consultation Report No CR01/2020, May 2020).
112. International Organization of Securities Commissions, 'Principles of Outsourcing' (Consultation Report No CR01/2020, May 2020) 25.
113. Gary Richardson, 'Bank Distress During the Great Contraction, 1929 to 1933, New Data from the Archives of the Board of Governors' (Working Paper No. 12590, National Bureau of Economic Research Cambridge, Mass., USA, 2006).
114. Gary Richardson, 'Banking Panics of 1930-31', *Federal Reserve History* (Essay, 22 November 2013) https://www.federalreservehistory.org/essays/banking-panics-1930-31.

Accordingly, the legal features used in banking payment systems to manage concentration risk deserve consideration for incorporation into the legal foundations of open banking.

### 9.4.4 Incorporating Concentration Risk Management in Open Banking

The management of concentration risk in banking payment systems is still evolving and significant concerns remain on the exposure taken to technological single points of failure. However, aspects of the approach to its management could be applied in open banking systems. This would require participants to provide regulators with sufficient transparency on their material service providers so that the risks of many participants relying on the same provider for the communication or storage of customer data can be assessed and monitored. This would also require binding contracts to be in place with the providers so that steps could be taken before one provider becomes a single point of failure and threatens the credibility of an open banking system. If risks increase, then alternative approaches which have been suggested for managing this risk could also be considered. These include generating competition amongst the providers (for example by mandating access, requiring diversification of service providers, requiring rotation between providers, or facilitating data sharing between the providers), or more direct regulatory intervention (by requiring licensing, requiring changes to technical functionality, encouraging or regulating the providers as public utilities).[115] A further alternative is to ensure that there is 'the ability to bring data back or applications back on-premises in a way that ensure continuous adequate performance' by the participant, despite the service provider's failure.[116]

115. *See, e.g.*, Dirk A Zetzsche et al., 'Digital Finance Platforms: Towards a New Regulatory Paradigm' (2020) 23(1) *University of Pennsylvania Journal of Business Law* 273.
116. Financial Stability Board (n. 111) 15.

## Chapter 10

# Allocating Liability in Open Banking

This chapter compares the legal foundations for the allocation of liabilities between participants in open banking systems. It compares the legal relationships established between participants which support this function in the Australian and UK open banking systems and evaluates them against the equivalent legal relationships established under banking payment systems. The analysis addresses three questions:

- What should the legal relationships be between participants?
- How should liabilities be allocated between participants?
- How should customers be compensated for losses?

The answers to these questions are fundamental to an open banking system's performance of its *connectivity* and *accountability* functions.

### 10.1 WHAT LEGAL RELATIONSHIPS SHOULD BE BETWEEN PARTICIPANTS?

Admission to participate in banking payment systems does not, of itself, define the legal relationships between the participants which enable fair and competitive participation. Instead, those relationships are defined by the 'rules of the game' of the banking payment system,[1] being the bilateral contracts and other legal relationships which 'are stitched together and subsumed within a framework of multilateral rights and duties'.[2] These legal relationships need to be established with 'a high degree of certainty' if risk

1. Stephen Millard, Andrew Haldane and Victoria Saporta, 'The Future of Payment Systems' in Stephen Millard, Andrew Haldane and Victoria Saporta (eds), *The Future of Payment Systems* (Routledge, 2008), 6.
2. Roy Goode, 'The Concept and Implications of a Market in Commerical Law' (1990) 24(2) *Israel Law Review* 185-210, 190.

management in banking payment systems is to be 'sound and efficient'.[3] The previous chapter showed how the relationships between participants in an open banking system, and with those indirectly participating, create a network of interdependencies in relation to the sharing and use of customer data. This means that the 'rules of the game' between participants in open banking systems are also critical.

The legal requirements relating to the legal relationships between participants are comparatively analysed below, followed by evaluation against the legal relationships established in banking payment systems.

### 10.1.1 Comparison of Legal Relationships Between System Participants

#### *(a) Multilateral Contracts*

In Australian open banking, the *CCA* creates a separate contract between a data holder to which a binding Australian Standard applies and each accredited person.[4] Under the terms of that contract, each of the data holder and the accredited person agrees to observe the binding Australian Standard and to engage in the conduct which it requires.[5] The purpose of this contract is to enable either a data holder or an accredited person to enforce the right which they have under the Australian system to access data in accordance with the Australian Standards.[6] However, the legislation does not limit the contractual rights to those needed to access data and they are granted to data holders (banks) as well as data recipients.[7]

In contrast, in UK open banking, the *PSR* does not establish any contractual relationship between banks and data recipients. Indeed, it makes it clear that there is no requirement for any contract between them in order for data to be shared under the UK system.[8] The FCA has clarified that this does not prohibit contractual arrangements between a bank and data recipient to address liability between them, or to permit access on more favourable terms (e.g., more frequent access) or more functionality (e.g., access to non-payment accounts) provided that the contract is not a precondition to access required under *PSR*.[9] Nor do the UK Guidelines address this absence. Whilst they 'describe and provide direction on the roles and responsibilities' of participants in

3. Committee on Payment and Settlement Systems, 'Core Principles for Systemically Important Payment Systems' (Core Principles, Bank for International Settlements, January 2001) [7.1.2].
4. *Competition and Consumer Act 2010* (Cth) ('*Competition and Consumer Act*') ss 56FD(1)(a), (b).
5. *Ibid.* s. 56FD(1)(c), (d).
6. Explanatory Memorandum, Treasury Laws Amendment (Consumer Data Right) Bill 2018 (Cth) [1.15] ('CDR Bill EM') [1.271].
7. The *CCA* provides that the rights to seek directions from the Court also apply to the contractual provisions requiring the performance of binding data standards: *CCA* (n. 4) s. 56FE (3). However, the intention is clear that they can also be separately enforced: CDR Bill EM (n. 6) [1.271].
8. *Payment Services Regulation 2017* (UK) ('*PSR*') reg. 70(2)(c).
9. Financial Conduct Authority, 'Payment Services and Electronic Money – Our Approach' (Approach Document, June 2019) [17.41].

the UK system,[10] they are not expressed to create binding legal obligations between banks and data recipients.[11]

### *(b) Effect of Contractual Arrangements*

The creation of contracts between banks and data recipients under Australian system represents a significant difference in the legal relationships between their participants. The Explanatory Memorandum to the Bill which enacted the Australian system described these arrangements to be a 'multilateral contract' which operates when a data standard applies to a data holder or an accredited person,[12] and also referred to the multilateral contracts established under the operating rules of financial markets licensed under the *Corporations Act*.[13] These references are curious. Multilateral contracts normally arise between parties when 'contracting parties do not deal directly with each other [and] [i]nstead they deal only with a central organiser'.[14] This results in the parties having contractual privity with each other, and not just that central organiser with whom they directly contracted. This is the effect of the statutory contract created under the *Corporations Act* between participants in licensed financial markets.[15] It is also the result of court decisions in both Australia and the UK when different participants agree to comply with the same rules with the same central party.[16] However, the statutory note accompanying the relevant provision in the *CCA* makes it clear that 'the data holder will be taken to have a separate contract with each accredited person'.[17] Accordingly, the legislative intention is a series of bilateral contracts each between a data holder and a data recipient, rather than a multilateral

10. Open Banking Implementation Entity, 'Open Banking Guidelines for Read/Write Participants' (Guidelines, May 2018) 5 https://www.openbanking.org.uk/wp-content/uploads/Guidelines-for-Read-Write-Participants.pdf.
11. There are references in the *CMA Order* to binding arrangements between the OBIE and banks, particularly in relation to the 'composition, governance arrangements, budget and funding for the Implementation Entity': *Retail Banking Market Investigation Order 2017* (UK) ('*CMA Order*'). However, recipients are not parties to these arrangements.
12. CDR Bill EM (n. 6) [1.270].
13. *Ibid.* [1.265].
14. John Dyson Heydon, *Heydon on Contract – The General Part* (Lawbook Co., 2019) [2.100].
15. The *Corporations Act* provides that the operating rules of a licensed market have effect as a contract under seal between the licensee and each market participant, and also between each participant and each other participant: *Corporations Act* (n. 31) s. 793B.
16. *See Clarke v. Earl of Dunhaven* [1897] AC 59 ('*Clarke v. Earl of Dunhaven*'); *Raguz v. Sullivan* [2000] NSWCA 240 ('*Raguz v. Sullivan*'). In the context of financial markets its effect is to 'underpin each bilateral sale and purchase contract with a multilateral network of market rules': Ewan McKendrick, *Goode and McKendrick on Commercial Law* (LexisNexis, 6th ed., 2020) 199. The constitution of a company has a similar effect as a contract between the members: Nick Seddon and Fred Ellinghaus, *Cheshire and Fifoot's Law of Contract* (LexisNexis Butterworths, 9th Australian ed., 2008) [3.6]. Indeed, this is the historical basis of the multilateral contract provision relating to financial markets in the *Corporations Act*: Corporations Law Amendment (ASX) Bill Explanatory Memorandum 1997 (Cth) [7.46], [7.47] ('ASX Bill EM').
17. *CCA* (n. 4) s. 56FG.

contract between all of them.[18] That being said, this should not impair the effectiveness of the provision to achieve this particular purpose, namely:

> if a data holder or an accredited data recipient is unwilling or unable to provide the designated data set in a format that is consistent with the data standards, then the party who is seeking the information is able to seek redress.[19]

The absence of any equivalent legal relationship between the bank and the recipient deprives participants in UK open banking of an important source of legal protection. It is noted that each system provides its regulator with rights to take action against a participant for breach of its data-related obligations.[20] Whilst each system also grants similar rights to affected persons,[21] under *PSR*, these are granted only to 'private persons', which would not include other participants in UK open banking.[22] Consequently, the primary legal protection for a bank or data recipient against the non-performance of another's obligations under UK open banking is enforcement by the FCA. If there is a breach by a participant and the FCA elects not to take any action (perhaps because no customers have been harmed) then there is no clear avenue for legal redress.[23] The impact of this difference between the Australian and UK systems is particularly apparent in the allocation of liability between participants.

### 10.1.2 Evaluation Against Legal Relationships in Banking Payment Systems

The legal relationship between banks that make and receive payments in banking payment systems depends on the payment mechanism used.

In correspondent banking, there is a 'chain' of agency relationships. Each agent bank has duties to its principal under its contract of appointment (which could be its account terms) but 'it is not liable to anybody else in the chain with whom it is not in immediate privity'.[24] For example, the correspondent bank appointed by a customer's

18. Whilst it is arguable that these bilateral contracts could themselves be sufficient to imply a true multilateral contract between the data recipients under the principles of *Clarke v. Earle of Dunhaven* and *Raguz v. Sullivan*, this should not be the case where it is contrary to the expressed legislative intention.
19. CDR Bill EM (n. 6) [1.270]. This does not require data recipients to have contracts with each other. Even though the reciprocity under the Australian system can require data recipients to share data with other data recipients, when doing so they are characterised as data holders: *see* section 3.3 above.
20. *See* section 6.2.2.
21. *See* section 6.2.2.
22. *PSR* (n. 8) reg. 148.
23. In enforcing the *PSR* the FCA's aim is to 'change the behaviour of the person who is the subject of the action, deter future non-compliance by others, eliminate any financial gain or benefit from non-compliance and, *where appropriate*, remedy the harm caused by non-compliance': Financial Conduct Authority, 'Payment Services and Electronic Money – Our Approach' (n. 9) (emphasis added) [14.3]. In choosing whether to refer a case for investigation and enforcement, the FCA considers its 'statutory objectives, business priorities and other issues, such as the response of the person to the issues': *ibid.* [14.5]. These criteria make it clear that the FCA may choose to not enforce every breach.
24. Philip R Wood, *Set-Off and Netting, Derivatives, Clearing Systems* (Sweet & Maxwell, 2019) Ch. 19.

bank does not have contractual duties to the customer.[25] Ultimately, the payment is settled across the accounts of a bank with whom both the payer's bank (or its correspondent bank) and the payee's bank (or its correspondent bank) hold an account.[26] The contractual relationship which they each have is with the bank across whose accounts the payment is made, rather than a separate contract between them, governs that payment.[27] This is not a multilateral contract and there is no contractual relationship between the payer and its bank when it is acting as receiving bank.

Payments through multilateral payment networks are also settled across the accounts which participants hold with the same bank being, for most payment systems, the central bank. However, in contrast to correspondent banking, the legal relationships for payments made through payment systems:

> depend upon multilateral contracts whereby each member bank is bound by the system rules. Each member will contract with the system provider to conform to the system rules. The members will then be deemed to have contracted between themselves on the terms of their individual undertakings.[28]

These rules are binding between the banks, new members are required to adhere to them in order to participate, they can inform customary banking practice,[29] and they are relevant to the disputes between them.[30] Also, the role that these contracts amongst the participants perform is fundamental to the payment system, and because they are one of the key tools used to mitigate systemic risk, they need to be 'enforceable in all relevant jurisdictions'.[31]

The nature of the legal relationships under UK system is more like those in correspondent banking whilst those under Australian open banking are more like those in a payment system. The UK system establishes no legal relationship between the bank, which is sharing the customer data, and the recipient, whilst the Australian system establishes a contractual relationship between them. As noted above, this

25. *Royal Products Ltd v. Midland Bank Ltd* [1981] 2 Lloyd's Rep. 194 ('*Royal Products v. Midland Bank*').
26. 'Any account transfer must ultimately be achieved by means of two accounts held by different beneficiaries with the same institution': *Libyan Arab Foreign Bank v. Bankers Trust Co* [1989] QB 728, 750 ('*Libyan Arab Foreign Bank v. Bankers Trust*').
27. It has also been found that there can be a claim of negligence by the paying bank against the receiving bank in these circumstances: *Royal Bank of Canada v. Stangl* (Ontario Court, General Division, Ferrier J, 28 February 1992) ('*Royal Bank of Canada v. Stangl*'). However, it has also been doubted that a duty of care between them arises: *Abou-Rahmah v. Abacha* [2005] 1 Lloyd's Reports 484 ('*Abou-Rahmah v. Abacha*').
28. Michael Brindle and Raymond Cox, *Law of Bank Payments* (Sweet & Maxwell, Thomson Reuters, 5th ed., 2018) [3-085]. *See also* John Odgers, *Paget's Law of Banking* (LexisNexis, 15th ed., 2018) [22.44] and Ross Cranston et al., *Principles of Banking Law* (Oxford University Press, 3rd ed., 2017) 242.
29. *Tidal Energy Ltd v. Bank of Scotland Plc* [2015] 2 All ER 15 ('*Tidal Energy Ltd v. Bank of Scotland Plc*').
30. *See State Bank of New South Wales v. Swiss Bank Corporation* (1995) 39 NSWLR 350 ('*State Bank v. Swiss Bank*'). *See also Tayeb v. HSBC Bank plc* [2004] 4 All ER 1024 ('*Tayeb v. HSBC Bank plc*'); Brindle and Cox (n. 28) [3.120]; Cranston et al. (n. 28) 242.
31. *See* Committee on Payment and Settlement Systems and International Organization of Securities Commissions, 'Principles for Financial Markets Infrastructures' (Standards, Bank for International Settlements, April 2012) 21.

deprives participants in the UK system of the certainty of the contractual rights which exist under the Australian system. It might be argued that these should not be necessary as they are not present in correspondent banking. However, certainty under correspondent banking arises through the contractual connection which each of the payer's and payee's intermediary banks have with the bank with whom they both hold accounts. This allows for liability to be allocated. There is no equivalent to this under either open banking system as each is a peer-to-peer system.[32] The Australian system addresses this absence through the contractual relationships it establishes between banks and data recipients, whilst the UK system does not address it at all.

This failure in the UK system to provide this certainty for the transferee and transferor of value means that it relies entirely on the actions of the regulator to ensure the proper functioning of the system, and the regulator's preparedness to investigate and take action. Whilst involvement of the regulator is important, sole reliance is not placed on regulation for the legal relationships under banking payment systems. Whilst there is an incentive for banks to not resort to legal action for all errors, losses and disputes which occur in banking payment systems, there is a difference between a bank making this choice knowing that its rights to take legal action exist, and not being able to take any action at all. Further, the availability of a separate right to take legal action means that participants themselves perform a role in encouraging and requiring the compliance of others. The impact of this is particularly apparent from the evaluation against the allocation of liability for funds transfers, considered next.

## 10.2 HOW SHOULD LIABILITIES BE ALLOCATED IN OPEN BANKING?

A critical part of the legal foundation of an open banking system is the allocation of liability when things do not go as planned. As the liability sought to be allocated is legal liability, the legal relationships between participants form the fundamental basis for this. Otherwise, the allocation of liability is solely regulatory, and solely dependent on regulatory action for its efficacy.

The legal requirements relating to the allocation of liabilities in open banking are comparatively analysed below, followed by evaluation against the liability allocation in banking payment systems.

### 10.2.1 Comparison of Liability Allocation Between Participants

#### *(a) Legislative Allocation of Liability*

The *CCA* contains the foundation of the liability allocation between participants in Australian open banking. It provides that any data holder or accredited data recipient

32. There is the potential to use 'designated gateways' in the Australian system 'to facilitate the transfer of data between a data holder and accredited data recipient or the consumer': CDR Bill EM (n. 6) [1.95]. However, there is no designated gateway for sharing banking data: *Consumer Data Right (Authorised Deposit Taking Institutions) Designation 2019* (Cth) ('*Open Banking Designation*').

who provides, or provides access to, CDR data to another person in good faith and in compliance with the *CCA*, its regulations and the *CDR Rules*:

> is not liable to an action or other proceeding, whether civil or criminal, for or in relation to the matter [of providing the CDR data or access to it].[33]

A person who wants to rely on this protection bears the evidential burden of proof in substantiating its requirements.[34] This was described as 'appropriate given that the person will know whether or not they received evidence of a valid consent or request and otherwise met the obligations in the CDR regime'.[35] Accordingly, a bank or an accredited data recipient that has complied with all of its obligations in relation to sharing data under the Australian system in good faith is protected from liability to others for doing so. However, if a bank or an accredited data recipient has not so complied with its obligations, then the protection does not apply and direct rights of recourse under the *CCA* and the *CDR Rules*,[36] and the statutory contract between participants described in the previous chapter, will be available. Whilst there are dispute resolution processes included in the Australian system, these do not allocate liability between participants.

Allocation of liability between banks and recipients in UK open banking is less clear. There are no provisions for the allocation of liability between banks and recipients in the *CMA Order*. There are liability allocation provisions in *PSR*, but they apply only to payment transactions rather than data sharing.[37] Those provisions can apply to failures in sharing data which result in an unauthorised payment transaction and if 'liability is attributable to an AISP'.[38] However, the *PSR* is silent on liability allocation for data sharing failures which do not result in unauthorised payment transactions,[39] and in these circumstances, the FCA recommends that 'the customer should, in the first instance, complain to the AISP and escalate any issues to the Financial Ombudsman Service'.[40] The FCA does not comment on the position of another participant in the UK system in these circumstances.[41] The OBIE has created a

33. *CCA* (n. 4) s. 56GC.
34. *Ibid.*
35. CDR Bill EM (n. 6) [1.467].
36. *See* section 6.2.2.
37. *See* section 10.2.2(a).
38. Financial Conduct Authority, 'Payment Services and Electronic Money - Our Approach' (n. 9) [8.214].
39. This was a contentious issue in the implementation of PSD2 in the UK: *see* Financial Services Consumer Panel, 'HM Treasury Consultation on the Implementation of the Revised EU Payment Services Directive PSDII', *Financial Services Consumer Panel* (Letter, 16 March 2017) https://www.fs-cp.org.uk/sites/default/files/fscp_response_hmt_implementation_of_the_revised_eu_payment_services_directive_ii.pdf.
40. Financial Conduct Authority, 'Payment Services and Electronic Money - Our Approach' (n. 9) [8.215].
41. Curiously, the CMA initially considered that the allocation of liability for unauthorised payments in PSR should have been sufficient to 'deal with any concerns over redress': Competition and Markets Authority, 'Retail Banking Market Investigation' (Final report, 9 August 2016) [13.75].

voluntary 'Dispute Management System' (DMS).[42] This provides a communication and information exchange process in which banks and data recipients can voluntarily participate 'to facilitate the speedy resolution of customer related issues in order to deliver better customer experiences'.[43] It also offers banks and data recipients a technological process to resolve disputes with each other.[44] However, the DMS does not offer any legal basis for liability allocation.

### *(b) Certainty in Allocation of Liability*

The allocation of liability between participants is a substantive difference between the systems. There was a clear intention in the design of the Australian system to 'establish clear principles of liability to ensure that there is no uncertainty about the rights and liabilities of consumers, data holders or data recipients',[45] namely:

- customers have rights to take legal action against each of their bank and their data recipient for breaches of their respective obligations to the customer;
- banks and data recipients have rights to take legal action against each other if the other breaches their obligations under the Australian Standards; and
- as noted above, banks and data recipients are protected from legal liability for providing access to CDR data in accordance with the *CCA* and the *CDR Rules*.

The result of these principles is that a participant is liable for its own non-compliance with their legal obligations under the Australian system, but if they comply with their legal obligations, then they are not responsible for the non-compliance of other participants.[46] Some gaps in the clarity of allocation of liability remain in the Australian system. For example, there is no clear process for determining whose fault has caused a particular loss and it is not clear how liability is shared if both the bank and the data recipient are at fault. However, these are not significant in comparison to the liability gaps in the design of the UK system. UK open banking does not provide comprehensive rights for all customers to take legal action for non-compliance, nor does it establish any contractual or other legal rights of action between banks and recipients or provide protection against liability for complying participants. The only protection provided to participants is a voluntary technological mechanism to be used for resolving disputes which does not have a legally binding foundation. This absence

42. Open Banking Implementation Entity, 'Dispute Management System (DMS) Code of Good Practice' (Code of Conducy No DMS 2.1 v0.11, October 2019) https://www.openbanking.org.uk/wp-content/uploads/COGP-2.0.pdf.
43. *Ibid*. 3.
44. *Ibid*. Appendix 1 (definitions of 'claimant', 'complaint', 'dispute').
45. Australian Treasury, 'Consumer Data Right' (Explanatory Guide, 9 May 2018) 6.
46. The Australian Government's Open Banking Review recommended that '[P]articipants in the Open Banking system should be liable for their own conduct but not the conduct of other participants': Australian Treasury, 'Inquiry into Future Directions for Consumer Data Right: Giving Consumers Choice, Convenience and Confidence' (Report, October 2020) 68.

represents a surprising, and recognised, flaw in its design which warrants evaluation against banking payment systems.[47]

### 10.2.2 Evaluation Against Legal Relationships in Banking Payment Systems

The allocation of liability under the frameworks can be evaluated against two bases of liability allocation under banking payment systems, being the legal arrangements between participants and regulation.

#### *(a) Allocation under Legal Relationships Between Participants*

The contractual and agency relationships which form the legal foundation of banking payment systems allocate liability between their participants. When acting as agent, such as in correspondent banking, a bank is liable to its principal for a failure to discharge its agency duties with due care and skill,[48] and it can be vicariously liable for the negligence or default of a correspondent bank which it appoints.[49] When acting as a contracting party, under both correspondent banking and payment system rules, it is liable to those with whom it has contractual privity for its own failure to perform its contractual obligations, but not the failure of others to perform their own obligations.[50]

This is comparable with the principles of liability allocation under Australian open banking which, as the analysis above shows, results in participants being liable for their own failure but not that of others. For example, the protection from liability offered to a participant under the *CCA* applies only if they comply with their obligations under the Australian system.[51] There is a further requirement that they do so in good faith, which is not dissimilar to the requirement for a bank to exercise reasonable care and skill in carrying out its customer's instructions to pay or receive funds. As noted above, there are no equivalent legal principles for liability allocation under the UK system for the sharing of data against which these can be compared.

#### *(b) Allocation under Payments Regulation*

Although the UK system makes no allocation of liability for data sharing, the *PSR* does allocate liability for payment initiation. If a payment initiated through the framework is not made, is defective or is made late, then the bank must refund to the customer the amount of the payment.[52] On request, the payment initiation service provider (PISP) must compensate the bank for the losses incurred as a result, unless the PISP proves

47. *See* Bank of England, Future of Finance: What it means for the UK Financial System (Report, June 2019) [1.13].
48. *See* Chapters 5 and 6 above.
49. *Royal Products v. Midland Bank* (n. 25).
50. Except those who the bank has itself appointed to perform the bank's obligations on the bank's behalf.
51. *CCA* (n. 4) s. 56GC.
52. *PSR* (n. 8) reg. 93.

that the payment order was received by the bank and the transaction was 'authenticated, accurately recorded and not affected by a technical breakdown or other deficiency' within the PISP's 'sphere of influence'.[53] If the liability of a bank under these provisions is attributable to another ASPSP or an intermediary, then they need to compensate the bank.[54]

The UK system does not apply these funds transfer liability principles to data sharing, even though the funds transfer and data sharing are both regulated by the *PSR*. If they were applied to data sharing, then liability would be allocated to the recipient, unless it could prove that it properly implemented the request for the sharing of data, in which case the liability would be allocated to the bank. This would be broadly equivalent to the protection granted to a data recipient under the Australian system if it can prove that it complied with its obligations in good faith. However, if the bank has also complied with its obligations under the Australian system in good faith, then neither the bank nor the recipient has any liability to the other. The residual liability of the bank for funds transfers is the difference between the regulatory allocation of liability for funds transfers under the *PSR* and the allocation of liability for data sharing under the Australian system.

Whilst the absence of liability allocation under the UK system has already been identified as a problem in its design, it is worth evaluating whether this absence of residual liability on the bank is also a problem in the design of the Australian system. In payments regulation in both Australia and the UK, a similar approach is taken in allocating liability for unauthorised funds transfers by requiring the bank to compensate the customer for losses (potentially less a nominal amount) unless the customer is proven to have been fraudulent.[55] This avoids the 'hopelessly complicated' problem of determining fault in order to compensate a customer.[56] Also, it reflects the belief that the bank is in the best position to assess the risks in a payment transaction:

> It is the payment service provider that provides the payments system, makes arrangements to recall misplaced or wrongly allocated funds and decides in most cases on the intermediaries involved in the execution of a payment transaction.[57]

Further, this allocation is also justified on the basis that the bank is 'the best loss absorber and redistributor'.[58]

---

53. *Ibid.*
54. *Ibid.* reg. 95.
55. *Ibid.* regs 75, 76, 90.8) regs 75, 76, 90. A similar allocation is made in Australia under the ePayments Code: Australian Securities & Investments Commission, 'ePayments Code' (Code of Conduct, 29 March 2016) https://download.asic.gov.au/media/3798542/epayments-code-published-29-march-2016.pdf.
56. Particularly in relation to customer's negligence and its causal link to loss: Benjamin Geva, *Bank Collections and Payment Transactions: A Comparative Study of Legal Aspects* (Oxford University Press, 2001) 420.
57. *Directive 2015/2366/EU of the European Parliament and of the Council of 25 November 2015 on Payment Services in the Internal Market, amending Directives 2002/65/EC, 2009/110/EC, and 2013/36/EU and Regulation (EU) No 1093/2010 and repealing Directive 2007/64/EC* OJ L 337/35 Preamble para 85 ('*PSD2*').
58. Geva, *Bank Collections and Payment Transactions: A Comparative Study of Legal Aspects* (n. 56) 420.

Whilst the problems in allocating fault would be no less complicated in the open banking systems, this reasoning does not apply to the same extent. Unlike a paying customer who has a contractual relationship with its bank but not the payee's bank, in sharing data, the customer has a direct relationship with both the bank and the recipient. Accordingly, the customer has rights against each if they fail to provide the services to the agreed standard.[59] Also, it is not fair to say that in open banking systems, it is the bank which provides the system and decides on the intermediaries involved. Instead, it was compelled to respond to customer requests to share data made by intermediaries chosen solely by the customer.[60] Further, the argument that the bank is in the best position to assess the risks, or the best absorber of losses, is weakened where the recipient might be a bank, and the holder of the data which is to be shared might not be a bank. In fact, it could be that neither is a bank. One or both might be a fintech company or a multinational technology and data firm.

For these reasons, the absence of an allocation of residual liability to the bank under the Australian system should not be regarded as a problem in its design, as the relationships with the customer differ from those relevant to unauthorised payments.

## 10.3 HOW SHOULD CUSTOMERS BE COMPENSATED FOR LOSSES?

The previous part of this chapter has shown that neither open banking system requires that the bank always must compensate the customer for any losses caused to the customer by the misuse of the customer data which the customer has requested that it share. It has also shown why such a requirement, common in payment regulation, would not necessarily be appropriate given the different roles performed in open banking systems. For this reason, the customer compensation arrangements imposed on recipients as part of their authorisation requirements are crucial.

The customer compensation requirements of the Australian and UK open banking systems are comparatively analysed below, followed by an evaluation against deposit protection in banking payment systems.

### 10.3.1 Comparison of Responsibilities for Customer Compensation

As analysed in Chapter 6, in Australian open banking, CDR consumers have a statutory right to take direct action against an accredited person for the damages caused by the entity's non-compliance.[61] Similarly, under UK open banking, there is a direct right of

59. In one sense, this is similar to (although conceptually reversed) a funds transfer between two account holders with the same bank, where disputes are dealt with through the relationship which each has with the bank: *see Momm and Others v. Barclays Bank International Ltd.* [1977] QB 790 (*'Momm v. Barclays Bank'*).
60. An alternative way to look at this is that the bank's liability for unauthorised payments is due to 'the role of the bank as a depositary for the customer's funds, responsible for their safekeeping': Geva, *Bank Collections and Payment Transactions: A Comparative Study of Legal Aspects* (n. 56) 420. Due to the bank's duty of confidentiality the bank's role in the safekeeping of the customer's information is not dissimilar.
61. *CCA* (n. 4) s. 82(1)(d).

action contained in the *PSR* for 'private persons' that suffer loss as a result of a contravention of the *PSR*.[62] In addition, as explained in the first section of this chapter, under the Australian system participants become parties to a statutory contract with each other in relation to their compliance with binding data standards.

### *(a) Requirements for Insurance*

Neither Australian nor UK open banking requires participants to hold a minimum amount of capital to ensure that they are able to meet their liabilities. Instead, under each system, in order to be authorised, a recipient must have adequate insurance, or a comparable guarantee.[63] The risk being covered by this requirement differs slightly between the systems. In the Australian system, the insurance is to cover:

> the risk of CDR consumers not being properly compensated for any loss that might reasonably be expected to arise from a breach of obligations

under the *CCA*, any regulations made under it, or the *CDR Rules*, to the extent they are relevant to the management of CDR data.[64] The insurance is expressed to be needed to 'reduce the risk of CDR consumers not being properly compensated due to an accredited person's lack of financial resources'.[65] This is why it is not required for data recipients that are ADIs,[66] as their prudential regulation and capital requirements should adequately ensure sufficient financial resources to compensate CDR consumers.

In contrast, in the UK system, the insurance is to cover:

> the applicant's potential liability to account servicing payment service providers and payment service users resulting from unauthorised or fraudulent access to, or use of, payment account information, up to such amount as the FCA may direct.[67]

It is expressed to be needed for 'strengthening the liability regime governing the interactions between the different actors involved in electronic payment transactions'.[68]

62. *PSR* (n. 8) reg. 148.
63. *Competition and Consumer (Consumer Data Right) Rules 2020* ('*CDR Rules*') r. 5.12(2)(b); *PSR* (n. 8) reg. 18.
64. *CDR Rules* (n. 63) r. 5.12(2)(b).
65. Australian Competition and Consumer Commission, 'Accreditation Guidelines' (Guide, 9 December 2020) 14.
66. *CDR Rules* (n. 63) sch. 3 r. 7.4.
67. *PSR* (n. 8) reg. 18(4). For this purpose, the FCA has directed that the amount be that which is determined in accordance with guidelines issued by the European Banking Authority in respect of *PSD2*: Financial Conduct Authority, 'Payment Services and Electronic Money – Our Approach' (n. 9) [3.59]. The guidelines are issued under Article 5(4) of *PSD2*: European Banking Authority, 'Guidelines on the Criteria on How to Stipulate the Minimum Monetary Amount of the Professional Indemnity Insurance or Other Comparable Guarantee under Article 5(4) of Directive (EU) 2015/2366 (PSD2)' (Final Report No EBA/GL/2017/08, 7 July 2018).
68. European Banking Authority, 'EBA Publishes Final Guidelines on Professional Indemnity Insurance' (Press Release, 7 July 2017) https://www.eba.europa.eu/eba-publishes-final-guidelines-on-professional-indemnity-insurance-under-psd2.

Although, the *PSR* does require minimum capital be held by providers of other payment services,[69] capital is not required to be held by AISPs under the UK systems because data recipients do not hold customer's funds.[70]

### *(b) Issues with Insurance Cover*

Even though under each system insurance is required to take the place of the recipient's capital in covering liabilities, there is a subtle difference in these requirements. In the Australian system, it does so on the assumption that the recipient won't hold enough capital to cover its liabilities unless it is a bank, whilst under the UK system, it does so on the assumption that the recipient should not be required to hold enough capital to cover its liabilities unless it also holds customers' money. Each of these assumptions is flawed, particularly in the context of established companies becoming recipients (who would be required to obtain insurance despite having sufficient economic capacity to meet any claims) and the increasing recognition of the value of customer information (which would mean that both money and information are valuable to the customer). Further, it fails to recognise that the risk against which capital is held in banking payment systems, credit risk, does have an equivalent in open banking systems: performance risk, as explained in Chapter 6. However, the impact of these flaws is smaller than those created by relying on insurance to ensure the data recipient's creditworthiness. This analysis is continued in section 10.3.2 below.

Another difference is in relation to the scope of the insurance. Under the UK system, it is to compensate for claims made by both banks and customers but only in respect of unauthorised or fraudulent access or use of customer data. Under the Australian system, the insurance is to compensate for claims by customers only, but it is not limited to particular types of claims. In different ways, the scope of each is more limited than the other, either with respect to the object of the covered liability or the nature of the liability covered. The UK limitation should not be practically meaningful, as it is difficult to see the sources of the data liability relating to the shared data beyond those which relate to the unauthorised or fraudulent access or use of those data. There could be liability for the AISs provided by the AISP if they are performed negligently, and theoretically these might not be covered by the required insurance, but neither would they be covered by insurance under the Australian system as the insurance is not required to cover the provision of the goods or services requested by the customer.[71] In contrast, the limitation on insurance in the Australian system is more significant. The absence of a requirement for insurance to cover liabilities owed to persons other than customers is anomalous as the data recipient also has potential liabilities to banks under the Australian system under the separate contract between a data holder and each accredited person created under the *CCA*.[72] It probably reflects

69. *PSR* (n. 8) reg. 6(3).
70. *Ibid*. sch. 3 pt 1. *See also PSD2* (n. 57) recital 35.
71. This is because these are not obligations owed under the *CDR Rules*.
72. *CCA* (n. 4) ss 56FD(1)(a)-(b).

the compensation provisions to protect retail clients of holders of an Australian Financial Services Licence under the Australian *Corporations Act 2000* (Cth).[73] However, that regime differs from Australian open banking as it does not contemplate a network of regulated entities sharing responsibilities.

### 10.3.2 Evaluation Against Deposit Protection in Banks

Bank regulation not only ensures that bank's promises *can* be met, but it also provides confidence to depositors that they *will* be met. The regulatory tools used for this purpose include imposing capital requirements to ensure that losses can be absorbed, liquidity requirements to meet deposit withdrawals, lender of last resort arrangements to provide liquid funds against illiquid assets, and deposit insurance arrangements. Without these, if there is any disruption to a bank, depositors may seek to withdraw funds at the earliest opportunity, threatening the solvency of the bank as illiquid assets are sold at a loss to meet depositors' claims.[74] By providing depositors with assurance from a third party that their claims will be met if the bank defaults, deposit protection provides the confidence needed to make banking work. Deposit protection in Australia is provided by the Financial Claims Scheme established under the *Banking Act 1959* (Cth), and in the UK by the Financial Services Compensation Scheme established under the *Financial Services and Markets Act 2000* (UK). Both represent deposit protection provided by the state. Diamond and Dybvig have argued that deposit insurance ought to be provided by governments rather than private insurers because of the unconditional nature of the guarantee.[75]

The insurance required to be held by data recipients is intended to perform a similar function in Australian and UK open banking – to guarantee the creditworthiness of the data recipient sufficiently for claims against it to be met, in the absence of capital requirements. However, its performance of this function is not as effective as deposit protection. This is because both Australian and UK open banking contemplate the insurance to be professional indemnity insurance.[76] Customarily, this insurance does not entitle the customer to claim directly against the insurer. Instead, the recipient is required to make a claim and the amount received increases the assets which it has available to compensate others. However, the data recipient will not be able to do so if it is in breach of its contractual policy obligations, the claim falls under a policy exclusion, the claim is within the policy excess or the claim is in excess of the policy

73. Holders of an Australian Financial Licence must have compensation arrangements for retail clients to cover losses suffered as a result of breaches by the licensee: *Corporations Act 2001* (Cth) s. 912(d).
74. *See* Douglas W Diamond and Philip H Dybvig, 'Bank Runs, Deposit Insurance, and Liquidity' (2000) 24(1) *Federal Reserve Bank of Minneapolis Quarterly Review* 14-23, 15.
75. *Ibid.*
76. *See PSR* (n. 8) reg. 18(4). In Australia, the ACCC contemplates both professional indemnity insurance and cyber insurance, but notes that the latter is often limited in nature: Australian Competition and Consumer Commission, 'Supplementary Accreditation Guidelines – Insurance' (Guidelines, 25 May 2020) 4.

cap.[77] Most importantly, the value of the insurance can diminish in the insolvency of the data recipient, which is when it is most needed, as customers will not be able to be fully compensated by making a claim against an insolvent data recipient. Although there are statutory protections of the priority to insurance proceeds in an insured's insolvency,[78] it is still necessary that a claim arises and is made by the insured before the policy is cancelled. This is relevant because cancellation of the policy on the commencement of insolvency is a common occurrence because the insolvency administrator can take the view that further premium payments should not be made as they can only benefit some and not all creditors.[79] For these reasons, although professional indemnity insurance provides some assurance, it is unable to sufficiently guarantee the data recipient's creditworthiness to ensure that a customer will be compensated for a breach by the data recipient of its information security or other obligations. Consequently, when evaluated against the deposit protection customarily available to bank depositors, it is not as effective in supporting the accountability function of open banking. For the same reason, to the extent that the insurance obtained by a recipient under UK open banking also covers liabilities to other participants as well as customers, those other participants are not guaranteed to benefit from claims made on the policy.

## 10.4 HOW CAN LEGAL FOUNDATIONS SUPPORT ALLOCATING LIABILITY?

### 10.4.1 Summary of Comparison and Evaluation

This chapter has examined the implications of the legal foundations of Australian and UK open banking for the allocation of liability through a comparison of the legal relationships between participants, the allocation of liabilities amongst those participants and the compensation for participants' failure, and an evaluation against equivalent legal features of banking payment systems.

The analysis has shown that UK open banking is lacking the legal foundations found in both Australian open banking and banking payment systems which establish binding legal relationships between participants, depriving participants in the UK system of a source of confidence as to the compliance by others with their obligations, resulting in reliance on the choices of regulators to enforce non-performance. It has also shown that the legal foundations of UK open banking do not allocate liability in relation to data sharing between participants, in contrast to the Australian open banking system which follows principles which are comparable to those used in banking payment systems. Further, the analysis has shown the legal foundation which

77. *See* St. John, Richard, 'Compensation Arrangements for Consumers of Financial Services' (Report, Australian Government, April 2012).
78. For example, the protection for third parties to which the insolvent has incurred the relevant liability *Corporations Act* (n. 73) s. 562.
79. Also, insurance policies which continue after the insolvency of the insured are not generally available: Australian Securities & Investments Commission, 'RG 126: Compensation and Insurance Arrangements for AFS Licensees' (Regulatory Guide, July 2020) [RG126.11].

supports compensating others for participant failure, being the requirement for participants to hold professional indemnity insurance, is not as effective in ensuring accountability as the deposit insurance found in banking payment systems.

The consequences of these differences is that there are stronger legal foundations to support connectivity and accountability in banking payment systems than in Australian and UK open banking, and that the legal foundations offer the least support in UK open banking. This is illustrated in Figure 10.1.

*Figure 10.1 Illustration of Evaluation and Comparison Relating to Allocating Liability*

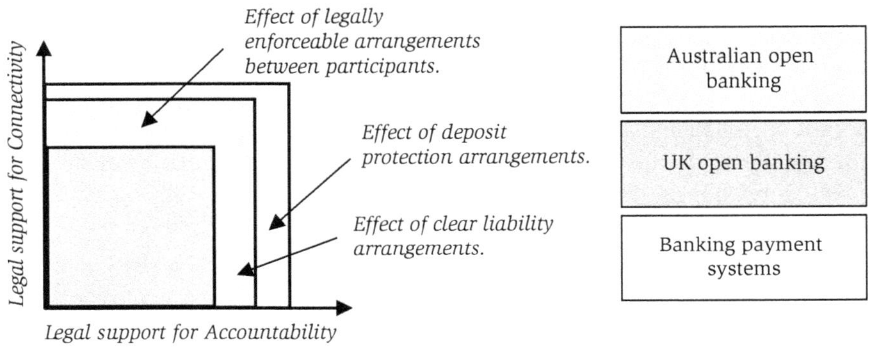


This analysis shows the need to balance connectivity and accountability in designing the legal foundations for allocating liability between participants. It also demonstrates the importance of managing validity risk. This risk is explained next, followed by an illustration of the comparable legal risk in banking payment systems, and a discussion of how legal risk management methods could be included in the legal foundations of open banking systems.

### 10.4.2 Validity Risk in Open Banking Systems

As explained in Chapter 6, validity risk arises from a lack of *legal support* for the performance of open banking's functions, instead of a weakness in the actual performance of those functions. If everything and everyone performs as intended, and there are no externalities which challenge that performance, then validity risk should not affect the effectiveness of the systems in achieving their objectives. However, if this is not the case, then the validity risks become evident as the inability to legally compel performance, or legally manage non-performance, affecting the system's effectiveness and credibility.

The impact of the validity risk identified in this chapter's analysis is particularly relevant for the trust and confidence necessary for open banking systems to achieve their objectives. As noted in previous chapters, customers are required to trust recipients to perform their obligations with customer data. Participants are also required to trust each other to perform their respective obligations under the open banking system. The trustworthiness needed for that trust is intended to be established through the imposition of appropriate obligations on participant's performance and requirements to be authorised to participate. However, if those obligations are not enforceable, or if there is no ultimate accountability for their non-performance because there are insufficient resources to compensate those who have been harmed, then they will undermine trust in open banking rather than support it. The obligations become evidence of the weakness of the system's structure, rather than its strength. If, despite the open banking system purporting to govern dealings with a customer's valuable information, it has insufficient legal support for its operation, then this is likely to be a serious and potentially fatal impact on its credibility and, as a result, its effectiveness in performing any of its functions.

To further explain validity risk, the next section sets out an illustration of the comparable risk in banking payment systems, *legal risk*.

### 10.4.3 Illustration of Legal Risks in Banking Payment Systems: Commercial Bank of Australia

As noted in Chapter 6, legal risk is the risk caused by a poor legal framework or legal uncertainties. Legal risk associated with inadequate legal relationships between participants is illustrated by aspects of the collapse of the Commercial Bank of Australia ('Commercial') in 1893, the most significant bank collapse in the most severe depression and banking crisis in Australia's history.

In the 1890s, Australian banking was unregulated with 'no credible restrictions on assets, liabilities or bank capital'.[80] Further, there was no government guarantee of deposits, nor was there any central bank, or banking clearing house which could manage a bank's default. However, there was a voluntary association of private banks called the 'Associated Banks of Victoria' ('Associated Banks'), which had made announcements that they would financially assist each other. Although these arrangements were not expressed as creating legal obligations between the banks, they were interpreted in the press as doing so. Despite this, the Commercial (the largest bank in Victoria at the time) suspended payment in April 1893 without any support from the Associated Banks. Following the failure of Commercial, 13 of Australia's 22 trading banks suspended operations and by mid-1893, 54 of the 64 institutions which called themselves banks in 1891 had permanently closed. Although the causes of the crisis were to be found in now familiar issues such as dependence on offshore funding and high leverage on assets with volatile values, it is the role played by the lack of legal arrangements between banks in the lack of support for the Commercial which is most relevant.

There was a strong belief that the other banks should have rescued the Commercial in order to prevent the panic which followed. However, a key factor which

80. Charles R Hickson and John D Turner, 'Free Banking Gone Awry: The Australian Banking Crisis of 1893' (2002) 9(2) *Financial History Review* 147-167, 147.

prevented such support being provided was that there was no legal framework in place under which such support could be provided. There were no legal obligations between members of the association to comply with prudential criteria nor rights and obligations in the case of a member's default. In the words of a leading economic historian, the Australian banks 'were simply too small, unsophisticated and single mindedly competitive to have allowed self regulatory agencies to emerge or to have functioned'.[81] As a result, the competition between the banks, lack of information as to value of assets and constraints on resources prevailed, with the result that the Commercial failed. Had there been enforceable legal obligations between the banks, as there was between the banks in the US who were members of the Clearing House, then the clarity which that provided might have enabled a rescue to have been made:

> The fundamental weakness of Australian banking in the late nineteenth century was that 'market discipline' was incapable of maintaining prudential standards in an increasingly risk laden environment. No institutional mechanism existed, be it an industry wide deposit insurance scheme with universal coverage, a clearing house association or a Bank of England-style bank, that could impose a code of behaviour of bank management.[82]

In fact, it was the collapse of the Commercial without the 'promised' assistance which proved that there were no legal obligations on which confidence could be based.

It is plausible that a lack of clarity in the allocation of legal liability of participants to each other, and to customers, could detrimentally affect an open banking system giving rise to risks similar to those which resulted in the failure to rescue Commercial. This could arise, for example, through an information security failure in a significant participant. Whilst addressing the consequence of that failure might necessitate cooperative action from all participants, this might not be forthcoming if there is a lack of certainty as to who is responsible for any losses which arise. Accordingly, participants may choose to act in their own self-interest and not participate in any remedial action. Concerns of this nature have arisen in the context of large cyber-attacks outside of open banking systems. An inability for participants to legally require other participants to comply with standards is also comparable. Whilst a regulator might be able to enforce compliance, it may choose not to do so, resulting in a similar circumstance for other participants as that of other banks in Commercial's default – desiring compliance to occur before default, but being unable to compel it. As with Commercial, the other participants' inability to require compliance by a non-complying participant removes a safety measure which could prevent the default of an important participant.

Accordingly, the legal features used in banking payment systems to manage legal risk deserve consideration for incorporation into the legal foundations of open banking.

81. David T Merrett, 'Preventing Bank Failure: Could the Commercial Bank of Australia Have Been Saved by Its Peers in 1893?' (1993) 64(2) *Victorian Historical Journal (1987)* 122-142, 124.
82. *Ibid.* 139.

### 10.4.4 Incorporating Legal Risk Management in Open Banking Systems

As noted in Chapter 8, a strong legal basis is a foundational requirement for a banking payment system. The management of legal risk requires a 'well founded, clear, transparent, and enforceable legal basis for each material aspect of its activities'.[83] These activities need to be supported by legally enforceable contracts or rules, which provide a high degree of legal certainty, and which clearly define the rights and interests of participants and customers. This is often ensured by obtaining independent legal analysis which confirms the existence and enforceability of the legal relationships, and then sharing that analysis amongst participants to promote confidence and transparency. 'In general, there is no substitute for a sound legal basis and full legal certainty'.[84]

There seems no reason to take a different approach in the legal design of open banking systems. Much of the trust and confidence necessary for the system to function is based on the strength of its legal foundation. Accordingly, to avoid the confusion and inaction able to be caused by legal uncertainty it is important that open banking systems create clear enforceable obligations between participants which are used as a basis for allocating liability between them. This provides the certainty of risk allocation needed for participants to make investments in the ecosystem.

It is also important that these legal obligations are supported by customer compensation arrangements which are more like deposit insurance. Whilst it might take time to develop the insurance market to provide less qualified insurance cover for open banking participants, this would be important to support the confidence placed in the systems as a whole and it would enable the insurance obtained by recipients to perform a similar function to depositor protection in banking payment systems,[85] by 'providing advance protection against future deviant outcomes or compensation for accomplished misdeeds'.[86]

83. Committee on Payment and Settlement Systems and International Organization of Securities Commissions (n. 31).
84. *Ibid.* [3.1.12].
85. *See ibid.*
86. Susan P Shapiro, 'The Social Control of Impersonal Trust' (1987) 93(3) *American Journal of Sociology* 623-658, 643.

CHAPTER 11

# Ensuring Credibility of Open Banking

This chapter completes the analysis by comparing the legal foundations for ensuring credibility of open banking systems. It compares the legal relationships established between participants and with regulators which support the credibility of the Australian and UK open banking systems and evaluates them against the equivalent legal relationships established under banking payment systems. The analysis addresses two questions:

- When should participants be removed?
- How should participant insolvency be managed?

The answers to these questions are fundamental to an open banking system's performance of its *connectivity* and *accountability* functions.

## 11.1 WHEN SHOULD PARTICIPANTS BE REMOVED?

Since its introduction in Chapter 1, the role of trust in the efficacy of open banking systems has been referred to in many of the previous chapters. One aspect of this trust is the confidence which customers have in the competence and reliability of the recipients with whom they have chosen to share their data. Both Australian and UK open banking impose requirements for authorisation to receive shared data to ensure that the recipients can be worthy of that trust:

> Consumers will only be able to use the right to direct the transfer of their data to trusted third parties. All data recipients who receive consumer specific data must be accredited.[1]

The legal foundations for this authorisation under the Australian and UK open banking systems were analysed in Chapter 9. However, as Chapters 1 and 4 explained,

1. Australian Treasury, 'Consumer Data Right Overview' (Explanatory Guide, 9 May 2018) 7.

this is not the only relevant support for trust in open banking. In addition to confidence in the performance of recipients, it is also necessary for there to be confidence in the open banking system as a whole, to ensure its credibility. Fundamental to this is the ability to suspend or terminate a participant's authorisation when it threatens other participants or the system itself.

The legal requirements relating to the removal of recipient's from participation under Australian and UK open banking are comparatively analysed below, followed by evaluation against the removal of authorisation to participate in banking payment systems.

### 11.1.1 Comparison of Removal of Participants from Open Banking Systems

#### *(a) Legislative Provisions Enabling Removal of Participants*

Under Australian open banking, the *CDR Rules* provide the ACCC with the power to suspend or revoke an accreditation of a data recipient if it is satisfied that the data recipient was granted accreditation on the basis of materially false or misleading information, has been found to have contravened a law relevant to the management of CDR data, or is no longer a fit and proper person to hold that level of accreditation. Accreditation can also be suspended or revoked by the ACCC if the accredited person ceases to be an ADI (if it was an ADI when accredited), if a term in a 'relevant contract' with the CDR consumer is found to be unfair,[2] is found to have breached one or more data standards or if the ACCC reasonably believes that suspension or revocation is necessary to protect consumers or to protect the security, integrity and stability of either the Register of Accredited Persons, or the information and communication technology systems that are used by CDR participants.[3] The ACCC has a further power to suspend (but not revoke) the accreditation of a data recipient if it reasonably believes that the data recipient has contravened one or more of the Australian Standards, or provisions of the *CCA* which amounts to an offence or is a civil penalty provision, or that a relevant contract with the CDR consumer has an unfair term.[4] The ACCC can also vary the conditions on a data recipient's accreditation, including by adding new conditions.[5] This can be done without notice if notice would create a real risk of harm or abuse to an individual or adversely impact the security, integrity and stability of either the Register of Accredited Persons or the information and communication technology systems that are used by CDR participants to disclose or collect CDR data.[6]

---

2. A 'relevant contract' for this purpose is a 'a standard form contract that is a consumer contract or a small business contract within the meaning of section 23 of the Australian Consumer Law' which arises from the good or service the consumer requested in connection with the sharing of the CDR data: *Competition and Consumer (Consumer Data Right) Rules 2020* ('*CDR Rules*') r. 5.17(2).
3. *CDR Rules* (n. 2) r. 5.17.
4. *Ibid*. r. 5.17 items 6, 10.
5. *Ibid*. r. 5.10.
6. *Ibid*. r. 5.10(3).

Under UK open banking, a recipient may be removed from the Directory if their regulatory status is revoked.[7] The FCA can cancel a person's registration as an AISP if the person obtained their registration through false statements or any other irregular means, the person no longer meets the conditions for registration, the person has provided payment services other than in accordance with their authorisation, the person's provision of payment services is unlawful, the person's continuation of its payment services business would constitute a threat to the stability of, or trust in, a payment system, or the cancellation is desirable to protect the interests of consumers.[8] The *PSR* also empowers the FCA to vary a person's registration for similar reasons, and that variation can take effect immediately, on the FCA providing notice.[9]

### (b) Conceptual Differences in Provisions Enabling Participant Removal

Australian and UK open banking share common elements in the cancellation of authorisations – each enables removal on the grounds of breaching obligations, providing false and misleading information or no longer meeting the requirements to be authorised.[10] Also, each system grants the regulator the ability to change the conditions on an authorisation.[11] However, there is one interesting, and three important, differences.

The interesting difference is that a data recipient's accreditation under Australian open banking can be suspended if there is an unfair term in their contract with a CDR consumer arising from a good or service requested in connection with the sharing of customer data. There is no equivalent to this in the UK system relating to the contract for the provision of the relevant AIS. Its inclusion is interesting because it extends the connection between the sharing of data and the supplies of particular goods or services which required that data beyond the data minimisation requirements explained in Chapter 6. This is more than protecting consumers in sharing their data, it is protecting consumers in relation to what they consume from sharing their data. Conceptually, it is a divergence from the principles encapsulated in the authorisation framework for the Australian system explained in Chapter 9, which sought not to apply to the service provided using the shared data.

The three important differences relate to urgent suspension, the consequences for shared data and the system being protected.

#### (i) Urgent Suspension

Under each system, a process is required to be followed before a revocation or cancellation of authorisation takes effect including notification and an opportunity for

7. Open Banking Implementation Entity, 'Open Banking Guidelines for Read/Write Participants' (Guidelines, May 2018) [5.5.2] https://www.openbanking.org.uk/wp-content/uploads/Guidelines-for-Read-Write-Participants.pdf.
8. *Payment Services Regulation 2017* (UK) ('*PSR*') regs 10(1), 19.
9. *Ibid.* regs 12(1), 19.
10. *CDR Rules* (n. 2) r. 5.17; *PSR* (n. 8) regs 10(1), 19.
11. *CDR Rules* (n. 2) r. 5.10; *PSR* (n. 8) regs 12(1), 19.

the authorised person to be heard.[12] However, Australian open banking also allows accreditation to be suspended without following this process if, in the opinion of the ACCC, there are urgent grounds for the suspension and, as a result, it is not possible to comply with that process beforehand.[13] There is no equivalent under UK open banking, or even an ability to suspend, rather than cancel, a recipient's authorisation. It is possible that the power to vary conditions on an authorisation without notice (which exists under both frameworks) could be used by the FCA to achieve a similar effect. Despite this, the absence of an express suspension right is notable, and is in contrast to the rights of the FCA with respect to some other authorisations which it grants.[14]

#### *(ii) Consequences for Shared Data*

Under Australian open banking, a recipient whose authorisation is suspended must cease to collect any more CDR data and notify each person who has consented to their collection of CDR data of their suspension and that their consents may be withdrawn.[15] A person whose accreditation is revoked must cease to collect any more CDR data and delete or de-identify the CDR data held by them in accordance with the processes described in Chapter 8.[16] There are no equivalent provisions which set out any data-related obligations following cancellation of authorisation under the UK system.

#### *(iii) System Being Protected*

Each framework enables the relevant regulator to remove a recipient where it is needed to protect the system's stability,[17] but the relevant 'system' being protected in each is different. In the Australian system, it is the Register of Accredited Persons or the 'information and communication technology systems that are used by CDR participants to disclose or collect CDR data'.[18] In the UK system, it is 'a payment system'.[19] These are not the same. A threat to the stability of the information and communication technology systems used to share open banking data which would justify removal of a participant from the Australian system would not be sufficient to remove the participant under the UK system unless it also threatened the stability of a payment system. It could be argued that this should be a matter for the OBIE, rather than the FCA, as it is operating the Directory which enables information transfer under the UK system.

12. *CDR Rules* (n. 2) rr. 5.18, 5.19. 5.20; *PSR* (n. 8) regs 10(2), 10(3).
13. *CDR Rules* (n. 2) r. 5.21.
14. The FCA has noted that its suspension power under *The Electronic Money Regulations 2011* (UK) is additional to what it possesses under the *PSR*: Financial Conduct Authority, 'Payment Services and Electronic Money – Our Approach' (Approach Document, June 2019) [14.11].
15. *CDR Rules* (n. 2) r. 5.23.
16. *Ibid. See* section 8.1.1(b) above.
17. *CDR Rules* (n. 2), r. 5.17.(1) item 4; *PSR* (n. 8) regs 10(1)(g).
18. *CDR Rules* (n. 2) r. 5.17.
19. *PSR* (n. 8) reg. 10(1)(g).

However, the OBIE is not a regulator, and it has said that it will remove an ASPSP or an AISP from the Directory if their relevant regulatory status is revoked.[20]

Combined, these three represent a material difference in the legal design of Australian and UK open banking. The focus of the provisions of the UK system is on the *payment systems* which could be affected by the use of the shared data, rather than open banking as *a system for sharing data*. Consequently, the legal foundations which can preserve the credibility of the system by excluding those who weaken it are stronger under Australian open banking. This is evaluated against banking payment systems in the next section.

Before evaluating the legal foundations for the exclusion of defaulting participants under open banking against those in banking payment systems, it is necessary to consider the exclusion of the holders of shared data from open banking, rather than the recipients. The Australian system does not provide a clear mechanism for the exclusion of a bank from its obligations to share customer data with data recipients. Participation as a data holder under Australian open banking does not require any authorisation under the Australian systems legislation and is based on the authorisation provided under the Australian *Banking Act*. The bank's participation under Australian open banking would cease once it ceased to be an ADI under that legislation, but withdrawal of that authorisation is not a matter for the ACCC and would have catastrophic consequences for its banking business. The consequences are not improved under UK open banking. The circumstance under the CMA9 banks would be even worse, as there is no basis under the *CMA Order* to exclude one of those banks from their obligation to share data. For other banks, to be excluded from the obligation to share data, they would have to cease to be ASPSPs, which would cause similar disruption. Accordingly, under each system, there is no clear legal basis for removing or suspending a bank if its participation was threatening other participants, or the system itself.

### 11.1.2 Evaluation Against Removal from Participation in Banking Payment Systems

Due to the systemic risks which payment systems can exacerbate through the connectivity of their participants, it is common for there to be a right to suspend the participation of failing participants urgently if they threaten the system's stability.[21] This can be found in the regulations governing the primary interbank payment systems of Australia and the UK.[22] The importance of this can be seen in the legal obligations (with criminal penalties) imposed on all participants of these systems in Australia to inform the operator of the insolvency of any participant.[23] It is also shown in the *PSR*

20. Open Banking Implementation Entity, 'Open Banking Guidelines for Read/Write Participants' (n. 7) [5.5.2].
21. *See* Committee on Payment and Settlement Systems, 'Core Principles for Systemically Important Payment Systems' (Core Principles, Bank for International Settlements, January 2001) [7.9.8].
22. *See* Reserve Bank of Australia, 'RITS Regulations' (Regulations, 18 November 2020) reg. 27.2; Bank of England, 'CHAPS Rules' (Rules, 31 March 2021) r. 6.8.
23. *Payment Systems and Netting Act 1998* (Cth) s. 7 ('*Payment Systems and Netting Act*'). The requirements in the UK are not imposed on all participants: *The Financial Markets and*

itself which, as noted in the section above, includes threatening the stability of a payment system as a basis for the cancellation of the authorisation of a payment service provider.[24] Importantly, these rights are not limited to suspending banks which are receiving funds, they also include the suspension of banks that are paying funds.

Australian open banking includes a comparable express right of urgent suspension of the accreditation of a data recipient.[25] There is no equivalent under UK open banking. Instead, cancellation of a data recipient's authorisation under the UK system requires a warning notice, an opportunity to make representations in response, a decision notice and an opportunity to appeal.[26] The absence of a right to urgently suspend a participant which is endangering the UK system is difficult to understand. It is possible that, carefully implemented, the power to vary the conditions on an authorisation under UK open banking could be used to achieve the same effect.[27] However, this would not fully address the issue as it lacks the transparency needed to deter activities which would warrant suspension and to underpin the confidence of customers and other participants in the framework.[28] Alternatively, the suspension power might not have been thought necessary in the knowledge that it would be included in the rules of the relevant payment system.[29] However, this misses the point. The suspension power under the Australian system is intended to manage risks in the data sharing network, not risk in other networks such as those that enable payments to be made. The OBIE might be thought of as the 'operator' of UK open banking, but it has no equivalent suspension right. The result is that there is no transparent basis for removing a recipient urgently even if they are threatening the data sharing system's stability. This deprives UK open banking of an important means of ensuring its credibility as a communication system if a participant defaults when it is evaluated against the rights provided under banking payment systems, and under Australian open banking.

As noted above, neither system contemplates the suspension of a bank's participation if it is threatening the stability of the open banking system. This could be on the basis that a bank is expected to either not fail or to be subject to an event which could cause harm to other participants. However, recent history of bank collapses and cyber-attacks show this assumption to be false, even if less likely than the failure of a recipient. Accordingly, each system is lacking a legal foundation which fully contemplates the cessation of participation in the case of participant failure. This becomes particularly important when a participant becomes insolvent.

*Insolvency (Settlement Finality) Regulations 1999* (UK) SI No. 2979 reg. 22, sch para 5 ('*Settlement Finality Regulations*').

24. *PSR* (n. 8) reg. 10(1)(g).
25. *CDR Rules* (n. 2) r. 5.21.
26. *PSR* (n. 8) reg. 10(2)-(5).
27. *Ibid.* regs 12(1), 19.
28. 'The rules of the system should provide for clearly specified procedures for orderly withdrawal of a participant from the system, either at the participant's request, or following a decision by the system operator that the participant should withdraw': Committee on Payment and Settlement Systems, 'Core Principles for Systemically Important Payment Systems' (n. 21) [3.9.2].
29. *See Settlement Finality Regulations* (n. 23) sch para 6.

## 11.2 HOW SHOULD PARTICIPANT INSOLVENCY BE MANAGED?

The insolvency of a participant in a banking payment system is a catastrophic event, not only for the customers of the participant who were relying on it for both storage and liquidity of value but also the other direct and indirect participant which were relying on its performance for their own. For these reasons, the enforceability of the legal foundations of banking payment systems in the circumstances of a participant's insolvency is crucial. Similarly, the treatment of participant insolvency in an open banking system is also crucial.

The legal foundations to the management of participant insolvency in open banking are comparatively analysed below, followed by evaluation against the management of participant insolvency in banking payment systems.

### 11.2.1 Comparison of Management of Participant Insolvency in Open Banking

#### *(a) No Provisions Contemplating Participant Insolvency*

Neither the Australian nor UK system expressly contemplates the insolvency of a participant. Under each, a recipient's insolvency would be a sufficient basis for the revocation (under the Australian system) and cancellation (under the UK system) of its authorisation.[30] As noted above, under the Australian system, this would result in an obligation to delete or de-identify the data held by the recipient, whilst under the UK system the recipient would have a legal obligation to no longer use the data. However, a recipient's insolvency is the result of its failure to perform its legal obligations,[31] and the further performance of legal obligations by the recipient, including those relating to customer data, cannot be assumed. Further, the functions of insolvency proceedings and the duties of the insolvency practitioner appointed to conduct them can complicate the performance of these obligations.

#### *(b) Complexity in Data-Related Obligations on Insolvency*

The complexity of the interaction between insolvency law and data-related obligations can be seen from two English cases. The first, *Southern Pacific Personal Loans*,[32] concerned the voluntary liquidation of a member of the Lehman Brothers group of companies and the customer data on loans granted by the company which had been redeemed. These data were not needed for the company's business, but they were needed for the company to comply with its obligations as a data controller to meet 'data

30. For example, as being desirable, or necessary, in order to protect the interests of consumers: *PSR* (n. 8) regs 10(h), 19 and *CDR Rules* (n. 2) r. 5.12(1).
31. Namely, the obligation to pay its debts: *see Corporations Act* (n. 31) s. 95A and *Insolvency Act 1986* (UK) s. 122 ('*Insolvency Act*').
32. *Southern Pacific Personal Loans Ltd* [2013] EWHC 2485 ('*Southern Pacific Personal Loans*').

subject access requests' under the *Data Protection Act 1998* (UK) (*DPA*).[33] As the cost of meeting these requests was many times the fees able to be charged for them, the liquidators sought clarification from the court that they were not data controllers, and that they may dispose of the data. The court found that the liquidators were only agents of the company, including with respect to data rights and obligations, and they were not bound by the *DPA* as data controllers.[34] Further, the court found that as the data were 'no longer required for any business of the company or for any purposes of the liquidation',[35] the data could (and should)[36] be deleted except to the extent they were needed for data requests already made, or for the liquidation.[37] The court did not find that the liquidators could ignore the company's obligations under the *DPA* because '[e]nforcement action might be taken and orders might be made against the company, notwithstanding that it is in liquidation',[38] but treated the liquidators' relationship with the data under the company's control similar to that which exists with the company's property.[39]

These principles were taken further in *Green v. SCL Group*,[40] which also concerned a 'subject access request' given under the *DPA* and a company in the Cambridge Analytica group of companies. Subsequent to the request being made, the company was placed into administration and the case concerned the impact of the administration on the 'data rights' which arose in respect of that request. The court was clear that such 'data rights' have no special status in insolvency, and the administrators were under no general duty to investigate 'data breaches' occurring before their appointment.[41] Instead the duties of the administrators were to achieve the objectives of the administration, namely:

> achieving an economic return to the creditors (not to investigating the company's compliance with data protection laws), to fulfilling their statutory duties to investigate the directors, and to exiting from the administration in an appropriate way.[42]

The court said that as insolvency is 'a class remedy in which individual legal rights are transformed into rights to participate in the insolvency process, that process itself being conducted in the interests of the general body of creditors',[43] the holder of 'data rights' was entitled to participate in the insolvency by proving a monetary claim. Further, the court did not find that the administrators were guilty of misconduct in

33. *Data Protection Act 1998* (UK) ('*DPA*').
34. *Southern Pacific Personal Loans* (n. 32) [34], [35].
35. *Ibid.* [39].
36. In accordance with the fifth data protection principle of the *DPA*, namely that personal data should not be kept for longer than is necessary for this purpose for which they were processed: *ibid.*
37. *Ibid.* [40].
38. *Ibid.* [38].
39. The court refrained from deciding that the data was property, and instead noted that this is 'a complex subject': *ibid.* [34].
40. *Green and another v. SCL Group Ltd and others* [2019] BCLC 664 ('*Green v. SCL Group*').
41. *Ibid.* 684.
42. *Ibid.*
43. *Ibid.* 683.

ignoring an enforcement notice given under the *DPA* as it was given to the company, and not to them, as the data controller, and it was not inappropriate for the administrators to determine that the costs of compliance with such a notice were more burdensome on creditors than non-compliance. In summary, the court was dismissive of data-related obligations having special status in insolvency and concluded that 'the administration was not being run with a view to providing [the data subject] with his data'.[44]

These cases show that the performance of statutory data-related obligations cannot be relied on in the data recipient's insolvency. This is because the insolvency practitioner conducting the insolvency proceedings 'would not be held to account for breaches of data protection laws, where it is a regulatory requirement for a controller or other officer to be appointed and assume responsibility for the handling of that data'.[45] Instead, like other obligations owed by the insolvent, they are to be converted to a monetary claim so that the creditor may participate in the sharing of the insolvent's remaining assets. There is no reason to believe that the result would be materially different under Australian insolvency law, as the relevant substantive principles are the same.[46]

However, each case was a challenge by the insolvency practitioners to ongoing obligations with respect to continuing to hold the relevant data, not the data's deletion. In *Southern Pacific Personal Loans* the insolvency practitioners wanted to delete the relevant data because of the ongoing obligations which the data created, whilst in *Green v. SCL Group*, the data had already been seized by the Information Commissioner's Office. What was missing in each case was a clear way for the insolvency practitioners to legally rid themselves of the relevant data and the associated ongoing non-monetary obligations. Accordingly, the clear statutory obligations to delete the customer data under the Australian system should be complied with if the recipient loses its authorisation and becomes subject to insolvency proceedings. The absence of similar clear obligations under the UK system means that the consequences of insolvency are more obscure and represent a significant difference between Australian and UK open banking. This is evaluated in the next section.

### 11.2.2 Evaluation Against Insolvency Law Protection for Banking Payment Systems

#### *(a) Legislative Protection from Insolvency Laws*

Due to the importance of their functions, both banks and payment systems are often protected by legislation from the operation of ordinary insolvency laws.[47] These protections quarantine deposits from those laws in the case of a bank's default and

44. *Ibid.* 687.
45. Robert Walters, 'Insolvency and Data Protection' (2021) 42(1) *Business Law Review*, 4.
46. *See* Philip R Wood, *Principles of International Insolvency* (Sweet & Maxwell, 3rd ed., 2019).
47. *See Banking Act 1959* (Cth) ('*Australian Banking Act*'); *Banking Act 2009* (UK) ('*UK Banking Act*'). *See also Payment Systems and Netting Act* (n. 23) and *Settlement Finality Regulations* (n.

grant priority to payment system rules over those laws in the case of a participant's default,[48] including by permitting payments to be settled in accordance with those rules even after the insolvency of a participant has commenced.[49] These protections are an important feature in managing the stability of the payment system, the systemic risk if there is a participant default and, as a result, the confidence in the system as a whole.

Neither of the Australian nor UK open banking systems has any similar legal protections of the legal rights and obligations with respect to customer data in the insolvency of a data recipient. However, due to an important difference between customer data and customer funds, managing this risk for open banking systems should not require the same form of legal protection as for payment systems. As explained in Chapter 8, customer data are non-rivalrous and, unlike customer funds, are not lost to the customer when they have been shared with a data recipient. For the customer to avoid losing value on a data recipient default, it is only necessary to compel the data recipient to delete the customer data rather than returning the data or transferring the data to another data recipient. There isn't a need to protect the continued operation of the open banking system's rules relating to the custody and use of customer data by the data recipient if the data are deleted on the data recipient's insolvency. As noted in above, this exists in Australian open banking but not UK open banking. Whilst it could be expected that an insolvency practitioner would comply with this obligation, to further protect the customer, and confidence in the open banking system, it would be more aligned with the protections afforded to payment systems if it were clarified that this deletion of customer data is required even in the insolvency of the data recipient. This would enhance the confidence which customers and participants have in the open banking system.

### *(b) Default Management Processes*

In addition, banking payment systems also include rules which manage the consequences of participant default. The purpose of these rules is to facilitate the continued functioning of the system by managing the settlement of outstanding transactions, limiting disruptions to the market, and minimising losses for non-defaulting participants.[50] To enable this to happen, the system needs to have clear rules for identifying

23). *See also* Kristin van Zwieten (ed.), *Goode on Principles of Corporate Insolvency Law* (Sweet & Maxwell, 5th ed., 2018) Ch. 1 pts 5, 6; Wood, *Principles of International Insolvency* (n. 46).

48. Creating a 'safe harbour' against the operation of those rules: Ross Cranston et al., *Principles of Banking Law* (Oxford University Press, 3rd ed., 2017) 355.

49. Namely, on the same day thus overriding the 'zero-hour rule'. *See Payment Systems and Netting Act* (n. 23) ss 6, 6A; *Settlement Finality Regulations* (n. 23) reg. 20. The same protections do not apply for payments made through correspondent banking arrangements as the commencement of insolvency proceedings can revoke the authority of an agent: *In re Farrow's Bank, Limited* [1921] 2 Ch. 164 ('*Farrow's Bank*'). *See also Pacific and General Insurance Co Ltd v. Hazell & Ors.* [1997] BCC 400 ('*P & G Insurance v. Hazell*').

50. *See* Committee on Payment and Settlement Systems and International Organization of Securities Commissions, 'Principles for Financial Markets Infrastructures' (Standards, Bank for International Settlements, April 2012) [3.13.1].

and declaring a default, what actions can be taken following a default, the consequences of those actions, and the roles of other parties in the management of the default.[51] This can include loss sharing arrangements between participants such as 'defaulter pays' arrangements where the participant in default pays for the losses caused to other participants, and 'survivor pays' arrangements where the other participants share the remaining losses in order to ensure the survival of the system.[52] Such arrangements require agreement between the participants to be effective. For example, 'defaulter-pays' followed by 'survivors-pay' was agreed between the settlement banks in two UK payment systems in 2005.[53] Its purpose was to guarantee that settlement takes place under those systems, even if the largest direct participant defaults under its obligations to other participants.[54] In the view of the Bank of England, this agreement 'protects the public from the disruption the closure of these systems would cause' and reduces systemic risk.[55]

Neither Australian nor UK open banking has any equivalent protection of their rules from the operation of insolvency laws nor any equivalent default management rights to clearly articulate how the continued functioning of the system will be protected from the insolvency of its participants. If, for example, a participant were suspended from the Australian system because it threatened the 'security, integrity and stability' of the 'information and communication technology systems that are used by CDR participants to disclose or collect CDR data',[56] it is not clear what actions would be taken afterwards to remedy the damage caused or to appropriately share the costs of doing so. There is nothing which articulates 'the roles, obligations, and responsibilities of the various parties, including the non-defaulting participants' or 'the existence of other mechanisms that may be activated to contain the impact of the default'.[57] In the case of a default triggered by cyber-security issues this could be particularly constrained as the focus of each system is on the information security of each participant, rather than the system as a whole.[58] Also, there is nothing that sets out how the costs for dealing with the threat will be allocated amongst the defaulting and surviving participants. In this regard, both systems are confusing. As the analysis in Chapter 10 above shows, the Australian system grants contractual rights to banks and recipients against each other with respect to breaches of the Australian Standards. However, as the analysis in that chapter also shows, the insurance which a data recipient is required to hold does not cover liabilities to other participants in the

51. *Ibid.* [3.13.2].
52. Committee on Payment and Settlement Systems, 'Core Principles for Systemically Important Payment Systems' (n. 21) [7.3.7].
53. Bank of England, 'Strengthening Financial Infrastructure' (2005)(June) *Financial Stability Review* 79.
54. Committee on Payment and Settlement Systems, 'Payment, Clearing and Settlement Systems in the CPSS Countries Volume 2' (Red Book, Bank for International Settlements, November 2012) 455.
55. Bank of England, 'Strengthening Financial Infrastructure' (n. 53) 86.
56. *See* section 11.1.1 above.
57. Committee on Payment and Settlement Systems and International Organization of Securities Commissions (n. 50).
58. *See* Chapter 8.

system. In contrast, the insurance required in the UK system does require insurance to cover those liabilities. However, UK open banking does not require there be any contractual basis under which those liabilities are owed. Accordingly, there is no clear way to ensure that the 'defaulter pays' and the 'surviving' participants will bear any costs or damage which fall upon them as a result of the participant's default against which they cannot be compensated. Further, no basis is established to share the costs to remedy the consequences on a framework of a participant's default amongst the remaining participants. When evaluated against the features of banking payment systems, this lack of consideration of dealing with the consequences of insolvency in the legal foundations of each system will potentially constrain their credibility if a participant should fail.

## 11.3 HOW CAN LEGAL FOUNDATIONS SUPPORT ENSURING CREDIBILITY?

### 11.3.1 Summary of Comparison and Evaluation

This chapter has examined the implications of the legal foundations of Australian and UK open banking for ensuring the credibility of the systems through a comparison of their legal features relating to the treatment of defaulting participants and the management of participant insolvency, and an evaluation against equivalent legal features of payment systems.

The analysis has shown that the legal foundation of UK open banking is lacking the features found in Australian open banking which enable the urgent removal of defaulting recipients or the removal of a participant which is a threat to the open banking system, as opposed to a payment system. This feature is also found in banking payment systems, where it is applied to all participants and not just those who receive payments. It has also shown that both Australian and UK open banking are lacking the legal features found in banking payment systems which preserve the system's ability to function despite a participant's default, and to fairly allocate the losses caused by that default between participants.

The consequences of these differences is that the legal foundations of UK open banking offer less support for its provision of accountability and credibility than the legal foundation of Australian open banking. Neither offers the same level of support as the legal foundation of banking payment systems. This is illustrated in Figure 11.1.

*Figure 11.1 Illustration of Evaluation and Comparison Relating to Ensuring Credibility*

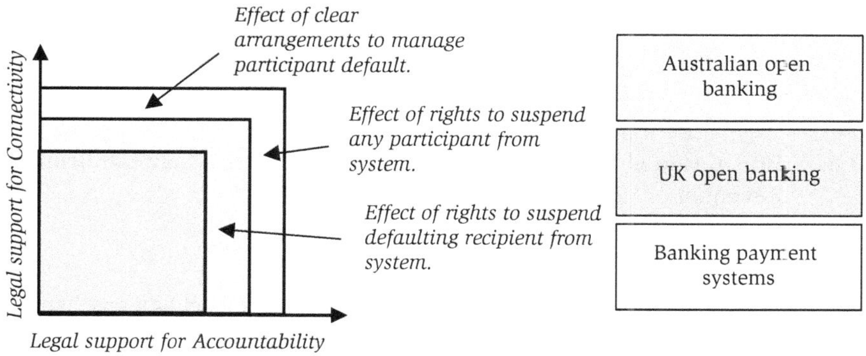


This analysis shows the need to balance connectivity and accountability to ensure credibility in open banking systems. This also demonstrates the importance of managing network risk. This risk is explained next, followed by an illustration of the comparable systemic risk in banking payment systems, and a discussion of how systemic risk management methods could be included in the legal foundations of open banking systems.

### 11.3.2 Network Risk in Open Banking Systems

Chapter 4 explained that open banking systems should develop into complex ecosystems, with many participants offering different services to each other and connected with each other to differing extents. Chapter 9 showed how the design of authorisation arrangements facilitated this development. In addition to the potential for increased competition and innovation, this could result in many participants relying on the services of only a few other participants, or a few participants could provide customers with access to a large number of other participants.

The failure of one of these highly connected participants could cause harm to many others in the system. Due to their high level of connectivity, if such a participant were to suddenly cease to provide those services, then not only might many of their customers suffer an interruption in their own business, but also other recipients may not be able to provide their own services to others. Also, if such a participant were to be subject to a cyber-attack which spread from its systems to others, then it could cause widespread damage due to its connectivity. As with other networks, interdependence created in the open banking systems could lead to 'cascading failures', 'breakdown avalanches' or 'domino effects' or, in the case of banking payment systems, 'systemic failure'. Further, as these participants directly face customers, unlike the outsourced service providers discussed in Chapter 9, the sudden withdrawal of services would cause customers to lose confidence in the open banking system, affecting still more participants, as 'information contagion' spreads. A further critical element in understanding this aspect of network risk is the role which confidence in the system plays in open banking. As noted in Chapter 4, credibility can be lost quickly in network failures. This risk can challenge the credibility needed for the open banking system to achieve its objectives.

To further explain this network risk, the next section sets out an illustration of the comparable risk in banking payment systems, *systemic risk*.

### 11.3.3 Illustration of Systemic Risk in Financial Systems: Lehman Brothers Revisited

Systemic risk in banking payment systems is:

> the risk that the inability of one of the participants to meet its obligations, or a disruption in the system itself, could result in the inability of other system participants or of financial institutions in other parts of the financial system to meet their obligations as they become due.[59]

The management of systemic risk is essential to the preservation of banking payment systems as it cannot be efficiently managed by participants acting on their own, because it results in the costs of a party's default being imposed beyond those with whom it directly transacts. The failure to fully understand this risk was a major contributor to the occurrence and impact of the 2007-2009 global financial crisis, as explained by the British Academy to Her Majesty Queen Elizabeth II:

> So in summary, Your Majesty, the failure to foresee the timing, extent and severity of the crisis and to head it off, while it had many causes, was principally a failure of the collective imagination of many bright people, both in this country and internationally, to understand the risks to the system as a whole.[60]

The relevance of systemic risk can be seen from revisiting the failure of Lehman Brothers ('Lehman'). As explained in Chapter 6, Lehman was a significant player in the global derivatives market, having a portfolio valued at the time of its failure of approximately $35 trillion, representing approximately 5% of the global derivatives market. Although not the direct cause of Lehman's collapse, derivatives played a large role in Lehman's failure. One aspect of their contribution was a lack of transparency as regulators did not know their number or value. Another was the risk created by the interconnectedness of the different derivative positions. A third was the 'run' created by its derivatives portfolio as counterparties demanded more and more collateral to protect their exposure. This spread beyond Lehman itself and led to a 'credit crunch' more globally. This was not just because of a cascade of losses through defaulting

59. Committee on Payment and Settlement Systems, 'Core Principles for Systemically Important Payment Systems' (n. 50).
60. Tim Besley and Peter Hennessey, 'Letter in Response to a Question of Queen Elizabeth' (2009) *British Academy of Science, London*. *See also* Jeremy Fouliard, Michael Howell and Hélène Rey, 'Answering the Queen: Machine Learning and Financial Crises' (BIS Working Paper No. 926, Bank for International Settlements, February 2021).

counterparties, but also because the 'information contagion' spread as a signal to markets that their perception of risk was faulty, which exacerbated the crisis. The resulting aversion to risk led to a breakdown of interbank money markets.

The benefits of rights to intervene to manage default and systemic risk can be seen in the treatment of Lehman's derivatives portfolio. Lehman's more than one million derivative transactions complicated the resolution of its bankruptcy proceedings and were the source of a significant loss of value in the bankruptcy. These derivatives consisted of two types, the minority were held in centralised clearing arrangements whilst the majority were held as bilateral contracts, or 'over-the-counter' transactions. The difference in the management of default of each is instructive.

- *Management of default through bilateral contracts*: The counterparties for the bilateral contracts needed to rely on the exercise of contractual rights to manage the impact of Lehman's default. This process was complicated by the difficulty of calculating replacement costs in illiquid markets, the need to construe complex legal documents and the sheer number of contracts terminated (more than 900,000 contracts and more than 6,000 claims filed in the bankruptcy proceedings). Through this process, counterparties to Lehman entities 'faced considerable uncertainty and complexity'.[61] The result was protracted and expensive and contributed to the disruption of the financial markets through the crisis.
- *Management of default through clearing arrangements*: In contrast, the resolution of the cleared derivatives position was simple. Critically, the process involved the suspension (within hours of default) of the Lehman entities from participation in the relevant markets by authorities so that no further risks could accumulate, and the outstanding derivative positions were either closed out or, in the case of transactions entered into on behalf of Lehman's clients, transferred to other brokers. As a result, most of Lehman's clients had access to their accounts within weeks. This process was so successful that the mandatory clearing of derivatives was implemented globally as part of the G20 reforms following the financial crisis.

The management of Lehman's cleared derivatives on its default shows the benefits of intervention to suspend a defaulting participant and coordinate the response to its failure. It is plausible that the failure of a highly connected participant in a mature open banking system could give rise to network risks similar to those which eventuated in the collapse of Lehman. This could arise, for example, through an information security failure causing spreading losses in data integrity. If such a participant cannot be urgently suspended, then more participants will be affected. Like the bilateral derivatives, customers and other participants will be left to fend for themselves and the resulting complexity and confusion will cause a significant drop in the credibility of the system. In part, this will be because the replacement cost of the unperformed data-related obligations may be extremely difficult to determine. It is important to

61. Reserve Bank of Australia, 'Financial Stability Review – March 2009' (Report, March 2009) 70.

reiterate that the contagion does not need to be spread by financial losses. It could be spread by losses of trust in the system itself.

Accordingly, the legal features used in banking payment systems used to manage systemic risk deserve consideration for incorporation into the legal foundations of open banking.

### 11.3.4 Incorporating Systemic Risk Management Features in Open Banking

The management of systemic risk is critical to the safety of banking payment systems. Of particular importance are rules and procedures which are 'designed to ensure that the [system] can take timely action to contain losses' and 'limit the potential for the effects of a participant's failure to spread to other participants'.[62] Transparency and clarity with respect to these rules are fundamental so as to provide certainty and predictability and minimise confusion if they are required to be used. Key aspects include the actions which can be taken when default occurs, the extent to which actions are automatic or discretionary, changes to normal operational practices, expected treatment of participant and customer value, the order in which actions are likely to be taken, the roles of various parties in the process and the existence of other mechanisms which might be activated to manage the default.

The financial crisis also made it clear that the regulation of a system required more than the regulation of the individual participants. Depositor protection was not enough in itself to protect banks' stability. A similar approach should be considered in the legal design of open banking systems, given the potential for network risk to be spread by a highly connected defaulting participant. A starting point is clear legal rights to remove a participant that is threatening the system's stability, or to urgently suspend a defaulting participant to avoid the accumulation of further risks. This would prevent the impact of the default of a participant (such as in relation to an information security failure) from being able to be spread to other participants through the system's connections. This chapter has shown that rights of this nature are included in Australian open banking.

The treatment of open banking as an entire system, rather than merely bilateral arrangements, also requires an assessment of what is required to preserve the continuance of the system's effectiveness despite the default of a significant participant. Banking payment systems do this through the articulation of the roles, obligations and responsibilities of non-defaulting parties in the case of a participant default. In addition to meeting actual costs, this might include how monetary losses are allocated to non-defaulting participants in order to ensure the system's continued operation. Such an allocation also helps to reinstate the confidence in the continuance of the system. Some adjustment will be required in adopting this approach in open banking. The 'losses' which an open banking system suffers due to the failure of a significant participant are more likely to be losses of trust and confidence due to the

62. Committee on Payment and Settlement Systems and International Organization of Securities Commissions (n. 50) 78.

loss or misuse of customer data which has resulted. Reinstating this trust and confidence might not be able to be addressed merely by the payment of money because in some circumstances money may not be able to mitigate the adverse effects suffered by customers. Instead, it may require cooperative efforts to be made by the surviving recipients to recover missing customer data, to re-establish lost customer identities and, if possible, to identify those who received customer data so that obligations for the data's deletion can be imposed on those recipients who are within jurisdictional reach. These arrangements should contribute to re-establishing confidence in the open banking system, particularly through the 'shared interest' demonstrated in the continuance of the system's operation. Similarly, it will be important that the risks of recurrence of the failures are seen to be eliminated or minimised. This will require a 'whole of system' approach, and the performance of mutually supporting obligations.

The steps described above cannot be expected to achieve perfect results. But if steps of this nature are not taken to manage network risk, then the legal foundations of an open banking system could pose a challenge to its credibility and its ability to perform any of its functions and achieve any of its objectives. The need to take great care in establishing strong legal foundations to manage network risk can be seen in the consequences which have arisen from unmanaged systemic risk in banking payment systems.

CHAPTER 12

# Open Banking and Banking Laws

Open banking is changing banking across the globe by empowering customers to benefit from sharing their banking data. However, like many other areas of rapid adoption of technology in society, there can be concern that the application of existing laws does not fully address the issues which arise. The analysis in the previous chapters has sought to address this by developing and then testing a banking law based framework to use with open banking. It has analysed the legal rights, responsibilities, and relationships for sharing customer data under open banking in Australia and the United Kingdom and evaluated them against banking laws performing similar functions for customer funds. The result of this assessment is summarised next, followed by a summary of the themes which have emerged for the design of open banking, the conclusions which can be drawn for the further use of banking law in open banking, and discussion of further questions to be answered in the future design and development of open banking law.

## 12.1 WHAT IS THE ASSESSMENT OF AUSTRALIAN AND UK OPEN BANKING?

The preceding chapters have analysed and compared the legal foundations of the Australian and UK open banking systems, namely those which govern the supply of customer data for sharing, sharing customer data, utilising shared customer data, preserving the value of shared customer data, enabling participation in open banking systems, allocating liability between participants and ensuring the credibility of an open banking system. These foundations have been evaluated in their performance of the core functions of open banking, being customer autonomy, data portability, recipient accountability and participant connectivity, by reference to the legal foundations of banking payment systems which perform equivalent functions. The analysis has also included an examination of the key risks which arise from the design of these rights, responsibilities and relationships and the consideration of the circumstances where similar risks have arisen in banking payment systems, and the applicability of the steps taken to manage them.

This analysis, evaluation, examination and consideration enables important conclusions to be drawn on the comparative strengths and weaknesses of the legal foundations of the two open banking systems when evaluated against open banking systems. These conclusions are summarised below, by reference to where the differences impact effectiveness and safety of the open banking system.

### 12.1.1 Support of System Effectiveness by Legal Foundations

The analysis has shown there to be issues in the legal foundations of the open banking systems which affect their efficacy in performing their functions, as summarised in Table 12.1.

*Table 12.1 Issues in Legal Foundations of Australian and UK Open Banking Systems*

<table>
<tr><th>Chapter</th><th>Identified Differences</th><th>System</th><th>Functions Affected</th></tr>
<tr><td rowspan="3">Supplying data</td><td>Customers cannot give payment initiation instructions.</td><td>Aus.</td><td rowspan="3">Autonomy<br>Portability</td></tr>
<tr><td>Customers can share data from payment accounts only.</td><td rowspan="2">UK</td></tr>
<tr><td>Customers cannot require data recipients to share data.</td></tr>
<tr><td rowspan="3">Sharing data</td><td>Customers cannot request their own data.</td><td>Both</td><td rowspan="3">Portability<br>Autonomy</td></tr>
<tr><td>Substantive legal rights in technical standards only.</td><td rowspan="2">UK</td></tr>
<tr><td>Business customers' enforcement of rights to share data limited.</td></tr>
<tr><td rowspan="3">Preserving value</td><td>Data quality requirements do not apply to business customers.</td><td rowspan="3">UK</td><td rowspan="3">Accountability<br>Autonomy</td></tr>
<tr><td>No obligation to delete business customer data after use.</td></tr>
<tr><td>No requirement to delete data when authorisation expired.</td></tr>
<tr><td rowspan="2">Facilitating Participation</td><td>Data able to be shared beyond scope of system's authorisations.</td><td rowspan="2">UK</td><td rowspan="2">Connectivity<br>Accountability</td></tr>
<tr><td>Limited visibility of outsourced service providers.</td></tr>
</table>

| *Chapter* | *Identified Differences* | *System* | *Functions Affected* |
|---|---|---|---|
| Allocating Liability | No enforceable legal relationships between participants. | UK | Accountability Connectivity |
| | No allocation of legal liability between participants. | | |
| | Limitations on insurance used to compensate customers. | Both | |
| | Participants' insurance not required to cover other participants. | Aus. | |
| Ensuring credibility | No right to remove participant for threat to framework. | UK | Connectivity Accountability |
| | No right to suspend a defaulting participant. | | |
| | No rights to manage impact of participant default. | Both | |

These differences demonstrate that:

- the customers' legal rights to share their data at their direction;
- the recipient's legal responsibilities in dealing with shared data; and
- the legal relationships between participants;

in the open banking systems offer less support for the performance of autonomy, portability, accountability and connectivity functions in the open banking systems than the support offered for the performance of the equivalent functions of liquidity, custody, and participation functions by equivalent legal foundations of banking payment systems. It follows from this analysis that the legal design of the open banking systems could benefit from incorporating legal features from banking payment systems to improve their efficacy.

The analysis has also shown that some differences between the legal foundations of open banking systems and banking payment systems do not impair the efficacy of the open banking systems because they are needed due to the differences between the fundamental nature of data and money, as summarised in Table 12.2.

*Table 12.2 Differences in Legal Foundations of Open Banking and Banking Payment Systems*

| *Chapter* | *Identified Differences* | *Reasoning* |
|---|---|---|
| Supplying data | Banks do not act as agent of customers in sharing customer data as they do in paying customer funds. | Data is non-rivalrous and does not constitute property of the customer |
| Sharing data | Recipients do not act as agent of customers in receiving customer data as banks do in receiving customer funds. | |

| *Chapter* | *Identified Differences* | *Reasoning* |
|---|---|---|
| Utilising data | Banks are not subject to controls in receiving and using customer funds which are equivalent to the data minimisation and customer consent constraints in open banking. | The value of data is subjective and use dependent |
| Preserving value | Data recipients do not have unconditional obligations to protect customer data as banks do in protecting customer funds. | Data is the object of, but does not define, obligations and data's value can be protected by their deletion |
| Allocating liability | Banks are not allocated residual liability for unauthorised use of shared data in the same way as they are allocated residual liability for unauthorised use of transferred funds. | Customers have direct relationship with recipients and banks perform different roles |

These differences primarily relate to the accountability to customers for the holding and use of their data. Importantly, a number of these differences relate to matters which are already addressed by privacy law and where the legal responsibilities are aligned with those laws. These differences do not negate the functional equivalence between open banking systems and banking payment systems as networks for communicating valuable information, particularly with respect to their autonomy, portability and connectivity functions. Accordingly, the legal features of banking payment systems remain a valuable benchmark against which the legal features of the frameworks can be evaluated.

### 12.1.2 Support of Risk Management by Legal Foundations

The analysis of the earlier chapters of this book also shows the risks which could develop from the issues identified in the legal foundations of the open banking systems and banking payment systems as summarised in Table 12.3.

*Table 12.3 Risks Arising from Issues in Legal Foundations of Open Banking Systems*

| *Primary Risk* | *Identified Issues* | *System* |
|---|---|---|
| Availability | Customers cannot give payment initiation instructions. | Aus. |
| | Customers can share data from payment accounts only. | UK |
| | Customers cannot require data recipients to share data. | |
| Performance | Customers cannot request their own data. | Both |
| | Limitations on insurance used to compensate customers. | |
| | Data able to be shared beyond scope of system's authorisations. | UK |

<table>
<tr><th>Primary Risk</th><th>Identified Issues</th><th>System</th></tr>
<tr><td rowspan="3">Value</td><td>Data quality requirements do not apply to business customers.</td><td rowspan="3">UK</td></tr>
<tr><td>No obligation to delete business customer data after use.</td></tr>
<tr><td>No requirement to delete data when authorisation expired.</td></tr>
<tr><td rowspan="5">Network</td><td>No visibility of outsourced service providers.</td><td rowspan="3">UK</td></tr>
<tr><td>No right to remove participant for threat to framework.</td></tr>
<tr><td>No right to suspend a defaulting participant.</td></tr>
<tr><td>Participants' insurance not required to cover other participants.</td><td>Aus.</td></tr>
<tr><td>No rights to manage impact of participant default.</td><td>Both</td></tr>
<tr><td rowspan="4">Validity</td><td>Substantive legal rights in technical standards only.</td><td rowspan="4">UK</td></tr>
<tr><td>Business customers' enforcement of rights to share data limited.</td></tr>
<tr><td>No enforceable legal relationships between participants.</td></tr>
<tr><td>No allocation of legal liability between participants.</td></tr>
</table>

This shows that the open banking system's legal foundations offer less support for the management of the risk that:

- data are not available to be shared by the customer;
- participants do not perform their data-related obligations;
- the value of the customer's data is not protected;
- the default of one participant causes the default of others; and
- the law will not recognise the validity of the frameworks' obligations;

than that offered by the legal foundations of open banking systems for the management of equivalent risks. No issue was identified in relation to the management of the risk that data are not able to be accurately sent or received because the Australian and UK system both use mandatory and specific standards. Nevertheless, it follows from this analysis that the legal design of the open banking systems could benefit from incorporating legal features from banking payment systems which manage risks in order to improve their trustworthiness.

The risk analysis also demonstrates that some of the methods for managing liquidity, credit and systemic risks in banking payment systems cannot be applied to manage availability, performance and network risks in open banking systems, due to specific issues related to differing features of customer data and customer funds. Namely, that customer data are non-rivalrous, non-fungible, and their value subjective, such that there is no 'settlement asset' which can finally discharge data-related obligations and that those obligations continue for as long as the data is held, and money may be insufficient to compensate for the losses caused if they are not performed. It also shows that, as a result, the management of some risks requires the development of new approaches to ensure performance of obligations and management of participant failure, which will need to be the subject of further policy, legal and technological development. However, the analysis also shows that these differences do not negate the comparability of these risks nor the adoption or adaptation of risk management methods from banking payment systems. These exceptions do not invalidate the use of the legal features of banking payment systems as a benchmark against which the legal features of open banking systems are evaluated.

The themes for the legal design and development of open banking which arise from this analysis are explained next.

## 12.2 HOW SHOULD OPEN BANKING BE DESIGNED AND DEVELOPED?

The analysis in this book establishes that open banking systems should, with respect to the sharing and use of customer banking data, include many of the comparable legal features of banking payment systems for the payment and use of customer money.

Appropriately incorporated, those legal features would support the performance of the functions of open banking systems so that they are effective in achieving their objectives, and support the management of risks in open banking systems so that they are safe, just as they support efficiency and safety in banking payment systems. Although customer funds and customer data are not the same, they both represent valuable information and the lessons learned in the design and re-design of banking payment systems should be heeded in establishing and developing open banking systems.

Four themes emerge from this analysis for the design and development of the legal foundations of open banking systems. Namely that those foundations should establish rights, responsibilities and relationships which support customers:

- in making choices;
- in deriving value;
- in looking after their value; and
- in trusting open banking;

with respect to their data. These are described below in turn.

### 12.2.1 Empowering Customers to Make Choices

As explained at the beginning of this book, customers are the subject and not the object of open banking. The legal design of open banking systems should support the choices which the customer should be able to make with respect to customer data. Empowering customers to choose whether or not to share their data, what data to share, with whom those data should be shared, for what purpose and for how long, is fundamental to the autonomy function to be performed by open banking, and to the management of availability risks.

Despite this, the importance of enabling customer choice can be overlooked in the design of open banking. This is because an over-emphasis on consumer protection or privacy in the design of an open banking system can compromise the choices which customers should be able to make with their data. A desire to use open banking to protect customers from the choices they make to share their data over-estimates the role of open banking. As the data are already available to the customer, open banking can enable those data to be shared but cannot prevent those data from being shared. For example, a customer could choose to email their bank statements to a data recipient if they could not share those data through open banking. This means that an effort to protect some customers from the choices they might otherwise make can result in customers using less reliable means of sharing data, defeating the consumer protection objective which was sought to be achieved.

Accordingly, it is important that the legal design of open banking takes a balanced approach to the objectives, principles, and functions of open banking systems in determining the legal features which should be included. A focus on supporting customer choices facilitates this. The autonomy function of open banking means that customers should be able to choose what they do with their data, with the result that systems themselves need to compete with other methods of data sharing. If open banking does not offer a better alternative than what customers already use, or what is otherwise available for them to choose, then it will not be used. For open banking to achieve all of its objectives, the legal design should balance the need for customer protection with customer choice, instead of assuming that customer protection is the primary objective to be achieved. A comparable balance has been reached in the design of banking payment systems where customers have rights to transfer their funds as they choose, subject to some customer protections which are considered fundamental to confidence in the system.

### 12.2.2 Enabling Customers to Derive Value

The legal design of open banking systems should enable the use of customer data for the benefit of the customer. The analysis has shown that the value of customer data is derived from the use of those data and open banking needs to facilitate sharing of those data by customers with recipients to enable that use. The sharing and use of customer data is fundamental to the portability function of open banking and to the management of communication risks which arise in open banking systems.

The importance of enabling customers to derive value from data can be missed because of a tendency to treat open banking as merely ancillary to established fields of law which primarily relate to data protection or payments. As noted in Chapter 1, much of the legal academic analysis of open banking has taken a privacy perspective, and the legal foundation for the UK system is the regulation of payment services. Whilst data protection and payments regulation support aspects of the effectiveness of systems in achieving their objectives, they cannot achieve those objectives by themselves. If they could, then open banking would not be needed. Accordingly, privacy laws and payments regulation are insufficient to form the foundation of the legal design of effective open banking systems (in this regard, payments regulation differs from the breadth of laws and legal principles applicable to banking payment systems). A privacy or payments regulation focus does not offer sufficient support for the derivation of value for customers from the use of their data.

Additionally, this need to focus on customer value means that it is important that the legal design of open banking regulates the sharing and use of the customer data but not the regulation of the services which that sharing and use enables. Whilst those services are the means by which the value of the customer data is derived by the customer, and data minimisation makes those services fundamental to the sharing and use of the customer data, it is not necessary for open banking systems to seek to regulate the services provided with the shared data. To do so risks regulatory confusion and over-regulation, as those services will already be subject to regulation beyond open banking. The result is likely to be that some other method of sharing the customer data will be used instead of open banking, to avoid the unnecessary regulation. A comparable approach is taken in banking payment systems where the regulation of transfers of funds does not seek to also regulate the provision of each good or service which can be acquired with those funds.

### 12.2.3 Encouraging Customers to Look after That Value

The legal design of open banking should encourage customers to look after the value of their customer data by establishing appropriate legal rights, responsibilities and relationships amongst customers, banks, recipients and the intermediaries who provide services to them. The analysis has shown this requires that legal obligations are incurred and performed. These legal obligations ensure that the customer benefits from the value of their customer data. This is fundamental to the accountability function to be performed by open banking systems, and to the management of performance, value and validity risks.

Despite the obvious importance of legal protections to the design of open banking systems, the need for the law to preserve customer value in their data can be ignored as shown by the open banking systems which seek to establish no legal rights and obligations between participants. The technological requirements of open banking are more apparent, because the uses of customer data which deliver value to the customer are primarily based in technology. Whilst the technological foundation is critical for the operation of open banking, it does not provide a sufficient basis for its entire governance. One reason is because the technical standards, which form the foundation of the technological governance, are insufficiently accessible, and inadequate in scope, to regulate all aspects of the interactions between participants in open banking. Another is they are not legally enforceable on their own.

The need for legal protection of customer value may not be fully understood until something goes wrong. Open banking systems have not been in existence for long enough to be tested by significant failures in participant performance. The experience with failures in banking payment systems shows that those failures should be expected to occur at some time and that the resolution of those failures is dependent on clear and certain legal rights and obligations. Whilst future participant failure is unlikely to be at the forefront of concerns in establishing a new technological framework to enable customers to share their data, the lessons from banking payment systems teach us that it should be, and that technological complexity of networks for the communication of valuable information, whether customer funds or customer data, should be supported by clear and enforceable legal rights, responsibilities and relationships.

### 12.2.4 Ensuring Customers Can Trust Open Banking

The legal design of an open banking system should support the credibility of the system so that customers can trust it for the sharing and use of their data. The analysis has shown that, in order to be effective, open banking systems should develop to be complex and connected networks of interdependence between participants and that continued participation relies on the credibility of the system and the confidence which customers and participants have in it. This is a consequence of the performance of the connectivity function of open banking frameworks, and to managing the network risks which arise.

Whilst the need for trust in open banking's success is often noted, the need for all customers and participants to have confidence in the system as a whole, rather than merely trust in those with whom they interact is not always recognised. This is curious given that this is a consequence of open banking developing as networks and the concept of a network is not new to either technology or banking. However, the function of an open banking system as an interdependent network can be obscured by the focus on the individual roles of the participants rather than the holistic outcome of the performance of their roles. For example, the competition objective of open banking systems is based on the information asymmetry which banks enjoy in relation to customer data and, as a result, a key focus of the design is to ensure that customers can require their bank to share their customer data. The role of the customer is to request their bank to share their data, the role of the bank is to share those data, and the role of the recipient is to provide a service to the customer with those data. This appears more like a transaction than part of a system and, as a result, a transactional focus can be taken in open banking system design. Banking payment systems are also built from many individual transactions similar in concept to these, but there is a key difference. In banking payment systems, there is an understanding that a bank might be either paying or receiving customer funds in any transaction. This clarifies the interdependence between the participants, and the reliance that each is placing on the others. This is a key element in the importance of reciprocity in open banking systems. Not only is the ability for customers to require that recipients also share customer data important for a system's performance of its portability function, but it is also important in understanding open banking as an entire system. Once it is understood that any participant could be required by a customer to share data with another participant, the understanding that each relies on each other's performance is no longer obscured.

## 12.3 WHY IS BANKING LAW NEEDED FOR DESIGNING OPEN BANKING?

As explained in Chapter 1, this book has sought to derive and demonstrate a banking law foundation for designing and developing open banking. It has not sought to address other issues relating to banking or data, such as those which are determined by the application of privacy or competition laws. These other perspectives are most often taken by legal analyses of open banking. This is understandable, given that open banking was established in the UK to remedy a competition problem, and with extensive reliance on existing privacy laws. These other legal contexts remain critical in establishing and analysing open banking systems, as they are an important foundation in achieving open banking's objectives, particularly the competition and consumer protection objectives articulated in Chapter 1.

However, this book demonstrates that competition and privacy laws are not the sole perspectives through which open banking systems should be analysed. This book provides a foundation for analysing the autonomy, portability, accountability and connectivity functions of open banking in a manner similar to which the liquidity, custody and access functions are analysed in banking payment systems. It also provides a new basis for analysing the risks which can arise in open banking systems based on those used in banking payment systems and shows how the methods for managing those risks in banking payment systems can be applied to open banking systems. The foundations, functions, features, and risks identified, analysed and assessed, in this book would not be as evident from an analysis of open banking from privacy and competition law perspectives. Also, although the competition and privacy principles support accountability functions which need to be performed by open banking in order to achieve its objectives, they do not do so comprehensively and are not well placed to identify or support open banking's autonomy or connectivity functions.

In this context, the perspective of banking law explored and explained in this book is an important addition to the legal analysis and design of open banking. Banking law principles enable a different perspective to be taken on open banking systems, as systems for *deriving value*, rather than as a means of protecting confidentiality, or achieving a better competition outcome in a market. This alternative perspective enables an assessment of the legal support provided in the systems for the *value* of the customer data, separate from the content from which that value is derived, or on the outcomes which arise from those data's use. As this book shows, this allows for a different analysis of risks which can arise in open banking and a different basis for recommending design features to manage those risks. Importantly, using banking law principles in the assessment and design of open banking allows open banking to benefit from the extensive history and development of banking payment systems, and the laws which have evolved to support them.

The in-depth comprehensive analysis, comparison and evaluation of the Australian and UK open banking systems in this book should be useful for those working in, or working on, those laws and regulations. However, it is also intended that this book be useful for those designing other open banking systems, by demonstrating how banking law can be applied in the design of open banking. Although open banking systems are still emerging, and despite their significant use of technology and digital transformation, this book shows that the design of open banking systems could, and should, benefit from the lessons learned in the legal design of banking payment systems in encouraging efficiency and managing risk over many years. In doing so, this book provides a new set of 'design principles' which can be used to design open banking in any jurisdiction which seeks to implement it, enabling the principles of banking law in that jurisdiction to be used as a reference point in the design of open banking rather than the laws of a foreign jurisdiction.

The significance of this book in open banking design extends beyond the legal context. One element of this significance is the provision of an additional legal benchmark against which open banking design decisions can be made, particularly to balancing different objectives (such as innovation and consumer protection). By facilitating an assessment of open banking systems as networks for the transfer of valuable information, this book enables open banking systems to be designed as *banking systems for data*, rather than merely technological systems for communicating banking data. The use of these design principles in implementing open banking can ensure that when customers are 'banking on data', they are supported and protected by legal rights, responsibilities and relationships equivalent to those which support and protect them when banking with their money.

## 12.4 WHERE NEXT FOR THE LEGAL DESIGN OF OPEN BANKING?

Despite the length and depth of its analysis, this book has barely scratched the surface of the legal issues associated with open banking. Beyond its scope there are many opportunities for further research. For example, how the foundations, functions, features, and risks identified, analysed and assessed in relation to the Australian and UK open banking systems would apply to an open banking system in a jurisdiction which has a different basis of banking law, such as a civil law jurisdiction, and how they would apply when open banking systems are extended beyond banking into other sectors, as is already happening in Australia and is anticipated in the UK.

Further opportunities for additional research have been touched on in the analysis too. For example:

- Research into the legal significance of the similarities and differences between customer data and customer funds, particularly in the context of cryptographic methods used in 'crypto-assets' and decentralised finance, which result in data being rivalrous rather than non-rivalrous.
- Research into how a legal and technological framework can be developed to establish the performance of data-related obligations so that an equivalent concept to a 'settlement asset' can be developed.
- Research into the legal requirements for insurance coverage to be developed to provide further comfort to those exposed to the performance of data recipient's obligations in order to reinforce the trust in open banking systems.
- Research into the nature of the legal connections required to ensure the resilience of a data sharing framework, such as an open banking system, in the case of the failure of large participants, given the differences in the nature of data and money.

These are only some examples, and other opportunities for legal research exist, such as with respect to the connection between the legal and the technological aspects of open banking, and into the interaction between data protection, competition and banking law perspectives in contributing to open banking's success in achieving its objectives. Legal research into open banking is critical for that success. If the evolving trend of open banking could change the traditional business model of banking, the relationship between bank and customer and revolutionise financial management for customers,[1] then further research will be important to continue to guide the way for those designing and participating in the open banking systems which enable 'banking on data'.

1. *See* Bank for International Settlements, 'Report on Open Banking and Application Programming Interfaces' (Report, November 2019).

# Bibliography

## Articles, Books, Reports


Acharya, Viral V and Tanju Yorulmazer, 'Information Contagion and Inter-bank Correlation in a Theory of Systemic Risk' (Discussion Paper No. 3743, Centre for Economic Policy Research, February 2003)

Advisory Committee on Open Banking, 'Final Report of Advisory Committee on Open Banking' (Report, April 2021) https://www.canada.ca/content/dam/fin/consultations/2021/acob-ccsbo-eng.pdf

Amihud, Yakov and Haim Mendelson, 'The Pricing of Illiquidity as a Characteristic and as a Risk' (2015) 19(3) *Multinational Finance Journal* 149-168

Armour, John, et al., *Principles of Financial Regulation* (Oxford University Press, 2016)

Association of Banking in Singapore and Monetary Authority of Singapore, 'ABS-MAS Financial World: Finance-as-a-Service API Playbook', November 2016) https://abs.org.sg/docs/library/abs-api-playbook.pdf

Australian Competition and Consumer Commission, 'Accreditation Guidelines' (Guide, 9 December 2020)

Australian Competition and Consumer Commission, 'Supplementary Accreditation Guidelines – Insurance' (Guidelines, 25 May 2020)

Australian Competition and Consumer Commission, 'Participant On-boarding Guide' (Guide, June 2021) https://www.cdr.gov.au/sites/default/files/2021-07/CDR_Participant%20On-boarding%20Guide_v1.3_6.pdf

Australian Prudential Regulation Authority, 'Register of Authorised Deposit-Taking Institutions', 30 November 2020) https://www.apra.gov.au/register-of-authorised-deposit-taking-institutions

Australian Prudential Regulation Authority, 'Outsourcing Involving Cloud Computing Services' (Information Paper, 24 September 2018)

Australian Prudential Regulation Authority, 'APRA's Policy Priorities' (Information Paper, 1 February 2021)

Australian Securities & Investments Commission, 'ePayments Code' (Code of Conduct, 29 March 2016) https://download.asic.gov.au/media/3798542/epayments-code-published-29-march-2016.pdf

Australian Securities & Investments Commission, 'RG 126: Compensation and Insurance Arrangements for AFS Licensees' (Regulatory Guide, July 2020)

Australian Treasury, 'Review into Open Banking: Giving Customers Choice, Convenience and Confidence' (Report, December 2017)

Australian Treasury, 'Consumer Data Right Overview' (Explanatory Guide, 9 May 2018)

Australian Treasury, 'Inquiry into Future Directions for the Consumer Data Right: Giving Consumers Choice, Convenience and Confidence' (Report, October 2020)

Australian Treasury, 'Government Response to the Inquiry into Future Directions for the Consumer Data Right' (Report, December 2021)

Australian Treasury, 'Statutory Review of the Consumer Data Right' (Report, September 2022)

Australian Treasury, 'Strategic Assessment: Outcomes' (Report, January 2022)

Awrey, Dan and Kristin van Zwieten, 'The Shadow Payment System' (2017-2018) 43 *The Journal of Corporation Law* 775

Bank for International Settlements, 'Outsourcing in Financial Services' (Report, Joint Forum, February 2005)

Bank for International Settlements, 'Big Tech in Finance: Opportunities and Risks' (Annual Report part III, June 2019) www.bis.org/publ/arpdf/ar2019e.htm

Bank for International Settlements, 'Report on Open Banking and Application Programming Interfaces' (Report, November 2019)

Bank of England, 'Strengthening Financial Infrastructure' (2005) (June) *Financial Stability Review* 79

Bank of England, 'CHAPS Rules' (Rules, 31 March 2021)

Bank of England, Financial Conduct Authority and Pay.uk, 'Access to UK Payment Schemes for Non-Bank Payment Service Providers' (Information Paper, December 2019)

Barabási, Albert-László and Réka Albert, 'Emergence of Scaling in Random Networks' (1999) 286 *Science* 509-512

Baudino, Patrizia, Jon Thor Sturluson and Jean-Philippe Svoronos, 'The Banking Crisis in Iceland' (FSI Crisis Management Series Paper No. 1, Bank for International Settlements, March 2020)

Becher, Christopher, Stephen Millard and Kimmo Soramaki, 'The Network Topology of CHAPS Sterling' (Working Paper No. 355, Bank of England, 24 November 2008)

Benediktsdóttir, Sigríður, Gauti B Eggertsson and Eggert Þórarinsson, 'The Rise, the Fall, and the Resurrection of Iceland' (2017) *Brookings Papers on Economic Activity*

Bennett, Colin J and Charles D Raab, *The Governance of Privacy: Policy Instruments in Global Perspective* (MIT Press, 2nd and updated ed., 2006)

Benoliel, Daniel, 'Technological Standards, Inc.: Rethinking Cyberspace Regulatory Epistemology' (2004) 92 *California Law Review* 1069

Bernanke, Ben S, 'Stabilizing the Financial Markets and the Economy' (Presentation, Economic Club of New York, New York, 15 October 2008)

Besley, Tim and Peter Hennessey, 'Letter in Response to a Question of Queen Elizabeth' (2009) *British Academy of Science, London*

Black, Julia, 'The Development of Risk Based Regulation in Financial Services: Canada, the UK and Australia' (Research Report, ESRC Centre for the Analysis of Risk and Regulation, January 2004)

Bollen, Rhys, *The Law and Regulation of Payment Services: A Comparative Study* (Kluwer Law International BV, 2012)

Borgogno, Oscar and Giuseppe Colangelo, 'Data Sharing and Interoperability: Fostering Innovation and Competition Through APIs' (2019) 35(5) *Computer Law & Security Review* 105314

Borgogno, Oscar and Giuseppe Colangelo, 'The Data Sharing Paradox: BigTechs in Finance' (2020) *European Competition Journal* 1-20

Bossone, Biagio and Massimo Cirasino, 'The Oversight of the Payments Systems: A Framework for the Development and Governance of Payment Systems in Emerging Economies' (Research Series, The World Bank, July 2001)

Botsman, Rachel, *Who Can You Trust?: How Technology Brought Us Together – And Why It Could Drive Us Apart* (Penguin UK, 2017)

Brindle, Michael and Raymond Cox, *Law of Bank Payments* (Sweet & Maxwell, Thomson Reuters, 5th ed., 2018)

Buckley, Ross P, Natalia Jevglevskaja and Scott Farrell, 'Australia's Data-Sharing Regime: Six Lessons for Europe' (2022) 33(1) *King's Law Journal*

Burdon, Mark and Tom Mackie, 'Australia's Consumer Data Right and the Uncertain Role of Information Privacy Law' (2020) 10(3) *International Data Privacy Law* 222-235

Burton, Gregory, et al., *The Law Relating to Banker and Customer in Australia* (Thomson Reuters, 2022)

Byers, Wayne, 'Peering into a Cloudy Future' (Speech, Curious Thinkers Conference, Sydney, 21 September 2018)

Bygrave, Lee A., *Data Protection Law: Approaching Its Rationale, Logic, and Limits* (Kluwer Law International, 2002)

Carriere-Swallow, Yan, Vikram Haksar and Manasa Patnam, 'India's Approach to Open Banking: Some Implications for Financial Inclusion', *Open Banking* (Oxford University Press, 2022)

Colangelo, Giuseppe and Oscar Borgogno, 'Data, Innovation and Competition in Finance: The Case of the Access to Account Rule' (2020) 31(4) *European Business Law Review* 573

Committee on Payment and Settlement Systems, 'Settlement Risk in Foreign Exchange Transactions' (Report, Bank for International Settlements, March 1996)

Committee on Payment and Settlement Systems, 'Core Principles for Systemically Important Payment Systems' (Core Principles, Bank for International Settlements, January 2001)

Committee on Payment and Settlement Systems, 'A Glossary of Terms Used in Payments and Settlement Systems' (Report, March 2003)

Committee on Payment and Settlement Systems, 'General Guidance for National Payment System Development' (Report, Bank for International Settlements, January 2006)

Committee on Payment and Settlement Systems, 'Payment, Clearing and Settlement Systems in the CPSS Countries Volume 2' (Red Book, Bank for International Settlements, November 2012)

Committee on Payment and Settlement Systems, 'Reducing the Risk of Wholesale Payments Fraud Related to Endpoint Security' (Report, Bank for International Settlements, May 2018)

Committee on Payment and Settlement Systems and International Organization of Securities Commissions, 'Principles for Financial Markets Infrastructures' (Standards, Bank for International Settlements, April 2012)

Competition and Markets Authority, 'Retail Banking Market Investigation' (Terms of Reference, 6 November 2014) https://assets.publishing.service.gov.uk/media/545a981c40f0b6130e000011/Terms_of_reference_retail_banking.pdf

Competition and Markets Authority, 'Retail Banking Market Investigation' (Final Report, 9 August 2016)

Competition and Markets Authority, 'The Future Oversight of the CMA's Open Banking Remedies' (Response to Consultation, 21 March 2022)

Congressional Research Service, 'Open Banking, Data Sharing, and the CFPB's 1033 Rulemaking' (Insight, CRS Report, 9 September 2021) https://crsreports.congress.gov/product/pdf/IN/IN11745

'Consumer Data Right – Exposure Draft Legislation to Enable Action Initiation', *Australian Government, The Treasury* (Exposure Draft Legislation, 26 September 2022) https://treasury.gov.au/consultation/c2022-317468

Cork, Julian, 'Banking as a Platform', *The Book on Open Banking: A Series of Essays on the Next Evolution of Money* (Bud Financial Limited, 2018) 85

Cranston, Ross, et al., *Principles of Banking Law* (Oxford University Press, 3rd ed., 2017)

Dal Pont, Gino, *Law of Agency* (Butterworths, 4th ed., 2020)

Data Standards Body, 'Consumer Data Standards v 1.6.0', *Consumer Data Standards*, 23 December 2020) https://consumerdatastandards.org.au

Data Standards Body, 'Consumer Experience Guidelines' (Guidelines, v 1.4.0 17 July 2020)

De Hert, Paul, et al., 'The Right to Data Portability in the GDPR: Towards User-Centric Interoperability of Digital Services' (2018) 34(2) *Computer Law & Security Review* 193-203

De la Mano, Miguel and Jorge Padilla, 'Big Tech Banking' (2018) 14(4) *Journal of Competition Law & Economics* 494-526

Delbridge, Arthur, John RL Bernard and David Blair, *The Macquarie Dictionary* (Macquarie Library Sydney, 1981)

Department of Finance Canada, 'Consumer-Directed Finance: The Future of Financial Services' (Report, February 2020)

Diamond, Douglas W and Philip H Dybvig, 'Bank Runs, Deposit Insurance, and Liquidity' (2000) 24(1) *Federal Reserve Bank of Minneapolis Quarterly Review* 14-23

Didenko, Anton, 'Cybersecurity Regulation in the Financial Sector: Prospects of Legal Harmonisation in the EU and Beyond' (2020) 25(1) *Uniform Law Review* 125

Didenko, Anton N and Ross P Buckley, 'The Evolution of Currency: Cash to Cryptos to Sovereign Digital Currencies' (2018) 42 *Fordham International Law Journal* 1041

Dixon, Victoria (ed.), *Goode on Payment Obligations in Commercial and Financial Transactions* (Sweet & Maxwell, 4th ed., 2020)

Earle, Timothy C, 'Trust, Confidence, and the 2008 Global Financial Crisis' (2009) 29(6) *Risk Analysis: An International Journal* 785-792

Elias, Peter, Amiel Feinstein and Claude Shannon, 'A Note on the Maximum Flow Through a Network' (1956) 2(4) *IRE Transactions on Information Theory* 117-119

European Banking Authority, 'EBA Publishes Final Guidelines on Professional Indemnity Insurance' (Press Release, 7 July 2017) https://www.eba.europa.eu/eba-publishes-final-guidelines-on-professional-indemnity-insurance-under-psd2

European Banking Authority, 'Guidelines on the Criteria on How to Stipulate the Minimum Monetary Amount of the Professional Indemnity Insurance or Other Comparable Guarantee under Article 5(4) of Directive (EU) 2015/2366 (PSD2)' (Final Report No EBA/GL/2017/08, 7 July 2018)

European Banking Authority, 'Guidelines on the Security Measures for Operational and Security Risks of Payment Services under Directive (EU) 2015/2366 (PSD2)' (Final Report No EBA/GL/2017/17, 12/12/2017)

European Banking Authority, 'Opinion of the European Banking Authority on the Implementation of the RTS on SCA and CSC' (EBA Opinion No EBA-Op-2018-04, 13 June 2018)

European Banking Authority, 'EBA Guidelines on Outsourcing Arrangements' (Final Report No EBA/GL/2019/02, 25 February 2019)

European Data Protection Board, 'Guidelines 06/2020 on the Interplay of the Second Payment Services Directive and the GDPR' (Guidelines, 17 July 2020)

Farrell, Scott, 'Blockchain Standards in International Banking: Understanding Standards Deviation' (2019) 7(3) *Journal of ICT Standardization* 209-224

Farrell, Scott, 'Open For Better: Applying Open Banking to Small Business Banking' (2019) (2) *Australasian Journal of Applied Finance* 19

Farrell, Scott, 'Allocating Liabilities in Open Banking in Canada' (2022) 39 *Banking & Finance Law Review* 33

Farrell, Scott, 'Designing Data Rights for Canadian Open Banking: Lessons from Banking Law in Australia and United Kingdom' (2022) 85(2) *Saskatchewan Law Review* 165

Farrell, Scott, 'Embedding Open Banking in Banking Law: Responsibilities, Performance, Risk and Trust' (2022) 17(2) *Journal of Business & Technology Law*

Farrell, Scott, 'A Systemic Perspective for U.S. Open Banking: Ensuring Participation, Access, and Stability' (2023) 34(2) *Florida Journal of International Law* 1

Financial Conduct Authority, *FCA Handbook* (Financial Conduct Authority, 2013)

Financial Conduct Authority, 'Payment Services and Electronic Money – Our Approach' (Approach Document, June 2019)

Financial Conduct Authority, 'Approach to Final Regulatory Technical Standards and EBA Guidelines under the Revised Payment Services Directive (PSD2)' (Policy Statement No. PS18/24, December 2018)

Financial Conduct Authority, 'Guidance for Firms Outsourcing to the "Cloud" and Other Third-Party IT Services' (Finalised Guidance No. FG16, July 2016, updated September 2019)

Financial Conduct Authority, 'AISP Models under PSD2', (Guidance, 21 January 2020) https://www.fca.org.uk/firms/agency-models-under-psd2

Financial Conduct Authority, 'Guidance on the Scope of the Payment Services Regulations 2017' (Perimiter Guidance Manual, April 2021)

Financial Conduct Authority, 'Open Finance' (Feedback Statement No. FS21/7, March 2021)

Financial Crisis Inquiry Commission, United States, *The Financial Crisis Inquiry Report: The Final Report of the National Commission on the Causes of the Financial and Economic Crisis in the United States Including Dissenting Views* (Final Report, 1 May 2011)

Financial Services Consumer Panel, 'HM Treasury Consultation on the Implementation of the Revised EU Payment Services Directive PSDII', *Financial Services Consumer Panel* (Letter, 16 March 2017) https://www.fs-cp.org.uk/sites/default/files/fscp_response_hmt_implementation_of_the_revised_eu_payment_services_directive_ii.pdf

Financial Stability Board, 'Regulatory and Supervisory Issues Relating to Outsourcing and Third-Party Relationships' (Discussion Paper, 9 November 2020)

Firth, Simon, 'The English Law Treatment of Lehman's Derivative Positions' in Dennis Faber and Niels Vermunt (eds), *Bank Failure: Lessons from Lehman Brothers* (Oxford University Press, 2017)

Flannery, Mark J, 'Iceland's failed Banks: A Post-Mortem' (Report, Special Investigation Commission, Annex 3, November 2009)

Fleming, Michael J and Asani Sarkar, 'The Failure Resolution of Lehman Brothers' (2014) (December) *FRBNY Economic Policy Review* 177

Floridi, Luciano, 'Philosophical Conceptions of Information', *Formal Theories of Information* (Springer, 2009) 13-53

Floridi, Luciano, *Information: A Very Short Introduction* (Oxford University Press, 2010)

Floridi, Luciano, *The 4th Revolution: How the Infosphere Is Reshaping Human Reality* (Oxford University Press, 2014)

Fouliard, Jeremy, Michael Howell and Hélène Rey, 'Answering the Queen: Machine Learning and Financial Crises' (BIS Working Paper No. 926, Bank for International Settlements, February 2021)

Fox, David, *Property Rights in Money* (Oxford University Press, 2008)

Fox, David and Sarah Green, *Cryptocurrencies in Public and Private Law* (Oxford University Press, 2019)

Fox, David, Francois Velde and Wolfgang Ernst, 'Monetary History Between Law and Economics' in David Fox and Wolfgang Ernst (eds), *Money in the Western Legal Tradition: Middle Ages to Bretton Woods* (Oxford University Press, 2016)

Fracassi, Cesare and William J Magnuson, 'Data Autonomy' (2021) 74(2) *Vanderbilt Law Review* 327

Fridriksson, Ingimundur, 'The Banking Crisis in Iceland in 2008' (2009) *The Central Bank of Iceland*

Frost, Jon, et al., 'BigTech and the Changing Structure of Financial Intermediation', BIS Working Paper No. 779 (April 2019)

Gal, Michal S and Daniel L Rubinfeld, 'The Hidden Costs of Free Goods: Implications for Antitrust Enforcement' (2016) 80(3) *Antitrust Law Journal* 521-562

Galati, Gabriele, 'Settlement Risk In Foreign Exchange Markets and CLS Bank' (2002) 4 *BIS Quarterly Review* 55-65

Garner, Bryan A, *Black's Law Dictionary – Ninth Edition, West, St* (2009)

Georg, Co-Pierre, 'The Effect of the Interbank Network Structure on Contagion and Common Shocks' (2013) 37(7) *Journal of Banking & Finance* 2216-2228

Geva, Benjamin, 'The Concept of Payment Mechanism' (1986) 24 *Osgoode Hall Law Journal* 1

Geva, Benjamin, *Bank Collections and Payment Transactions: A Comparative Study of Legal Aspects* (Oxford University Press, 2001)

Geva, Benjamin, *The Payment Order of Antiquity and the Middle Ages: A Legal History* (Hart Publishing, 2011)

Geva, Benjamin, '"Bank Money": The Rise, Fall and Metamorphosis of the "Transferable Deposit"' in David Fox and Wolfgang Ernst (eds), *Money in the Western Legal Tradition: Middle Ages to Bretton Woods* (Oxford University Press, 2016)

Geva, Benjamin, 'Payment Transactions under the EU Second Payment Services Directive – An Outsider's View' (2018) 54 *Texas International Law Journal* 211

Gillespie, Nicole and Robert Hurley, 'Trust and the Global Financial Crisis', *Handbook of Advances in Trust Research* (Edward Elgar Publishing, 2013)

Gleick, James, *The Information: A History, a Theory, a Flood* (Vintage, 2011)

Global Association of Central Counterparties, 'Central Counterparty Default Management and the Collapse of Lehman Brothers' (Information Paper, April 2009)

Goldbarsht, Doron, Baskaran Balasingham and Jeremy Moller, 'Open Banking in Australia: Competition and Money Laundering, Risks and Benefits' (2021) 32(2) *Journal of Banking and Finance Law and Practice*

Goode, Roy, 'The Concept and Implications of a Market in Commercial Law' (1990) 24(2) *Israel Law Review* 185-210

Gozman, Daniel, Jonas Hedman and Kasper Sylvest Olsen, 'Open Banking: Emergent Roles, Risks & Opportunities' (2018) (183) *Research Papers*

Gozman, Daniel and Leslie Willcocks, 'The Emerging Cloud Dilemma: Balancing Innovation with Cross-Border Privacy and Outsourcing Regulations' (2019) 97 *Journal of Business Research* 235-256

Graef, Inge, Martin Husovec and Nadezhda Purtova, 'Data Portability and Data Control: Lessons for an Emerging Concept in EU Law' (2018) 19(6) *German Law Journal* 1359-1398

Graef, Inge, Martin Husovec and Jasper van den Boom, 'Spill-Overs in Data Governance: The Relationship Between the GDPR's Right to Data Portability and EU Sector-Specific Data Access Regimes' (TILEC Discussion Paper No. DP 2019-005, Tilburg University, April 2019)

Greenleaf, G. W., *Asian Data Privacy Laws: Trade and Human Rights Perspectives* (Oxford University Press, 2014)

Greenleaf, Graham and Alan Tyree, 'Bankers' Duties and Data Privacy Principles: Global Trends, and Asia-Pacific Comparisons' in Sandra Booysen and Dora Neo (eds), *Can Banks Still Keep a Secret* (Cambridge University Press, 2017) 31-61

Greenspan, Alan, *The Age of Turbulence: Adventures in a New World* (Penguin, 2008)

Haldane, Andrew G, 'Rethinking the Financial Network', *Fragile stabilität–stabile fragilität* (Springer, 2013) 243-278

Hermstruwer, Yoan, 'Contracting Around Privacy: The (Behavioral) Law and Economics of Consent and Big Data' (2017) 8 *Journal of Intellectual Property, Information Technology and Electronic Commerce Law* 9

Heydon, John Dyson, *Heydon on Contract – The General Part* (Lawbook Co., 2019)

Hickson, Charles R and John D Turner, 'Free Banking Gone Awry: The Australian Banking Crisis of 1893' (2002) 9(2) *Financial History Review* 147-167

HM Treasury, 'The Economic Value of Data: Discussion Paper' (Discussion Paper, 2018) www.gov.uk/government/publications

HM Treasury et al., 'Joint Statement on the Future of Open Banking' (Policy Paper, 25 March 2022)

HM Treasury and Financial Conduct Authority, 'Expectations for the Third Party Access Provisions in the Payment Services Directive II' (Statement, July 2017)

Hong Kong Monetary Authority, 'Open API Framework for the Hong Kong Banking Sector', 18 July 2018) https://www.hkma.gov.hk/media/eng/doc/key-information/press-release/2018/20180718e5a2.pdf

Information Commissioner's Office, 'Guide to the General Data Protection Regulation' (Guide, 1 January 2021)

Information Commissioners Office, 'Anonymisation: Managing Data Protection Risk Code of Practice' (Code of practice, November 2012)

Information Commissioners Office, 'The Information Commissioner's Response to the HM Treasury Consultation on the Implementation of the Revised EU Payment Services Directive II' (Consultation Response, 17 March 2017)

International Organization of Securities Commissions, 'Principles of Outsourcing' (Consultation Report No. CR01/2020, May 2020)

Jackson, John and Mark Manning, 'Central Bank Intraday Collateral Policy and Implications for Tiering in RTGS Payment Systems' in Stephen Millard, Andrew Haldane and Victoria Saporta (eds), *The Future of Payment Systems* (Routledge, 2008)

Jeng, Linda (ed.), *Open Banking* (Oxford University Press, 2022)

Jenkinson, Nigel and Mark Manning, 'Promoting Financial System Resilience in Modern Global Capital Markets: Some Issues' (2007) 3(Autumn) *Bank of England Quarterly Bulletin* 453

Jónsson, Ásgeir and Guillaume Cannat, *Why Iceland?* (McGraw-Hill, 2009)

Kahn, Charles M and William Roberds, 'Why Pay? An Introduction to Payments Economics' (2009) 18(1) *Journal of Financial Intermediation* 1-23

Kahn, Charles, Stephen Quinn and Will Roberds, 'Central Banks and Payment Systems: The Evolving Trade-Off Between Cost and Risk' Norges Bank Conference on the Uses of Central Banks: Lessons from History, June, 5-6 June 2014)

Kelleher, John D and Brendan Tierney, *Data Science* (MIT Press, 2018)

Kirby, Michael, 'The Fundamental Problem of Regulating Technology' (2009) 5 *Indian Journal of Law & Technology* 1

Kitchin, Rob, *The Data Revolution: Big Data, Open Data, Data Infrastructures and Their Consequences* (Sage, 2014)

Koops, Bert-Jaap, 'The Trouble with European Data Protection Law' (2014) 4(4) *International Data Privacy Law* 250-261

Kuner, Christopher Barth, *Transborder Data Flows and Data Privacy Law* (Oxford University Press, 2013)

Lacker, Jeffrey, 'Payment Economics and the Role of Central Banks' in Stephen Millard, Andrew Haldane and Victoria Saporta (eds), *The Future of Payment Systems* (Routledge, 2008)

Leibbrandt, Gottfried, 'Gottfried Leibbrandt on Cyber Security and Innovation' (Keynote Address, 14th Annual European Financial Services Conference, Brussels, 24 May 2016) https://www.swift.com/insights/press-releases/gottfried-leibbrandt-on-cyber-security-and-innovation

Leibbrandt, Gottfried and Natasha De Teran, *The Pay Off: How Changing the Way We Pay Changes Everything* (Elliot & Thompson, 2020)

Leonard, Peter, 'The Good Oil on Valuing "The New Oil"' (2018) 24(7) *Computer and Telecommunications Law Review* 167

Leonard, Peter G, 'Regulatory Trends and Emerging Practices in Access to Customer Data, Portability and Data Sharing in the Financial Services Sector' (2017) 2 *Data Synergies Pty Limited*

Lessig, Lawrence, *Code Version 2.0* (Basic Books, 2006)

Liu, Han-Wei, 'Shifting Contour of Data Sharing in Financial Market and Regulatory Responses: The UK and Australian Models' (2021) 10(3) *American University Business Law Review*

Lopez, Santiago Ramirez, 'Informing Consent' (2018) 9 *Journal of Intellectual Property, Information Technology and Electronic Commerce Law* 35

Lord Justice Briggs, 'How Has English Law Coped With the Lehman Collapse?' in Dennis Faber and Niels Vermunt (eds), *Bank Failure: Lessons from Lehman Brothers* (Oxford University Press, 2017)

Lubben, Stephen, 'Lehman's Derivative Portfolio: A Chapter 11 Perspective' in Dennis Faber and Niels Vermunt (eds), *Bank Failure: Lessons from Lehman Brothers* (Oxford University Press, 2017)

Malgieri, Gianclaudio and Bart Custers, 'Pricing Privacy: The Right to Know the Value of Your Personal Data' (2018) 34(2) *Computer Law & Security Review* 289

Mann, FrancisA, *The Legal Aspect of Money* (Oxford University Press, 1938)

Manning, Mark, Erlend Nier and Jochen Schanz, *The Economics of Large-Value Payments and Settlement: Theory and Policy Issues for Central Banks* (Oxford University Press, 2009)

Marchant, Gary E, Braden R Allendby and Joseph R Herkert, 'The Growing Gap Between Emerging Technologies and the Law', *The Growing Gap Between Emerging Technologies and Legal-Ethical Oversight* (Springer, 2011) 19-33

Martens, Bertin, 'An Economic Perspective on Data and Platform Market Power' (JRC Digital Economy Working Paper No. 2020-09, European Commission, JRC Technical Report, 2021)

Mayer-Schönberger, Viktor and Kenneth Cukier, *Big Data: The Essential Guide to Work, Life and Learning in the Age of Insight* (John Murray, 2nd ed., 2017)

Mayer-Schönberger, Viktor and Thomas Ramge, *Reinventing Capitalism in the Age of Big Data* (Basic Books, 2018)

McAndrews, James and Simon Potter, 'Liquidity Effects of the Events of September 11, 2001' (2002) *FRBNY Economic Policy Review* 59

McKendrick, Ewan, *Goode and McKendrick on Commercial Law* (LexisNexis, 6th ed., 2020)

McLeay, Michael, Amar Radia and Ryland Thomas, 'Money Creation in the Modern Economy' (2014) *Bank of England Quarterly Bulletin* Q1

Meese, James, Punit Jagasia and James Arvanitakis, 'Citizen or Consumer?: Contrasting Australia and Europe's Data Protection Policies' (2019) 8(2) *Internet Policy Review* 1

Merrett, David Tolmie, 'The Australian Bank Crashes of the 1890s Revisited' (2013) 87(3) *Business History Review* 407-429

Merrett, David T, 'Preventing Bank Failure: Could the Commercial Bank of Australia Have Been Saved by Its Peers in 1893?' (1993) 64(2) *Victorian Historical Journal* 122-142

Millard, Stephen, Andrew Haldane and Victoria Saporta, 'The Future of Payment Systems' in Stephen Millard, Andrew Haldane and Victoria Saporta (eds), *The Future of Payment Systems* (Routledge, 2008)

Millard, Stephen and Victoria Saporta, 'Past, Present and Future' in Stephen Millard, Andrew Haldane and Victoria Saporta (eds), *The Future of Payment Systems* (Routledge, 2008)

Moses, Lyria Bennett, 'Recurring Dilemmas: The Law's Race to Keep Up with Technological Change' (2007) *University of Illinois Journal of Law Technology & Policy* 239

National Bank of Belgium, 'Financial Stability Review' (Review, 2007)

Newman, John M, 'Antitrust in Zero-Price Markets: Foundations' (2015) 164 *University of Pennsylvania Law Review* 149-206

Nicholls, Christopher C, 'Open Banking and the Rise of FinTech: Innovative Finance and Functional Regulation' (2019) 35(1) *Banking & Finance Law Review* 121-151

Nussbaum, Arthur, *Money in the Law: National and International: A Comparative Study in the Borderline of Law and Economics* (Foundation Press, 1950)

Odgers, John, *Paget's Law of Banking* (LexisNexis, 15th ed., 2018)

Office of the Australian Information Commissioner, 'Consumer Data Right Privacy Safeguard Guidelines' (Guidelines, July 2020)

Office of the Australian Information Commissioner and Data 61, 'The De-Identification Decision-Making Framework' (Guidance, 18 September 2017)

Open Banking Implementation Entity, 'Customer Experience Guidelines' (Standard, v3.1.10) https://standards.openbanking.org.uk

Open Banking Implementation Entity, 'Customer Experience Guidelines Checklist v 3.1.10', *Customer Experience Guidelines*) https://standards.openbanking.org.uk/customer-experience-guidelines/customer-experience-checklist/explanation-of-the-customer-experience-checklist/latest/

Open Banking Implementation Entity, 'Open Banking API Specifications ' (Standard, v3.1.10) https://standards.openbanking.org.uk

Open Banking Implementation Entity, 'Open Banking Security Profiles' (Standard, 2018-2019) https://standards.openbanking.org.uk/security-profiles/

Open Banking Implementation Entity, 'Open Banking Guidelines for Read/Write Participants' (Guidelines, May 2018) https://www.openbanking.org.uk/wp-content/uploads/Guidelines-for-Read-Write-Participants.pdf

Open Banking Implementation Entity, 'Dispute Management System (DMS) Code of Good Practice' (Code of Conduct No DMS 2.1 v0.11, October 2019) https://www.openbanking.org.uk/wp-content/uploads/COGP-2.0.pdf

Open Banking Implementation Entity, 'Directory 2.0 Technical Overview v1.5', *Open Banking Developer Zone* (Technical Specification, 29 December 2020) https://openbanking.atlassian.net/wiki/spaces/DZ/pages/1150124033/Directory + 2.0 + Technical + Overview + v1.5

Open Banking Implementation Entity, 'Enrolling onto the OBIE Directory' (Guide, November 2020) https://www.openbanking.org.uk/wp-content/uploads/Enrolling-Onto-Open-Banking-Guide.pdf

Open Banking Implementation Entity, 'How to Enrol with Open Banking', *Open Banking – Third Party Providers* (Guide, 2021) https://www.openbanking.org.uk/providers/third-party-providers/

Open Data Institute and Fingleton, 'Open Banking, Preparing for Lift Off' (Report, 2019)

Organisation for Economic Co-operation and Development, *Exploring the Economics of Personal Data: A Survey of Methodologies for Measuring Monetary Value* (OECD Publishing, 2013)

Palmieri, Alessandro and Blerina Nazeraj, 'Open Banking and Competition: An Intricate Relationship' (2021) 6 *EU and Comparative Law Issues and Challenges Series (ECLIC)* 217-237

Plaitakis, Ariadne and Stefan Staschen, 'Open Banking: How to Design for Financial Inclusion' (Working Paper, CGAP, 2020)

Proctor, Charles, et al., *Mann on the Legal Aspect of Money* (Oxford University Press, 7th ed, 2012)

Productivity Commission, *Data Availability and Use* (Report No. 82, 2017)

Prudential Regulation Authority, 'CBEST Threat Intelligence-Led Assessments' (Implementation Guide, January 2021)

Prudential Regulation Authority, 'Outsourcing and Third Party Risk Management' (Policy Statement No. PS7/21, March 2021)

Prudential Regulation Authority, 'Supervisory Statement SS2/21 Outsourcing and Third Party Risk Management' (Supervisory Statement, March 2021)

Purtova, Nadezhda, 'Default Entitlements in Personal Data in the Proposed Regulation: Informational Self-Determination Off the Table ... And Back on Again?' (2014) 30(1) *Computer Law & Security Review* 6-24

Purtova, Nadezhda, 'The Illusion of Personal Data as No One's Property' (2015) 7(1) *Law, Innovation and Technology* 83-111

Purtova, Nadezhda, 'The Law of Everything: Broad Concept of Personal Data and Future of EU Data Protection Law' (2018) 10(1) *Law, Innovation and Technology* 40-81

Rahmatian, Andreas, 'Money as a Legally Enforceable Debt' (2018) 29(2) *European Business Law Review* 205-236

Reimsbach-Kounatze, Christian, 'Enhancing Access to and Sharing of Data: Striking the Balance Between Openness and Control Over Data' in German Federal Ministry of Justice and Consumer Protection and Max Planck Institute for Innovation and Competition (eds), *Data Access, Consumer Interests and Public Welfare* (Nomos Verlagsgesellschaft mbH & Co. KG, 2021) 25-68

Remolina, Nydia, 'Open Banking: Regulatory Challenges for a New Form of Financial Intermediation in a Data-Driven World' (2019) (2019/05) *SMU Centre for AI & Data Governance Research Paper*

Reserve Bank of Australia, 'Financial Stability Review – March 2009' (Report, March 2009)

Reserve Bank of Australia, 'Financial Stability Review' (Report, October 2018)

Reserve Bank of Australia, 'Exchange Settlement Account Policy', *Payments and Infrastructure* (Policy, 26 July 2019) https://www.rba.gov.au/payments-and-infrastructure/esa/

Reserve Bank of Australia, 'RITS Regulations' (Regulations, 18 November 2020)

Reynolds, Faith, et al., 'Consumer Priorities for Open Banking' (Research Report, June 2019) https://www.openbanking.org.uk/wp-content/uploads/Consumer-Priorities-for-Open-Banking-report-June-2019.pdf

Richardson, Gary, 'Bank Distress During the Great Contraction, 1929 to 1933, New Data from the Archives of the Board of Governors' (Working Paper No. 12590, National Bureau of Economic Research, Cambridge, Mass., USA, 2006)

Richardson, Gary, 'Banking Panics of 1930-31', *Federal Reserve History* (Essay, 22 November 2013) https://www.federalreservehistory.org/essays/banking-panics-1930-31

Robinson, Neil, et al., 'Review of the European Data Protection Directive' (Technical Report, Information Commissioner's Office, May 2009)

Roth, Felix, 'The Effect of the Financial Crisis on Systemic Trust' (2009) 44(4) *Intereconomics* 203-208

Rule, James B. and Graham W. Greenleaf, *Global Privacy Protection: The First Generation* (Edward Elgar, 2008)

Ryan, Philippa, *Trust and Distrust in Digital Economies* (Routledge, 2019)

Sainz de Vicuna, Antonio, 'An Institutional Theory of Money' in Mario Giovanoli and Diego Devos (eds), *International Monetary and Financial Law: The Global Crisis* (Oxford University Press, 2010)

Schenk, Catherine R, 'Summer in the City: Banking Failures of 1974 and the Development of International Banking Supervision' (2014) 129 (540) *The English Historical Review* 1129-1156

Schweitzer, Heike and Robert Welker, 'A Legal Framework for Access to Data: A Competition Policy Perspective' in German Federal Ministry of Justice and Consumer Protection and Max Planck Institute for Innovation and Competition (eds), *Data Access, Consumer Interests and Public Welfare* (Nomos Verlagsgesellschaft mbH & Co. KG, 2021) 103-154

Scott, Hal S, 'The Importance of the Retail Payment System' (Article, Retail Payment Systems Conference; Harvard Law School Program on International Financial Systems, 26 February 2015)

Seddon, Nick and Fred Ellinghaus, *Cheshire and Fifoot's Law of Contract* (LexisNexis Butterworths, 9th Australian ed., 2008)

Seltzer, Andrew J, 'The Functions of Australian Banks' Branch Networks: The Diversification of Risks and Spatial Allocation of Capital' (2018) 58(3) *Australian Economic History Review* 338-361

Shannon, Claude, *Claude Ellwood Shannon: Collected Papers* (IEEE Press, 1993)

Shannon, Claude E, 'A Mathematical Theory of Communication' (1948) 27(3) *The Bell System Technical Journal* 379-423

Shapiro, Susan P, 'The Social Control of Impersonal Trust' (1987) 93(3) *American Journal of Sociology* 623-658

Sleijpen, Olaf, 'How to Make Open Finance a Success: Lessons from PSD2' (Keynote Speech, DeNederlandscheBank, 4th Annual Conference on FinTech and Regulation, Brussels, 3 March 2020)

Smith, Adam, *The Wealth of Nations: An Inquiry into the Nature and Causes of the Wealth of Nations* (Wordsworth Editions, 2012)

Soramäki, Kimmo et al., 'The Topology of Interbank Payment Flows' (2007) 379(1) *Physica A: Statistical Mechanics and Its Applications* 317-333

St. John, Richard, 'Compensation Arrangements for Consumers of Financial Services' (Report, Australian Government, April 2012)

Strategy, Department for Business Energy & Industrial, 'Next Steps for Smart Data' (Report, September 2020) https://assets.publishing.service.gov.uk/government/uploads/system/uploads/attachment_data/file/915973/smart-data-consultation-response.pdf

Tellez, Eduardo, 'Mapping the Australian Banking System Network' (2013) *RBA Bulletin* 45-54

U.S. Office of Financial Research, '2017 Financial Stability Report' (Report, 5 December 2017) https://www.financialresearch.gov/financial-stability-reports/2017-financial-stability-report/

van Zeeland, Ine and Jo Pierson, 'In Banks We Trust: Banks as Custodians of Personal Data in Open Banking Ecosystems', SSRN (Research Paper, 30 July 2021) https://papers.ssrn.com/sol3/papers.cfm?abstract_id=3896405

van Zwieten (ed.), Kristin, *Goode on Principles of Corporate Insolvency Law* (Sweet & Maxwell, 5th ed., 2018)

Vezzoso, Simonetta, 'Fintech, Access to Data, and the Role of Competition Policy' (2018) *Competition and Innovation, São Paulo: Scortecci*

Vezzoso, Simonetta, 'The Dawn of Pro-Competition Data Regulation for Gatekeepers in the EU' (2021) *European Competition Journal* 1-16

Walters, Robert, 'Insolvency and Data Protection' (2021) 42(1) *Business Law Review*

Walters, Robert, Leon E Trakman and Bruno Zeller, *Data Protection Law: A Comparative Analysis of Asia-Pacific and European Approaches* (Springer, 2019)

Watts, Peter and Francis MB Reynolds, *Bowstead and Reynolds on Agency* (Sweet & Maxwell, 22nd ed., 2020)

Weaver, Warren, 'Recent Contributions to the Mathematical Theory of Communication' (1953) *ETC: A Review of General Semantics* 261-281

Weinberger, David, *Too Big to Know: Rethinking Knowledge Now That the Facts Aren't the Facts, Experts Are Everywhere, and the Smartest Person in the Room Is the Room* (Basic Books, 2011)

Wicker, Elmus, 'A Reconsideration of the Causes of the Banking Panic of 1930' (1980) 40(3) *The Journal of Economic History* 571-583

Wood, Philip R, *Principles of International Insolvency* (Sweet & Maxwell, 3rd ed., 2019)

Wood, Philip R, *Set-Off and Netting, Derivatives, Clearing Systems* (Sweet & Maxwell, 2019)

Zachariadis, Markos, Pinar Ozcan and Dize Dinckol, 'The Economics and Strategy of Platforms: Competing in the Era of Open Banking', *The Book on Open Banking: A Series of Essays on the Next Evolution of Money* (Bud Financial Limited, 2018) 59-70

Zachariadis, Markos and Pinar Ozcan, 'The API Economy and Digital Transformation in Financial Services: The Case of Open Banking' (SWIFT Institute Working Paper No. 2016-001 2017)

Zech, Herbert, 'A Legal Framework for a Data Economy in the European Digital Single Market: Rights to Use Data' (2016) 11(6) *Journal of Intellectual Property Law & Practice* 460-470

Zech, Herbert, 'Data as a Tradeable Commodity – Implications for Contract Law' in Josef Drexl (ed.), *Proceedings of the 18th EIPIN Congress: The New Data Economy between Data Ownership, Privacy and Safeguarding Competition, Forthcoming* (Edward Elgar Publishing, 2017)

Zeller, Bruno and Andrew M Dahdal, 'Open Banking and Open Data in Australia: Global Context, Innovation and Consumer Protection' (2021) (*Qatar University College of Law, Working Paper Series, Working Paper* 2021/001)

Zetzsche, Dirk A, et al., 'The Evolution and Future of Data Driven Finance in the EU' (2020) 57 *Common Market Law Review* 331-360

Zetzsche, Dirk A, et al., 'Digital Finance Platforms: Towards a New Regulatory Paradigm' (2020) 23(1) *University of Pennsylvania Journal of Business Law* 273

Zunzunegui, Fernando, 'Digitalisation of Payment Services' (2018) (5) *Ibero-American Institute for Law and Finance Working Paper*

# Table of Cases

# Table of Legislation

## INTERNATIONAL BANKING AND FINANCE LAW SERIES

1. Jan Job de Vries Robbe, *Innovations in Securitisation. Yearbook 2006*, 2006 (ISBN 90-11-2533-7).
2. Jim Bartos, *United States Securities Law: A Practical Guide*, Third edition, 2006 (ISBN 90-411-2362-8).
3. Hui Huang, *International Securities Markets: Insider Trading Law in China*, 2006 (ISBN 90-411-2557-4).
4. Barth et al., *Financial Restructuring and Reform in Post-WTO China*, 2007 (ISBN 90-411-2573-6).
5. Zhongfei Zhou, *Banking Laws in China*, 2007 (ISBN 978-90-411-2519-4).
6. Jan Job de Vries Robbe & Paul Ali, *Expansion and Diversification in Securitization Yearbook 2007*, 2007 (ISBN 978-90-411-2661-0).
7. Ross Buckley, *International Financial System. Policy and Regulation*, 2008 (ISBN 978-90-411-2746-4).
8. Jan Job de Vries Robbe, *Securitization Law and Practice: In the Face of the Credit Crunch*, 2008 (ISBN 978-90-411-2715-0).
9. Phoebus Athanassiou, *Hedge Fund Regulation in the European Union: Current Trends and Future Prospects*, 2009 (ISBN 978-90-411-2856-0).
10. Jan Job de Vries Robbe, *Structured Finance: On from the Credit Crunch: The Road to Recovery*, 2009 (ISBN 978-90-411-2787-7).
11. Gaetane Schaeken Willemaers, *The EU Issuer-Disclosure Regime: Objectives and Proposals for Reform*, 2011 (ISBN 978-90-411-3394-6).
12. Panagiotis Delimatsis & Nils Herger (eds), *Financial Regulation at the Crossroads: Implications for Supervision, Institutional Design and Trade*, 2011 (ISBN 978-90-411-3355-7).
13. Raffaele Scalcione, *The Derivatives Revolution: A Trapped Innovation and a Blueprint for Regulatory Reform*, 2011 (ISBN 978-90-411-3430-1).
14. Douglas Arner & Ross Buckley, *From Crisis to Crisis: The Global Financial System and Regulatory Failure*, 2011 (ISBN 978-90-411-3354-0).
15. Anton P. Trichardt, *Letters of Comfort: A Trans-Systemic Analysis*, 2012 (ISBN 978-90-411-3600-8).
16. Eddy Wymeersch, *Alternative Investment Fund Regulation*, 2012 (ISBN 978-90-411-3690-9).
17. Asif H. Qureshi & Xuan Gao (eds), *International Economic Organizations and Law: The Perspective and Role of the Legal Counsel*, 2012 (ISBN 97890-411-3427-1).
18. Rhys Bollen, *The Law and Regulation of Payment Services: A Comparative Study*, 2012 (ISBN 978-90-411-3818-7).
19. Ramandeep Kaur Chhina, *Standby Letters of Credit in International Trade*, 2012 (ISBN 978-90-411-4560-4).

20. Dirk Zetzsche (ed.), *The Alternative Investment Fund Managers Directive*, Third Edition, 2020 (ISBN 978-94-035-0910-5).
21. Lorenzo Sasso, *Capital Structure and Corporate Governance: The Role of Hybrid Financial Instruments*, 2013 (ISBN 978-90-411-4843-8).
22. Pablo Iglesias-Rodríguez, *The Accountability of Financial Regulators: A European and International Perspective*, 2013 (ISBN 978-90-411-3874-3).
23. Seraina Neva Grünewald, *The Resolution of Cross-Border Banking Crises in the European Union: A Legal Study from the Perspective of Burden Sharing*, 2014 (ISBN 978-90-411-4909-1).
24. Megan Bowman, *Banking on Climate Change: How Finance Actors and Transnational Regulatory Regimes are Responding*, 2015 (ISBN 978-90-411-5223-7).
25. Jin Sheng, *China's Listed Companies: Conflicts, Governance and Regulation*, 2015 (ISBN 978-90-411-5925-0).
26. Sven Schelo, *Bank Recovery and Resolution*, Second Edition, 2020 (ISBN 978-94-035-1881-7).
27. Luis M. Hinojosa–Martínez & José María Beneyto (eds), *European Banking Union: The New Regime*, 2015 (ISBN 978-90-411-5263-3).
28. Gill North, *Effective Company Disclosure in the Digital Age*, 2015 (ISBN 978-90-411-3815-6).
29. Hanneke Wegman, *Investor Protection: Towards Additional EU Regulation of Investment Funds?*, 2016 (ISBN 978-90-411-5252-7).
30. Ruth Plato-Shinar, *Banking Regulation in Israel: Prudential Regulation versus Consumer Protection*, 2016 (ISBN 978-90-411-6791-0).
31. Bader Alkhaldi, *Saudi Capital Market: Developments and Challenges*, 2017 (ISBN 978-90-411-8351-4).
32. Yves Mauchle, *Bail-In and Total Loss-Absorbing Capacity (TLAC): Legal and Economic Perspectives on Bank Resolution with Functional Comparisons of Swiss and EU Law*, 2017 (ISBN 978-90-411-8998-1).
33. Uzma Ashraf Barton, *Rethinking Regulation of International Finance: Law, Policy and Institutions*, 2018 (ISBN 978-90-411-8838-0).
34. Phoebus L. Athanassiou, *Digital Innovation in Financial Services: Legal Challenges and Regulatory Policy Issues*, 2018 (ISBN 978-90-411-8781-9).
35. Gu Bin, *The Law and Governance of the Asian Infrastructure Investment Bank*, 2019 (ISBN 978-94-035-0631-9).
36. Gerald Nels Olson, *Money, Morality and Law: A Case for Financial Crisis Accountability*, 2019 (ISBN 978-94-035-0941-9).
37. Scott Farrell, *Banking on Data: Evaluating Open Banking and Data Rights in Banking Law*, 2023 (ISBN 978-94-035-3116-8).